Pastimes

The Context of Contemporary Leisure

Third Edition

Ruth V. Russell

Sagamore Publishing L.L.C.

Champaign, Illinois

Interior Design and layout: K. Jeffrey Higgerson
Cover Design: K. Jeffrey Higgerson

Cover images © Ruth V. Russell

Library of Congress Catalog Card Number: 2004116703
ISBN 1-57167-564-7

Printed in the United States.

For Pat, again and more than ever.

CONTENTS

Preface ix
Acknowledgments ix

Part I .1
Leisure as a Condition of Being Human—Personal Context

Chapter One 3
Meanings of Leisure

Preview 3
The Humanities of Leisure 4
   Leisure and Literature 4
   Leisure and Art 9
   Leisure and Music 13
Classical Meanings of Leisure 16
   The Kingdom of Kush: Adornment of Daily Life . . .17
   Ancient Greece: The Good Life 17
   Ancient Rome: Leisure as Spectacle 21
   Ancient China: Life Balance 23
   Muhammad's Early Empire: Relaxation 25
   Ancient New World Societies: Ceremony 26
   Medieval Europe: The Work Ethic 28
   The Renaissance: Humanism 29
Today's Meanings 30
   Leisure as Free Time 31
   Leisure as Recreational Activity 32
   Leisure as State of Mind 33
Summary: What We Understand 34
Applications to Professional Practice 34
References 37

Chapter Two 39
Having Fun

Preview 39
Freedom 40
Intrinsic Reward 42
Happiness 44
Pleasure 46
Play 49
Game 54
Humor 56
Relaxation 57
Ritual 59
Solitude 60
Commitment 61
Spirituality 64
Risk 65
Summary: What We Understand 66
Applications to Professional Practice 67
References 69

Chapter Three 71
Explanations

Preview 71

Situation Factors Explaining Leisure Behavior .72
Theories Explaining Leisure Behavior 78
   Compensation and Spillover 79
   Kelly's Types 82
   Neulinger's Paradigm 84
   Flow 89
   Adventure Experience Paradigm 93
   Self-As-Entertainment .95
   Theory of Anti-Structure 96
Summary: What We Understand 98
Applications to Professional Practice 99
References 102

Chapter Four 105
Leisure and Life Span

Preview 105
The Meaning of Age .106
Physical Development 109
Emotional Development 114
Intellectual Development 120
Social Development .125
Summary: What We Understand 131
Applications to Professional Practice 132
References 134

Part II 137
Leisure as a Cultural Mirror—Societal Context

Chapter Five 139
Leisure's Anthropology

Preview 139
How Culture Influences Leisure 141
   Characteristics of Culture 141
   Cultural Change 146
Hunches About the Earliest Human Cultures . .153
Leisure and Cultural Development 157
Leisure and Modernity 161
   Postmodernism 163
   Well-being 164
Summary: What We Understand 166
Applications to Professional Practice 166
References 168

Chapter Six .171
Leisure's Geography

Preview 171
Leisure as Space 175
   Crowding in Leisure 178
   Leisure and Distance .180
Leisure as Place 182
   Place Attachment 184
   Place Identity 185
Environmental Impact 188

CONTENTS

Summary: What We Understand 192
Applications to Professional Practice 192
References 197

Chapter Seven .199
Common Culture

Preview 199
Characterizing Common Culture 200
Television 204
Popular Music 210
Popular Print 213
Films 216
Theme Parks 220
Role of Entertainment 227
Summary: What We Understand 229
Applications to Professional Practice 229
References 232

Chapter Eight .235
Leisure and Technology

Preview 235
Technology and Quality of Life 238
Computer Assisted Leisure 242
Technology as Leisure 248
Summary: What We Understand 252
Application to Professional Practice 253
References 255

Chapter Nine .257
Taboo Recreation

Preview 257
Leisure and Deviance 260
Why Taboo Recreation? 261
Taboo Recreation That Injures Self 268
Taboo Recreation That Injures Others 274
The Dilemma of "Goodness" 278
Summary: What We Understand 281
Applications to Professional Practice 282
References 284

Part III 287
Leisure as a Social Instrument–
Systems Context

Chapter Ten 289
Using Leisure for Social Good

Preview 289
Colonial America 291
Transitions of the 1800s 294
Birth of Organized Leisure Systems 300
The Movement's Zenith 309
Leisure as Community-Maker Today 310
Summary: What We Understand 313

Applications to Professional Practice 313
References 315

Chapter Eleven 317
Paying For It All

Preview 317
The Web of Leisure and Economics 319
    Economic Development 319
    Capitalism 323
    Consumerism 326
How Leisure Benefits an Economy 331
    Expenditures and Investments 332
    Employment 334
    Taxes 335
    Property Values 336
How Leisure Harms an Economy 336
    Accidents 337
    Balance of Payments 339
Summary: What We Understand 340
Applications to Professional Practice 340
References 342

Chapter Twelve 343
Of Time and Work

Preview 343
Time 345
    Types of Time .346
    Time Tyrannies 351
    Time for Leisure 355
Work 360
    The Intention of Work 361
    Worker Rewards and Dissatisfactions 364
    Leisure and Work 365
Summary: What We Understand 371
Applications to Professional Practice 372
References 374

Chapter Thirteen 377
Leisure and Equity

Preview 377
How Leisure Both Restricts and Enables Equity . .379
Examples 383
    Women 383
    Gays and Lesbians 387
    Racial and Ethnic Minorities 391
    Immigrants 394
    At-Risk Youth 397
    Persons with Disabilities 400
Summary: What We Understand 404
Applications to Professional Practice 404
References 406
Index 409

Preface

The purpose of this third edition of Pastimes is to bring attention to new concepts about leisure. In addition, I wanted to make it more fun. In other words, in this edition, Pastimes accomplishes the same things as the first two editions, only more.

First, as an introduction to the concept of leisure, the book must always be contemporary. Momentous change, actual and alleged, has always been the lifeblood of leisure. Now, again, Pastimes gathers together state-of-the-art practices in leisure sciences and studies, reflecting a wide range of material from the disciplines of sociology, psychology, economics, political science, anthropology, media and cultural studies, and the humanities. In addition, this edition contains two new chapters featuring leisure as geography and leisure and technology. More than being a text that teaches the foundational meanings and roles of leisure, however, Pastimes is very much a point of view. Leisure is presented as a human phenomenon that is individual and collective, vital to survival and frivolous, historical and contemporary, good and bad.

Second, as a teaching tool, this third edition teaches more. It contains more illustrations of concepts through field-based case studies, current research studies, and biographical features. To make the material more personally relevant, new boxes featuring exploratory activities are offered, and a new section in every chapter features applications to professional practice. There are more definitions of terms in the margin, and even more photographs! Throughout, I have chosen to use the most interesting, relevant, exciting, and fun information and approach possible. This wasn't at all difficult! Leisure simply is a very intriguing subject.

Acknowledgments

This book is the result of years of engagement with leisure theory, research, and personal and professional practice. Signs of my worldwide wanderings are also evident. It has all come together from decades of study and conversation about the character of modern societies and their leisure. I have enjoyed every minute of it.

Through these journeys I am grateful to many. To begin, I am indebted to my family, friends, and pets for helping me learn. Learning is the greatest of joys, and I have been lucky to be able to devote my life to it. In addition, I thank the administration of Indiana University, in particular Deans David Gallahue and Jerry Wilkerson, and Chair Lynn Jamieson, who over the years have awarded me with free time, material support, and travel funding. I also thank my students at Indiana University, who always helped me see the point, and my colleagues at universities around the world, who read the first two editions and contributed both compliments and complaints that were directly instructive in the preparation of this edition.

LEISURE AS A CONDITION OF BEING HUMAN

PERSONAL CONTEXT

We begin our explorations of leisure by considering its significance for us personally. Leisure helps shape us as human beings. It is expressed throughout our lives and is revealed in our histories, growth, health, and behaviors.

Chapter 1

illustrates leisure's meanings for us through the humanities, and by contrasting ancient and contemporary definitions.

Chapter 2

discusses the qualities of leisure: happiness, freedom, pleasure, intrinsic reward, and others.

Chapter 3

offers some explanations about our leisure behaviors and interests.

Chapter 4

traces the ways leisure helps us grow, mature, adjust, thrive, and age throughout our lives.

Leisure *helps to shape who we are as human beings.*

Even though we may think of **leisure** *casually as having* **fun**, *scientists have taken the matter quite* **seriously**.

Imagination *is more important than knowledge.*

Meanings of Leisure

Preview

What is leisure?

Leisure is a dynamic concept with different meanings depending on the context.

Can we find meanings of leisure through the humanities?

Perhaps leisure can be most meaningfully understood through music, art, and literature. In a short story, individual meanings of leisure are revealed; a song expresses a particular group's use of leisure; and a painting depicts an entire era's interpretation of leisure.

Are there clues to meanings of contemporary leisure in ancient history?

From the beginning of human history, leisure has been a part of everyday life. Legacies from ancient cultures endure today.

How is leisure defined now?

Most commonly, leisure is defined today as free time, recreational activity, and a special attitude.

Key Terms

Humanities 4
Aesthetic 9
Impressionism 9
Culture hearths 16
Aristotle 18
Olympian 19
Schole 21
Ludi 22
Feudalism 28
Work ethic 29
Renaissance 29
Humanism 30
Discretionary time 32

Skiing through a pine forest. Watching a movie on television. Baking a cake. Leafing through a magazine. Knitting a sweater. Winning a game of Monopoly. Coaching a Little League team. Conversing in an electronic chat room. Playing in a soccer match. Planting geraniums. These and a wide world of other experiences are our pastimes—our leisure.

To have leisure is one of the earliest dreams of human beings—to be free to pursue what we want, to spend our time meaningfully in pleasurable ways, to live in a state of grace (Godbey, 1999). Living life on our own terms is a central idea for people, and in this chapter we set the stage for understanding the essential humanness of leisure by exploring the foundational meanings of our pastimes.

Since leisure is a complex concept that has different meanings depending on the people, place, and time, defining it requires journeys to different peoples, places, and times. First, we define leisure through its reflections in the humanities: literature, art, and music. Next, we examine some of the enduring meanings of leisure by exploring their origins in ancient cultures. Finally, we summarize leisure's contemporary meaning according to its common connotations.

The Humanities of Leisure

Leisure is a part of the humanities because the humanities are those areas of creation whose subject is human experience. The humanities include

> **Humanities:** areas of creation whose subject is human experience

the arts, such as music, paintings, poems—a record of human experience. Broadly speaking, the arts focus on artificial objects or events created by human beings; however, the term "artificial" does not mean "phony." In its original sense it simply means "not from nature," that is, something made by humans. In fact, the word "art" comes from the same root.

In creating songs, stories, sculptures, and other art forms, composers, writers, and artists begin with their own experiences. When we listen to a musical performance or read a short story, we understand something about the life of its creator. Because leisure is so basic to being human, it is often expressed in their creations.

Leisure and Literature

Literature, in the broadest sense, is widely apparent in everyday life. Magazine articles, greeting card verses, hymns, and novels are all forms of literature. For example, in the United States and Canada people spend about $36 billion a year on books (Association of American Publishers, 2003).

Fiction writers, dramatists, and poets often write about their feelings, what they believe, their times, and the lives they lead. Like looking into a mirror, literature offers the context of life. For example, during the early 1900s in the United States, literature expressed the optimism and conservative ideals of the Victorian Age. Authors of the 1920s wrote about disillusioned and rootless characters. Literature of the 1930s protested unjust social conditions. Today, literature often features the pains of human relationships.

For example, in John Updike's story "Still of Some Use," first published in 1987, notice how the loss of family unity is described through the loss of a family pastime.

> When Foster helped his ex-wife clean out the attic of the house where they had once lived and which she was now selling, they came across dozens of forgotten, broken games. Parcheesi, Monopoly, Lotto: games aping the strategies of the stock market, of crime detection, of real-estate speculation, of international diplomacy and war; games with spinners, dice, lettered tiles, cardboard spacemen, and plastic battleships; games bought in five-and-tens and department stores feverish and musical with Christmas expectations; games enjoyed on the afternoon of a birthday and for a few afternoons thereafter and then allowed, shy of one or two pieces, to drift into closets and toward the attic. Yet, discovered in their bright flat boxes between trunks of outgrown clothes and defunct appliances, the games presented a forceful semblance of value: the springs of their miniature launchers still reacted, the logic of their instructions would still generate suspense, given a chance.
>
> "What shall we do with all these games?" Foster shouted, in a kind of agony, to his scattered family as they moved up and down the attic stairs.
>
> "Trash 'em," his younger son, a strapping nineteen, urged.
>
> "Would the Goodwill want them?" asked his ex-wife, still wife enough to think that all of his questions deserved answers. "You used to be able to give things like that to orphanages. But they don't call them orphanages anymore, do they?"
>
> His older son, now twenty-two, with a cinnamon-colored beard, offered, "They wouldn't work anyhow; they all have something missing. That's how they got to the attic."
>
> "Well, why didn't we throw them away at the time?" Foster asked, and had to answer himself. Cowardice, the answer was. Inertia. Clinging to the past.
>
> His sons, with a shadow of old obedience, came and looked over his shoulder at the sad wealth of abandoned playthings, silently groping with him for the particular happy day connected to this and that pattern of coded squares and colored arrows. Their lives had touched these tokens and counters once; excitement had flowed along the paths of these stylized landscapes. But the day was gone, and scarcely a memory remained.

"Toss 'em," the younger decreed, in his manly voice.

For these days of cleaning out, the boy had borrowed a pickup truck from a friend and parked it on the lawn beneath the attic window, so the smaller items of discard could be tossed directly into it. The bigger items were lugged down the stairs and through the front hall and out; already the truck was loaded with old mattresses, broken clock-radios, obsolete skis, and boots. It was a game of sorts to hit the truck bed with objects dropped from the height of the house. Foster flipped game after game at the target two stories below. When the boxes hit, they exploded, throwing a spray of dice, tokens, counters, and cards into the air and across the lawn. A box called Mousetrap, its lid showing laughing children gathered around a Rube Goldberg device, drifted sideways, struck one side wall of the truck, and spilled its plastic components into a flower bed. As a set of something called Drag Race! floated gently as a snowflake before coming to rest, much diminished, on a stained mattress, Foster saw in the depth of downward space the cause of his melancholy: he had not played enough with these games. Now no one wanted to play.

(From *Trust Me* by John Updike. Copyright © by John Updike. Reprinted by permission of Alfred A. Knopf Inc.)

Updike, whose fiction usually includes deep uneasiness mixed with humor over changes of relationships within a family, has used in this story "fun and games" as an explanation of family loss. Can you remember the end of a particular family custom that your parents expected to continue, such as playing cards on the patio in the summer, going to sports events together, or spending vacations at the same place?

In comparison, Maya Angelou's poem "Harlem Hopscotch," uses the rhythm of a chant for a children's street game to express a serious problem in society.

HARLEM HOPSCOTCH

One foot down, then hop! It's hot.
> *Good things for the ones that's got.*
Another jump, now to the left.
> *Everybody for hisself.*
In the air, now both feet down.
> *Since you black, don't stick around.*
Food is gone, the rent is due,
> *Curse and cry and then jump two.*
All the people out of work,
> *Hold for three, then twist and jerk.*
Cross the line, they count you out.
> *That's what hopping's all about.*

Both feet flat, the game is done.
They think I lost. I think I won.

(From *Just Give Me a Cool Drink of Water 'Fore I Die* by Maya Angelou. Copyright © 1971 by Maya Angelou. Reprinted by permission of Random House, Inc.)

In the poem Angelou uses the children's game of hopscotch to vent frustration and a sense of betrayal. Although the poem is about the injustices of race and social class, it makes light of it by putting it into a rhythm of a classic children's pastime. Or does it? What do you think is meant by the game's outcome in the last line?

And, finally, from a novel by John Knowles:

Underseas diving I knew to be a nerve-racking sport, that's why I chose it. I had never understood people who sought "peace and quiet." I looked for peace in the middle of a howling hurricane of action, in the silent eye at the center.

(From *Morning in Antebes* by John Knowles. Copyright © 1961 by John Knowles.)

The Study Says
Fairy Tale Drinking
Box 1.1

Directions: Players need two full pitchers of beer for the table and one empty glass per person, plus one extra glass. Float the extra glass in one of the pitchers. The lip of the glass should protrude about an inch above the surface of the beer. To begin, players fill their glasses from the second pitcher and take turns pouring beer from their glasses into the floating glass. Each player is responsible for an out-loud count of five while pouring beer into the floating glass. The glass then becomes the responsibility of the next player. The perfect pour is one that causes the glass to sink to the bottom in six seconds, because the player in whose turn the glass drops to the bottom of the pitcher must drink all of its contents.

In this study, a narrative analysis of the drinking game "Dunk the Duchess" reveals that at least part of the appeal is that the game is a fairy tale. Fairy tales have three characteristics, as this drinking game demonstrates: character roles, binary oppositions, and archetypal narrative trajectory.

For the characters, the role of princess is played by the floating glass, the object of the action. In fact, the very name of the game refers to the floating glass as "the duchess." The floating glass also plays the role of villain. It controls the outcome of the story and has the power to bring both safety and harm to players. The beer in the pitcher containing the floating glass is like the fairy godmother in "Cinderella": It instructs the princess/glass in what to do. Meanwhile, the role of hero is played by the individual players' glasses of beer. Yet the hero is a false one. As the game story proceeds and more and more beer is poured into the glass/toward the princess from players' glasses, it is revealed that while appearing to nurture and care for the princess/glass, ultimately the beer is transformed along with the princess/glass into a villain.

The study also suggests that drinking games are fairy tales according to their binary oppositions. Basic to any narrative is the establishment of conflict. Binary oppositions, or pairs of opposing forces, often identify the conflict. In drinking games, the opposition of these forces creates the excitement of the action. In "Dunk the Duchess" these competing forces are:

Weak	–	Strong
Unskilled	–	Skilled
Female	–	Male
Chugging	–	Not chugging
Passed out	–	Not passed out
"Winning"	–	"Losing"

Finally, the narrative trajectory of the game can be observed. In the typical fairy tale plot, there is preparation, complication, transference, struggle, return, and recognition. In "Dunk the Duchess" the preparation phase is the gathering of players, pitchers, beer, and glasses. Players' roles are also negotiated. Next, the plot involves a complication. In this game the fine motor skill of pouring beer accurately is required. The complication phase of the plot begins when the villain's (floating glass's) efforts to manipulate the princess succeed, and the princess (also the floating glass) is unable to sustain the quantity of beer. There is transference in the plot's trajectory and a struggle ensues. All is ended when the "winning" player chugs and passes out, to the enthusiasm of the other players.

(From "Snarfing, Booting, and Dunk the Duchess A Narrative Tale of College Drinking Games" by Ruth V. Russell. Paper presented at the Leisure Research Symposium, Nashville, TN, 1999.)

Leisure and Art

People have always had an interest in the beauty of order. We enjoy certain patterns of contrast and balance for their own sake. We doodle during class, wear jewelry, and make patterns with the lawnmower in our yard. We receive an **aesthetic** experience from it. The use of pattern also has a commemorative function. The most important events in our religious, social, and political lives are reflected in art. For example, when we take pictures of relatives at family reunions, we record the occasion in visual form to make it memorable.

> **Aesthetic:** sense of beauty

In other words, art mirrors what we consider to be beautiful and important. Since our curiosity here is about leisure, let's continue our humanities exploration by finding what is considered beautiful and important about leisure through sculpture and painting.

To the ancient Greeks, a human being's health and happiness were supremely important. In particular, they admired the beauty and agility of the human body (Fig. 1.1). Since it was through the perfection of their bodies that human beings most resembled the gods, sports were a spiritual as well as physical expression. The numerous ancient Greek sculptures of humans remaining today communicate that life was good and meant to be enjoyed. The nude male body in action at gymnasiums was a daily experience, and sculptors had ample opportunity to observe the body's proportions and musculature.

Perhaps one of the most readily recognized reflections of leisure in art comes from the **impressionist** period in Europe. Impressionism is a style of art that presents an immediate "impression" of an object or event. Impressionist painters try to show what the eye sees at a glance, and the composition seems spontaneous.

> **Impressionism:** an art style that achieves a vividness simulating reflected light

Figure 1.1

The Ancient Greeks greatly respected the beauty and agility of the human body. Photo of a sculpture of Nike loosening her sandal, Acropolis. © Ruth V. Russell

Although painters and other artists have created impressionistic works in several periods of history, the term is most commonly applied to the work of a group of painters exhibiting in Paris from about 1870 to 1910. What is the impression of leisure in this art?

The painting Terrace at Sainte-Adresse by Claude Monet depicts vacationers (Fig. 1.2). Painted in 1866, it is the view from a window of his aunt's villa in France where Monet stayed that summer. Out in the water are a number of ships, varying from the pleasure boats moored on the left to the steamers on the right. The ships include a mixture of old and new ships, which represent the transition of sail to steam. Another related transition is represented in the painting. In the middle distance is a fishing boat (just above the parasol), suggesting the local and traditional life at Sainte-Adresse before its transformation by tourists. This mirrors what was happening at that time in most of coastal France. Fishing villages were being changed into resorts, marked by broad avenues, sidewalks, formal gardens, and huge buildings. Shortly after the scene depicted in Monet's painting, municipal authorities and owners of villas began filling in or leveling land, pushing landings, porches, and roads out toward the water, and creating artificial spaces for the visiting Parisians, leaving nothing for the fishermen and shopkeepers who had once lived there (Herbert, 1988).

Figure 1.2

Claude Monet. Terrace at Sainte-Adresse. 1866. (The Metropolitan Museum of Art, purchased with special contributions and purchase funds given or bequeathed by friends of the Museum, 1967. 67.241)

Mary Cassatt's Woman in Black at the Opera, painted in 1879, presents a woman in "matinee" clothing using her upward-tilted opera glasses to scan the audience (Fig. 1.3). With a bit of humor, Cassatt also has a man in the distance leaning out of his box to point his glasses in her direction, emphasizing the fun of spying on one's society (Herbert, 1988). We also learn from the painting that leisure defined the upper social class of this era.

Figure 1.3

Mary Cassatt. Woman in Black at the Opera. 1879. (The Hayden Collection. Courtesy Museum of Fine Arts, Boston)

Enjoying restaurants and cafes was also an important pastime for upper-class Parisians at the time. Many paintings from the impressionist period depict women and men enjoying each other's company over food and drink. Pierre-Auguste Renoir's painting The Luncheon of the Boating Party, begun in the summer of 1880, shows the terrace of the Restaurant Fournaise (Fig. 1.4). Renoir shows us something about interrelationships. Notice the young man leaning over, intent on the young woman seated at the front table, while her tablemate looks away and across the table. But the object of his gaze is a woman occupied with her puppy, and the man standing behind her is gazing across the terrace at someone else. Could we say that this painting reflects isolation, however relaxed, that can be part of anyone's experience at a party?

Figure 1.4

Pierre-Auguste Renoir. The Luncheon of the Boating Party. 1881. (The Phillips collection, Washington, D.C.)

In Profile

Le Restaurant Fournaise
Box 1.2

By the close of the 19th century, Paris was overflowing with any number of restaurants and cafes where one could sample a variety of wines and robust cuisine. Especially popular were the restaurants on the outskirts of Paris at the banks of the Seine River. On Sundays they teemed with boating Parisians who fled the city for a bit of fresh air and romance. One popular establishment was Le Restaurant Fournaise. Best known for its depiction in The Luncheon of the Boating Party (1881) by Renoir (Fig. 1.4), the restaurant had a lively atmosphere. The Fournaise became quite popular among the Parisian upper classes, and it was not uncommon to see finely dressed men and women, nobility included, amid the bare-armed, undershirt-clad canoeists dining on cabbage soup, bacon omelets, fried fish, roast chicken, and potato salad—all washed down with a good Bordeaux. Diners were served on the red-and-white canopied terrace overlooking the river, and at midday a majestic view of sunlight flickering on the Seine gave way to a veritable parade of 300 to 400 boats passing (Leaf, 1994).

Even this brief glance at leisure through the impressionist art of the late 1800s reveals that leisure was paramount in Paris. Indeed, idle hours and entertainment greatly expanded during this time, particularly for the upper class. By the end of the century, daily life there was dominated by theaters, operas, cafes, restaurants, dances, racetracks, gardens, and parks. Tourists began to flock to Paris to enjoy the elegant urban culture and to the seaside to take in the peaceful beauty. All this is portrayed in the thousands of paintings by impressionist artists.

Leisure and Music

Music is perhaps the most basic and universal activity of humankind. Beginning as the simple and natural sound of the human voice, music has existed in some form from the earliest days. Through the centuries, music has taken many forms and reflected many ways of life. Today in Western cultures, people often express themselves through jazz, rock, rhythm and blues, country, rap, gospel, classical, folk, and other musical styles. For example, U.S. recording companies in 2001 shipped 968 million CDs, representing $13.7 billion (Recording Industry Association of America, 2004).

In keeping with our exploration of expressions of leisure through the humanities, how might music portray leisure? Let's consider rock and roll and begin with Elvis Presley, who remains rock's most indelible image worldwide. Rock and roll would have happened—and was already happening—without Elvis, but it would have been very different and would never have reached the spectacular heights nor had the sweeping impact that it did without Elvis (Gass, 1994). In Elvis, millions of young people found more than a new entertainer; they found themselves, or at least an idealized image of themselves that stood in stark, liberating contrast to the repressed atmosphere of the 1950s. Thus, through a popular form of leisure—rock and roll music—masses of young people found a liberating identity.

What was this new identity? 1956 and 1957 were the glory years for Elvis. During that period he held down the number-one position on the charts for a staggering 58 weeks (Gass, 1994). For example, "Hound Dog" was just one half of an amazing 1956 single released by Elvis; the flip side was "Don't Be Cruel," a pairing that resulted in the highest-selling single record of the decade, and one which provides a tidy summary of the image Elvis' music represented to young people of the time. While the straight rock of screaming guitars and drums in "Hound Dog" emphasizes a wild and raucous sound, "Don't Be Cruel" has a lighter beat and gentler accompaniment that focuses attention on a sweet melody and lyrics. This makes for a big difference between the sexually aggressive "Hound Dog" and the playfully innocent "Don't Be Cruel." And just like the two sides of this one single, youth of the 1950s were bumping, although timidly, against the outer edges of a sort of rebellion.

Rock and roll provides many other reflections of leisure as well. While some rock songs—like those by Elvis—defined the character of youth, others spoke to the youth creed—having fun. One of the best examples, perhaps, is "All Summer Long" by The Beach Boys.

> *Sittin' in my car outside your house*
> *(Sittin' in my car outside your house)*
> *'Member when you spilled Coke all over your blouse*
>
> *T-shirts, cut-offs, and a pair of thongs*
> *(T-shirts, cut-offs, and a pair of thongs)*
> *We've been having fun all summer long*
>
> *(All summer long you've been with me)*
> *I can't see enough of you*

(All summer long we've both been free)
Won't be long till summertime is through
(Summertime is through)
Not for us now

Miniature golf and Hondas in the hills
(Miniature golf and Hondas in the hills)
When we rode the horse we got some thrills
Every now and then we hear our song
(Every now and then we hear our song)
We've been having fun all summer long
Won't be long till summertime is through
(Summertime is through)

(Excerpt from "All Summer Long," by The Beach Boys—Brian Wilson, Irving Music, Inc., Recorded 5/6/64 and
5/7/64. Reprinted with permission.)

The Beach Boys made bright harmonies and falsetto voices as central to rock and roll as guitars and drums. Their songs were full of in-group surfing references that sounded positively exotic to the rest of us, along with celebrations of hot rods, drag races, dance parties, going steady, and other rites of teenage life. And the purpose of that life was to have fun. Unlike Elvis' soft–hard youth rebellion, The Beach Boys brought teenage concerns to playing at the beach all summer long.

We can find the meaning of leisure in musical forms other than rock and roll as well. For example, nearly two centuries before Elvis and The Beach Boys, Vivaldi's classical work "The Four Seasons" portrays a description of the powerful emotions associated with the change of nature's seasons. The celebration in the music of things pastoral is poignant, since the composer was sickly and often housebound, yet it also reflects the eighteenth century's fashionable preoccupation with the idealization of nature. In the rap song "People Everyday," recorded in the early 1990s by the group Arrested Development, leisure is expressed as hanging out in the park with a radio tape player, resting, and putting one's soul at ease. Michael Jackson, in the song "Remember the Time," expresses the park differently. Here the park is remembered as a place for falling in love. Leisure is sometimes used as a metaphor in music, as illustrated by k.d. lang's "Wash Me Clean," where desiring someone romantically is like swimming— "swimming through my veins."

There are, of course, many more sculptures, paintings, stories, poems, compositions, and songs that we could use to extend this excursion into the portrayal of leisure in the humanities. Try one of the activities in Box 1.3 for additional references to the meaning of leisure.

In Your Own Experience

A Potpourri
Box 1.3

What other examples of the meaning of leisure in the humanities can you find? Here is a potpourri of experiences that will help you find them:

1. Who is your favorite recording artist? Listen to a CD that samples this music and determine how many references to leisure you can find. How is leisure defined?
2. Visit your campus or community art museum. Check out any of the galleries (Western art, Eastern art, ancient art) and determine how leisure is portrayed in the paintings and sculptures.
3. Pick up a copy of your favorite magazine. By just glancing at each page from beginning to end, how many references to leisure can you find in the ads, stories, articles, and photographs? How is leisure depicted?

After your personal adventures with this you might form small discussion groups to share and compare the results.

Classical Meanings of Leisure

It is not really known where civilization, that is, settled community life and the social institutions necessary to support it, originated. However, the story of how it evolved once it began is known. The retreat of the last glaciers (about 11,000 years ago) initiated successive periods of cultural evolution from primitive hunting-and-gathering societies to the development of agriculture and animal husbandry, and ultimately to the urbanization and industrialization of modern societies. As people gathered together into communities, more formalized rules of conduct naturally emerged, including governments, religions, and work occupations.

Geographers term these original centers of community development **culture hearths.** Arising in separate areas of the world, at different times, and under differing circumstances, the earliest culture hearths were in the areas

Culture hearths: original centers of civilization. Significant innovations made them cornerstones for the development of more advanced civilizations around the Mediterranean Sea, the Indian subcontinent, northern China, Southeast Asia, and in several locations in Africa and South America (Rubenstein, 2003). Our contemporary meanings of leisure were shaped by the histories of these early culture hearths. Let's explore some of them.

The Kingdom of Kush: Adornment in Daily Life

Africa has been called the "birthplace of the human race." The oldest evidence of human like creatures found anywhere in the world consists of bones and other fossils discovered at many sites in eastern and southern Africa. Also, the fertile soils of the Nile Valley in northern Africa supported some of the earliest and greatest civilizations in the world, including a kingdom called Kush, which arose in about 4,000 BC (Bayley, Baynes, & Kendall, 2004).

Kush was perhaps the earliest center for the exchange of ideas, especially in politics and religion. The Kushites also developed new styles in art and architecture, including the use of metal and wood. For example, in excavations of burial tombs, such as the one at Karanog, decorative clothing, jewelry, and vessels for food and drink were found. Items needed for personal adornment included eye makeup containers and tweezers. Elaborate oil flasks, bronze cups, and wine jars were also discovered. (Pan-African Market Place, 1993). Such avid use of art and craft in daily life appears to be the Kush legacy for leisure.

Ancient Greece: The Good Life

Our leisure inheritance from ancient Greece is significant. The search for a good life and ways to attain it are particularly of Greek origin, and we can trace this through the ancient Greek philosophers.

The philosopher Plato, for example, was interested in the benefits of music and gymnastics. He believed that there were spiritual and physical rewards to be gained from participation in such activities. Socrates believed that knowledge was required in choosing the best pleasures. That is, the good life was a life of right choices and conduct. Throughout his writings, Aristotle also conveyed ideas and, more importantly, ideals about the role of leisure in attaining the good life. In fact, to understand the classical perspective of leisure, there is no better teacher than Aristotle.

Aristotle (Fig. 1.5) believed leisure activities were performed for their own sake. Leisure was the freedom from having to be occupied (thus, from having an occupation) and was the necessary condition for happiness. He believed the goodness of anything was found in the realization of its uniqueness, and for human beings, he considered the most unique quality to be the power to think. Thus, Aristotle believed a life of contemplation was the proper use of

Figure 1.5
Aristotle (Christopher B. Stage)

leisure. He also believed that a lifetime should be devoted not only to thinking noble and divine thoughts, but to doing civic and productive good deeds as well (Hemingway, 1988).

Aristotle: 384-322 BC; Greek philosopher and scientist who shares with Plato and Socrates the distinction of being the most famous of ancient thinkers

In Profile

Aristotle
Box 1.4

Aristotle (384-322 BC) was a Greek philosopher, educator, and scientist. He grew up in the northern Greek town of Stagira, the son of the personal physician to the king of nearby Macedonia. Some historians believe that Aristotle may have lived his early years recklessly but soon made his way to Plato at the Academy in Athens and studied under this master teacher for 20 years (Simpson, 1989).

Aristotle left Athens and became the tutor to Alexander, grandson of the Macedonian king. This new assignment paid off when Alexander later conquered all of Greece and ascended to the throne. Under the support of Alexander, Aristotle returned to Athens and founded the Lyceum. This new school immediately surpassed Plato's Academy in prestige and was particularly noted for its teaching of the natural sciences.

In spite of this, the Athenian citizenry remained at odds with Aristotle because of his friendship with Alexander, who had conquered them. When Alexander unexpectedly died, the Macedonian rule in Athens quickly fell, and Aristotle was forced to leave Athens to avoid the same fate as Socrates. Only a few months after fleeing Athens, Aristotle became ill and died.

How ancient Greeks interpreted the advice of their philosophers in daily life provides a legacy in expressions of leisure of today. For example, daily leisure included such intellectual pursuits as philosophy and mathematics, or cultural activities such as poetry and music, politics, and sports. Yet social distinctions were prominent in ancient Greek leisure. What Plato, Socrates, and Aristotle taught about leisure was available only to aristocrats. In Athens at the time, native-born males who were citizens were a privileged leisure class. Their control of a system of slaves and limitations on the rights of women empowered their lives of leisure. An immediate example of this legacy can be found in the lives of wealthy plantation owners in the colonial Americas.

Privileged ancient Greek children played with toys widely recognized by today's children: jacks (called knuckle bones because the jacks were the knuckle bones of an animal), kites, and marbles. Amphitheaters provided entertainment in music, dance, and drama. Even proxemos, whose prime function was to assist fellow citizens traveling abroad, were the forerunners of today's tour guides.

Another legacy may be found in organized sport. Scholars believe that sport contests might have originally been offered at the funerals of fallen heroes to give their spirits pleasure. Excavation at the ancient Olympic site in western Greece shows that the first formalized Olympic Games took place in 776 BC. Originally named for the god **Olympian**, these games were later held in honor of Zeus. Part religious event and part sports event, the Olympic Games were held every four years, and in the first 13 Olympiads, a footrace of about 180 meters was the only event.

Through the years longer running races were added, as well as other types of competition, such as horse races, weight lifting, boxing, and the pen-

> **Olympian:** one of the ancient Greek gods; being like the god, especially in being calm and untroubled by ordinary affairs

tathlon (which consisted of javelin and discus throwing, a sprint foot race, the long jump, and wrestling). A savage and sometimes deadly sport called pancratium, which combined boxing and wrestling, was introduced in 648 BC. Scholars tell us that pancratium was like a form of extreme wrestling in which the only hits not allowed were gouging with the thumb and biting.

Of course, athletes in the games were the aristocratic young men who had the privilege of leisure. Yet there is some evidence that women had their own games in Olympia (Pausanias, 1918). These were the Heraea Games held every four years to honor the goddess Hera, the consort of Zeus. Here unmarried women competed in foot races, with winners receiving the Olympic olive branch garland and, according to Pausanias, part of the cow sacrificed to Hera.

Although we commonly think that the end of the ancient Olympic Games occurred with the Roman conquest, their demise actually began before this when a wave of interest in books and the arts swept through Greece. Youth turned their attention away from sports, and later when the Romans did conquer Greece, stadiums were turned into amphitheaters, and athletes were replaced with slaves. Eventually, since this caused a decline in the quality of the games, the Emperor Theodosius ordered them ended in 394 AD and none were held for more than 1,500 years.

In Focus

Are Today's Olympians Too Commercial?
Box 1.5

These days you don't have to look far to see the connection between commercialism and sports. For example, at Olympic competitions, athletes' uniforms and equipment bear the discreet but readily identifiable trademarks of their manufacturers. After the Games we see winning Olympians endorsing all manner of products, such as cereals. They become celebrities and appear on television shows, make movies, go on the talk circuit, and do other things to cash in on their fame.

Is it all too much? Do you ever wish we could return to the "pure" notion of the sports competitions of the ancient Olympic Games?

But wait a minute! Even without Wheaties, ancient Greeks honored and even "marketed' their athletic heroes. Although a garland of olive leaves from a tree at Zeus' shrine was the official prize awarded, an Olympic victory was often lucrative. Poets were often commissioned to celebrate these victories with odes, and sculptors were employed to render an image of the athlete to be placed in a sanctuary. Coins were also minted to commemorate athletic victories, and some city-states awarded stipends to Olympic winners or allowed them to dine at public expense for life (Martin, 1996).

Questions to Consider and Discuss

1. *Who is your favorite "commercial" athlete? In what ways has this person been commercialized?*

2. *Do you consider the treatment of favorite athletes from the ancient games to have been commercial according to today's practice? How is it similar? Different?*

3. *Do you think the commercialization of athletes helps or hinders the sport? Why?*

Afterward, leisure became more studious. To emphasize this, it is worth noting that the ancient Greek term for leisure was **schole**, "meaning to use free time wisely for oneself" (Ibrahim, 1991). Toward this goal, Plato established the Academy, a place for reading, writing, discussion, and thinking forms of pastimes, as well as music, poetry, oratory, debate, and inquiry about nature. It may surprise you that this Greek word for leisure, schole, was the origin of the English word school.

> **Schole:** an ancient Greek term for leisure, meaning to use free time wisely for oneself

Putting it all together, then, we can conclude that for the ancient Greeks, leisure was both intellectual and physical. It was the importance of developing both the mind and the body through participation, learning, and zestful living. The good life of leisure for the Greeks was a very complex ideal: Knowledge and health led to virtuous choices and conduct, which in turn led to true pleasure. Leisure, then, was not just a weekend or a vacation. For the privileged, it was a way of conducting all of life.

Ancient Rome: Leisure as Spectacle

Quite a different meaning of leisure that we might also find evident today is from ancient Rome. Rome began its rise to power around 200 BC. It ruled and prospered under a policy of expansion by using both military and political methods until around 200 AD. Although ancient Romans borrowed a good deal of Greek philosophy and copied Greek art and architecture, they had a more practical notion about leisure.

As Rome conquered its neighbors (Greece, Syria, Egypt, and Macedonia), the problem of overseeing an immense empire meant that the need for social order took precedence over the individual's need for personal freedom. Discipline and careful regulation were required. Further, as Rome's military prizes increased, so did the free time of the growing middle class. The governing empire responded with large-scale entertainment. As opposed to the Greek idea of leisure as both intellectual and spiritual, Romans participated in mass recreation. There were heated public baths, parade grounds for various ball games, and grand athletic exhibitions. Often, the middle classes were spectators to absurd pleasures: Gladiators often fought each other to the death, and condemned political prisoners and criminals were sometimes thrown to wild animals. Leisure was used as a form of social control based on the policy of "bread and circuses." The recreation exhibitions became a means whereby rulers and officials could win popular favor, as they had great drawing power among the masses.

Beginning about 31 BC, the **ludi**, or public games, became annual events in the Roman calendar (Ibrahim, 1991). For example, the Ludi Plebei, games of the commoners, lasted from November 4 to 17. By the end of the Roman Empire, the calendar included 175 official holidays, with 101 of them for the-

Ludi: a Latin word for public games

atrical entertainments, 64 devoted to chariot races, and 10 given over to gladiatorial combats (Roberts, 1962).

Specialized facilities were provided throughout the Empire for these events. The oldest of these, the Circus Maximus, was built for horse races, trick-riding, mock cavalry battles, and chariot races. Amphitheaters hosted gladiatorial combats, with the largest, the Colosseum, holding thousands of spectators (Fig. 1.6). The Colosseum also hosted the naumachiae, a ship battle requiring the flooding of the Colosseum floor. The greatest of all naumachiae was staged by Claudius outside Rome in Lake Fucine.

Figure 1.6

The Colosseum in Rome today. © Ruth V. Russell

A total of 19,000 men boarded a fleet of 50 ships and battled each other beginning at 10:00 am, and by 3:00 pm, 3,000 of them were dead (Butler, 1971).

Ironically, such excesses in the name of leisure finally degraded the Roman people and their culture. Although rich cultural developments occurred during this time in sculpture, painting, and poetry, the leisure tastes of the masses led to a depravity that some historians consider an important factor in the demise of the Roman Empire. The preponderance of passive and barbaric entertainment, which sapped the will of the spectators, perhaps was too much for the constant pressure of aggressive invaders.

Ancient China: Life Balance

According to ancient Chinese belief, the area we call China is situated, cosmologically, at the center of the universe. Thus, the idea of centricity has been prevalent in over 4,000 years of Chinese philosophy. For example, the quest for harmony, life balance, calmness, order, and peace is central to the teachings of Confucius. Does this provide a legacy for today's leisure?

The story of leisure in ancient and medieval China is framed by the histories of the imperial dynasties, in particular the Han and Tang Dynasties (Table 1.1, Fig 1.7). With the arrival of the Han Dynasty, for example, China was united politically, and a lifestyle resembling that of the ancient Greeks evolved (Ibrahim, 1991). It was during this time that Confucianism became the official doctrine, which among other things resulted in an educated upper class devoting itself to fine arts. The goal was to prepare a broadly cultivated person in both the literary and martial arts, following an ideal of a harmonious body and mind. Later, the Tang Dynasty contributed another important chapter to leisure's beginnings. Culturally, this was a period of enormous vitality. China became a cosmopolitan society—one rich in music, literature, and the visual arts (Tregear, 1985). Even today, poems dating from the Tang Dynasty are regarded

Table 1.1
An Abbreviated Chronology of Chinese Dynasties

Dynasty	Time period	Theme
Xia	ca. 2000–1500 BC	Its existence is debated
Shang	ca. 1600–1111 BC	Aristocratically minded
Zhou	ca. 1111–221 BC	Unsettled and warring
Qi	221–207 BC	Initiated imperial rule
Han	206BC–220AD	Revived artistic endeavors
Tang	618–907	Golden age of literature and art
Song	960–1279	Commerce and agriculture
Ming	368–1644	Economic, technical development
Qing	1644–1911	End of imperial rule

Figure 1.7

Tourists at the Great Wall of China today. Over 2000 years old, today the wall is maintained for tourism by the Chinese government. © Ruth V. Russell

as unsurpassed. Interestingly, based on the idea of a square world, the Tang capital (the city of Xi'an today) was laid out like a chess board.

Two types of people evolved during the dynasty periods: the governing class and the peasants. The governing and merchant classes of people, the male gentry, lived in a large household with many servants, wives, concubines, children, and grandchildren. These buildings were set at right angles and were separated by a series of courtyards. Each building was designed to render something special, such as admiring the moonlight, making music, painting chrysanthemums, or having banquets. Specialized servants for recreation were kept, such as chess players, painters, acrobats, and musicians. An ancient text cited by Ibrahim (1991) lists 55 varieties of such recreation talents, including tellers of riddles and obscure stories, imitators of street cries, sleight-of-hand experts, and kite flyers.

The masses in ancient China, on the other hand, were peasants who tilled the land. Although they were legally free, they could be sold to other households. During the Song Dynasty, however, the peasants became more prosperous and had more free time for play and entertainment (Fitzgerald, 1933). "Pleasure grounds" were vast covered markets where crowds gathered to watch a theatrical presentation, see a marionette show, take lessons in singing, or be entertained by dancing turtles!

Muhammad's Early Empire: Relaxation

Muhammad, which means "praised one," was the founder of the religion of Islam and one of the most influential people of all time. Within 100 years after his death, in 632AD, Muslims had carried his teachings into other parts of the Middle East, North Africa, Europe, and Asia. Today, Islam is the second largest religion, with about 1.3 billion followers (22 percent) throughout the world (Adherents.com, 2002).

Included in the teachings of Muhammad is another meaning of leisure still retained by people today. Early Muslims learned Muhammad's philosophy of leisure through one of his sayings: "Recreate your hearts hour after hour, for the tired hearts go blind" (from the Hadith). In the Qur'an (the Islamic holy book), paradise for the faithful is envisioned as an expression of leisure. It consists of a verdant garden where chosen men recline on beautiful carpets next to rippling water and delight in the fragrance of flowers. The vision of these lush gardens for relaxing were recreated by wealthy ancient Muslims and Arabs alike, who spent hours there among the pavilions, pools, and fountains. During the day they relaxed, conversed with friends, and played chess. At night, entertainment was provided by salaried musicians, and dancers performed until dawn.

As early as this ancient period, women were already segregated from men (Ibrahim, 1991). Even though Muhammad had sought to limit the practice of polygamy (marriage to more than one wife), the upper-class wealthy man typically kept several wives and their children in a special place within the palace called the harem. The harem lifestyle also focused on relaxation: Wives and their children received visitors, played quiet games, read, and told stories.

Ancient New World Societies: Ceremony

Now let's think about the early societies in the Americas. In North America we can cite the ancient civilization of the Cahokia people who lived around 700AD near what is today St. Louis. From studying the drawings on excavated pottery remains, archeologists believe Cahokia was the ceremonial center for a larger metropolis that served a series of villages within a 50-mile radius.

Meanwhile, the history of the Mayas and the Aztecs offers a more extensive glimpse of a ceremonial meaning of leisure. For example, the Mayas, who around 300AD developed a magnificent civilization in what is now part of Mexico and Central America, considered the religious festival to be a favorite pastime. The Mayan year was divided into 18 months of 20 days each, leaving an extra five-day "lucky" period. Each month had its special festivals (Ibrahim, 1991) with drummed music, dancers, and dramatists. The passion of the Mayas, however, was the game of pok-a-rok. Similar to today's basketball, pok-a-rok was played with a ball on a long, rectangular court with spectators seated on both sides. The goal was to pass the ball through a stone ring—often as high as 30 feet, using only the elbows, knees, and hips (Fig. 1.8).

Figure 1.8

Remains of a pok-a-rok court in Mexico's Yucatan region. © Ruth V. Russell

Similarly, for the Aztec people who ruled a mighty empire in what is now Mexico around the 1400s, religious ceremony was central to life. The Aztecs had one of the most advanced civilizations in the world, building cities as large as any in Europe at that time. The Aztecs worshiped hundreds of gods and goddesses, each of whom ruled one or more human activities. Most religious celebrations took place inside walled ceremonial centers. They included a temple, gardens, living quarters for the priests, sacred water pools for ceremonial cleansing, and racks to hold the skulls of sacrificed victims. In addition, another game resembling basketball, tlachtli, was played in the ceremonial centers. Anthropologists have generally been awed by speculated luxuries within these centers, including dancers kept for amusement, royal zoos, and of course chocolate!

In Focus

Ancient Inuit Endurance Contests
Box 1.6

One sign of the meaning of leisure today is the popularity of endurance sports. Testing the limits of human (and animal) endurance for the fun of it is illustrated by the masses who participate in the New York City and Boston marathons, in any number of triathlons (which combine swimming, bicycling, and running), and even in equestrian endurance rides. These and other sporting events are designed to test an athlete's physical and mental stamina. A modern idea?

In ancient civilizations, endurance sport was often used as a means to test stamina. For example, in the desolate lands near and above the Arctic Circle in today's Canada, the various tribes of Inuit seemed particularly fond of games of endurance (Craig, 2002). These often involved some type of unique contortion of the human body, often creating humorous results. Others seem to have been more a test of a person's pain threshold. For instance, the ikuskikmiag has been described by anthropologists as an elbow-ear walk. Why not try it yourself! Bend down and support yourself by only your toes and elbows. Meanwhile, grasp your ears with your hands. Now see how far you can travel before giving out or toppling over. Or how about tulu-gauyak? In this ancient Inuit competition, both the legs and the arms were placed in the sleeves of a parka, and in this position, the athletes raced to a predetermined mark. In another endurance event, two players would stand face-to-face, wrap their right arm around their opponent's head, and then insert their fingers in his mouth and pull, with the person turning his head toward the pull being declared the loser. This was called igiruktuk.

Questions to Consider and Discuss

1. Do you consider these ancient Inuit endurance events to be cruel and barbaric? Why or why not?

2. What legacy can you trace between these ancient expressions of leisure and such contemporary activities as boxing or "professional" wrestling?

3. Do you consider today's endurance sports to be cruel and barbaric? Why or why not?

Medieval Europe: The Work Ethic

The Middle Ages, or the medieval period, describes the era between ancient and modern times in Western Europe extending from the end of the Roman Empire (about 400AD) to the 1500s. The former Roman Empire was divided into large estates called kingdoms ruled by wealthy landowners. Later, this evolved into the system of **feudalism.**

Feudalism meant a social class-based expression of leisure. In medieval Europe there were three types of people: the wealthy noblemen who owned the land, the clergy who served the church, and the peasants who worked on the land to support themselves, the clergy, and the noblemen.

> **Feudalism:** fragmented political power in which private ownerships prevail

The lives of the noblemen centered on fighting, so as might be guessed, they were particularly interested in hunting and tournaments (Labarge, 1965). Hunting with hounds and falconry were the most popular, and tournaments were mock fighting events. When the events turned into wild melees, a new variation of the tournament developed—the Round Table (Labarge, 1965), which was also a social occasion accompanied by jousting with blunted weapons, wrestling, darts, and even skipping contests. The nobleman's castle was also a setting for pleasures. Minstrels (who were musicians, acrobats, jugglers, and storytellers all in one), entertained, and guests also played dice, backgammon, checkers, and chess. In fact, to be good at chess was a mark of distinction (Ibrahim, 1991). The clergy were wealthy noblemen who devoted their lives to the church, yet they also enjoyed pastimes much like other noblemen. Even though officially regarded as sinful, pastimes included social drinking, gambling, secular music, and theatrical performances, all of which were tolerated because they were linked to religious events (Chubb & Chubb, 1981).

Meanwhile, the peasants, who had few rights and were mostly at the mercy of their lords, had very little free time. Although the church sought to censure it, dancing, singing, and general partying typically filled Sundays and certain church-declared saint's days. Fairs, held for the peasants on church holidays, featured the antics of trained monkeys and such performers as fire-eaters and sword swallowers. The songs of the day were usually sacrilegious and vulgar (Ibrahim, 1991).

As you might already suspect, the story of leisure during the Middle Ages includes a controversial subtext. Life was difficult for everyone. People lived only an average of 30 years. Very few people could read and write. In the midst of this hardship, the Catholic Church became the main civilizing force, and according to church doctrine, the main goal of life was abstinence from worldly pleasures. Thus, the church maintained that the way to a higher quality of life was through hard work, good deeds, and self-deprivation. Thus, officially, leisure was considered to be against church teachings. This is why this period of early human history is often considered to be the birth of the **work ethic.** Whereas to the ancient Greeks, work was a curse, during the Middle Ages, work provided social status.

The Renaissance: Humanism

By about 1300 medieval Europe began to give way to modern Europe, a period in European history called the **Renaissance.** Renaissance is a French word meaning "rebirth," and in this 300-year period, it meant changes in ways of experiencing leisure.

> **Work ethic:** a cultural norm placing a positive moral value on work for its own sake

This was the age of such painters as Michelangelo, Raphael, and Leonardo da Vinci; sculptor Donatello; playwright William Shakespeare; and author Cervantes. This was also an age of adventure. People were fascinated with the world and other people. They set out on dangerous voyages to explore unknown lands. Books about travel began to flood England, and it became a widespread practice for young gentlemen to complement their education with

> **Renaissance:** the transitional era between medieval and modern times in Europe, marked by a humanistic revival of the arts

travel (Hudman, 1980). Drama, music, and dance also flourished. Under the sponsorship of nobles and royalty, theaters and opera houses were constructed, and troupes of actors, singers, musicians, and dancers were in high demand. The wealthy arranged formal dances, exhibitions, banquets, hunts, and masquerades, whereas the middle class tried to copy the upper class by participating in less extravagant festivities. Even children's activities stressed creative pastimes, such as studies in art, music, and science (Bucher, Shiver, & Bucher, 1984).

In short, the Renaissance was a time of renewed interest in those things human, including art, literature, and drama. This emphasis formed a new philosophy known as **humanism**, which glorified and celebrated the human being. The legacy of humanism today can be found in both religious doctrine and individual beliefs. Although it has many current interpretations, humanism includes the idea of human happiness as its own justification. Like leisure, life is to include freedom of expression, awareness of beauty, and harmoniously combining personal satisfaction with self-improvement.

> **Humanism:** a philosophy that emphasizes the importance of human beings

Today's Meanings

By tracing the meaning of leisure in the humanities and in ancient history, we can see that it means many things depending on the place, the time, and the people. Next we consider the contemporary meanings of leisure. As in the humanities and in ancient history, our definitions of leisure today are also a matter of perspective. Individual experiences and cultural biases continue to define leisure in a number of ways. Because of this, leisure is a difficult concept to define. As described by Kelly and Freysinger (2000), "It is an experience, but in

---

Table 1.2
Contemporary Definitions of Leisure

Leisure is . . .

Free time—time free from obligations
"To me, leisure is the weekend."

Recreational activity—nonwork kinds of activity
"To me, playing golf and watching TV are leisure."

Attitude—self-actualized life perspective
"To me, getting the most out of the day is leisure."

In Your Own Experience
Definition Interviews
Box 1.7

Why not understand the differences in definitions of leisure for yourself!
Here's one way:

1. Randomly and quickly ask at least 20 of your friends and family members what leisure means to them. Ask them to give you one-word or one-phrase definitions. Record every definition you are given.

2. Next, select for more formal and lengthy interviews two people you don't know very well and who are different from your friends and family. For example, you might choose someone from another country or a person quite a bit older or younger than you. Ask them about the role(s) of leisure in their lives. How do they experience leisure? What do they like best (and least) about their leisure? How important is leisure in their life?

3. Summarize the results of both the quick and extensive interviews in writing. Bring it to class to compare with the results of other interviews. Discuss how the meaning of leisure is contextual.

context. It has form, but is not defined by form. It takes place in time, but defines the time rather than being defined by it" (p. 16). Therefore, as we consider the contemporary meanings of leisure, be aware that clear boundaries are not possible.

As summarized in Table 1.2, the meaning of leisure today can generally be described in three ways. First, leisure is free time. Next, leisure is nonwork activity. Finally, leisure is a state of mind, or special attitude.

Leisure as Free Time

Today leisure is commonly considered time available after obligations—time to use as one pleases. There is a small but important distinction here. For most people who consider leisure as free time, their perspective goes beyond considering simply the residual time that remains after such tasks as work, study, and personal maintenance are completed. The concept of **discretionary time**

> Discretionary time: time that is free of obligation

perhaps best describes the essence of leisure as time—that is, leisure is time available for making personal choices.

This definition of leisure means that it is quantifiable and that it is possible to refer to leisure in terms of amounts possessed. We often look forward to weekends and holidays because we will have more leisure. When we retire from employment we look forward to more leisure. This quantifiable definition of leisure as free time has led to comparative research. Time–budget studies make it possible to contrast the leisure of different population groups and different cultures. For example, in comparing annual paid vacations required by law across countries, we note that the Dutch receive nine weeks, Swedes get five weeks, the Irish have three weeks, and Canadians and Americans usually receive one to two weeks (Schor, 2001). Further, in North America, teens have more free-time than do middle-aged adults, single men have more than married men, and employed single mothers have the least of all (Kelly & Freysinger, 2000).

These differences in the amount of leisure are due to situational differences. And this is one of the problems with the free-time definition of leisure. People have differing obligations; thus, to have leisure, people must overcome multiple constraints. For example, employed single mothers have many more obligations in their daily lives than do employed single men. Does this mean they have less entitlement to leisure? Also, the free-time definition of leisure is subject to differences in people's perceptions. For example, if free time is regarded as a privilege, it is more likely to be important to use leisure wisely by filling it with experiences that are personally and socially beneficial. In contrast, if free time is perceived to be an empty space that, if left unfilled, becomes something negative, leisure becomes intimidating.

Leisure as Recreational Activity

A second definition of leisure is action based. This definition refers specifically to how we use our time when we are not working. In this sense, we define leisure by the form of our recreational activities. According to the U.S. Census Bureau (2002), 76 percent of Americans participate in exercise programs, 66 percent go to the movies, 66 percent make home improvements, 57 percent visit amusement parks, 45 percent play sports, 43 percent do charity work, and 40 percent pursue computer hobbies as recreational activities.

Even though we may define leisure as nonwork pursuits, it does not mean purposeless activity. According to Dumazedier (1974), leisure activity achieves the purposes of relaxation, diversion, refreshment, and re-creation of the spirit. Thus, accordingly, only those pursuits that satisfy these purposes can be considered leisure. Is it truly this simple?

Some scholars have pointed to the contradiction in this qualification. For example, in considering the purpose of relaxation, can we achieve this by sleeping in on Saturday morning, competing in a triathlon, baking a cake, window-shopping at the mall, playing Solitaire on the computer, and even digging a ditch? Are all of these activities, then, the same form of recreational activity? Scholars have also pointed to another problem in defining leisure as an activity. Is tennis leisure when it is played on Saturday at the local park and something else when played in a required physical education class? When is washing the dishes a leisure activity?

As with the free-time definition, leisure defined as recreational activity means it can be counted and compared across different population groups and cultures. For example, in the U.S. only 35 percent of women as compared with 56 percent of men play sports, and whereas 68 percent of people aged 18 to 24 years engage in computer hobbies, only seven percent of those 75 years old and over do (U.S. Census Bureau, 2002).

Leisure as a State of Mind

Defining leisure as time free after obligations and as recreational activities helps us understand leisure objectively. That is, we can observe, count, and compare leisure when considering it as time and as activity. But is there more to it than this in today's connotation of leisure? Defining leisure as a state of mind or as a special attitude, although more subjective, rounds out our understanding of the meaning of leisure. This third definition asserts, in fact, that time and activity are irrelevant—that only personal meaning counts (Kelly & Freysinger, 2000). That is, leisure is defined as a psychological condition, that is, by the meaning it holds for us, as a philosophy about living. Almost poetically, Pieper (1963) explains it this way: "Leisure, like contemplation, is a higher order than the active life. . . . It involves the capacity to soar in active celebration, to overstep the boundaries of the workaday world".

To illustrate this concept, a team of researchers (Hull, Steward, & Yi, 1992) studied the states of mind of hikers during a short but strenuous day hike. In general, the hikers described their feelings during the hike as complete satisfaction. This is not surprising given the scenic beauty of the area. Yet these feelings of satisfaction were found to be quite independent of the activity and setting. Feelings of self-satisfaction, positive outlook, and happiness varied little with the type of scenery being viewed, the degree of exertion (downhill vs. uphill), or with the accomplishment of reaching the destination. These feelings were more an attitude, or state of mind.

Although this study suggests that the psychological condition of leisure is simply a matter of "feeling good," it is more than this. Leisure, according to the state-of-mind definition, is an entire way of being—one that involves acting on opportunities for building meaningfulness into life. Leisure is self-expression and self-actualization.

Summary: What We Understand

Leisure is a complex concept. To understand its contemporary expression, this chapter explored its various definitions from three perspectives: the humanities, the history of ancient cultures, current connotations. After studying this chapter, you should know that:

- Leisure is contextual. That is, its meaning depends on the place, the time, and the people.

- Literature, art, and music offer glimpses of leisure as integral to the human experience.

- In ancient cultures leisure has meant many things and varied in its importance.

- Our contemporary meanings and uses of leisure are derived in part from the legacies of ancient cultures.

- Contemporary meanings of leisure include free time, recreational activity, and the state of mind.

Applications to Professional Practice

In many societies, leisure opportunities and resources are provided for people. In North America, these are typically classified according to the type of sponsor. For example, federal, state/provincial, and local governments provide leisure for people, and so do nongovernmental, nonprofit agencies. Private clubs and commercial for-profit businesses also provide for the leisure needs of people. Employers often offer facilities and programs for leisure as an employment benefit. Colleges and universities accommodate the leisure interests of students, and recreation services are part of the treatment for hospital patients. These and many other examples form the diverse "industry" of leisure service organizations.

In general, these many examples can be categorized according to three types. Commercial agencies provide leisure services as a business. Private agencies, in contrast, offer facilities and programs for their members, and public agencies are government sponsored and available to all people. Table 1.3 compares these types.

Table 1.3
Leisure Services Sponsor Types

	Public	Private	Commercial
Purpose	To see that all citizens have a high quality of life	To meet the leisure needs of members	To sell leisure in order to make a profit
Example	Toronto Parks & Recreation Department	YMCA	Blockbuster, Inc.
Users	Available to all	Available to members only (according to age, gender, religion, etc.)	Available to those who can afford to pay for the service
Services	Sports, cultural arts, outdoor recreation	Sports, social recreation, hobbies, voluntary service	Sports, entertainment, travel, cultural arts
Agencies	Federal, state/ provincial, county, city government	Clubs, fraternities, associations	Corporations, franchises, companies, business partnerships
Funding	Taxes, gifts, grants, user fees	Membership dues, gifts, endowments, fundraisers	Admission fees, purchases, owner investments
Facilities	Community centers, parks, athletic fields, playgrounds, museums, zoos, golf courses	Youth centers, fitness centers, athletic fields, clubs, camps, marinas	Theaters, restaurants, bowling centers, amusement parks, stadiums
Leadership	Individuals with professional preparation in recreation and volunteers	Individuals with professional preparation in recreation and volunteers	Business- and sales-oriented individuals

As you can see from studying the table, although all organizational types deliver leisure services, they do so in slightly different ways. This is because leisure is defined in different ways. For example, a public recreation agency, such as a city parks and recreation department, is likely referring to the recreational activity definition of leisure in its focus on providing facilities and programs that enable people to participate in sports, cultural arts, or outdoor pursuits. On the other hand, a private recreation agency, such as a skilled-care nursing facility, may consider leisure as free time in its mission of enabling meaningful uses of the time of terminally ill patients. Finally, an illustration of the state-of-mind definition of leisure might be interpreted from the motives of commercial recreation agencies. If their services can create positive feelings of satisfaction, then clients are likely to continue paying for these services, thus enhancing the organization's profit.

For Further Information

Thousands and thousands of career employment positions can be found in all three types of leisure service agencies. There are also numerous avenues to finding out about openings, including your university professors and career services center, state job listings, specific agency job listings nationwide, and national job listings. For example, one such U.S.-focused national job listing is that provided by the National Recreation and Park Association. To check it out go to www.nrpa.org and link to "professional services" and then to "career center." Looking down the list of current available positions, would you say that this service focuses primarily on public, private, or commercial careers?

References

Adherents.com. (2002). *Religions by size.* Retrieved January 17, 2004, from http://www.adherents.com/Religions_By_Adherents.html

Association of American Publishers. (2003). *Industry statistics.* Retrieved January 14, 2004, from http://www.publishers.org/industry/index.cfm.

Bayley, R., Baynes, M., & Kendall, T. (2004). *NubiaNet.* Retrieved January 17, 2004, from http://www.nubia.net.org/

Bucher, C. A., Shivers, J. S., & Bucher, R. (1984). Recreation for today's society. Englewood Cliffs, NJ: Prentice-Hall.

Butler, J. (1971). *The theatre and drama of Greece and Rome.* San Francisco: Chandler.

Chubb, M., & Chubb, H. R. (1981). *One-third of our time? An introduction to recreation behavior and resources.* New York: John Wiley & Sons.

Craig, S. (2002). *Sports and games of the ancients.* Westport, CT: Greenwood Press.

Dumazedier, J. (1974). *Sociology of leisure.* New York: Elsevier North-Holland.

Fitzgerald, C. P. (1933). *China: A short cultural history.* New York: Praeger.

Gass, G. (1994). *A history of rock music: The rock & roll era.* New York: McGraw-Hill.

Godbey, G. (1999). *Leisure in your life: An exploration* (5th ed.) State College, PA: Venture.

Hemingway, J. L. (1988). Leisure and civility: Reflections on a Greek ideal. *Leisure Sciences,* 10: 179–191.

Herbert, R. L. (1988). *Impressionism: Art, leisure and Parisian society.* New Haven, CT: Yale University Press.

Hudman, L. E. (1980). *Tourism: A shrinking world.* Columbus, OH: Grid.

Hull, R. B., Steward, W. P., & Yi, Y. K. (1992). Experience patterns: Capturing the dynamic nature of a recreation experience. *Journal of Leisure Research,* 23(3), 240–252.

Ibrahim, H. (1991). *Leisure and society: A comparative approach.* Dubuque, IA: Wm. C. Brown.

Kelly, J. R., & Freysinger, V. J. (2000). *21st century leisure: Current issues.* Boston: Allyn and Bacon.

Labarge, M. W. (1965). *A baronial house hold of the thirteenth century.* New York: Barnes & Noble.

Leaf, A. (1994). *The impressionists table: Recipes and gastronomy of 19th century France.* New York: Rizzoli.

Martin, T. R. (1996). *Ancient Greece: From prehistoric to Hellenistic times.* New Haven, CT: Yale University Press.

Pan-African Market Place. (1993, September). Come home to Sudan, a nation full of potential and promise! *Pan-African Market Place,* 1–2.

Pausanias. (1918). *Description of Greece* (Vols. 1–4). (W. H. S. Jones & H. A. Ormerod, Trans.). Cambridge, MA: Harvard University Press.

Pieper, J. (1963). *Leisure: The basis of culture.* New York: New American Library.

Recording Industry Association of America. (2004). *Industry statistics.* Retrieved January 15, 2004 from http://azaz.com/music/fetures/0008.html

Roberts, V. M. (1962). *On stage: A history of theatre.* New York: Harper & Row.

Rubenstein, J. M. (2003). *The cultural landscape: An introduction to human geography.* Upper Saddle River, NJ: Prentice Hall.

Schor, J. (2001). Real vacations for all. Retrieved January 26, 2004, from www.futurenet.org/17work/schor.htm

Simpson, S. (1989). Aristotle (384–322 BC) In H. Ibrahim (Ed.), *Pioneers in leisure and recreation.* Reston, VA: The American Association of Health, Physical Education, Recreation, and Dance.

Tregear, M. (1985). *Chinese art.* New York: Thames and Hudson.

U.S. Census Bureau. (2002). *Statistical abstracts of the United States: 2001.* Retrieved January 27, 2004, from www.census.gov/prod/2002pubs/01statab/arts.pdf.

CHAPTER TWO

Having Fun

Preview

Is it important to have fun?

Even though we may casually think of leisure as "just having fun,"
philosophers and scientists have taken the matter quite seriously.

What do we mean when we say we are having fun?

Having fun involves the leisure qualities of happiness, pleasure, freedom, intrinsic reward, play, game, humor, relaxation, ritual, solitude,
commitment, spirituality, risk, and others.

Is leisure all these qualities?

For any single experience, leisure can be characterized by one or
more of these qualities, but usually not all of them. For example, a
quick climb to the top of a rock face may be experienced as risk,
freedom, spirituality, and even game.

Key Terms

Intrinsic reward 42
Extrinsic reward 44
Eudaimonia 44
Cynicism 47
Skepticism 47
Stoicism 47
Epicureanism 47
Hedonism 48
Agon 56

Alea .56
Mimicry 56
Ilinx 56
Ritual 59
Decorum 60
Serious Leisure 62
Self-efficacy 65
Cultural capital 67

Are you having fun? Although this may seem a trivial question, much of our lives is spent in pursuit of a good time. Having fun is often what is thought of when considering leisure, and almost everyone wants it. What is it that makes leisure fun? That is, what are the qualities of leisure? In this chapter, we portray the nature of leisure by characterizing its experience and expression. In doing this, we go far beyond the definitions of leisure explored in the last chapter. We focus on the variety of ways leisure is felt.

Freedom

Foremost, leisure makes us feel free. In fact, scholars suggest that leisure cannot survive when freedom is curtailed. There are primarily two understandings of the rapport between leisure and freedom: leisure as freedom "from," and leisure as freedom "to."

First, leisure is temporary freedom "from" the necessary routine of life. That is, leisure frees us from obligations and provides a compensation for work. Leisure also provides us the opportunity to experience freedom from coercion in how we choose to live our lives. Leisure as freedom "from" has been labeled by scholars as a negative freedom because it carries the connotation that it must be earned. For example, can one experience the freedom of leisure if one is retired from a paid job?

This concern has led to another idea about leisure and freedom. Leisure as freedom "to" is considered a more positive freedom. Here the focus is on freedom of choice, or freedom to experience a particular personal expression. This means that in order to have leisure, we must grasp the possibilities of choice through our pastimes. Leisure as freedom "to" means being able to expand beyond the limits of the present to experience wonderfully fulfilling possibilities.

To illustrate this distinction, I'll cite a series of interviews I conducted a few years ago with women who were "serving time" in prison. I wanted to explore how leisure was experienced with almost all constraints of obligation removed. Their daily responsibilities included only three meals and one hour of yard exercise. By the conclusion of the study, I realized that these women felt they had absolutely no leisure. In spite of having almost unlimited freedoms "from," because they experienced no freedoms "to," they were incapable of having leisure.

What is required to experience leisure as freedom "to"? According to the investigations of Bregha (1991), freedom in leisure is a matter of possessing personal qualities, having the means, and receiving permission. First, freedom "to" in leisure requires having the knowledge, physical ability, personality, and other personal qualities needed. This includes having information about what is available or permissible, as well as knowledge about oneself, including the consequences of actions. Similar to the ancient Greek ideal, this means that leisure requires the ability to choose with intelligence and responsibility.

Second, for Bregha (1991) leisure involves having the means. Throughout history, wealth has always been perceived as a factor in having leisure. As illustrated during the European Medieval period, wealth (especially the possession of property) was often a requirement for leisure. In fact, during the 19th century, the wealthy were tagged "the leisure class." To a great extent, unfortunately, this link still exists today. Many forms of recreational activity require participation fees, equipment, clothing, transportation to special locations, and expensive instruction and training. Have you priced jogging shoes or admission to a theme park lately?

Third, to Bregha (1991) the ability to choose leisure requires permission. Since few forms of leisure, except perhaps daydreaming and contemplation, can be experienced without at least the passive consent of our neighbors or civic authorities, the ability to experience leisure requires sanction from others. For example, there are city ordinances against playing music too loudly, restaurants are open only at specific times and days, and to jog on private property we must have authorization from the owners.

Is this discussion of freedom beginning to make it seem like leisure is fragile and almost impossible? Leisure is our most precious expression of freedom. It gives us freedom to choose, but choice, in turn, requires awareness, a sense of direction, possessing the means, and ultimately, the authority. In other words, leisure is as much freedom to do something as freedom from something.

In Focus

The Downshifting Movement
Box 2.1

After graduating from college, Jeff and his girlfriend, Liza, moved to Seattle and into an old house in a nice neighborhood. They share the place with another friend, each paying $312 per month rent. Jeff works for himself as a medical and legal interpreter. Nicely dressed, he doesn't look too different from other 25-year-old college graduates, but there is one major distinction: Jeff is living on about $10,000 a year.

Patty, a 28-year-old New Yorker, recently sold her car, moved out of a huge apartment and into something smaller, and gave away much of her wardrobe. Michael, 29, quit his high-tech job, sold his beach home in Malibu, and moved home. Two years after college, Maggie rejected her high-paying marketing job in Miami and took a part-time job at a small college in Baltimore so she could volunteer at a riding stable, add yoga to her daily routine, and spend lunch hours reading and writing poetry.

Jeff, Patty, Michael, and Maggie are examples of what is called "downshifting," or voluntary simplicity. Fed up with the slavery of working hard in order to spend more money, in order to work harder, in order to spend even more money, they are pursuing a different path. They learn to want less, live more simply, and slow down. Downshifters believe spending less does not reduce their quality of life—in fact, they believe it raises it. Their experience is that less spending gives them more time, peace of mind, physical health, friendship, and appreciation of what they do spend (adapted from Schor, 1998, pp. 133–135).

Questions to Consider and Discuss

1. *Do you know anyone who has made a lifestyle change to live more simply? What was his or her life like before and after the change? Why did he or she make the change?*

2. *Might Jeff and the others have made their decisions based on the ideas of freedom presented in this chapter? Are they choosing freedom "from" or freedom "to"? Have they therefore chosen more leisure?*

Intrinsic Reward

So what is the ultimate reward of freedom? What might feeling free in leisure do for us? This book is about the many benefits (and harms) of leisure, but perhaps foremost is the benefit of intrinsic reward. **Intrinsic reward** comes from doing something for its own reasons. Cross-country skiers often exclaim about sensations of peaceful-

Intrinsic reward: doing something for its own reasons

ness while gliding along; artists may value working with clay on the potter's wheel because of the elastic, smooth substance responding in their hands; and dancers often describe dancing as moving to a rhythm within (see Csikszentmihalyi, 1975). Intrinsic reward is perhaps the main reason we continue to pursue a particular form of leisure. When the activity is its own reward, we are motivated to experience it more (see Table 2.1).

Table 2.1
Types of Intrinsic and Extrinsic Reward

Intrinsic reward
Stimulation–Engaging in a pastime for the simple pleasure of doing it
" I ride a bicycle for the thrill of pedaling fast."

Accomplishment–Engaging in a pastime to feel efficient or competent
" I swim for the satisfaction I get from perfecting my strokes."

Knowledge–Engaging in a pastime to learn something new
" I play video games in order to learn new ways of winning."

Extrinsic reward
Identified regulation–Engaging in a pastime because it is important
" I'm in the karate class because I want to be able to protect myself from crime."

Introjected regulation–Engaging in a pastime so as not to feel guilty for not doing it.
"I play basketball in order to be in good shape."

External regulation–Engaging in a pastime to avoid a punishment
"I hang out with peers so I'm not left out of the group."

Note. Taken from Pelletier (1995).

   To create intrinsic reward, motivational theory outlines two needs that must be met. First, people need to be self-determining. They need to feel that they are the origin of their own behavior—that they are not being controlled. Second, they need to feel competent. Feelings of failure are not present with intrinsic reward. What happens when we do not feel self-determining or competent in our leisure? Extrinsic reward is the result.

Extrinsic reward is the consequence when we engage in a particular form of leisure for reasons other than its own sake. Our motivation is from the outside. For example, we sign up for an exercise class because we want to lose weight, not because we want to experience the exhilaration of moving our bodies (see Table 2.1).

> **Extrinsic reward:** doing something for a payoff

A particularly fascinating aspect to this is how intrinsic reward can turn into extrinsic reward. One example comes from a classic study of preschool children (Lepper, Greene, & Nisbett, 1973). Children who initially showed a high interest in drawing were chosen for the study. They were divided into three groups: Children in the first group were told that if they would draw pictures, they would receive a "good player award." Children in the second group received the same reward but were not told about it in the beginning. In the third group, children were neither told they would receive an award nor did they receive an award. Two weeks later, the children were unobtrusively observed in their classrooms, and the amount of time they spent drawing pictures was monitored. Those children who expected the reward showed less interest in drawing than those in the unexpected and no award groups. In addition, the pictures the children drew in the expected award group were judged to be poorer quality than those drawn by the children in the other two groups. In other words, the children who were offered a prize switched from intrinsically to extrinsically motivated behavior, and it was no longer as much fun to draw pictures.

Happiness

The search for happiness is universal. Yet happiness is often elusive because it is a quality of the heart. Happiness, morale, psychological well-being, and a positive life attitude are all indicators of the overall quality of our inner experience. And one way of characterizing leisure is as the inner experience of happiness that comes from living well. How does this occur? We answer this question from two perspectives: classical philosophies and current understandings about achieving happiness.

This was the question that occupied much of the thinking of Aristotle—How should the good life be lived? His answer was that the best life comes from **eudaimonia,** which most translations today interpret as "happiness" or "personal well-being" (Sylvester, 1991). Unlike today's understanding of happiness as a psychological condition, Aristotle meant something else: Eudaimonia was not determined by positive feelings, but rather by good actions. To Aristotle, happiness was having the ability to choose and engage in worthy pursuits. Rather than being a subjective concept, it was an objective one: Some actions are better than others. Unhappiness, then, occurs when one cannot do good things.

> **Eudaimonia:** a feeling that comes from good actions; Aristotle's idea of happiness

Thus, for leisure to bring happiness, it must entail only moral and "good" activities. Otherwise unhappiness results.

Thinking about happiness by focusing on unhappiness was, centuries later, the approach of philosopher Bertrand Russell. In a classic book devoted to the subject, Russell (1968) considers people who suffer from unhappiness. He concludes the causes of unhappiness are competition, boredom, fatigue, and envy. The "cure," Russell claims, is zest. Happiness is the possession of a zestful attitude toward life: "The secret of happiness is this: let your interests be as wide as possible, and let your reactions to the things and persons that interest you be as far as possible friendly rather than hostile" (p. 111).

Even more recently, hundreds of studies have sought to answer the question of what makes us happy. Some have predicted that age is a factor, that younger people are happier than older people. Some studies suggest women are happier than men, and that having good health makes one happy. Having friends, a spouse or partner, enough money, a good education, and a meaningful career have also been connected to happiness in research studies, as have being creative and having a nurturing personality. But what about the specific role of leisure in happiness?

In one study (Larson & Richards, 1998), adolescents revealed that their emotional high points were on Fridays and Saturdays, especially among ninth to 12th graders. Their mood drops on Sunday, before returning to school, and remains low during the week, as they spend much of their time in adult-structured settings such as school. It begins to rise again on Thursday. To explain these findings, the researchers noted that as teens move from junior high to high school, the frequency of going out on their own with friends—to movies, sporting events, and parties—increases dramatically. Researchers call this a "cultural script" for what is supposed to happen, and teens who fall short of the script (i.e., who spend weekend evenings at home) often experience profound loneliness.

In another study (Putnam, 2000), the role of specific forms of leisure in adult happiness was examined: attending club meetings, volunteering to help others, entertaining at home (Fig. 2.1), and attending church regularly. The results indicated that all four leisure activities were related to higher levels of happiness than is average for adults. Those who were active in clubs, volunteered, entertained at home, and went to church were happier than most. However, the researchers also discovered a diminishing return to this conclusion. Doing too many of these activities reduced happiness. They discovered that the best frequency was slightly less than once a week.

Figure 2.1

Research indicates that entertaining at home is related to happiness in adults.

(© Ruth V. Russell)

Pleasure

Leisure is pleasing. In almost all characterizations of leisure, pleasure is included. It can come from listening to your favorite music, petting your dog, or eating a handful of popcorn. What is pleasure, and how does leisure bring pleasure to us?

One way of explaining pleasure is via the concept of biological evolution. According to this view, pleasure results when one does something that, in the past, had been useful for survival. It comes from a chemical stimulation of a particular neural receptor that the organism previously needed for optimal functioning (Csikszentmihalyi, 1993). For example, when our very distant ancestors lived in the sea, their bodies adapted to a salty environment. Although we have lived for many millions of years on land, we still need a constant supply of salt, and with time, the taste of salt has become pleasurable, such as in a handful of popcorn.

There is also a social evolutionary concept for explaining pleasure. In their book *The Evolution of Leisure* (1988), leisure philosophers Goodale and Godbey describe the social roots of pleasure. Originating with the ancient Greeks, these include the ideas of cynicism, skepticism, stoicism, epicureanism, and hedonism.

Cynicism refers to the belief, established in the 4th century B.C. by Antisthenes, a disciple of Socrates, that virtue rather than pleasure is the chief goal of life. The wise person looks with contempt on all the ordinary pleasures of life. Today we use the word cynicism to sneer at the idea that human nature is good. **Skepticism** was another philosophical movement originating in ancient Greece. As in the current use of the word, skeptics doubted everything. Although we can thank proponents of this view for challenging and clarifying such ideas as astrology and magic, skeptics also taught people to withhold judgments if they wanted mental peace—that is, to accept whatever was conventional.

Cynicism: virtue rather than pleasure is life's goal

Skepticism: accepting whatever is conventional

Stoicism holds the middle perspective about pleasure. It compromises between the rejection of pleasure by cynicism and skepticism, and the promotion of pleasure in epicureanism and hedonism. Ancient Greek, and later Roman, philosophers believed that people achieve their greatest good by following reason, freeing themselves from passions, and focusing on only those things they could control. Thus, even today, stoics accept good fortune without joy and misfortune without complaint—"You win a few, you lose a few!"

Stoicism: indifference to both pleasure and pain

Named after the ancient Greek philosopher Epicurus, **epicureanism** holds that pleasure should be in moderation, and that the best pleasures (such as contemplation and appreciation) are intellectual. According to epicurean understanding, the more inferior pleasures were those that responded to the

Epicureanism: pleasure of certain forms in moderation

In Profile

Epicurus
Box 2.2

Epicureanism, a system of philosophy, is based on the teachings of the Greek philosopher Epicurus (341-270 bc). In his school in Athens, which was called "the Garden," the importance of balancing pleasure and pain through the virtues of justice, honesty, and prudence was taught. This is why Epicurus preferred friendship to love (it was less disquieting) and intellectual pleasures to sensual ones (they did not disturb peace of mind). In his own words, *No pleasure is a bad thing in itself: but the means which produce some pleasures bring with them disturbances many times greater than the pleasures themselves.* (Principle Doctrines, 3-4)

As an organized school, epicureanism went out of existence in the 4th century, but its ideas have attracted many eminent persons from many countries (including Thomas Jefferson in the United States), and epicureanism is regarded as one of the leading schools of moral philosophy of all time.

senses, such as sexual drives and hunger. Finally, **hedonism** held that pleasure is the highest goal of life. In fact, the term comes from the Greek hedone, meaning "pleasure." Whereas those who believed in epicureanism considered pleasures of the mind to be the most valued, followers of hedonism included the body, fame, power, and wealth as other sources of pleasure.

> **Hedonism:** pleasure is life's goal

All five of these ancient perspectives about pleasure have influenced contemporary notions of leisure as pleasurable. For example, some consider certain forms of leisure, such as dancing, to be pleasurable because of sensations in the body (hedonism). For others, such physical pastimes are considered immoral because of their sensual nature (cynicism).

A contemporary casting of the various kinds of pleasure that may result from our pastimes include the sensory, expressive, and intellectual (Smith, 1991). Sensory pleasures are often found in such everyday activities as eating, listening to music, having sex, and playing sports. These expressions are pleasurable because they stimulate the body directly. For example, by measuring people's physiological responses to musical tones (a facial electromyograph technique), researchers discovered that tones of low intensity (75 dB) were more pleasing to listeners than tones of high intensity (95 dB). (What do these find-

Figure 2.2
The sculpture The Napper perhaps gave expressive pleasure to its creator, Duane
Hanson, and can give intellectual pleasure to travelers in the Orlando, Florida, airport.
(© Ruth V. Russell)

ings suggest about the pleasure of really loud music?) Expressive pleasures
from leisure, on the other hand, are based on the use of creativity. As a result
of an experience, something is produced that gives pleasure (Fig. 2.2). To distinguish, listening to rap music may trigger sensory pleasure, whereas creating
a rap song more likely offers expressive pleasure. Finally, intellectual pleasure
from leisure seems to belong to thinking activities. These might include fantasizing, daydreaming, and studying.

Play

Play is human nature itself. It is a spontaneous act that elevates us to the seriousness of frivolity. It involves the existential suspension of consequences; it is
motivated by sheer enjoyment in living.

Although play is usually associated with the activities of children, the
notion of play as childlike did not emerge in Western cultures until the early
17th century (Kando, 1980). This is because prior to this, the concept of "child"
did not exist. During the Middle Ages in Europe, there were two types of people: adults and little adults. As the paintings by Dürer and Brueghel show, the
facial traits, clothing, and behaviors of children are rendered as adultlike.

Currently, we know that play has a pervasive influence in all human
activity, for both children and adults. This is the perspective of Johan Huizinga
(1949), who argued that the character of play as out of the ordinary and open

Figure 2.3
According to Huizinga (1949), it is in play that innovation occurs. (© Ruth V. Russell)

is fundamental to being human. Because play is the context for exploration, Huizinga considers play to be not only the best source of innovation (Fig. 2.3), but at the center of all civilization. That is, culture itself, including social and economic development, arises from play.

But the question that has been most enduring for scientists and philosophers is, Why do people play? Since the 18th century, according to Ellis (1973), at least 15 different theories have emerged to explain play. These theories have been derived from the knowledge bases of biology, psychology, and sociology. In reviewing the more common of these theories, we'll use Ellis' classification system: first the older theories, then the more recent theories, and finally, the most contemporary explanations (Table 2.2).

One of the oldest and most often quoted theories of play is the surplus energy theory. It claims that play serves as a safety valve for burning up stored physical energy. Another early theory viewed play as preparation for adulthood. This biologically based theory explains that children play because of the instinctual urges required for survival. Finally, the relaxation theory explains play as an activity that provides recuperation from fatigue and stress. Opposite the surplus energy explanation is the relaxation perspective, which claims that play restores energy.

These and other theories, which date back to the early part of the 20th century, were often labeled "armchair" theories because they had limited research

Table 2.2
A Brief Comparison of Play Theories

Theory	Definition	Example	Critique
Surplus energy	Burning up excess energy	Children chasing each other around the playground	Helps justify the role of physical play for problem youth; doesn't explain non-physical play
Preparation	Practice for adult life	Children playing house or doctor	Doesn't explain adult play
Relaxation	Recuperation	Playing solitaire as a study break	Doesn't explain play that is similar to work
Catharsis	Letting off emotional steam	Playing the piano after an argument	Has intuitive appeal in its field of application, yet aggressive behavior often increases aggressive behavior
Behavioristic	A response to a pleasurable stimulus	Going out and playing basketball after your team has won the tournament	Overlooks the role of individual differences, yet has boosted play as a topic worthy of serious study
Psychoanalytic	Mastering disturbing events or thoughts	A child yelling at her stuffed animals after her schoolteacher has scolded her	Initiated the practice of careful observation of play as therapy
Arousal seeking	Seeking optimal stimulation	Bored students counting a professor's mannerisms in class	Has more research support
Competence-effectance	Having an effect on things	Making snow angels in the yard	Requires more research testing

support. More recent theories represent attempts to make the explanation of play more scientific. For example, the catharsis theory is similar to the surplus energy theory except that it focuses on pent-up emotional energy rather than surplus physical energy. Play is viewed as a socially acceptable way to purge negative feelings. Another more recent theory is the behaviorist explanation, which labels play as a form of learning. Based in the work of behavioral psychologists such as B. F. Skinner, play is connected with the stimulus–response mechanisms. That is, play is considered a pleasurable activity that receives praise and recognition; thus, it is learned and repeated. Finally, the psychoanalytic explanation, first developed by Sigmund Freud, viewed many forms of play as symptoms of psychological illness. That is, play was a method of mastering disturbing events or thoughts.

Since these more recent theories have been substantiated by research data, they have been useful in furthering the investigation of play. They are still explored in studies today and remain credible as at least partial explanations of why people play. The most contemporary explanations, in fact, have often been composites of these earlier theories. For example, the arousal-seeking theory claims the main goal of play is both intellectual and physical stimulus. That is, play serves to generate complexity as a guard against boredom. And the competence-effectance theory refers to the need to produce effects, to be a cause of things taking place or being produced.

Each of these contemporary theories of play, as well as others such as attribution theory, conflict-enculturation theory, and recapitulation theory, have an element of truth, yet none are sufficient to fully explain why we play. However,

In Profile

The Yo-Yo

Box 2.3

Invented in China more than 2,500 years ago, the yo-yo is the second-oldest known toy, after the doll.

Half a billion yo-yos have been sold since the 1930s.

The most expensive yo-yo ever was auctioned for $16,000. It was an autographed gift to country music star Roy Acuff from president Richard Nixon.

The world's largest workable yo-yo weighs 897 pounds and measures 10 feet 4 inches.

The first yo-yo traveled to space on the space shuttle Discovery in 1985. Without gravity, the astronauts discovered that when the yo-yo was released, it moved slowly and gracefully along the string but would not sleep.

(from Roper, 2001)

Animal Play
Box 2.4

Behold the puppy! At about three weeks of age, this tiny ball of fur has already begun gnawing, pawing, and tugging at its littermates. At four to five weeks, its antics rival those of a rambunctious school-age child, chasing, stalking, and wrestling with its siblings at all hours of the day and night.

Such behavior is not unusual among social mammals. From human children to monkeys, whales, and sewer rats, many groups of mammals (and some birds) devote a significant amount of their youth to various forms of play (McDonald, 1995). A steady accumulation of research evidence over the past two decades has begun to reveal why mammals play. Here are some of the findings.

First, some research suggests that play helps animals, such as wolves and monkeys, form bonds with other members of their group and trains them to behave according to the norms of their social hierarchy. In addition, some scientists think that the intense physical activity associated with play helps infant mammals burn off excess energy, generate body heat, and prevent the accumulation of fat—all important physiological factors in staying alive in early life. Finally, in some animals, researchers have found that play is necessary for the development of proper sexual and maternal behavior. For example, in her experiments with rats, Susan Brunelli of Columbia University found that those that did not play as infants lacked maternal instincts as adults (McDonald, 1995).

But not all animals play. Hamsters, for example, play hardly at all, even though they are closely related to rodents that play a lot. According to Gordon Burghardt of the University of Tennessee, animals that play are generally cared for by parents, given more food as infants than they need for growth, raised in relatively protected environments, and tend to be warm-blooded. This may explain why play is not seen in reptiles, which are cold-blooded animals born fully capable of fending for themselves, and why domestic dogs and cats typically play more than their wild counterparts (McDonald, 1995).

this should not cause us to lose sight of play and playfulness as a core characteristic of leisure. Perhaps play does not occur because it is useful. Perhaps it is simply an enchanted place outside ordinary life.

Game

Did you know that over 10 million people in the world regularly play chess? Millions more frequently play board games, card games, computer games, dice games, Internet games, party games, video games, deck games, fantasy games, trivia and word games, and even war games. Games are of great interest to people. They are also of great interest to scientists. For example, mathematicians and computer programmers use game strategy to help solve particular problems. Psychologists and psychiatrists use games, such as psychodrama, as a therapeutic tool.

So how are games a quality of leisure? One clue may be the origin of the word. The English word game is related to the old German word *gaman*, which

Figure 2.4

These Girl Scouts are playing a game that requires open space, a bedsheet and ball, and cooperation with each other to win. (© Ruth V. Russell)

means "glee." Thus, the original meaning of game was not far from that of play, meaning spontaneous, nonserious, and joyful expression. More recently, however, social scientists have understood a game to be different from play—as being a more structured, organized, and regulated form of activity.

A game is a contest (Fig. 2.4). It may be a contest with yourself, such as the card game of solitaire, or it may occur between two or more people or teams. Through cunning, manipulation, logic, luck, or even cooperation, the desired outcome is winning. This means that a game must have rules. This is what distinguishes games as simple or complex: Complex games have more rules. In watching children play a game, you may notice how the number of rules often increases as the game continues. Games differ in terms of where they occur (a special table, court, field, or room) and in terms of the equipment required (cards, dice, markers, racquet, or ball). Some games last only a few minutes, whereas other games, such as Monopoly, can last for days.

In Profile

Monopoly
Box 2.5

In the heart of the Great Depression in the United States, when the average person was either broke or about to be, unemployed Charles Darrow offered an illusion of wealth. He dreamed of escaping the summer heat of Philadelphia and going down to the cool breezes on the boardwalk of Atlantic City. One day, Darrow sat down at his kitchen table and put his fantasy on paper. He invented a board game using the street names that intersect with Atlantic City's boardwalk. Each player would get $1,500 to restart life by the shore and another $200 every time they circled the neighborhood. He called the game Monopoly.

People began dropping in at Darrow's house to play Monopoly. As demand for the game increased, Darrow went to work producing 100 sets in his basement, which he sold for $4 each. But making all those deeds, hotels, houses, and $100 bills by hand quickly exhausted him, so Darrow brought the game to Parker Brothers in New York. Although the Parker Brothers executives played Monopoly all afternoon, they said it had too many design errors and rejected it. Meanwhile, Monopoly was spreading by word of mouth, so a local printer began to help Darrow make the games. Within a year, 17,000 orders had come from stores across the United States, Parker Brothers reconsidered, and Darrow retired at age 46 to raise orchids in the countryside.

Monopoly, the idea of amassing money and property, has sold over 200 million copies in 80 countries. It has been translated into 26 languages, and it remains a best seller. (http://www.hasbro.com/monopoly/, Retrieved 1/30/04)

Perhaps the most important characteristic of games is that they are in some way artificial. They take place as a synthetic counterpart to real life. The contest of the chess match is the artificial enactment of a medieval war. Monopoly is the counterfeit experience of capitalism.

The type of play required in a game is the final characteristic. Callois (1961) distinguished four types of play in games: agon, alea, mimicry, and ilinx. **Agon,** which means "competitive" and requires some skill, includes most sports and games. **Alea** games, such as Bingo, require luck, and winning is a matter of fate. **Mimicry** games, typically video games, involve role playing. **Illinx** games involve vertigo and other types of sensory stimulation, such as in drinking games. Some games, of course, involve more than one of these forms of play. For example, playing the card game of poker likely involves both competitive skill and luck. Thanks to this categorization, we understand that games have a wide range of meanings. It also is useful in describing some of the harmful uses of games, such as in drinking games and video games.

| Agon: competitive |
| Alea: luck |
| Mimicry: role-playing |
| Ilinx: sensory |

Humor

"Angels fly because they take themselves lightly," says an old Scottish proverb. Humor is essential to human beings. Researchers at Stanford University have

The Study Says

Effects of Humor on Mood
Box 2.6

The hypothesis that 20 minutes of humor would result in benefits to mood comparable to those of a 20-minute session of aerobic exercise was investigated by Szabo (2003). Thirty-nine university students were tested three times, at weekly intervals, on running or jogging at a self-selected pace, watching a humorous stand-up comedy video, and watching a documentary video. Mood was determined by a questionnaire five minutes before and after each event. The study results demonstrated that both humor and exercise had an equally positive effect on increasing a sense of positive well-being. However, humor had a greater impact than exercise on reducing anxiety. Based on these results, it was concluded that humor could induce positive psychological changes that are at least comparable, if not superior, to the effects of exercise.

reported, for example, that laughter aids digestion, stimulates the heart, strengthens muscles, activates the brain's creative function, and keeps you alert (Jones, 1992). Jokes, cartoons, parodies, puns, silliness, imitations, and tall tales are good for us! Because humorous moments contribute to well-being, humor can be considered a quality of leisure.

What is humor? Morreall (1983) claims that humor is simply a pleasant psychological shift—a natural expression of pleasure. The source of this pleasure is often an embarrassment, some sudden and unexpected event, or the release of pent-up energy. These most often occur during leisure—they make us feel good and we laugh.

Why do we laugh? The oldest, and probably still most widespread, theory of laughter is that it is an expression of feeling superior. Labeled the superiority theory (Morreall, 1983), in this view laughter is seen as self-congratulatory, involving malice toward other people. The relief theory, on the other hand, claims that laughter is physiological, used to vent nervous energy. We laugh (such as at a cartoon about sex) as a release against denied feelings or social restrictions (Spencer, 1911). Another explanation of laughter is the incongruity theory (Morreall, 1983). Accordingly, laughter is viewed as an intellectual reaction to something that is unexpected, such as in the punch line of a joke.

Humor is therapeutic. In a hospital near Atlanta, Georgia, there is a "laughing room" in which patients are encouraged to watch funny movies and read humorous books. The purpose is to help them get well. The hospital reports that the laughing room decreases people's need for pain medication and serves as an antidepressant because it stimulates endorphins in the brain. Voltaire once noted, "The art of medicine consists of amusing the patient while nature cures the disease."

Relaxation

For many of us, leisure is found in doing meaningless things or in doing nothing at all (Fig. 2.5). A child drawing pictures in the beach sand that a wave immediately erases, a tourist wandering without an itinerary, and two friends rocking in silence on the front porch are relaxing, and through relaxation, they are experiencing being "leisurely."

Perhaps the most important proponent of this quality of leisure was Josef Pieper, a German scholar from the 1950s who declared: "Leisure is not the attitude of mind of those who actively intervene but of those who are open to everything; not of those who grab hold, but of those who leave the reins loose and who are free and easy themselves" (1963, p. 41). For Pieper, leisure meant being truly and abundantly relaxed. Doug Kleiber, a contemporary American scholar, agrees with Pieper and claims that true leisure is comfort in

Figure 2.5

Relaxation in leisure is perhaps more important to modern life than we think. (© Ruth V. Russell)

just being appreciative, contemplative, and peaceful. He writes, "Leisure is most essentially a position of relaxation, of faithful openness to immediate reality and ease of movement and thinking" (Kleiber, 2000, pp. 83–84).

This quality of leisure may be difficult for us to grasp because we live in societies that celebrate effort and accomplishment. Thus, relaxation is considered nonproductive. Even if we highly value relaxation, it is for leisure's ability to recharge us so we might be productive later. But we must also revere relaxation as an end in itself. In *Freedom and Destiny*, psychoanalyst Rollo May (1981) refers to it as "the pause." The pause is critical to our lives because it signifies an interruption to the dogged automatic chain of cause and effect. Intervening is imagining, reflecting, and pondering. Without the pause, we sacrifice the richness of wonder.

Further comments about relaxation and leisure come from Steffan Linder (1971). More than 30 years ago, he wrote that being "harried" (to use his word) is the absence of leisure. Linder argued that when we devote too much time and energy to acquiring things, and then to taking care of them, we are too tired and time-poor for leisure. To Linder, leisure was simplicity.

Ritual

How do you enter a swimming pool for the first time? Do you usually jump in off the side, dive in from the board, use the ladder, or walk down the shallow end steps? Most of us follow a consistent pattern for this. Or how does your family celebrate Thanksgiving? Would it be an outrage if certain foods and preparations were missing from the dinner table? These and many other examples demonstrate the ritual nature of leisure. In fact, much of our leisure is ritualized: Americans vacationing in Florida must visit Walt Disney World, and can't possibly miss watching the annual Super Bowl football game on television. Let's explore this a bit more.

First, **ritual** is defined as a set of acts (originally involving religion or magic) with their sequence established by tradition and stemming from everyday life (Ibrahim, 1991). In addition, ritual may begin as an individual pattern but later evoke collective behavior. Ritual is perhaps born from the human need for regular and mutual affirmation (Ibrahim, 1991). For all of these reasons, ritual is pervasive in leisure. Many forms of leisure involve ritual, and even more directly, leisure itself has been ritualized.

> **Ritual:** any customarily repeated act

Holidays provide a rich illustration of leisure as ritualized. As in ancient societies, there are many holidays in our contemporary lives. Today, we ritualistically experience patriotic holidays (Canada Day), as well as holidays considered seasonal (New Year's Day), or religious (Hanukkah). In addition, there are unofficial holidays that inspire specific rituals, such as the opening of deer hunting season.

Holidays in North America have evolved from a variety of cultures worldwide and have greatly changed in their meanings and how they are ritually celebrated (Godbey, 1999). In fact, for many holidays, the occasion is increasingly marked by rituals that have little relation to their origin. For example, Groundhog Day (February 2) is the American version of Candlemas Day, which originated in Europe as an observance of the purification of the Virgin Mary. The belief that if Candlemas Day were sunny, winter would continue was somehow transferred to the groundhog's shadow when the tradition came to this country (Godbey, 1999).

Many illustrations of ritual can be found in tourism as well. For example, MacCannell (1999) claims that modern international sightseeing possesses its own rituals that actually serve as a sort of moral structure to behavior. Modern guided tours are extensive ceremonial agendas involving long strings of obligatory rites. If one goes to Europe, one must see Paris; if one goes to Paris, one must see the Louvre Museum; if one goes to the Louvre, one must see the Mona Lisa. What an agenda! MacCannell declares that the ritual attitude of the tourist originates in the act of travel itself, which itself originated as a pilgrimage to holy places. In anthropological studies, a special term has been identified for this behavior: sight sacralization. A particular destination becomes a tourist attraction because, for social, historical or cultural reasons, it represents something morally good. The next time you're seeing the Mona Lisa, notice how reverent the other tourists are in its presence.

The examples of holidays and tourism work because ritual and leisure share certain characteristics. For example, both involve intrinsic reward, having meaning in and of themselves (Grimes, 1982). In addition, much of the ritual of leisure is of the type labeled by Goffman (1959) as interaction ritual, or decorum. **Decorum** is nonessential, as is decoration, but is practiced because it enhances social interaction. Golf, for example, is considered one of the most decorum-rich sports. Where to stand while others are playing, how to mark your ball on the green, and when it's your turn to play can intimidate a new player unaware of the ritual.

Decorum: socially useful decoration

Solitude

Time spent alone is an integral and important part of living. Solitude returns us to ourselves by providing opportunities for growth and creativity (Storr, 1988). Returning to ourselves is characteristic of leisure. Although we typically think of leisure as a social and companionable experience, being alone at leisure can produce great fulfillment. When we are free to totally be ourselves, accountable only to ourselves and free of obligations and duties, we are at leisure. Let's illustrate with a common leisure experience—reading (Fig. 2.6).

Reading is not necessarily easy; it makes demands on our skills by requiring our concentration and our attention. Have you noticed how reading isolates the reader from the ordinary action around her or him? The fun of reading, then, like so many solitary activities, is in its escapist nature. Everyday routines are forgotten for a

Figure 2.6
Some pastimes, such as reading, return us to our own world. (© Ruth V. Russell)

moment. The leisure pursuit of reading provides for us a special and separate form of being; it returns us to our own world, or a "sphere of privacy" (Davies, 1989, p. 111). How does leisure grant us a world of our own? Leisure, in a sense, is a form of **narcissism.** Through moments of solitude in leisure, we are allowed to return to ourselves, to "love" ourselves. Here's how writer May Sarton expresses it in her journal:

> September 15th
>
> *Begin here. It is raining. I look out on the maple, where a few leaves have turned yellow, and listen to Punch, the parrot, talking to himself and to the rain ticking gently against the windows. I am here alone for the first time in weeks, to take up my "real" life again at last. That is what is strange—that friends, even passionate love, are not my real life unless there is time alone in which to explore and to discover what is happening or has happened. Without the interruptions, nourishing and maddening, this life would become arid. Yet I taste it fully only when I am alone here and the house and I resume old conversations.*
>
> (Sarton, 1973, p. 3)

Contemporary cultures make solitude difficult to attain. The cell phone, paging beeper, and computer are ever-present threats to privacy. In cities, it is impossible to get away from the intrusions of other people and their noise. Most occupations require working with and around other people. This may be why some people describe driving in a car as leisure. It is considered refreshing simply because they are alone and temporarily unavailable to others. (Unless, of course, you have your cell phone turned on!)

Commitment

Do you know anyone who is so committed to a particular pastime that it holds absolute primacy in life's priorities? After being asked, "How bad would it be if you were unable to downhill ski anymore?" a 57-year-old man responded,

> *It would be very bad. Very bad. Skiing is a very important part of my life. Not just of my leisure life, but of my real life. It is part of being me. Your question is the hard one that I am not ready to deal with.*
>
> (Russell, 2000)

For some people, leisure supplies the main source of personal identity and meaning in life. For some, it is the definitive answer to "Who am I?" and is therefore taken very seriously. The underlying theme is the commitment to developing skill and experience in an activity that becomes central to life.

There are several ways to consider the serious quality of leisure. One is to focus on how expert someone is in a particular pursuit. Some people spend many years perfecting the skills and knowledge needed to do a pastime well. Another approach is to consider leisure as a commitment in terms of the longevity of a particular pursuit across the life span. That is, an individual who has consistently and regularly pursued a pastime from childhood through old age demonstrates she or he is serious about this pastime. We might also consider the serious quality of leisure in terms of specialization. For example, people committed to fishing typically progress from simply casting lures to catching the most fish, to using the more refined fly-casting method of catching particular kinds of fish.

Beginning in the mid-1980s, the term **serious leisure** made its debut in the leisure studies literature. Over the years, the concept has been extensively researched and contemplated by scholars. Serious leisure is "the systematic pursuit of an activity that participants find so substantial and interesting that, in the typical case, they launch themselves on a career centered on acquiring and expressing its special skills, knowledge, and experience" (Stebbins, 1992, p. 3). In other words, it is high-investment leisure.

Serious leisure: the substantial and systematic pursuit of an activity

Serious leisure can be contrasted with casual leisure. In casual leisure, such as in watching television, engaging in social conversation, or eating and drinking, even though there may be an immediate intrinsic reward, little or no training is required to enjoy it. Serious leisure continues over a long time, requires a great deal of effort and preparation, and provides strong personal identification. To review, the qualifications for serious leisure include:

- a long-term commitment to developing appropriate skills
- a high standard of performance
- participation for the experience of it (intrinsic reward)
- a set of values, resources, and schedules constructed around the activity
- involvement in groups engaged in the same activity
- self-identification with the activity
- continued interest in the challenge of increasing skill levels (Stebbins, 2001)

But commitment in leisure is a matter of degree. In serious leisure we are perhaps referring to the highest degree of commitment. A little milder on the commitment scale might be those Stebbins (1999) refers to as hobbyists, meaning persons who, although enthusiastic about their pastime, do not participate according to all of the qualifications of seriousness listed above. In other words, their passion for stamp collecting might provide intrinsic reward, long-term involvement, and skilled conduct without requiring that it be prioritized above everything else in the daily routine or be used for self-identification.

In Your Own Experience

Spiritual Health
Box 2.7

	Rarely	Sometimes	Most of the Time	Always
1. I believe life is a precious gift that should be nurtured.	1	2	3	4
2. I take time to enjoy nature and the beauty around me.	1	2	3	4
3. I take time alone to think about what's important in life—who I am, what I value, where I fit in, and where I'm going.	1	2	3	4
4. I engage in acts of caring and goodwill without expecting something in return.	1	2	3	4
5. I feel confident that I have touched the lives of others in a positive way.	1	2	3	4
6. I am content with who I am.	1	2	3	4
7. I go for the gusto and experience life to the fullest.	1	2	3	4

Total your scores. An ideal spiritual health score is 28. Scores of 27-20 are outstanding. Your answers show you are aware of the importance of spirituality to your health. Scores of 19 to 10 show that although you experience some spirituality in life, there is room for growth. Study the items you answered "sometimes." What changes could you make to improve your score? For scores 9 and lower, your spiritual health is at risk. Why do you think this is so?

(Adapted from: U.S. Health and Human Services, 1981. Health style: A self test. Washington, DC: Public Health Service.)

Spirituality

Everyone's life draws on some form of spirituality. In fact, more and more, spirituality is considered a requirement for our health (Heintzman & Mannell, 2003). Not only does our belief system provide important coping resources for dealing with stress, but it also enhances our overall quality of well-being. Spirituality fosters a "sense of meaning, inner wholeness, connection with others, a unity with all nature and the universe" (Walsh, 1999, p. 6). Living spiritually can give us hope, optimism, forgiveness, and internal peace. Spirituality may involve believing in a supreme power or may simply be a means to greater harmony in life.

Some even refer to spirituality as a kind of intelligence. For example, Zohar and Marshall (2001) consider spiritual intelligence to be our capacity for meaning, vision, and value. Our "spiritual quotient," or SQ as it is called, underlies the things we believe in and the role our beliefs and values play in the actions we take. We have a longing for something that takes us beyond the present moment, for something that gives us and our actions a sense of meaning. When we have high spiritual intelligence, we are able to satisfy this longing. The SQ is the ability to let go of the confines of our ego and, according to Zohar and Marshall, is a necessary foundation for the effective functioning of both our intellectual and emotional intelligence.

Where does leisure come in? Although leisure, with its connotation of pleasure, may appear to be an inappropriate context for spirituality, there is perhaps no more compatible connection in our lives than leisure and spirituality. It also matters how you define leisure (as time, activity, or state of mind), and there are at least three ways to examine this connection: leisure as a means of connecting with a supreme power, leisure as a means to personal meaning, and leisure as a way to connect with others (Karlis, Grafanaki, & Abbas, 2002).

For some scholars, the link between spirituality and leisure is one that focuses on building a connection with a supreme power, or God. That is, leisure is viewed as necessary for religious development. For example, Lehman (1974) suggests that a leisure state of mind is one that helps us attain enlightenment, and for Pieper (1963), leisure is a meditative state in which one discovers God and the true meaning of life. Further, Lee (1964) sees leisure as providing an inner feeling of freedom, which is needed to fully experience God. Some consider the practice of such spiritual activities as prayer to be leisure-like.

Most scholars focus on the relationship between spirituality and leisure from the perspective of creating meaning in one's life (Heintzman, 2002). One of the most commonly cited illustrations of this is the out-of-doors. When playing in the natural world, we often find it easiest to think about our lives. The forces of nature help us understand our place in it and renew our spirit along the way. We need to go to the woods, oceans, plains, deserts, and rivers to discover the spiritual riches within ourselves because they instill a sense of "peace and serenity" (Kaplan, 1984).

Finally, leisure may be considered to have a spiritual quality because it is a way to connect with others. Activities such as camping may help us better connect not only with ourselves, but also with others with whom we share the experience. Through fellowship and service to others, that is, shared leisure, we may better understand each other. This is perhaps best illustrated through religious festivals and holidays. That is, the common link between leisure and spirituality is celebration. Pieper (1963), for example, declares that reverent celebration is the soul of leisure. In leisure, he argues, people celebrate with each other that which is good.

Risk

Ocean cruising is an exotic and esoteric way of life. Cruisers are people who sail the oceans of the world for years at a time just for fun. They forsake the security and safety of land-based life for the formidable challenges of the high seas. Many give up careers. Their lifestyle requires much effort, involves considerable danger, and provides no extrinsic rewards, such as fame or money. Why, then, do they do it?

Similarly, why do people scale vertical rock faces, shoot whitewater rapids in kayaks, skydive, and pursue other high-risk pastimes? What is the reward? Risk. Risk in leisure gives us a sense of freedom, control over ourselves and the environment, and an escape from the ordinary routines of life. We gain the knowledge that we are able to cope with our fears.

Let's consult some of the research to confirm this. First, a study by Priest and Bunting (1993) found that participation in a three-day whitewater canoeing trip resulted in decreases in feelings that the activity was risky and increases in feelings of competence. Similarly, Paxton (1998) measured **self-efficacy** gains from risky forms of leisure. Typically, these gains lasted for at least one year after the experience. Jones and Ellis (1996) concluded that the experience was physiological from studying participants

> **Self-efficacy:** considering oneself as able to produce the intended results

on a high-ropes course. They noted that levels of beta-endorphin (a naturally occurring opiate linked to pleasure) rose moderately.

We are not limited to considering the leisure quality of risk only on rock faces, on ropes courses, and in whitewater rapids. Other high-risk pursuits might include gambling, having a poem you've written read aloud to an audience, and baking a cake for friends using a new recipe. Nonetheless, it is clear that the deliberate use of risk is an important quality of leisure. Indeed, leisure that provides an opportunity for risk is attractive to millions of people (Ewert

& Galloway, 2001). Even though our societies are rightfully concerned about pastimes that are excessively dangerous and, by some measures, foolhardy, the natural desire for risk from leisure cannot be eliminated. It is one of the reasons for undertaking leisure activities.

Summary: What We Understand

There is no question that the experience of leisure is crucial:

- We all need leisure in our lives because it provides us with those qualities that make us human.
- Leisure provides freedom, intrinsic reward, pleasure, happiness, spirituality, solitude, ritual, humor, play, game, commitment, risk, and relaxation.
- We don't need all of these qualities at the same time and in the same pastime, but we do need some of them at least some of the time.
- This is because leisure is an intense engagement as well as an escape, simple as well as complicated, and deep as well as shallow.
- In fact, leisure has many more life-dependent qualities that are not presented in this chapter.

From Your Own Experience

It's Your Choice
Box 2.8

Ask yourself these questions:

1. If you had to choose between a society without sport and a society without art, which would you choose?
2. If you could learn only one new leisure skill in the next five years, what would you like to learn?
3. If you were banished to a remote island with no other people residing there, what three nonliving things would you take for your leisure?
4. You are responsible for choosing one leisure activity to take into the future for all humanity. What activity would you choose?

Now, of course, you need to think about the reasons for your answers. What were some of your own values or beliefs about leisure that came into play? What specific leisure qualities discussed in this chapter were behind your choices? (adapted from Stumbo, 1992)

Applications to Professional Practice

Where do our places for leisure come from? What is in our "stockpile" of resources for leisure? Because there are so many, a comprehensive list of leisure resources is impossible. To offer a sample, gymnasiums, ice rinks, playgrounds, tracks, trails, athletic fields, art centers, concert halls, libraries, museums, theatres, amusement parks, camps, marinas, fitness centers, resorts, church basements, club rooms, rivers, mountains, ski slopes, sport courts, and of course our own homes are included in our wide collection of leisure resources.

Why do we have so many? Why are leisure resources important to us? This chapter was devoted to answering this question in terms of the important qualities of leisure, but let's highlight one additional reason why having leisure resources is important. In a nutshell, leisure resources are needed to enhance life's successes. The specific concept that supports this claim is cultural capital. **Cultural capital** is defined as an individual's store of behaviors and knowledge (Bourdieu, 1977) that pays off in terms of succeeding in the culture. The importance of this concept for people is that the more a person's own cultural capital matches that which is most highly regarded by his or her culture, the more successful he or she will be in work and school. How does this relate to pastimes? Bluntly, it says that the way to success is via a shared experience in the pastimes of those at the top. Before we reject this notion as elitist, let's examine it a bit more closely.

> **Cultural capital: personal resources that are useful for achieving competence in a society's high-status culture**

Cultural capital is acquired through life experiences and interactions. The "capital" acquired in childhood is believed to affect not only success in school but also success later in occupations. According to Bourdieu (1977), the reason some children fail at school is that the school often requires cultural capital that is foreign to their lives. For example, the forms of music emphasized in school may not match the musical heritage of a child whose parents are not originally from that culture. Thus, what is necessary to succeed in the home often leads to failure in school, and later, at a job.

How can cultural capital be increased? Part of the answer is in the availability of leisure resources. For example, Katsillis and Rubinson (1990) found that high school students' participation in "high culture" activities (attending live theater, and visiting museums and galleries) was an important source of cultural capital that related positively to success in school. In the research of Downey and Powell (1993), those eighth graders who were more successful in school participated in scouting, hobby clubs, boys' or girls' clubs, 4-H, Y activities, and summer and other organized recreation programs.

Researchers at the University of California at Irvine (Rauscher, 1994) found that listening to music helps the brain manage complex mental functions, such as understanding mathematics. In their experiments preschool children who received eight months of music lessons demonstrated spatial reasoning skills that far outstripped those of preschoolers who didn't take lessons. For these and other studies, the answer to helping people be more successful in life is a rich leisure life.

For Further Information

Read more about the source of ideas on cultural capital by checking the Internet for sites devoted to Pierre Bourdieu's "Forms of Capital." Here are a few places to begin: http://enwikipedia.org/wiki/Cultural_capital and http://enwikipedia.org/wiki/Pierre_Bourdieu.

References

Bourdieu, P. (1977). Cultural reproduction and social reproduction. In N. Smelser (Ed.), *The handbook of sociology.* Beverly Hills, CA: Sage.

Bregha, F. J. (1991). Leisure and freedom re-examined. In T. L. Goodale, & P. A. Witt (Eds.), *Recreation and leisure: Issues in an era of change.* State College, PA: Venture.

Callois, R. (1961). *Man, play, and games.* Glencoe, IL: Free Press of Glencoe.

Csikszentmihalyi, M. (1975). *Beyond boredom and anxiety.* San Francisco: Jossey-Bass.

Csikszentmihalyi, M. (1993). *The evolving self: A psychology for the third millennium.* New York: Harper-Perennial.

Davies, M. (1989). Another way of being: Leisure and the possibility of privacy. In T. Winnifrith, & C. Barrett (Eds.), *The philosophy of leisure.* New York: St. Martin's Press.

Downey, D., & Powell, B. (1993). Do children in single-parent households are better living with same-sex parents? *Journal of Marriage and the Family, 55*, 55–71.

Ellis, M. J. (1973). *Why people play.* Englewood Cliffs, NJ: Prentice-Hall.

Ewert, A., & Galloway, S. (2001, February). Adventure recreation: What's new for resource managers, public policy analysts, and recreation providers. *Parks and Recreation, 26–35.*

Godbey, G. (1999). *Leisure in your life: An exploration.* State College, PA: Venture.

Goffman, E. (1959). *The presentation of self in everyday life.* New York: Doubleday.

Goodale, T. L., & Godbey, G. C. (1988). *The evolution of leisure: Historical and philosophical perspectives.* State College, PA: Venture.

Grimes, R. (1982). *Beginnings in ritual studies.* Lanham, MD: University Press of America.

Heintzman, P. (2002). A conceptual model of leisure and spiritual well-being. *Journal of Park and Recreation Administration, 20(4),* 147–169.

Heintzman, P., & Mannell, R. C. (2003). Spiritual functions of leisure and spiritual well-being: Coping with time pressure. *Leisure Sciences, 25,* 207–230.

Huizinga, J. (1949). *Homo Ludens: A study of the play element in culture.* London: Routledge & Kegan Paul.

Ibrahim, J. (1991). *Leisure and society: A comparative approach.* Dubuque, IA: Wm. C. Brown.

Jones, S. S. (1992). *Choose to live peacefully.* Berkeley, CA: Celestial Arts.

Jones, R. A., & Ellis, G. D. (1996). Effect of variation in perceived risk on the secretion of beta-endorphin. *Leisure Sciences, 18,* 277–291.

Kando, T. M. (1980). *Leisure and popular culture in transition.* St. Louis: C. V. Mosby.

Kaplan, R. (1984). Impact of urban nature: A theoretical analysis. *Urban Ecology, 8,* 189–197.

Karlis, G., Grafanaki, S., & Abbas, J. (2002). Leisure and spirituality: A theoretical model. *Society and Leisure, 25(1),* 205–214.

Katsillis, J., & Rubinson, R. (1990). Cultural capital, student achievement, and educational reproduction: The case of Greece. *American Sociological Review, 55(2),* 270–279.

Kleiber, D.A. (2000). The neglect of relaxation. *Journal of Leisure Research, 32(1),* 82–86.

Larson, R., & Richards, M. (1998). Waiting for the weekend: Friday and Saturday night as the emotional climax of the week. In A. C. Crouter, & R. Larson (Eds.), *Temporal rhythms in adolescence: Clocks, calendars, and the coordination of daily life.* San Francisco: Jossey Bass.

Lee, R. (1964). *Religion and leisure in America: A study in four dimensions.* New York: Abingdon.

Lehman, H. D. (1974). *In praise of leisure.* Kitchener: Herald Press.

Lepper, M. R., Greene, D., & Nisbett, R. E. (1973). Undermining children's intrinsic interest with extrinsic reward: A test of the "overjustification" hypothesis. *Journal of Personality and Social Psychology, 28(1),* 129–137.

Linder, S. (1971). *The harried leisure class.* New York: Columbia University Press.

MacCannell, D. (1999). *The tourist: A new theory of the leisure class.* Berkeley: University of California Press.

May, R. (1981). *Freedom and destiny.* New York: W. W. Norton.

McDonald, K. A. (1995, January 13). The secrets of animal play. *The Chronicle of Higher Education,* p. A8–A13.

Morreall, J. (1983). *Taking laughter seriously.* Albany: State University of New York.

Paxton, T. S. (1998). Self-efficacy and outdoor adventure programs: A quantitative and qualitative analysis. Unpublished doctoral dissertation, University of Minnesota, Minneapolis-St. Paul.

Pelletier, L. G. (1995). Loisirs et sante mentale: Les relations entre la motivation pour la pratique des loisirs et le bien-etre psychologique. *Canadian Journal of Behavioural Sciences, 27(2), 140–156.*

Pieper, J. (1963). *Leisure: The basis of culture.* New York: The New American Library.

Priest, S., & Bunting, C. (1993). Changes in perceived risk and competence during whitewater canoeing. *Journal of Applied Recreation Research, 18(4), 265–280.*

Putnam, R. D. (2000). *Bowling alone.* New York: Simon & Schuster.

Rauscher, F. (1994). *Music and spatial task performance: A causal relationship.* Irvine, CA: Center for the Neurobiology of Learning and Memory.

Roper, I. (2001). *Yo-Yos: Tricks to amaze your friends.* New York: HarperCollins.

Russell, B. (1968). *The conquest of happiness.* New York: Bantam.

Russell, R. V. (2000). Unpublished field notes.

Sarton, M. (1973). *Journal of a solitude.* New York: W. W. Norton.

Schor, J. B. (1998). *The overspent American: Upscaling, downshifting, and the new consumer.* New York: Harper-Perennial.

Smith, S. L. J. (1991). On the biological basis of pleasure: Some implications for leisure policy. In T. L. Goodale, & P. A. Witt (Eds.), *Recreation and leisure: Issues in an era of change.* State College, PA: Venture.

Spencer, H. (1911). On the physiology of laughter. *In Essays on Education, Etc.* London: J. M. Dent.

Stebbins, R. A. (1992). *Amateurs, professionals, and serious leisure.* Montreal, Quebec, Canada: McGill–Queen's University Press.

Stebbins, R. A. (1999). Serious leisure. In E. L. Jackson, & T. L. Burton (Eds.), *Leisure studies: Prospects for the twenty-first century.* State College, PA: Venture.

Stebbins, R. A. (2001). *New directions in the theory and research of serious leisure.* Lampeter, Wales, United Kingdom: The Edwin Mellen Press.

Storr, A. (1988). *Solitude: A return to the self.* New York: Ballantine Books.

Stumbo, N. J. (1992). *Leisure education II: More activities and resources.* State College, PA: Venture.

Sylvester, C. (1991). Recovering a good idea for the sake of goodness: An interpretive critique of subjective leisure. In T. L. Goodale, & P. A. Witt (Eds.), *Recreation and leisure: Issues in an era of change.* State College, PA: Venture.

Szabo, A. (2003). The acute effects of humor and exercise on mood and anxiety. *Journal of Leisure Research, 35(2), 152–162.*

Walsh, F. (1999). *Spiritual resources in family therapy.* New York: Guilford.

World Tourism Organization. (2003). Tourism Highlights. Retrieved January 30, 2004, from http://www.world-tourism.org.

Zohar, D., & Marshall, I. (2001). SQ: *Connecting with our spiritual intelligence.* New York: Bloomsbury.

CHAPTER THREE

Explanations

Preview

What influences our pastime choices?

Because leisure behavior is complex and dynamic, there are multiple explanations.

What role do life situation factors have on influencing our pastime choices?

Such demographic characteristics as our age, gender, income, education level, residence, and others shape our leisure interests and needs.

Can leisure be explained theoretically?

Several theories attempt to explain the conditions and functions of leisure behavior.

Are these theories supported by research?

Research has demonstrated that the theories do explain some aspects of leisure behavior, but more work is needed for a comprehensive explanation.

Key Terms

Demography	72	Paradigm	84
Gender	73	Autoelic	93
Lifestyle	77	Liminality	97
Theory	78	Communitas	97

W hy did you choose to take a vacation last summer? How did you choose where to go and what to do after you got there? As you begin to answer this (or the alternative question of why you chose not to have a vacation), you quickly begin to realize that your reasons are numerous and interrelated.

Perhaps this is what makes studying leisure so intriguing. Indeed, leisure has been the subject of scholarship by a wide range of writers and investigators representing a wide range of disciplines (Searle, 2000). Some of this study focuses on the causes of leisure behavior by particular life situation factors, such as age, level of education, and residence. Other explanations are derived from the development of theories that are then tested for validity through research studies. In this chapter we describe what we know about leisure behavior from both situational factors and theories.

Situational Factors Explaining Leisure Behavior

In explaining why each of us participates in leisure pursuits and the benefit we derive from them, one important source is demographic information. **Demography** is the study of human populations. It takes into account numerous social, cultural, and environmental factors that affect people's situations in life (Fig. 3.1). Demographic information about people includes age, gender, ethnicity, race, income, educational level, occupation, and residence. All of these factors play a role in determining what, why, and

> **Demography: the study of human populations**

how we pursue our pastimes.

To begin, one's age affects leisure interests and behaviors. This is one of the most highly researched factors. In spite of differences in individual personalities, age groupings dictate a great deal about our leisure pursuits. This is because age is an indication not only of maturation, but also of historical experiences, abilities, social

Figure 3.1

Leisure is uniquely expressed according to such demographic factors as age, race, gender, and health. Patient and recreation therapist enjoy a dance in a nursing home. (© Ruth V. Russell)

expectations, and social rights and privileges. For example, the various state and province regulations for minimum driving (and drinking) ages have a significant impact on the leisure choices of youth, as do restrictions against driving for the very elderly.

There are many illustrations of the effect of age on leisure. According to some research, for example, current generations of older women experience significantly lower levels of physical activity and sports participation than do younger generations (Kelly & Freysinger, 2000). This is perhaps because older women have not had the opportunities for physical skill development that younger generations have because of social restrictions against their participation in sports when of school age—the prime stage in life for learning physical skills.

Thus, age as a predictor of leisure experience operates in tandem with gender. In many cultures, gender is a central aspect of defining who we are. It is the focus of the structure and process of everyday life. What is gender? **Gender** is the set of social expectations attached to biological sex. This means that certain behaviors, physical appearances, social roles, attitudes, expressions of sexuality, and abilities are expected from individuals according to whether they are males or females (Kelly & Freysinger, 2000). The concept of gender suggests that what it means to be a woman or a man is more socially than biologically ascribed.

> **Gender: social expectations attached to biological sex**

A great deal of research has also been done on gender as an explanation of leisure interests and behaviors, most of which has focused on describing gender differences. For example, men and women are likely to engage in different sports. There are more women participants in group-exercise programs and more men participants in weightlifting programs. Further, boys are more likely to play video and computer games, and young boys' recreation is also more likely to involve large groups. Another gender difference is that women are more likely than men to experience leisure when outside the home. For men, home is more often a site of leisure. This is perhaps because, for women, home is more often associated with child and household care chores (Henderson, Bialeschki, Shaw, & Freysinger, 1996). Other than differences such as these, gender doesn't matter much in explaining some leisure behavior. For example, socializing with family and friends is as likely to be just as highly valued by men as it is by women (Kelly & Freysinger, 2000).

Our leisure is shaped not only by age and gender, but also by ethnicity and race. These factors are also descriptions of how our personal identity is socially defined, meaning that society has expectations of our leisure behavior based on skin color and ethnic origin. That is, the leisure choices of individuals from various ethnic and racial groups differ primarily because of cultural differences. For example, it is assumed that African Americans have more "natural ability" in team sports and that the leisure of Hispanic Americans is more family-oriented. Furthermore, how different ethnic and racial groups are portrayed on television and in games, music, and toys demonstrates a strong stereotyped notion of leisure based on this demographic factor (Kelly & Freysinger, 2000).

We must be very cautious in explaining leisure interests and behaviors based on race and ethnicity alone, because these factors are highly associated with two other demographic factors: level of education and income. Belonging to the opera guild and taking a two-week ski resort vacation probably have more to do with education and income levels than with race or ethnicity.

Income and education are therefore also powerful factors that influence how we express our leisure. Higher levels of education tend to accompany higher levels of personal income, which can be spent on pastimes. To illustrate, researchers in tourism report that tourists with higher incomes stay longer and spend more money per day than do those with lower incomes (Mill, 1986). In essence, in technological cultures leisure opportunities are more accessible to those with higher incomes. This is why poverty is such a double tragedy. Although participation in leisure activities improves the quality of daily life, it tends to be less available to economically disadvantaged people who perhaps need it most. There is another interesting connection between money and leisure. In some situations, leisure actually provides direct financial benefits to participants. Obvious examples are occupations in which participants are paid for engaging in their favorite pursuits, such as being fishing guides, fitness instructors, artists, musicians, and so on.

Like income, the contribution of education to leisure choices is direct. Education, in and of itself, can contribute to people's ability to participate in leisure. We learn to read, write, and manipulate numbers, which are frequently the skills required for certain leisure pursuits such as working puzzles and playing some card games. In addition, attitudes toward leisure can be altered by education. Those who learn while young that leisure is a valuable part of health and happiness are more likely to experience positive leisure experiences as adults. In school, curricula in art, music, dance, drama, the outdoors, sports, and literature teach us important leisure skills. Thus, beyond enabling higher levels of leisure spending, education is an important factor in determining our leisure interests.

Religion is also a demographic factor that commonly influences leisure behavior. Most religious organizations are concerned with human goodness and thus often teach doctrines that promote healthful expressions of leisure. Some religious organizations also use recreational activities as a means of spreading their particular creed. For example, the United Methodist Church provides a social club for young members with programs in community service, drama, music, social events, outdoor recreation, and trips.

Finally, leisure behavior is in part determined by residence. Where we live greatly affects the nature and accessibility of pastime opportunities. Some pastimes are not universally available because of climate, topography, and other elements of location. For example, in an urban location a wide range of commercial and cultural activities are available, yet activities requiring large space, such as hunting, are less common (Fig. 3.2). When a suburban residence is chosen, local government-sponsored youth sports may be more readily available, yet opportunities to attend live theater or enjoy diverse restaurant

Figure 3.2
Interests in activities such as bird watching are often determined by our residential location.
(© Ruth V. Russell)

cuisine may be more limited. Apartments and condominiums are often selected because of their ability to offer greater opportunities for leisure, such as swimming pools, tennis courts, jogging trails, and picnic shelters.

The demographic factors we have discussed (age, gender, race, ethnicity, income, educational level, religion, and residence), as well as others, impact our leisure choices and behaviors through another concept. This is lifestyle. Our lifestyle can be considered the "stew pot" of these demographic factors; it is here that they mix together and set the scene for how we live. **Lifestyle** is a pat-

In Focus

Noise
Box 3.1

Since the days of Sodom and Gomorrah, cities have been singled out as bad places. Some of the reasons some of us love to hate the city include its architecture, which restricts sunlight, forms wind tunnels, and traps heat. But these troubles don't usually head most city-bashing lists. The most often-cited source of urban problems is other people. City dwellers are assured of crowded, restrictive, and just plain noisy lives. For example, the quietest times in New Yorkers' apartments are louder than the noisiest small towns.

Noise is an almost entirely human-made plague that rarely occurs in nature. Often to a greater extent than air and water pollution, noise generated by people and their machines causes readily measurable physiological and psychological changes. Changes in blood pressure, respiration rate, hormone levels, muscle tension, and digestion can take a disastrous toll on well-being. Further, noise affects behavior. It lowers performance, mood, and sociability, and increases aggression.

So, you say, why not move out of the city to the peace and quiet of the suburbs? If you've spent even one summer's day in a suburban neighborhood, you'll quickly retort that there's no quiet there either. Thanks to the din of the internal combustion engine from a chorus of lawn mowers, weed whackers, hedge trimmers, and leaf blowers, there's a lot of noise there too! So let's head out to the lake, which, of course, turns out to be noisier than the New Jersey Turnpike, with the roar of jet skis, jet boats, cigar boats, and boom boxes (adapted from Gallagher, 1993, pp. 148-153).

Questions to Consider and Discus

1. How does noise affect you? Does it affect your enjoyment of your favorite pastimes?

2. How might the noisy city or the noisy suburban neighborhood affect the choice of leisure pursuits of people who live there?

3. Is the noise generated by particular leisure pursuits themselves justified? Or does it mean that some enjoy leisure at the expense of others?

tern of living. It is both what people do and how they do it. For example, let's consider a family reunion. There are many patterns for this simple event. How many are invited, where it is held, who does the food preparation, how often they are held, what is eaten, and what time of day are all decisions based on lifestyle

| Lifestyle: pattern of everyday living formed by demographic factors |

differences that vary for each family and ones that are governed by such factors as age, gender, income, and residence.

Numerous studies have attempted to categorize lifestyle types. For example, the VALS (Values and Lifestyles) typology divides people into eight lifestyle types according to such demographic factors as age, income, and education, as well as personal values (see Table 3.1). In the VALS typology, leisure is an important dimension of overall everyday styles that shape people's identities, priorities, and investments in life (Kelly, 1999). In return, people's identities, priorities, and investments shape their leisure style.

Table 3.1
Lifestyle Types According to the VALS (Values and Lifestyles) Survey

Lifestyle type	Description	Leisure interests
Actualizers	Successful, sophisticated, active, "take-charge" people with high self-esteem and abundant resources.	Wide range of interests, reflecting a cultivated taste for the finer things.
Fulfilleds	Mature, satisfied, comfortable, conservative, reflective. Many are retired.	Leisure interests tend to center around the home.
Achievers	Successful career- and work-oriented people who value predictability and stability over risk.	Social lives are structured around family, church, and career.
Experiencers	Young, vital, enthusiastic, impulsive, and rebellious. Seek variety and excitement, savoring the new, the offbeat, and the risky.	Their energy finds an outlet in exercise, sports, outdoor recreation, and social activities. Also avid consumers of music and movies.
Believers	Conventional people with concrete beliefs based on traditional, established codes of family, church, community, and nation. Income, education, and energy are modest but sufficient.	Follow established leisure routines organized around home, family, and religious organizations.
Strivers	Seek motivation, self-definition, and approval from the world around them. Unsure of themselves and low on economic, social, and psychological.	Impulsive and easily bored. Many seek to be stylish in leisure.

From Your Own Experience

What Is Your Lifestyle?
Box 3.2

From studying Table 3.1, identify which lifestyle type you think you are. To see how close you are, take the VALS (Values and Lifestyles) questionnaire yourself. Here's how. Go to the Web site http://www.sric-bi.com. From here, click on "VALS Survey" on the right side of the page. Notice the many options for reading more about the VALS system, and when you're ready, click on "Take the Survey" in the box at the bottom of the page. After answering all questions, click on "Submit," and in a few seconds your lifestyle profile will be reported. Compare the results to Table 3.1 again. Were you surprised by the results? Why or why not? How does your lifestyle type relate to your leisure interests?

Theories Explaining Leisure Behavior

Now we turn to other ways of explaining leisure behavior. That is, we consider the understanding we gain from theories. What is a theory? A **theory** is a set of interrelated, testable propositions. The goal of a theory is to summarize existing knowledge, provide an explanation for observed events, and predict the occurrence of as-yet-unobserved events on the basis of the principles of the theory.

> **Theory:** a plausible body of principles used to explain some behavior or event

Because of the multidisciplinary nature of leisure, numerous theories are used to explain it based on propositions in sociology, psychology, anthropology, and other disciplines. Some leisure theories are simpler propositions based on direct observation, whereas others are more comprehensive, with extensive testing. None of the theories completely explain all leisure behavior for all people. Yet they are pragmatically useful to those who provide leisure services because they help predict the needs and interests of clients (Fig. 3.3).

Figure 3.3
Understanding why people behave in leisure as they do has been used by managers of parks to respond to the needs of visitors. (© Ruth V. Russell)

Compensation and Spillover

For a long time, leisure choices have been explained as a response to work. That is, the nature of people's work directly influences their choice of pastimes. Illustrating this approach are two work-based theories: spillover and compensation. Even though these two theories provide opposite explanations, both are based on the idea that leisure is undertaken in reaction to work.

According to compensation theory, leisure makes up for the deadening rhythm of our workaday existence. Deprivations experienced at work are "compensated" for during leisure. This explanation claims that people participate in activities that satisfy needs they cannot satisfy at work. As described

In Focus

Leisure Quotes
Box 3.3

Following are some often-heard quotations about leisure. Each in its own way, these quotes comment on the relationship between work and leisure:

"To be able to fill leisure intelligently is the last product of civilization."

Arnold Toynbee

"Be temperate in your work, but don't carry the practice over into your leisure hours."

Monty Woolley

"Most people spend most of their days doing what they do not want to do in order to earn the right, at times, to do what they may desire."

John Brown

"You gotta be a man to play baseball for a living but you gotta have a lot of little boy in you, too."

Roy Campanella

"If you watch the game, it's fun. If you play it, it's recreation. If you work at it, it's golf."

Bob Hope

"If the world were not so full of people, and most of them did not have to work so hard, there would be more time for them to get out and lie on the grass, and there would be more grass for them to lie on."

Don Marquis
(from Stumbo, 1992, pp. 75–77)

Questions to Consider and Discuss

1. Which quote is your favorite? Why? How do you interpret its meaning?

2. Which quotes could be said to support the spillover theory? Which the compensation theory? Why?

3. What additional explanations about the relationship between work and leisure do the quotes suggest?

by Wilensky (1960), a person, particularly a worker engaged in repetitive, low-skilled, and machine-paced work, will seek the precise opposite for leisure. Compensation theory, then, explains why people who perform physical work choose to spend their free time resting, or why those who work indoors prefer outdoor pursuits.

In contrast to the compensatory explanation is the spillover effect for leisure (Wilensky, 1960). According to the spillover theory, work will "spill over" into leisure. This means that workers are thought to participate in leisure activities that have characteristics similar to their job-related tasks. For example, computer skills learned on the job may enable one to socialize on the Internet. According to this theoretical approach, leisure becomes an extension of the skills and attitudes used at work. It explains why people who are sedentary at work are often not interested in physical pastimes, or why those who work indoors might be uncomfortable outdoors.

Notice that these two theories are similar in some respects and different in others. On the one hand, leisure can be different from work (compensation theory) or a repeat of work (spillover theory). Yet for both of these theories, leisure is explained according to its relationship to work. One consideration that clarifies this seeming contradiction is whether work is satisfying. Which theory applies to a situation depends on the amount of satisfaction found in the work. For work that is satisfying, work activities and interests may spill over into leisure. On the other hand, when work is not satisfying, leisure may be needed to compensate for satisfactions not derived from work.

Also notice how these theories contribute to stereotypes about social status and leisure choices. They claim to explain why the construction worker goes bowling every week, likes fast motorcycles and boats, and watches professional wrestling on television, and why the corporate executive plays golf at the country club, travels to exotic places, and attends symphony concerts. Often such stereotypes are wrong and unfair. For example, you perhaps know a construction worker who enjoys listening to classical music on the radio while working or a corporate executive who unwinds on the weekend by driving drag racing cars.

Furthermore, research testing these theories has provided findings that are contradictory. Although there has been more support for spillover than compensation theory (Mannell & Reid, 1999), these theories have not been particularly useful in explaining how people organize leisure and work in their lives, or the impact of work–leisure relationships on life satisfaction (Chick & Hood, 1996). Finally, because the basis is work, the compensation and spillover theories do not explain the leisure behavior of those who do not work, for example, the retired, young children, and the unemployed.

Kelly's Types

Another theoretical approach that explains leisure by way of its contrast with work is that suggested by sociologist John Kelly (1972). Its basis is the nature of meaning and the amount of freedom. We can picture this theory as a diagram of four types of leisure. As shown in Figure 3.4, how much freedom and what sort of meaning we derive from leisure experiences defines what type of leisure we are experiencing. According to Kelly, some types of leisure are more "work-like" than others.

Figure 3.4

John Kelly's theory of types of leisure (Kelly, 1982).

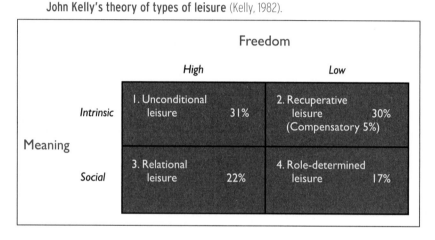

		Freedom	
		High	Low
Meaning	Intrinsic	1. Unconditional leisure 31%	2. Recuperative leisure 30% (Compensatory 5%)
	Social	3. Relational leisure 22%	4. Role-determined leisure 17%

In the first cell of the diagram, unconditional leisure occurs when an activity is chosen for its own sake, for the satisfaction intrinsic to participation (Kelly, 1972, p. 60). This is experience independent of work and freely chosen as an end in itself. Something about the activity is exciting, personally expressive, creative, or emotionally fulfilling. Although exactly what this activity is varies for each of us, the meaning and freedom characteristics are the same. That is, unconditional leisure is high in freedom of choice and is pursued for its intrinsic meaning.

In the second cell of the diagram, according to Kelly, recuperative leisure provides a compensation for some deficit or loss. For example, coming home from work and listening to music as a way to unwind, or taking a brisk morning walk as a way to clear the head for studying would be explained as recuperative leisure. The purpose is rest and recovery. This type of leisure provides a compensation for the constraining conditions of work, parenthood, school, caring for an aged parent, and even bad weather. That is, although this type of leisure is chosen for intrinsic reasons, it assumes a low freedom of choice.

In relational leisure (cell three), leisure expressions are chosen because of a desire to be with others. Leisure occurs as a way of being with people we enjoy. Relational leisure is done not so much because someone else expects it, but because it is a valued way of expressing the relationship. Going camping with your family because you enjoy their companionship, taking a child to the zoo because you want to spend some meaningful time with her or him, or having a midmorning cup of coffee with a work colleague because you are friends could all be explained as relational leisure. There is a high amount of freedom of choice and social meaning.

Finally, Kelly theorized about role-determined leisure (cell four). This is leisure that satisfies the expectations of others. A parent attends a Little League game to cheer for his or her child. A boss invites employees to a backyard cookout to show appreciation for their hard work. Leisure that is done with other people to meet a perceived role obligation, namely, as parent, boss, son, or roommate, is motivated by a desire to serve the relationship (Fig. 3.5). Here, there is social meaning and low freedom of choice.

Thus, the answer to why people choose particular pastimes is based on the nature of the meaning received from it and the amount of freedom of choice applied to it. Research on this theory has typically focused on the proportions of each type of leisure in people's lives. For example, a study of three American communities revealed a profile of what adults did for leisure and why (Kelly, 1978). A slight majority of the leisure reported (31 percent) was considered unconditional leisure. Thirty percent of the leisure was recuperative, 22 percent was relational, and 17 percent was role-determined (see Fig. 3.4).

Another line of research has focused on whether some activities tend to be of certain types. According to Kelly's (1982) research, although no activities always have the same meaning for everyone, some do tend to be chosen for intrinsic reasons and others are generally a response to perceived role expectations. For example, Kelly considers arts, crafts, hobbies, creative home projects, and some sports as primarily unconditional leisure. Also, reading, television viewing, listening to music, daydreaming, and some travel tend to be chosen for their ability to be recuperative. Activities such as eating out and attending parties are more likely chosen as relational leisure, and pastimes of any sort experienced with family members are typically determined by the role. Fine distinctions exist in this classification, however. As Kelly explained, "cultural activities tend to be more unconditional if they involve the effort of going somewhere on a schedule and more recuperative if they are passive and done at home" (1982, pp. 168–169).

Figure 3.5

Playing with children can be role-determined leisure for a parent. (© Ruth V. Russell)

Neulinger's Paradigm

John Neulinger developed a **paradigm** that also contrasts leisure to work, but

> **Paradigm:** a pattern or model for how something works

because Neulinger was a psychologist, the emphasis of his theoretical work was focused on the "states of mind" of leisure and work.

Neulinger's theory maintains that perceived freedom is the primary determining quality of the leisure state of mind. As with Kelly's theory of leisure types, perceived freedom means how much choice we feel we have in determining our own actions. Was it our choice completely (perceived freedom), or did we do it because we felt we had to (perceived constraint)?

To Neulinger, of secondary importance to the leisure state of mind is motivation. According to the theory, motivation for a person's actions is a matter of degree between intrinsic reasons, meaning doing it for its own sake, and extrinsic reasons, meaning doing it for a payoff or to avoid a punishment.

Neulinger divided these two qualities across a "state of mind" continuum to explain different leisure experiences. For example (Fig. 3.6), the paradigm makes the distinction between leisure and nonleisure along the dimensions of perceived freedom and intrinsic or extrinsic motivation. It does this by dividing these dimensions into six types of psychological states of mind (Neulinger, 1976).

1. *State of Mind One.* This represents the purest form of leisure—an expression freely chosen for its own sake. Pure leisure requires freedom from

In Profile

John Neulinger
Box 3.4

John Neulinger, at the time of his death in 1991, was professor emeritus of psychology at the City College of New York, and chair of the Society for the Reduction of Human Labor. Dr. Neulinger was widely recognized as one of the pioneers in the study of psychological aspects of leisure and the author of numerous articles and books on that topic. His perspectives on the relationship between freedom and leisure were influenced by his experiences in Nazi Germany before and during World War II. In his later years, he came to believe that society was rapidly moving toward a postindustrial phase in which technology would provide the means to minimize human labor, but that life would be denigrated unless beliefs and values to embrace such a change were developed

(from http://www.academyofleisuresciences.org/memory.htm).

external control, and it brings intrinsic rewards. Neulinger's pure leisure state of mind is the same as Kelly's unconditional leisure. It not only requires "a complete mastery of oneself in terms of total freedom from inner constraints, but it also implies the condition of being able to enjoy the satisfactions derived from intrinsic rewards without having to pay attention to potential extrinsic ones" (Neulinger, 1981, p. 31).

2. *State of Mind Two.* This type of leisure represents a wide range of experiences, all of which are freely chosen yet are both extrinsically and intrinsically rewarding. The activity is satisfying not only in itself but also in terms of its payoffs. For example, perhaps, for you, refinishing a piece of antique furniture, doing chores around the house, or gardening are characteristic of this leisure–work state of mind. An important distinction is that a person can quit whenever she or he pleases.

3. *State of Mind Three.* This is leisure–job according to Neulinger. It is a type of leisure one engages in without coercion, but the satisfaction comes from external payoffs. For some people, playing cards for money (when they don't need the money) or lifting weights in order to look better (not on a doctor's orders) might fit this state of mind. While reflecting an experience of perceived freedom, the activity is only extrinsically rewarding and thus resembles a job. Some consider this leisure–job state of mind to be the same as recreation, that is, doing something you freely choose for a reward external to the activity.

Figure 3.6

Neulinger's paradigm distinguishes leisure from nonleisure by the amount of perceived freedom and type of motivation (Neulinger, 1981).

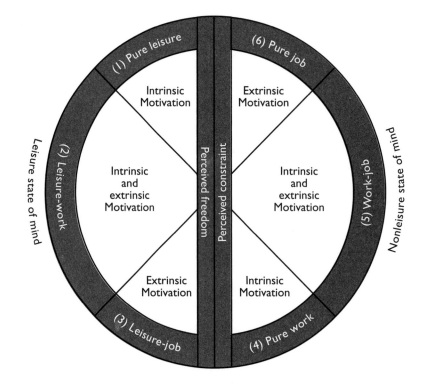

4. *State of Mind Four.* According to Neulinger's paradigm, the first three states of mind are considered to be leisure. Beginning with State of Mind Four, the second three states are considered to be nonleisure. The distinction between the leisure and the nonleisure states of mind is the presence or absence of the perceived freedom of choice. For example, State of Mind Four is not considered to be leisure because even though it is done for intrinsic reasons, it is under perceived constraints. Neulinger called it pure work (cell four). Examples could include doing homework when a student is interested and even enjoyably involved, but which is done nonetheless because of a teacher-made assignment. Given free choice, the student would not do the homework, even though he or she finds it engrossing.

5. *State of Mind Five.* This is work–job, namely, activities engaged in under constraints but having both intrinsic and extrinsic rewards. The typical employment situation may produce this state of mind. For example, in one study, the staff of a large municipal recreation and parks department rated their jobs as highly meaningful and usually personally satisfying, but they did complain about low salaries. They also indicated on the survey that they would quit or retire immediately if given the financial opportunity (Russell, 1993).

From Your Own Experience

Sampling the WAID
Box 3.5

To experience how Neulinger derived at his theoretical paradigm, try out a portion of the questionnaire he and other researchers used to determine leisure and nonleisure states of mind. Complete the modified excerpt of the questionnaire below.

Time	Activity	Freedom	Reason
10:00 am			
11:00 am			
Noon			
1:00 pm			
2:00 pm			
3:00 pm			
4:00 pm			
5:00 pm			
6:00 pm			
7:00 pm			
8:00 pm			
9:00 pm			
10:00 pm			

Thinking about your day yesterday (do not retrieve your appointment calendar, it is what you perceive about that day that is important), fill in the table columns. For the "activity" column, enter the main activity you recall experiencing at that time. For the "freedom" column, enter a number from 0 to 10 that reflects how much freedom of choice you perceived for each activity. For the "reason" column, enter a number from 0 to 10 reflecting how much intrinsic motivation you perceived for each activity. For both freedom and reason, a score of 0 represents no freedom/intrinsic motivation, up to a score of 10, which represents the highest possible amount of freedom/intrinsic motivation.

After completing the questionnaire, review your scores in the freedom and reason columns. Do you tend to have high scores (up to 10), midrange scores (4-6), or low scores (down to 0)? Accordingly, in comparing your own results with Neulinger's paradigm in Figure 3.6, in which state of mind do you think you spent your day yesterday? Why? Was it leisure or nonleisure? Why?

6. *State of Mind Six.* A state of mind in the pure job category is completely opposite pure leisure. It is an activity engaged in by necessity and under constraints. There is no reward in and of itself but only through a payoff resulting from it. Having to work at a job in its most negative connotation to earn a living only is categorized as pure job. It has no other redeeming qualities.

What is most important to realize about Neulinger's theoretical contribution to explaining leisure is that the paradigm claims that behavior is attributed solely to self rather than to external forces. This means that the explanation of leisure is psychological rather than sociological, as in the perspective of Kelly discussed in the previous section.

Many studies have used Neulinger's paradigm to explain quality of life. Through a data-collection questionnaire called What Am I Doing? (or WAID), research subjects indicate on a time diary how they feel about what they are doing throughout their day according to the amount of perceived freedom and intrinsic motivation. One of these studies was of college students (Hultsman, 1984). Students majoring in business were compared with students majoring in leisure studies. The hypothesis was that as a result of their education, students pursuing a degree in leisure studies would gain an appreciation of the value of leisure as a contributor to their quality of life; however, the study found no difference between the two majors. Leisure studies students did not perceive any more freedom or intrinsic motivation-and thus leisure—in their lives than business students.

Flow

Over the past 30 years, Mihaly Csikszentmihalyi and his colleagues have studied thousands of people who seemed to be spending time doing what they really want to. They have included interviews with rock climbers, chess players, and amateur athletes (Csikszentmihalyi, 1975), as well as surgeons, professors, clerical and assembly line workers, young mothers, retired people, and teens (Csikszentmihalyi, 1990). These inquiries have led to one of the more popular and universally accepted theories about leisure. It is called *flow*.

Flow is a word Csikszentmihalyi uses to describe a state of being in which you become so involved in some activity or experience that nothing else seems to matter. He writes, "Contrary to what happens all too often in everyday life, in moments such as these what we feel, what we wish, and what we think are in harmony" (Csikszentmihalyi, 1997, p. 29). The metaphor of flow is one that many people have used to describe the sense of effortless action they feel in moments that stand out as the best in their lives. Athletes refer to it as being "in the zone," religious mystics as being in "ecstasy," and artists and musicians as "aesthetic rapture." Csikszentmihalyi discovered that people reached this optimal experience through different activities but in similar ways. These common reasons have become the major elements of the flow theory. In his interviews, when people reflected on how it felt when their experience was most optimal, they mentioned at least one, and often all, of the following characteristics or conditions:

1. *The activity is challenging and requires skills.* Flow tends to occur when a person's skills are fully involved in overcoming a challenge that is just about manageable (Fig. 3.7). Optimal experiences usually involve a fine balance when there is some exertion for which we have the appropriate skills. If challenges are too high for our skills, we experience anxiety. If challenges are too low relative to our skills, we are bored. If both challenges and skills are perceived to be low, we feel apathetic. But when high challenges are matched with high skills, then the deep involvement that sets flow apart from ordinary life is likely to occur (Csikszentmihalyi, 1997). While a typical day is full of anxiety and boredom, flow experiences provide flashes of intense living. This is one of the great appeals of sport. For the skilled, the challenges of competition can be very stimulating. But when beating the opponent takes precedence over performing as well as possible, flow disappears.

2. *Action and awareness merge.* When we are experiencing an activity as flow, our attention is completely absorbed by that activity. There is no excess "psychic energy" left over to consider anything other than the activity. All our attention is focused; we become so involved in what we are doing that the activity becomes almost automatic. We stop being aware of ourselves as sepa-

In Profile

Mihaly Csikszentmihalyi
Box 3.6

Mihaly Csikszentmihalyi's interest in flow began as a very personal one. In October 1944 relatives argued with his mother that Venice, Italy, was not enjoyable at this time of year—too many mosquitoes—and that the theaters would all be closed. His mother ignored their advice and left Budapest, Hungary, with 10-year-old Mihaly and his sister on the early train. Later that day, the advancing Russian army bombed the bridges, placed Budapest under siege, and within three months, more than half of Mihaly's relatives were dead. He and his family had taken the last train out (Shore, 1990).

After the war, questions plagued Mihaly. He vividly remembered his relatives at the train station imploring them to stay in Budapest. "I wondered at the time, 'How can people be so mistaken about things?' This was an example of mass denial of reality that seemed extremely important for me to figure out" (Shore, 1990, p. 34).

In the winter of 1952, 18-year-old Mihaly was in Switzerland; his pockets were empty. He searched Zurich for an activity that would keep him warm and not cost anything. The solution was a free lecture given by a psychologist, Carl Jung. Inspired, he began to read Jung's books, then the works of Freud, and finally, anything he could find on psychology.

To fulfill this fascination, at the age of 22, Mihaly arrived at Chicago's Dearborn Street Station with $1.25 in his pocket. He knew no one and spoke only the little English he had picked up from reading American comics in a Rome newspaper. In five months he had passed the high school equivalency exam, and four years later he earned a B.A. in psychology from the University of Chicago.

As a doctoral student, Mihaly began to feel that much of psychology was consumed with the pathological aspects of life. He was interested in the positive dimensions as he continued to reflect on his earlier war concerns. He began to study creativity. For his Ph.D. dissertation, completed in 1965, he studied a group of art students. He recalled, "I was puzzled about why they were so taken with what they were doing without any extrinsic rewards, and I realized people seek activities for their own sake—and this was generally what people in the past called happiness" (Shore, 1990, p. 34). This became the basis for a lifetime of research on the theory of flow.

rate from the activity. We are completely absorbed by it. A rock climber put it this way: "You don't feel like you're doing something as a conscious being; you're adapting to the rock and becoming part of it" (Csikszentmihalyi, 1975, p. 86).

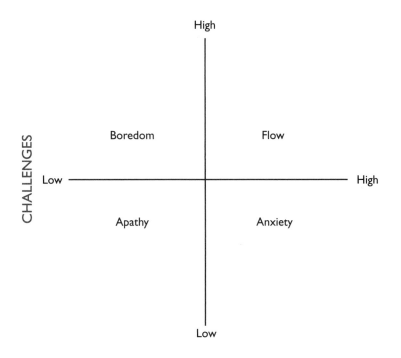

Figure 3.7
In flow theory, one condition of optimal experience is a balance of challenge and skill. Flow results when high challenges are matched with high skills (Csikszentmihalyi, 2000).

3. *Concentration is on the activity.* Related to the previous characteristic of flow, concentration on the action at hand also explains such optimal experiences. According to researchers, one of the most frequently mentioned dimensions of flow by study respondents is that while it lasts, one is able to forget unpleasant aspects of life. For example, a dancer describes how it feels during a good performance: "Your concentration is very complete. Your mind isn't wandering, you are not thinking of something else; you are totally involved in what you are doing" (Csikszentmihalyi, 1990, p. 53).

4. *Loss of self-consciousness.* When we engage in activities that require us to concentrate on the action at hand and that are experienced as a merging of action and awareness, a loss of self-consciousness is a natural by-product. Csikszentmihalyi (1990) describes this as feeling as though the boundaries of our being have been pushed forward. In flow there is no opportunity for self-scrutiny. If, for example, a basketball player is thinking, "I hope my boyfriend saw that great shot I just made," there is no loss of self-consciousness and flow isn't occurring.

5. *Clear goals and feedback.* It is possible to achieve such complete involvement in a flow experience partly because the goals of the activity are clear and the feedback is immediate (Fig. 3.8). It is easy to enter flow in games such as chess because they have goals and rules for action that make it possible for the player to act without questioning what should be done and how. After each move on the chess board, you can tell whether you have improved your position or not.

Figure 3.8
The feedback these children receive from releasing newly hatched turtles in a conservation project is immediate and clear. (© Ruth V. Russell)

6. *Sense of control.* The flow experience is also typically described as involving a sense of control. Although it is actually possible to lose control during a flow experience (e.g., a rock climber may fall and break a leg), the perception of being in control is an important aspect of the experience. Essentially, activities that produce flow, even the most risky ones, allow the participant to feel in control. This was demonstrated in the research of Larson (1988), who assessed high school students working on a research paper for English class. As might be imagined, students experienced a wide range of feelings during the writing experience. Some described their feelings as "flustered" and "overwhelmed" (p. 153). Others were bored. Some students, however, reported flow-like involvement in their writing that reflected their sense of being in control, such as, "I felt really powerful, like I had the information in the palm of my hand and could mold it any way I wanted" (p. 164).

7. *Transformation of time.* One of the most common descriptions of the flow experience is that time no longer seems to pass as it ordinarily does. In most situations, it seems to pass much more quickly. People in Csikszentmihalyi's research have reported that they lost track of time while experiencing flow. Csikszentmihalyi has concluded that "although it seems likely that losing track of the clock is not one of the major elements of enjoyment, freedom from the tyranny of time does add to the exhilaration we feel during a state of complete involvement" (1990, p. 67). Think about times when you've gone for a long run, read a good novel, or skied down a powdery slope. Remember how surprised you were when the activity was over?

8. *Autotelic.* According to the flow theory, a key element in optimal experience is that it is an end in itself. This means the activity is **autotelic**. As in Neulinger's paradigm and Kelly's leisure types, Csikszentmihalyi believes that a leisure experience is done not with the expectation of a future benefit, but because the doing itself is the reward. Ask anyone who has climbed a mountain why she or he did it, and the answer is likely, "Because it was there."

> **Autotelic:** an experience that has purpose in itself; intrinsically rewarding

Adventure Experience Paradigm

Another similar theory about optimal experience is the adventure experience paradigm (AEP) developed by Martin and Priest (1986). According to Priest (1992), the AEP is applicable to any leisure pursuit that has elements of uncertainty, regardless of whether individuals deliberately seek physical risks. In focusing on only the balance of skill and challenge characteristic from the flow theory, the AEP theory uses a balance of perceived risk and competence to determine a peak adventure experience (Fig. 3.9). Depending on this balance of perceived risk and competence, the AEP theorizes five conditions: devastation and disaster, misadventure, peak adventure, adventure, and exploration and experimentation.

Priest and Baille (1987) describe the condition of devastation and disaster as one in which the risks overwhelm the competence of the individual to the point of having a perception of the likelihood of injury or even death. Misadventure is described as a condition that occurs when competence does not quite match risk, possibly created by an incident such as tipping over a canoe. Peak adventure, on the other hand, occurs when the individual is concentrating intensely and experiencing a state of euphoria because competence and risk are perfectly balanced. Priest and Baille describe the condition of adventure as occurring when there is a slightly lower risk, giving participants a chance to put their competence to test, whereas the condition of exploration and experimentation happens when risk is low and competence high, which provides a more relaxed setting for practicing skills.

The Study Says

Flow in Daily Life
Box 3.7

Flow can seem an elusive phenomenon that, for most people, occurs only on rare occasions and only for special people (Voekl, Ellis, & Walker, 2003). Can the optimal experience of flow be a part of daily life for everyone? To study this question, researchers typically use a data-gathering technique called the experience-sampling method (ESM). Study participants carry an electronic pager for four to seven days; when beeped at random times during the day, they report on their immediate experience by completing a short questionnaire. From this approach, researchers have concluded that the daily experience can include combinations of the characteristics of flow, but not always at optimal levels. For example, in our day we might experience high levels of concentration but low levels of sense of control and time distortion (Voelkl et al., 2003). In other studies, the presence of flow in planned recreation programs has been investigated. For example, Walker (2002) compared the flow states of recreational and competitive athletes. Although these findings indicated that both types of athletes experienced flow during workouts, for recreational athletes flow was significantly more important in determining their satisfaction with participation, whereas performance success determined satisfaction for competitive athletes.

The AEP theory has been tested primarily with people who are kayaking and rafting whitewater rivers. What is distinctive from these studies is the difference between real and perceived risk and competence. That is, real risk and competence are primarily found in the most extreme limits of a situation, whereas in most cases, people are experiencing perceived risk and competence. For example, the real risk could be that there is little chance of rolling the kayak, whereas the perceived risk could be that rolling the kayak is probable.

Research has also demonstrated that the AEP and flow theories are practically identical. What is unique about the AEP theory compared with flow is its ability to be used by managers of leisure experiences to determine how best to meet the needs of clients. For example, by using the AEP's simple measures of risk and competence, leisure service managers can assess whether the activity offers their clients suitable challenges, and then manipulate them accordingly (Morgan, 2001/2002).

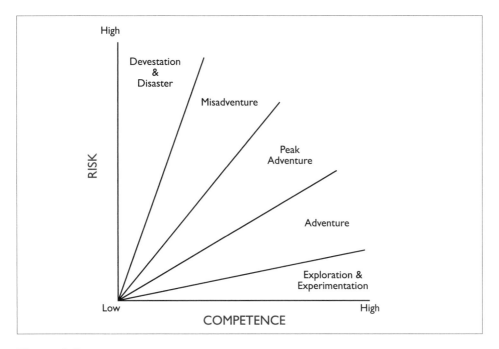

Figure 3.9
The adventure experience paradigm (AEP; adapted from Jones, Hollenhorst, & Perna, 2003, p. 20).

Self-As-Entertainment

Another theoretical perspective is the self-as-entertainment (S-A-E) construct developed by Mannell (1984). It focuses on solving the problem of boredom in leisure by focusing on individual personality differences. The S-A-E theory characterizes the ways people differ in their ability to fill free time with personally satisfactory activity. In other words, people who are high on the personality trait of S-A-E are able to fill free time satisfactorily. They do not experience time as "hanging heavily on their hands" or feel that their free time is "wasted." On the other hand, individuals low on this trait perceive that they have "too much free time" and that there is frequently "nothing to do" (Mannell, 1984, pp. 232–233).

In explaining the theory, Mannell has used the comments made by parents about their children. How often have we heard a parent make comparisons between children concerning their ability to play by themselves or to entertain themselves? This is the first factor of the S-A-E theory: People differ in their ability to fill free time satisfactorily. Some are seemingly always occupied with something, whereas others seem at a loss for what to do.

A second factor is that people also differ in the ways they seek diversion during their free time. Mannell hypothesized that some people use the "self" as the primary source of entertainment. They have the capability to occupy themselves in an enjoyable manner. Research has tentatively suggested that some prerequisite skills for this may be the ability to engage in fantasizing and make-believe, and the ability to use the knowledge stored in memory. Those who do not tend to rely on the "self" as the source of entertainment, Mannell indicated, seek diversion through external sources, such as by calling up friends on the telephone or watching television.

One particularly fascinating study reflecting the S-A-E theory is the early research by Singer (1961). It investigated fantasizing in nine- to 13-year-old children. Children clinically assessed as low and high fantasizers were brought individually into an office and told that astronauts (a highly desirable occupation for this group of children) must be able to wait patiently for extended periods of time. Each child was then asked to wait as long as he or she could while the researcher sat and worked at a desk in the same room. High fantasizers were able to wait three times as long as low fantasizers. The fantasizers were quickly lost in their daydreams and inner thoughts, whereas the nonfantasizers appeared restless and bored. One interpretation of these findings was that the high fantasizers were able to fill the time by using themselves as sources of entertainment.

Theory of Anti-Structure

Now we turn to the discipline of anthropology for another theoretical explanation of leisure. It is based on rituals in people's lives. One particular kind of ritual that has drawn considerable attention is the rite of passage, which occurs when members of a society are ritually transformed from one kind of social person into another, such as from child to adult, or from single person to married couple. The particular kind of rite of passage that is our focus here is the one that moves us from everyday life into a special existence (Fig. 3.10).

Proposed by Victor Turner, and often called the theory of anti-structure, the idea is that there are formal rituals that govern people's behavior both inside and outside everyday life (Turner, 1969, 1982). The rituals that are outside daily life separate people and events from their everyday experiences by being antagonistic to them. That is, they are "anti," or opposed to, everyday structure. This is how leisure exists, according to Turner, as a ritual that sets people outside their norm. Leisure is the anti-structure part of our lives. It's easy to see the usefulness of this theory when we consider vacations and media-based forms of entertainment, for example, as these leisure situations have their own distinct realities for the express purpose of being removed from the everyday routine.

One study of how anti-structure explains leisure is that of Deegan (1989) about the rituals of a college football game. Study findings revealed that the citizens of a state, community, and school experience this pastime as some-

Figure 3.10

This interpreter at the Polynesian Cultural Center in Hawaii is helping tourists dramatically transform out of their everyday lives and into the world of Fiji. (© Ruth V. Russell)

thing outside their everyday existence. Accordingly, their behaviors are different from the usual pattern. Other studies have demonstrated singles bars, auctions, and serial televisions shows (such as Star Trek) as anti-structure contexts as well. For example, auctions provide members of the community with ways to exchange goods that violate the everyday norms of doing business.

Two concepts help to extend our understanding of leisure as anti-structure. These are liminality and *communitas*. **Liminality** is a term that comes from the Latin, meaning "threshold." Turner uses it to refer to the transition from the everyday to outside the everyday. It is in this liminal stage of a rite of passage where a more pure form of play occurs, because it is free of societal norms and structures. Its transitional nature creates an environment conducive to fun (Turner, 1982, p. 40).

> **Liminality:** a transitional stage

People in the liminal stage tend to develop an intense comradeship with one another. Social distinctions that separated them before the ritual and that will separate them again afterward become irrelevant. Turner called this liminally produced social relationship *communitas*, by which he meant a loosely structured community of equal individuals. In thinking about the college football example in Box 3.8, we can see how the actions of the fans can be explained by the liminality and communitas concepts.

> **Communitas:** a temporary sense of social camaraderie

The Study Says

Go Big Red
Box 3.8

An excerpt from the field notes for a study of anti-structure in leisure by Deegan (1989):

Nebraska football is surrounded by ritual events. . . . On game day, there is a complete "rite of passage." Since many people travel great distances, their pilgrimage is elaborate and expensive. Parking is at a premium within a five- or six-block radius immediately prior to game time; the streets are filled with fans dressed in red, holding radios. One's class is evident outside of the stadium by one's means of transportation, access to privileged parking space, and participation in elite pregame program events. Inside the stadium, the fans become one, however, jointly sharing in the ritual of the game. They move as one, highly knowledgeable of the game and the players; their responses are immediate, facilitated by radios and televisions available to approximately one in 15 fans. The fans are not passive; they express their opinions in raucous jubilation or heated anger. Jumping up and down, congratulating each other, clapping, and yelling are all typical expressions of joy. Shaking one's arm in a vengeful fashion and booing are likely displays of anger. Often they pound each other on the back or yell obscenities. They are part of one "team." Their side is "number one." Children, old people, married couples, teens, college kids, farmers—any combination of potential rivals or enemies are "friends" in this setting.

According to the anti-structure theory, then, leisure is very important. Deegan (1989) states, "The ability to have something in common with strangers, to sing and yell and cry in public, to root for one's team, and to publicly participate and reaffirm one's values, are strong bonds that help us tolerate and give meaning to life" (p. 87).

Summary: What We Understand

The many ways of explaining leisure help us understand our own and others' pastimes. Beyond the excitement of knowing for the sake of knowing, understanding leisure is also useful to managers of recreation businesses, facilities, and programs. As a result of studying this chapter you should know that

- Leisure interests and behaviors are complex and unique, and thus difficult to explain.

- Nonetheless, leisure interests and behaviors can be explained in part by lifestyle, which is shaped by multiple demographic characteristics.

- Formal theories that explain leisure interests and behaviors come from the basic disciplines, such as psychology, sociology, and anthropology.

- All the theories discussed have research support, yet some are still at the conceptual level of theory development.

- Neither demographic characteristics nor the various theories are able to thoroughly explain leisure behavior.

Applications to Professional Practice

From earliest times, people have traveled. Trips taken by ancient peoples were mainly driven by religion, hunger, or to escape danger. The first trip for purposes of tourism was made by Queen Hatshepsut to the lands of Punt (now Somalia) in 1490 bc. Descriptions of her tour have been recorded on the walls of the Temple of Deit El Bahari, at Luxor, and are still admired by tourists today (McIntosh & Goeldner, 1986).

Indeed, tourism today is a much different expression of leisure. Millions of people now travel for pleasure. And tourism has become one of the fastest-growing social and economic phenomena in the 21st century. All predictions maintain that the number of tourists, both those who travel internationally and those who travel domestically, will continue to increase and that the geographic spread of tourism will continue to widen. Overall, the tourism industry is one of the world's largest. France is the top destination (over 77 million international tourists per year), followed by Spain (51 million), the United States (42 million), and Italy (40 million). The annual worldwide total of international tourists is over 702 million, who spend U.S.$474 billion (World Tourism Organization, 2003).

Indeed, tourism is perhaps the most frequent type of leisure activity. Why? Although traveling for pleasure today is not as arduous as it probably was for Queen Hatshepsut, it still takes time, costs money, and sometimes brings inconveniences. Why do so many do it? Let's answer this question in two ways: according to the demographics of tourists and their personalities.

First, travel tastes differ according to age, income level, educational level, personal health, stage in the family life cycle, occupation, and many other demographic factors. For example, some hotels cater specifically to the family market, such as Holiday Inn's Holidome, which features indoor playgrounds, miniature golf, game rooms, and swimming pools. Politics, health factors, and economies interact with tourist demographic profiles and thus also play a role. For example, in 2003, international tourism faced an exceptionally difficult year in which three negative factors came together to reduce international arrivals by 2 percent: the Iraq conflict, the SARS health scare, and weak economies (World Tourism Organization, 2003).

On the other hand, people's personality types also shape travel interests. To elaborate, in explaining why destination areas rise and fall in popularity, Plog (1974) classified tourists according to their personalities. He proposed a continuum ranging from the psychocentric at one end to the allocentric at the other. The pure psychocentric personality is self-centered, whereas the pure allocentric personality is interested in things beyond the self. Psychocentrics tend to focus on the events around their own lives, whereras allocentrics are outgoing and self-confident. They are willing to reach out and experiment with life.

Plog found that North American tourists were normally distributed along the continuum between these two extreme types, with most people falling in the midcentric range, a balance of both psychocentric and allocentric. His research was also able to identify the travel preferences of people according to where their personality was located on the continuum (Fig. 3.11). That is, allocentrics tended to travel far away and to unfamiliar places, whereas psychocentrics were happiest vacationing close to home.

Figure 3.11
Personality types and tourist destinations (McIntosh & Goeldner, 1986).

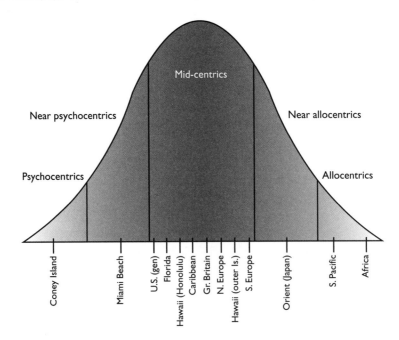

Professionals in the tourism industry are able to use both the demographic profiles of tourists and information about their personalities to plan and manage tourist attractions, services, marketing, and transportation. Thanks to research data such as those demonstrated here, companies such as the Holiday Inn Holidomes can meet the specific travel expectations of its most likely guests.

For Further Information

Is a career in one of the tourism industries right for you? If you are curious about other people and locales, have or plan to take advantage of a study abroad program while in college, or enjoy traveling, you might talk to your campus career counselor about it. A good place to start is the Web site of the Canadian Tourism Human Resource Council at www.cthrc.ca/careerplanning/.

References

Chick, G., & Hood, R. D. (1996). Working and recreating with machines: Outdoor recreation choices among machine-tool workers in western Pennsylvania. *Leisure Sciences, 18*, 333–354.

Csikszentmihalyi, M. (1975). *Beyond boredom and anxiety.* San Francisco: Jossey-Bass.

Csikszentmihalyi, M. (1990). *Flow: The psychology of optimal experience.* New York: Harper & Row.

Csikszentmihalyi, M. (1997). *Finding flow: The psychology of engagement with everyday life.* New York: Basic Books.

Csikszentmihalyi, M. (2000). The contribution of flow to positive psychology: Scientific essays in honor of Martin E. P. Seligman. In J. E. Gilham (Ed.), *The science of optimism and hope.* Philadelphia: Templeton Foundation.

Deegan, J. J. (1989). *American ritual dramas: Social rules and cultural meanings.* New York: Greenwood Press.

Gallagher, W. (1993). *The power of place: How our surroundings shape our thoughts, emotions, and actions.* New York: HarperPerennial.

Henderson, K. A., Bialeschki, M. D., Shaw, S. M., & Freysinger, V. J. (1996). *Both gains and gaps: Feminist perspectives on women's leisure.* State College, PA: Venture.

Hultsman, J. (1984, October). Leisure education as a correlate of quality of life. Proceedings: Symposium on leisure research, NRPA Congress for Recreation and Parks, Orlando, FL.

Jones, C. D., Hollenhorst, S. J., & Perna, F. (2003). An empirical comparison of the four channel flow model and adventure experience paradigm. *Leisure Sciences, 25*, 17–31.

Kelly, J. R. (1972). Work and leisure: A simplified paradigm. *Journal of Leisure Research, 4*, 50–62.

Kelly, J. R. (1978). Leisure styles and choices in three environments. *Pacific Sociological Review, 21*, 187–207.

Kelly, J. R. (1982). *Leisure.* Englewood Cliffs, NJ: Prentice-Hall.

Kelly, J. R. (1999). Leisure behaviors and styles: Social, economic, and cultural factors. In E. L. Jackson, & T. L. Burton (Eds.), *Leisure studies: Prospects for the twenty-first century.* State College, PA: Venture.

Kelly, J. R., & Freysinger, V. J. (2000). *21st century leisure: Current issues.* Boston: Allyn & Bacon.

Larson, R. (1988). Flow and writing. In M. Csikszentmihalyi, & I. S. Csikszentmihalyi (Eds.), *Optimal experience: Psychological studies of flow in consciousness.* Cambridge: Cambridge University.

Mannell, R. C. (1984). Personality in leisure theory: The self as entertainment. *Society and Leisure, 7*, 229–242.

Mannell, R. C., & Reid, D. G. (1999). Work and leisure. In E. L. Jackson, & T. L. Burton (Eds.), *Leisure studies: Prospects for the twenty-first century.* State College, PA: Venture.

Martin, P., & Priest, S. (1986). Understanding the adventure experience. Journal of Adventure Education, 3(1), 18–21.

McIntosh, R. W., & Goeldner, C. R. (1986). *Tourism: Principles, practices, philosophies.* New York: John Wiley & Son.

Mill, R. C. (1986). Tourist characteristics and trends. In *Literature review: The President's commission on Americans outdoors.* Washington, DC: Government Printing Office.

Morgan, D. J. (2001/2002). Risk, competence and adventure tourists: Applying the adventure experience paradigm to whitewater rafters. *Leisure/Loisir, 26*(1–2), 107–127.

Neulinger, J. (1976, June). The need for and the implications of a psychological conception of leisure. *The Ontario Psychologist, 8*, 15.

Neulinger, J. (1981). *To leisure: An introduction.* Boston: Allyn & Bacon.

Plog, S. C. (1974). Why destination areas rise and fall in popularity. *The Cornell Hotel and Restaurant Administration Quarterly, 14*(4), 55–58.

Priest, S. (1992). Factor exploration and confirmation for the dimensions of an adventure experience. *Journal of Leisure Research, 24*, 127–139.

Priest, S., & Baille, R. (1987). Justifying the risk to others: The real razor's edge. *Journal of Experiential Education, 10*(1), 6–22.

Russell, R. V. (1993). *Employee perceptions of work-place barriers to change.* Technical report prepared for the Indianapolis, IN, Department of Parks and Recreation.

Searle, M. S. (2000). Is leisure theory needed for leisure studies? *Journal of Leisure Research, 32,* 138–142.

Shore, D. (1990, Winter). The pursuit of happiness. *University of Chicago Magazine,* 28–35.

Singer, J. (1961). Imagination and waiting behavior in young children. *Journal of Personality, 29,* 396–413.

Stumbo, N. J. (1992). *Leisure education II: More activities and resources.* State College, PA: Venture.

Turner, V. (1969). *The ritual process: Structure and anti-structure.* Chicago: Aldine.

Turner, V. (1982). *From ritual to theatre: The human seriousness of play.* New York: Performing Arts Journal Publications.

Voelkl, J., Ellis, G., & Walker, J. (2003, August). Go with the flow. *Parks & Recreation.* 20–29.

Walker, J. (2002). Exploring the influence of the individual's ability to experience flow while participating in a group-dependent activity on individual satisfaction with a group's performance. Unpublished doctoral dissertation, Clemson University, South Carolina.

Wilensky, H. (1960). Work, careers and social integration. *International Social Science Journal, 12,* 4.

World Tourism Organization. (2003).Tourism highlights. Retrieved January 30, 2003, from http://www.world-tourism.org

CHAPTER FOUR

Leisure and Life Span

Preview

How is life span related to leisure?

Life is experienced both as a continuous process and as change. Leisure stimulates and eases the transitions of change yet remains constant throughout life.

How does leisure affect my physical development?

Leisure is a tool for developing motor control when young and an aid to staying physically vital when old.

How does leisure affect my emotional development?

Leisure teaches us joy, affection, and other positive feelings and helps us cope with anger, fear, anxiety, and other negative feelings.

How does leisure affect my intellectual development?

Leisure is a prime medium for learning and keeping sharp such skills as language, intelligence, and creativity.

How does leisure affect my social development?

Leisure helps us achieve and remain vibrant within a social network.

Key Terms

Life span development	106	Identity	116
Chronological age	106	Convergent thinking	120
Birth cohort	106	Divergent thinking	120
Core plus balance	108	Peer	125
Adolescence	111	Gender identity	125
Sociocultural	111	Autonomy	127
Emotions	115	Crowds	127
Locus of control	116	Cliques	127

We begin young, we mature and grow older, and we die. This is the cycle of life. Attendant to this process is the benchmark of age. This chapter is about the continuities and changes of age as they relate to leisure. How do our pastime expressions and interests change as we move through the life cycle? Does the significance and meaning of our pastimes stay with us our whole lives?

We will take a **life span development** approach, meaning that instead of studying each age group separately, we will view human life as an uninterrupted process. For the organization of this chapter, we will use tasks physical, emotional, intellectual, and social developmental tasks and examine how leisure relates to them across the life span. But first, we consider the meaning of age itself.

> **Life span development: the changes and continuities of life from birth to death**

The Meaning of Age

To begin to think about how and why age shapes and is shaped by leisure, it is important to think about the meaning of age itself and how the process of aging is conceptualized. On the simplest level, age is an indication of the years since birth. This is **chronological age.**

Even though simple to define, chronological age is complex, because we see it as an indication of maturation, requiring matching levels of physical, intellectual, emotional, and social ability. For example, as the expression "act your age" suggests, we expect a higher level of emotional self-control of a 26-year-old than we do of a six-year-old. Similarly, we use chronological age to define specific responsibilities and social roles. For example, 76-year-olds are not supposed to take up new hobbies or fly down hills on skateboards (Fig. 4.1)!

> **Chronological age: number of years since birth**

Another way to consider age is by **birth cohort.** Here age means a group of individuals who share the same year or decade of birth and subsequently share the same events in history. For example, in Canada prior to the early 1980s, people 65 years of age and older were not required to retire, whereas today's generations of older adults are because of the passage of mandatory retirement legislation. Therefore, cohorts of older adults are now experiencing different opportunities than earlier cohorts for life in old age. As another example of how generations have different life experiences, in the United States, Title IX has greatly enabled sports and physical recreation participation for girls and women. But this is true for only those cohorts born since 1972 when the law was passed. For those women in cohorts already

> **Birth cohort: shared history of the same birth year**

Figure 4.1
A 75-year-old on a skateboard. His wife learning to paint in watercolors. There are individual differences to age-related role expectations. (© Ruth V. Russell.)

In Profile

Generation Y
Box 4.1

- Born between 1980 and 2000
- In the United States, 70.4 million people, or 26 percent of the population
- The most ethnically diverse generation (one in three are not white)
- Spends an average of $100 per week of disposable income
- Concerned about social issues
- Prefers directness over subtlety, action over observation, and cool over all else
- Heavily influenced by peers
- Feels "crunched for time" (http://www.library.csuhayward.edu, Retrieved 2/5/04)

out of school at that time, there were relatively few opportunities for participation in interscholastic sports when young.

The story of the **relationship between age and leisure** is one of both continuity and change. What we are today is based in part on what we were yesterday, and on how we will be different tomorrow. For example, we may participate in outdoor recreation today because our parents often took us camping when we were children. Or at a party we may become outgoing and jovial even though our usual manner is reserved and quiet. There is both change and continuity in the types of leisure activities we choose, in the frequency of participation in leisure activities, and in our motivations for leisure choices (Freysinger, 1999).

This relationship between age and leisure has been labeled **core plus balance** (Kelly, 1999). That is, there is a persistent "core" of leisure activities that occupies most people most of their lives. These represent continuity in leisure. Our core pastimes are typically those activities that are easily accessible and low cost, such as watching television, taking walks, and shopping. In everyday life, these activities occupy the greatest amount of time. On the other hand, our lives include a variety of pastimes. This is our "balance" we enjoy leisure patterns that change throughout our life span. In these expressions, we seek variety and separation from daily life. They balance out our lives. For example, as a child you may have been intensely involved in playing saxophone in the band, and as

> **Core plus balance:** there is both a persistent core and a balancing variety in our pastimes across the life span

In Focus

Second Chances
Box 4.2

During her working years, Terryl Paiste supervised a group of writers and editors in the computer division of an insurance company. But at home, at night and on weekends, Terryl spent her time writing one-act comedies for senior theater, plays performed by mature actors and on themes appealing to older adult audiences. Now, after retiring from her 22-year career in computing, Terryl has more time to write. So far, she's written about 20 plays that have been performed at theaters around North America.

Retirement is still four to five years away for DeVance Walker, the small-business services director in a county Department of Economic Development. But when the day finally comes, DeVance will be ready to step into a new career as a college professor. Six years ago, he went back to his alma mater, Howard University, to study at night for a doctorate in political economics. He says he strongly believes that people should develop a plan for what they are going to do in retirement. "Find a profession that you love," he advises.

Life has come full circle for Thomas Hovis. As a young man interested in art, he graduated from college with a degree in commercial design. He went on to spend 20 years working for a large corporation handling sales of specialty chemicals. Now, in retirement, Thomas has returned to his artistic roots as founder of his own company, Art & Frame of Tysons Corner. He primarily sells to corporate and government clients who need wall decorations for new or renovated offices (Hinden, 2000).

Questions to Consider and Discuss

1. *What traces of both continuity and change in the life cycle do you see in these three cases?*

2. *How are their leisure interests important to their "second careers"?*

3. *Putting yourself at about age 50, what might you plan for your retirement?*

a young adult, your weekends were filled with whitewater kayaking. Then, as an older adult, you may throw yourself into gardening.

Physical Development

The strength of the relationship between leisure and physical development is constant across the life span, but the nature of the relationship changes. The physical benefits from leisure shift from developing motor control in children, to sustaining health during the middle years, to reducing the decline in physical capabilities in older adulthood.

Today, the average life expectancy is 85 years. This average is genetically set. If you live a healthy lifestyle, including regular exercise, you can expect to add up to 10 quality years to this. This means 85 years or more of physical movement in defiance of gravity! How does leisure assist with this? Let's begin our exploration of leisure and physical development across the life span by considering children.

In the beginning, infancy is a time when the newborn struggles to master her or his own body, and play provides an important tool in this struggle. Early learning is the result of movement, and an infant's egocentric and individualistic play is almost all movement based. Although an infant's movements seem random, such variety is important to his or her early movement experiences.

By two years of age, the baby has begun to develop basic motor skills, such as running and jumping, and such nonmotor skills as turning, pushing, pulling, and kicking. Early play experiences are crucial to acquiring these skills. Through physical play, babies also learn muscle control and coordination. Between the ages of about six and 12, the amount of muscle tissue doubles and flexibility increases in the typical child. Thus, physical movement continues to be a necessary developmental component, particularly for promoting normal bone growth. Playing with ropes, mastering climbing and balancing equipment, and learning to control balls give children opportunities to expand their neuromuscular coordination and strength as well.

From Your Own Experience

The Life Expectancy Calculator
Box 4.3

To calculate your own life expectancy, check out the Web site http://www.livingto100.com. As you complete the on-line questionnaire, notice the factors associated with living longer.

To put it bluntly, children would not grow up without adequate play. Increased motor control does not occur simply and automatically with maturation; the child's body develops in large part from the physical demands placed on it.

Are children in North America engaged in sufficient physical play experiences? Discouragingly, the answer is no. According to the Surgeon General (2004), approximately 13 percent of children between the ages of six and 11 years in the United States are overweight. In addition to improved eating habits, the recommendation is that children require at least one hour of moderate physical activity every day to maintain their proper weight. That's a surprisingly difficult standard to meet, as children today spend most of their free time watching television (about three hours per day), playing computer games, and surfing the Internet.

In other words, even though children are by nature an active age group, their current activity level isn't adequate for sound growth. Conditions such as increased body fat affect not only their physical capacity but their self-esteem and social development as well. In spite of this, participation in all types of physical activity declines strikingly as their age or grade in school increases. This spells trouble for adulthood, because childhood activity levels are strong predictors of physical activity later in life (Taylor, 1999).

So what happens to leisure and physical development for adolescents? Pinpointing the beginning (and end) of adolescence is very difficult, as individual human bodies mature at different rates. Two 13-year-old boys could actually be up to five years apart in physical maturity because of differences in their developmental timetables. Physical change is the major initiator of this wide-ranging passage from childhood to adulthood we term adolescence.

In fact, the word **adolescence** is Latin and means "to grow up." And the physical changes experienced by teenagers (growth spurts, changing body proportions, hormone increases, etc.) are large and rapid, more so than at any other phase in the life span. Thus, these changes, and the accompanying traumas, can affect concepts of self that go beyond the physical. If appropriately selected, active forms of leisure can help teens cope with their social and psychological awkwardness as well.

> **Adolescence:** the state or process of reaching physical maturity

For example, sports participation, particularly in competitive experiences, is important for teens, because it not only provides healthful exercise for developing strength, flexibility, height, endurance, and fine motor control, but it can also improve self-confidence and social status (Fig. 4.2). As one college student put it, "As a teenager entering high school, I decided to run cross-country. This decision was made partly because I was overweight. I cannot stress how important that one decision was. I lost weight and met many upperclassmen before school even started. As a result, my first day of high school was not so scary" (Evans, 1993, p. 2).

Unfortunately, for the teen, as for many other age groups, the passive experience of TV viewing remains the most preoccupying activity–about three hours a day. Furthermore, lingering **sociocultural** pressures in Western societies such as the United States and Canada encourage girls to reduce physical activity in adolescence. Indeed, in spite of such programs as Title IX, studies show that by age 16, 56 percent of black females and 31 percent of white females report they have no regular leisure-time physical activity in their lives (Center for Health and Health Care in Schools, 2002).

> **Sociocultural:** a combination of social and cultural factors, such as societal attitudes, rewards, and institutions

When individuals enter the workforce or attend college in late adolescence and early adulthood, their physical capabilities and energy are usually at a peak. Many seek a wide assortment of active forms of recreation, with participation in strenuous sports typically continuing from youth. Interest in high-risk activities, such as skiing and rock climbing, begin to develop fully as well.

Usually by the late 20s or early 30s, leisure and physical development begin to shift their relationship. Biological maturity, when bone density is greatest and most physical skills peak, occurs at about this time (Donatelle & Davis, 1996). Participation in strenuous and high-risk sports gradually decreases. This happens because of decreasing vigor as well as increasing time commitments to one's career and family. As a counterforce, however, is the high-level skill development that has taken place through years of practice, which makes some sports, such as golf, even more enjoyable for young adults.

Figure 4.2

Physical forms of leisure are just as important for teens as they are for children, yet studies show active leisure declines for adolescent girls. (© Ruth V. Russell.)

Perhaps what is most important about the role of leisure in physical development in adulthood, however, is its utility for sustaining health. Physical pastimes keep adults healthy. Indeed, for North Americans, the risk of such leading killers as heart disease, cancer, stroke, and chronic lung diseases can be significantly reduced by an active lifestyle. How? Among the benefits one can hope to achieve in adulthood through active leisure pursuits are:

- greater energy levels
- a stronger immune system
- improved cardiovascular functioning
- increased muscle tone, strength, flexibility, and endurance
- an improved ability to manage stress
- an improved self-concept
- a more positive outlook on life
- enhanced relationships with others
- enhanced levels of spiritual health

In Focus

Hearts N' Parks
Box 4.4

Hearts N' Parks is a community-based initiative supported by the National Institutes of Health and the National Recreation and Park Association (NRPA). Its aim is to reduce the growing trend of obesity and the risk of coronary heart disease in the United States by encouraging people of all ages to aim for a healthy weight, follow a heart-healthy eating plan, and engage in regular physical activity. The basis for the program is "magnet centers." Agencies of various types work in tandem in a particular geographic area to implement new strategies for helping people improve their heart health. Mostly this is done by incorporating heart-healthy information and activities into existing community programs. And there have been important results. For example, in just its first year, adults in the programs increased weekly active time from eight to 10 hours and decreased weekly sedentary time from 40 to 31 hours (NRPA, 2003).

Questions to Consider and Discuss

1. *How physically active are you? If you are of typical college age, you are probably pretty active. What about your parents and grandparents? Are they as physically active as you?*

2. *Check the Web site for the public (city, county, district) parks and recreation department in your community. Are they participating in the Hearts N' Parks initiative? If so, what is the nature of their involvement?*

3. *If you and your family members have access to a Hearts N' Parks program, do you think it might affect your levels of physical activity? How or how not?*

For those who face the challenges of a physical disability, leisure offers a special opportunity. It can bridge to fuller participation in the activities of daily living by increasing physical functioning. Through therapeutic recreation services, sport activities are often promoted as useful in maintaining and enhancing physical functioning. For example, a person who enjoyed downhill skiing before a double leg amputation can be taught how to continue this interest with special ski equipment. Indeed, in a study of participants in a wheelchair tennis program, results demonstrated that the experience increased their perceptions of physical competence (Hendrick, 1985).

For everyone, normal physiological changes that affect leisure continue to occur with advancing age. As all human bodies get older, they gradually become less flexible and endurance is reduced. After age 50, the number of muscle fibers steadily decreases. Yet even with up to 50 percent deterioration in many organ systems, an individual can still physically function adequately. In fact, the ability of human beings to compensate for age-related physical changes attests to a significant amount of reserve capacity, and in most instances, the normal physical changes of aging need not diminish a person's quality of life. By remaining physically vigorous through leisure, with some modifications, life's pleasures can continue. Even people who begin a regular exercise or sports program late in life can make significant improvements in their heart and lung capacity.

Nonetheless, the proportion of individuals starting vigorous pastimes declines with age (Iso-Ahola, Jackson, & Dunn, 1994), even though older adults identify physical exercise as one of the important needs satisfied by expressions of leisure (Donatelle & Davis, 1996). This may be changing, however. A recent study ("Research Suggests Positive Attitude Could Prolong Life," 2001) confirmed that people over 65 are more vigorous than ever—an 8.8 percent increase since 1982. This is because older persons are now better educated about healthy lifestyles and tend to take better care of themselves.

Emotional Development

All people go through the process of learning how to deal with their feelings. Some are very good feelings, such as joy, affection, and sensuality. Others, such as anger, fear, anxiety, jealousy, and frustration, are not pleasant at all. Leisure itself is often considered an emotional state, a feeling of joy or a positive state of mind; thus, its role in the development of emotional health is particularly intriguing. Let's begin again with children.

Young children have all the basic **emotions** of adults, but their expression is more immediate, impulsive, and direct. Most children grow up learning to manage their emotions by using coping strategies, so the immediacy is more controlled and socially appropriate. Play is an important ingredient in this emotional development.

> **Emotions:** psychic and physiological reactions

From Your Own Experience
Sportspersonship
Box 4.5

One of the most visible signs of emotional maturity in competitive sports is sportspersonship. Although there is no universal definition of it, people often declare they know it when they see it! This means you can develop your own definition. To help, indicate which of the following represent sportspersonlike behaviors to you:

[ ] Questioning officials by lodging an official protest
[ ] Questioning officials by having the team captain speak to them
[ ] Having coaches represent the team in arguing with officials
[ ] Treating all opponents with respect and dignity at all times
[ ] Obeying all league rules
[ ] Including a less-skilled player in the game
[ ] Making only positive comments to spectators
[ ] Leaving the game voluntarily when angry
[ ] Giving teammates only constructive criticism
[ ] Giving teammates positive encouragement

Share your results with classmates and try to come up with a consensus about what sportspersonship means.

One of the emotions children must learn to deal with is the tension caused by fear and anxiety. In a classic study of children's fear, Jersild and Holmes (1935) found that younger children are most likely to be afraid of specific things, such as strange people and noises. Children of about five to six years of age show an increased fear of imaginary or abstract things, such as fantasized creatures, the dark, and being alone. Freud (1955) argued that play helps children master fear and anxiety. He claimed that if children are not allowed to deal with traumatic events through play, they can become psychopathic adults.

In fact, later studies by Barnett (1984) supported the importance of fantasy play used by children to neutralize the anxiety they feel. For example, researchers have observed that children use fantasy play to reenact sources of emotional distress. This often happens by changing the outcome of the stressful event or reversing roles to achieve a more pleasant result.

Another way leisure aids in the emotional development of children is through a concept called **locus of control**. Locus of control is a personal perception about the source of power in life. With an external locus of control, we perceive that we have no control, that we are merely pawns moved by forces beyond our control. With an internal locus of control, we perceive that we are the origin of our own life events; the internal locus of control is related to coping successfully for both young and older persons. In terms of the role of leisure, we know that the more time children spend in a supervised, child-centered play program, the more internal their locus of control becomes.

Locus of control: the perception of the source of control in one's life

An example of this is the "playwork" or adventure playground movement in the United Kingdom and Western Europe (Brown, 2002). It is based on the philosophy that children should have command over their own play outcomes; thus, "playwork takes the agenda of the individual child as its starting point" (p. 52). On a playground this might mean that children design and control their own weekly play program within an enabling environment. At Bornenese Jord (The Children's Earth) in the city of Arhus, Denmark, for example, there is a large sand play area under shade trees with small farm animals to be cared for, two small child-built playhouses, and a stream with a paddle wheel, water-stopping wooden plugs, and a pulley system that let the children route the water through a series of troughs (Bruya, 1988).

In moving from childhood to young adulthood, adolescents often display a curious combination of emotional maturity and childishness. This mixture is often awkward, but it serves an important developmental function. Psychologists agree that in adolescence, an important emotional task to be accomplished successfully is the formation of an **identity**.

Identity: individuality, distinct uniqueness

The fundamental question of "who am I?" characterizes the early teenage period. The young person tries out many kinds of personal identities and explores his or her emotional capacities. This is a main function of leisure in adolescence; it provides a context for experimenting with one's identity. Finding out who we are is serious business and often takes place for teens on the playing field, in the band room, at the Scout meeting, or perhaps in the shopping mall. The more relaxed setting of recreational activities can be viewed as a safe haven in which teens can try things out.

In Focus

Kids and the Mall
Box 4.6

I'd heard about a kid in Florida whose mother picked him up after school every day, drove straight to the mall, and left him there until it closed all at his insistence.

(Kowinski, 1989, p. 348)

The mall is a common gathering place for a large number of North American youth. The findings of a 1996 study from the International Council of Shopping Centers might be eye-opening to some: Although teens make up an estimated 10 percent of the total population, they make up about 25 percent of total mall visitors. And they spend money–an average of $40 a week, every week, just at the mall. Some malls have taken steps to cater to their young customers, and certainly a glimpse at the types of stores in malls indicates retailers understand their importance. In fact, some view their mission as one of "training" teens for a life of hard-core shopping.

On the other hand, some sociologists (e.g., Lewis, 1989) suggest that kids who spend a lot of time at the mall are exhibiting a good deal of alienation from both family and school. They use the mall as neutral ground on which to create a fragile but mutually supportive community. According to Kowinski (1989), "Structure is the dominant idea, since true 'mall rats' lack just that in their home lives, and adolescents about to make the big leap into growing up crave more structure than our modern society cares to acknowledge" (p. 351).

Questions to Consider and Discuss

1. *Were you a "mall rat" when you were growing up? Did you know anyone from your school or neighborhood who spent a lot of time at the mall? What is your opinion of this situation?*

2. *Check the Web sites of several malls near you. What policies, if any, do they have about children and teens who hang out at the mall? Do you agree with these policies? Why or why not?*

3. *Considering the concept of locus of control as a developmental emotional task for children and teens, might the mall be helping them achieve this? If children learn about themselves through the mall, what developmental emotional tasks might they face as adults?*

Also for teens, there is a shift in their motivation for leisure. For example, research has indicated that as children progress through school, their motivation becomes increasingly extrinsic (Graef, Csikszentmihalyi, & Giannino, 1983). That is, such motivators as winning in games and sports become prime sources for developing a positive identity or sense of self.

College students are also engaged in discovering their identity. At this stage in the life span, leisure provides a vital context for breaking with the personal identities associated with family and home community. Several emotional transitions occur, such as the emergence of a focused sexuality and greater social and economic independence from the parents (Kelly, 1982). The college years are a final time to try out the new possibilities for an adult identity.

Universities and colleges aid in this process by providing "real-world" simulations. Students can participate in politics through student government and in a profession through practicums and internships. Likewise, social events, intramural sports, spring break trips, activity clubs, and other campus experiences are crucial for the development of the future selfhood. Campus organizations provide ways of experimenting with attitudes of influence, dissent, and cooperation (Fig. 4.3). Campus recreation also plays a role in reducing the stress some college students experience. For example, Ragheb and McKinney (1992) found that the more students participated in recreation activities, the less academic stress they experienced.

Figure 4.3

Campus organizations provide ways of experimenting with influence, dissent, and cooperation. (© Ruth V. Russell.)

The years from 35 to 45 have been called the "deadline decade," or the era of the "midlife crisis." Divorce and career changes occur with increasing frequency. Predictable at this point in life is a sense of stagnation. Some people experience tumultuous struggles within themselves and with others. Married persons with children often find their recreation patterns disrupted and restricted. Some resent the change from the lifestyle they enjoyed at earlier life stages. Others welcome the stable, noncompetitive, and predictable leisure patterns of family life.

The years between middle and old age have been labeled the reintegration period of the life cycle (Rapoport & Rapoport, 1975). Emotionally, this is the time in which adults reevaluate themselves and their lives, and the meaning and worth of their life commitments are weighed. A person may take a second look at her or his personal relationships, community, career, and pastimes. Are they producing the fulfillment they once promised?

The free-choice nature of leisure makes it a prime medium for life evaluation. New pastimes can be tried with minimal changes to one's relationship and work commitments. Often with increased free time and money, people in this reintegration life stage can bring former leisure interests back into their lives. There are exceptions, of course, but life during this stage can be very emotionally satisfying, involving many new and renewed pastime expressions. This pattern accompanies another change in adult leisure before retirement–an increase in the proportion of experiences chosen primarily for their own sake, for intrinsic reasons. Regardless of whether the activities change, the motivation seems to become more related to self-satisfaction.

As we approach the retirement years, one underlying emotional preoccupation is anticipation (Rapoport & Rapoport, 1975). This anticipation of the future may be positive or negative. Some look forward to retirement, to escaping the routine of the job, and to having time for leisure that is not restricted to weekends and holidays. Others are not as sure about what they will do without the structure of employment. Leisure can be a part of retirement preparation decisions. Should I buy a motor home so I can travel? Maybe I should move into a retirement center where the days are filled with planned recreational events.

Alongside these uncertainties is continuity as well. In this time of transition, people generally continue the pastimes of previous years. If they have fulfilling life patterns outside of work, this may be a time of excitement. Without leisure interests that are personally meaningful, the adjustments of retirement may be difficult. Although depression, loneliness, and apathy may characterize the feelings of some retirees, these tend to be people who have less emotional preparation for retirement. Expanding their favorite leisure interests can aid in these emotional adjustments. As our identities in leisure activities become more important, we will be rewarded with greater opportunities for fulfillment.

Some recent research findings dramatically illustrate this point ("Research Suggests Positive Attitude Could Prolong Life," 2001). In studying biographies written by respondents in their early 20s, researchers found that those who articulated more positive emotions lived as many as 10 years longer than those who expressed fewer positive emotions. That is, negative emotions such as anxiety, hatred, and anger can have a cumulative effect on the body over time.

Eventually, the death of a partner or spouse becomes a reality for many. One's companion in leisure is gone. Not only does the loss of a significant person create loneliness, but it also changes the context of leisure, which requires a rebuilding of other leisure roles. For most people, grief does not allow them to accept their new freedom until the process of working through the loss has been accomplished, but once begun, leisure can help with the emotional healing. Many widows and widowers demonstrate great powers of adaptation.

Intellectual Development

Beginning our exploration of leisure and intellectual development again with the childhood period of life, it has long been thought that one of the main contributions of a child's play is the development of cognitive skills. Specifically, play has been linked to the development of two modes of thought: convergent and divergent thinking (Fromberg & Bergen, 1998; Vandenberg, 1980).

An important function of play and games for children is enhanced problem-solving or **convergent thinking** ability. This is because a child's playful experience with objects and processes can be applied to real-life issues. By exploring objects in play, children not only learn the properties of those objects but also see their potential for application to various other problem situations (Barnett, 1990). For example, one study found that children who were allowed to play with materials that would later be used in a task actually performed that task better than children who had no opportunity for the same play experiences (Sylva, Bruna, & Genova, 1976).

Convergent thinking: using information to find one right answer

In addition, games and play contribute to **divergent thinking** ability. This is due to both the spontaneous and symbolic nature of these activities. Play provides the child with a broad repertoire of skills and responses that can be applied creatively to problem solving. Also, play enhances the child's transition from concrete to abstract thought processes because of the way children's play frequently uses unreal things to represent real ones (Fig. 4.4). Make-

Divergent thinking: thinking in different directions

believe play appears to be the key link. It creates a flexible attitude toward the world that can be carried into adulthood. The role of imagination is so important to intellectual development that it prompted Albert Einstein to note, "Imagination is more important than knowledge."

Figure 4.4
Make-believe play helps children develop divergent thinking ability. (© Jane Duffy.)

Another intellectual skill to which leisure contributes is language. Sounds, syllables, words, and phrases provide children with a rich source of play material. Infants discover the joy of vocal play when starting to babble. By the time they are uttering their first words and sentences, preschool children have begun to playfully manipulate grammar, rhyme, nonsense words, and multiple meanings. School-age children have an underground oral tradition of rhymes, jokes, and incantations that they have passed on to each other for generations. For example, do you remember "1, 2, 3, 4, I declare a thumb war; 5, 6, 7, 8, try to keep your thumb straight" that begins a thumb-wrestling match?

The idea that play and language are interrelated is not surprising, since both serve several joint functions in the young child's life: (a) Both involve a communicative function, and (b) children use both play and language to experiment and learn about themselves and others (Barnett, 1990). Whereas play clearly comes before language in the growth of a child, play is, in a sense, a form of language itself because it incorporates symbolic as well as social interactions.

Piaget (1936), a famous child psychologist, discovered that playing out a story forces a child to become actively involved in an experience. In order to re-create the events of a story, the child must create a mental representation of the events and then engage in social interaction to coordinate the playing. A number of studies support this, demonstrating a relationship between symbolic play and language during the early stages of language acquisition in children both with and without language disabilities.

In Profile
Jean Piaget (1896-1980)
Box 4.7

Jean Piaget, a Swiss psychologist, won fame for his studies on the thought processes of children. The research consumed most of his life, including constant study of his own three children. By the time of his death, he and his associates had published more than 30 books on the subject.

Piaget's goal was to define children's increasingly effective intellectual abilities. His work led him to conclude that children pass through four stages of mental development. First, during the sensorimotor stage from birth to two years, they obtain a basic knowledge of objects through their senses. At first, simple motor skills, such as grasping and holding objects, lay the groundwork for developing more complex thinking and language. By 15 to 18 months of age, children try to use objects as they were intended, and the play becomes still more realistic by 24 months. For example, toddlers take dolls out for walks and line up toy trucks and cars in the right direction.

Next, children enter the preoperational stage. From about ages two to seven years, they use language and imagination skills to help build some facsimile of the outside world. The child develops the ability to see adult action at one point in time, store that information in memory without performing the act, and imitate the act at a later time. Later, from about seven to 11 years of age, children begin to think logically. Essentially, this concrete operational stage is when children begin to use symbols. For example, whereas younger children require props to be similar to the real object for pretending play, older children can pretend using props that are only abstract representations of the object, such as a stick for a gun.

Finally, in Piaget's fourth stage of formal operations, which lasts from about 11 to 15 years of age, children begin to reason realistically about the future and to deal with abstractions and possibilities. Older children are more likely to approach a problem by imagining all the possible relationships. Their thought is richer, broader, and more flexible.

From a great number of investigations, it is clear that mental abilities increase rapidly from birth through adolescence, but not at the same rate. Such abilities as perceptual and psychomotor speed develop more rapidly. These abilities depend most heavily on flexibility, adaptability, and speed of information processing—the sorts of things practiced in some forms of games. On the other hand, word fluency and verbal comprehension develop more slowly. Thus, the average young person's score on perceptual psychomotor speed reaches 80 percent of her or his ultimate peak by about age 12, whereas the 80 percent level for verbal comprehension is not reached until age 18, and for word fluency it is later than age 20 (Conger & Peterson, 1984).

What happens next? Stereotypes about inevitable intellectual decline as we grow older have been largely refuted. "We used to think that the adult brain couldn't grow," says neurologist Jay Lombard (as cited in Merrell, 2003). "Now we know that it not only grows but also regenerates old cells that are out of use" (p. 18). Given an appropriate length of time, adults and older adults may learn and develop mental skills in a manner similar to younger people, and some mental abilities improve well into the middle years. Researchers have also determined that what many older people lack in speed of learning they make up for in practical knowledge. For example, longitudinal research suggests that those intellectual abilities that require experience, knowledge, and judgment are retained into the 60s and beyond. When compared with people between the ages of 20 and 40, those age 55 and over needed more time to complete tasks but were just as accurate (Goldman, 1996).

The best of it is that as you age, you can actually encourage brain growth and regeneration, and several studies have confirmed the contribution of leisure to this process (Riddick, 1993; Riddick & Daniels, 1984; Rothschadl, 1993). For example, keeping mentally sharp can be aided by engaging in intellectually challenging pastimes, such as playing board and card games, joining book clubs, attending lectures, and learning new hobbies. Being creative through leisure also encourages healthy mental functioning.

The Study Says

Smartening-Up Strategies
Box 4.8

Age is undeniably a factor in mental functioning, but people of any age can benefit from these leisure-based ways of keeping sharp. The brain is like a muscle: It can always use a little exercise. Here's what the research says.

1. *Play games often.* Classic games such as chess, checkers, bridge, and backgammon are perfect brain food. They force you to think ahead, to see the big picture, and to consider a number of options at once. Researchers have found that those who played games at least once a week cut their risk of developing dementia by at least half. The benefit increased with the number of times played, up to four times a week.

2. *Work crossword puzzles.* Crossword puzzling is to the brain as running on a treadmill is to the heart. In a recent study, elderly people who grappled with crosswords 4 days a week had a nearly 50% lower risk of developing dementia than those who did them only once a week.

3. *Choose right-brain hobbies.* Since we live in a mostly left-brain world where we are expected to think before acting, choose a leisure activity that gives you practice with right-brain thinking. For example, research shows that pinball, juggling, and some video games are all excellent right-brain activities because they force you to act on instinct. Also, doodling, looking at art, and listening to music offer this type of practice.

4. *Spend more time with favorite hobbies.* Enjoyable hobbies create more synapses. Research shows that pleasure is a crucial component of a healthy brain. Use your fingers (needlework or playing an instrument), keep a journal, and do balancing things (tai chi, yoga).

5. *Be active.* It is now irrefutable that exercise increases brain power. Aerobic exercise pumps more blood to the brain, bringing vitalizing oxygen and nutrients to cells. It also has a powerful effect on an intracellular messenger called brain drive neurotropin factor (BDNF), which slows the rate of normal brain-cell death.

(Merrell, 2003)

Social Development

Human infants are born into an environment rich with social expectations, norms, and traditions. A social heritage with standards of behavior awaits them. However, infants have no awareness of this. They have no sense of themselves as individuals or of their relationship with others around them. Thus, a dramatic series of changes takes place during the first two years, in which children become aware of their environment and the ways they can act on it. They become aware of family relationships, themselves as girls or boys, and what is good behavior and bad behavior. Play, of course, is a prime teacher in a child's social development.

The importance of the **peer** group in teaching social skills has been well documented. As children become increasingly more effective at communicating and better at understanding the thoughts and feelings of others, the amount and quality of peer interaction changes greatly. This is particularly evident in play. For example, early studies of peer relations in children have charted the development of six different levels of social interaction in play (Craig & Baucum, 2001; see Table 4.1). These levels of interactive play predominate at certain ages. Yet what matters is that children be given ample opportunities to experience these forms of interactive play as they develop. They perfect such social skills as empathy, role taking, self-control, and sharing.

> **Peer:** one who is of equal standing, usually based on age and economic status

As children grow older, their play begins to involve ritual. They make decisions about taking turns, setting boundaries, and stipulating rules about what is and what is not permitted. These rituals help them learn about winning and losing, about fitting their behavior into certain patterns of rules, and about how their actions affect others. Learning social roles is an important developmental achievement that relies on the benefits of play. For example, playing house helps children practice family roles, and pretending to be an athletics coach teaches them about adult work roles. Such play requires novel ways of interacting with peers.

Gender identity is another adult social domain learned through early play experiences. Child psychologists suggest that much of the basis for an individual's gender identity is acquired by age three and is primarily a result of the different ways parents treat male and female babies (Craig & Baucum, 2001). For older children, parents, teachers, peers, and even television characters reinforce sexual stereotypes. These stereotypes can be problematic for development because they provide arbitrary "scripts" for behavior. For example, in Western societies such as the United States and

> **Gender identity:** a person's perception of the self as relatively masculine or feminine in character

Canada, masculine characteristics (ambitiousness, assertiveness, competitiveness, and self-sufficiency) are more highly valued than female characteristics (being affectionate, cheerful, soft-spoken, and yielding).

Table 4.1

Levels of Play According to Peer Interactions

Level of play	Age	Interaction
Nonsocial play	Infant to one year	Unoccupied, unfocused. No peer interaction.
Solitary play	Infant to one year	Child plays alone. No peer interaction.
Onlooker play	two years	Child's interaction with peers is limited to just observing other children.
Parallel play	two to three years	Children play alongside each other but do not interact with each other.
Associative play	four to five years	Some interaction; children engage in separate activities but interact by exchanging toys and commenting on one another's behavior.
Cooperative play	six to seven years	Fully interactive with peers; children's actions are directed toward a common goal.

An easy way to understand such scripts is through ideas about gender-appropriate leisure behavior (Berk, 2003). For example, mothers and fathers play with male and female infants quite differently. Fathers' play tends to be physical and arousing rather than intellectual, as is the case with mothers' play. Parents allow boys more freedom to display aggressive behavior and to engage in more vigorous activities with toys. Boys receive more gross motor stimulation from parents, whereas girls receive more verbal stimulation. These differences carry forward to leisure choices. Whereas older boys usually stick to masculine pursuits, girls experiment with a wider range of options. Besides cooking, sewing, and babysitting, they join organized sports teams, take up science projects, and build forts in the backyard.

Some gender-based differences in children's play remain, however. Play for girls in middle and late childhood occurs more often in small groups and in private places, and it mimics adult social relationships. It is also more spontaneous, freer of rules, and more cooperative than boys' play. In contrast, boys at this stage experience more controlled competitive games and "weapon-based" fantasy play. These differences in play further reinforce gender identities and help ensure that children will grow up behaving in ways their society considers appropriate to their sex.

For adolescents, difficult changes in social development join those in emotional and physical development. If an adolescent is to become truly adult and not just physically mature, he or she must fit into a social world, achieve independence from his or her parents, and establish enduring relationships with peers. This means that the development of **autonomy** is central. The teen must become adjusted to the demands and the privileges of independence. An important context for developing autonomy is in peer group friendships and social leisure experiences.

> **Autonomy:** emotional, social, and physical independence from others; the ability to self-govern

Most teens are attached to a social group that has considerable power to shape their pastime interests and behaviors. During middle and late childhood, peer relationships tend to center around neighborhood play groups and same-sex groups. Largely informal at first, these children's groups become more highly structured with increasing age, and aspects of formal organization appear, such as special membership requirements and elaborate rituals. For the teenager, the world also widens, and the range of acquaintances broadens.

In general, the teen's peer relationships fall into three broad categories: the **crowd**, the **clique**, and individual friendships (Conger & Petersen, 1984). Teens experience a great deal of their leisure within these relationships. Such social recreational pursuits as parties, movies, dances, concerts, driving, and just "hanging out" with a friend, clique, or crowd provides a setting for adolescent social development. At their best, these forms of peer relationships can help teens accomplish positive social development. At their worst, worries over social acceptance and rejection are potent at these ages; thus, peer relationships can be painful and peer influences negative.

> **Crowds:** a large, loosely organized peer group in which membership is based on reputation and stereotype

> **Clique:** a small group of about five to seven peers who are friends

What influences the sorting of teenagers into cliques and crowds? In addition to personality and interests, family factors are surprisingly important. In a study of eight thousand 9th to 12th graders, teens who described their parents as authoritative tended to be members of "studious," "jock," and "preppie" groups. In contrast, boys with permissive parents aligned themselves with the "partying" crowd. And teens who viewed their parents as uninvolved more often affiliated with the partying and "headbanger" crowds (Durbin, Darling, Steinberg, & Brown, 1993). To a large extent, these findings indicate that many social group values are extensions of ones acquired at home.

The Study Says
Social Class and Peer Influence
Box 4.9

A study of Dutch youth focused on the degree to which adolescents associate with parents and peers in their leisure time. To the surprise of the researchers, much of what was discovered was based on social class differences.

For example, in terms of associative preferences, it was found that 10- to 12-year-old children from wealthier families were "family" kids. They spent a substantial part of their leisure time with parents and siblings. Fourteen- and 15-year-old boys from wealthier backgrounds strongly focused on peer groups, whereas girls of the same age and background had more of a preference for friendships with one other.

In terms of parental attitudes, 10- to 12-year olds, especially those from higher social classes, experienced the most parental interference in their leisure activities, and teenage girls from higher socioeconomic families encountered the most parental attention to peer contacts.

The researchers concluded that advocating more organized leisure programs for disadvantaged youth might help compensate for the reduced parental involvement (te Poel Zeijl, du Bois-Reymond, Ravesloot, & Janita Meulman, 2000).

Such peer groups also serve as the platform for the development of sexuality. "Romantic" leisure is important for testing sexuality and for establishing ways of relating lovingly to others (Fig. 4.5). In fact, sexuality is a preoccupation in the development of social selfhood for many adolescents, and sexual activity itself can be a major pastime.

To begin, teens often develop same-sex physical attachments. Crushes and sexual play with persons of the same sex are common for younger adolescents,

Figure 4.5
Most teens are attached to a social group that has considerable power to shape their pastime interests and behaviors, including those of a sexual nature. (© Ruth V. Russell.)

as both boys and girls form very deep relationships with best friends. For some, that special friendship takes the form of extended communication and helps develop peer trust. Some teens then move from the same-sex romantic relationship to the beginnings of opposite-sex relationships. Others develop their normative social pattern through homosexual relationships. Sources of sexual orientation (either homosexual or heterosexual) are not well understood, but they probably are the result of a combination of biological and environmental factors. Additionally, the importance of games and fantasy play for children, and of sport and social recreation for teens, suggests that the factors relevant to the development of sexual orientation should also be researched more fully.

At the point of leaving school, young adults are propelled into more adult social roles related to the social institutions of family, the economy, and the community. For many, these can be exciting times of exploring new possibilities for life and filling out their new social identities. More and more, young adults are taking on more work roles. Thus for them, leisure is predominantly social and commercial, taking place in bars, clubs, restaurants, resorts, and apartment complexes. On the other hand, some young adults get married, and the impact of this transition on leisure depends on whether residence, employment, and family size change as well. Regardless, the likelihood that their leisure will be expressed with a partner increases, as leisure becomes an important context for building the relationship. This may also mean that involvement in some pastimes formerly experienced separately will decrease.

Additionally, for young adults, the time and money spent for leisure tend to be restricted by the births of children. Typically, the first change in leisure that new parents realize is the loss of freedom. Parents of young children cannot engage in spur-of-the-moment pastimes outside the home, and at-home pastimes become more interrupted and crowded. At this life stage, then, leisure usually takes place in or near the home and with family.

Despite the old adage that "the family that plays together stays together," research suggests that this many not necessarily be so. As an example, a study by Freysinger (1994) found that leisure experienced between children and their parents was satisfying only for the fathers. This may be because leisure with children is one of the few ways fathers interact with their children; hence, it may be more valued by them. For the mothers, on the other hand, experiencing leisure with children may be perceived as just another duty of daily caregiving.

As children leave the family and assume their own lives more fully, their middle-aged parents grow more independent, although this varies by ethnic group. Three different leisure patterns seem to be the main options for the "empty nest" couple. First, some use their new freedom to turn back to the marriage for leisure partnership. For them, leisure may become more important as some of the pursuits laid aside during parenting are taken up again (Fig. 4.6). Others turn outward and seek new and separate social groups and activities. This can also be a renaissance time for middle-aged adults who have not reared children, as their careers stabilize and become financially rewarding. Finally, some pour themselves into a greater work engagement by launching new careers or increasing civic responsibilities, thus continuing the restrictions on their leisure time.

As people grow into old age, the nature of their social roles and relationships changes again. Spouses and partners may die, and socializing with coworkers on the job disappears with retirement. The way older people interact in their social worlds of family, friends, and neighbors is affected by physical, situational, and even economic changes. Sometimes circumstances can mean that social involvements diminish, paving the way for making new friends. Doing this is important, because older adults who are part of well-defined friendship groups–those who continue to feel "connected"–tend to have higher morale (Searle, Mahon, Iso-Ahola, Sdrolias, & vanDyck, 1995). In fact, some research has demonstrated that friends are more important than family in enhancing life satisfaction in old age (Adams, 1986). The explanation for this might be given from a leisure perspective: Friendship is more rewarding because it is not obligatory. Leisure often provides the context for friendship. For example, one of the primary benefits of living in age-segregated retirement communities is the availability of potential friends.

Figure 4.6
The "empty nest" couple sometimes seeks new social groups and activities. (© Ruth V. Russell.)

Summary: What We Understand

The cycle of life is both certain and uncertain, constant and changing. The role of leisure in human development from birth to death is likewise both expected and surprising. In either case, leisure is important throughout life. It is necessary for growing, maturing, and reaching old age. Although the nature of its role may change, leisure is constantly with us. As a result of reading this chapter, you should know that

- **Leisure helps children develop motor skills, and in the middle and later years it helps sustain physical capabilities.**

- **For children, leisure is a tool for learning; for adults, leisure is important in maintaining previously acquired mental abilities, as well as developing others more fully.**

- Although leisure itself is often considered an emotional state, it also plays a role in the development of emotions for children and in the maintenance of emotional health for adults.

- Finally, through leisure, children are able to acquire appropriate skills for social interaction, and when people grow into older adulthood, leisure is often their sole connection to the social world.

Applications to Professional Practice

Sport is another important resource that is typically managed by professionals in recreation and park services. Indeed, even casual observation of the average community demonstrates the priority of sport resources. Basketball hoops above garage doors, tennis courts behind apartment buildings, city swimming pools, private golf courses, jogging and fitness trails, health clubs, and of course, softball diamonds can be found everywhere. Because the role of sport in physical, emotional, intellectual, and social development was frequently cited in this chapter, let's consider its implications for professional practice.

It is estimated that 55 percent of adult Australians, 45 percent of adult Americans, and 34 percent of adult Canadians play sports. And by most accounts, these proportions are on the rise. Likewise, new sports soar to popularity, new highs are reached in attendance at sporting events, and new teams and leagues in amateur and professional sports are established. For example, according to a Canadian Curling Association survey (2001), more than 750,000 active curlers in the country now play in 1,298 clubs. The number of curlers is predicted to grow by 8.9 percent annually over the next 25 years–a growth rate that would put curling ahead of golf, hockey, tennis, and skiing (Bergman, 1992). Additionally, curling has become a major television draw, with upward of three million viewers tuning in for recent telecasts of the men's championships.

Many agencies and organizations provide resources for sports participation and spectating. Athletic clubs, community centers, clubs, religious groups, commercial stadiums and tracks, hotels, camps, cities, and schools are among the many examples. Through the provision of programs and facilities, community agencies attempt to serve a variety of sports interests. Common are facilities and programs for team sports, such as basketball, soccer, and softball. Private health and fitness clubs typically offer individual sports, such as jogging, walking, and weight lifting. Some private clubs specialize in providing opportunities for such individual sports as boating, tennis, golf, and swimming. Commercial establishments cater to such sports interests as bowling.

Leisure service organizations not only provide many types of sports, but they also serve a broad range of participants. Communities offer sports programs for the novice and the highly skilled, for the young and the old, for women and girls as well as men and boys. For example, in the United States there are 92 softball teams for players aged 70 and older (Senior Softball Summit, 2004). Sports for people with disabilities have also become more available, particularly golf, snow skiing, tennis, and basketball. Numerous organizations promote these opportunities, including Special Olympics International (2004), which trains and competes over one million participants with mental retardation in summer and winter events in 150 countries.

Even the home is an important sports resource. Typically, we think of the home as a place for solitary or social activities, such as conversation, playing card games, and watching television. However, as contemporary society embraces new technologies and as the cost of many away-from-home events increases, home has become more important for such active pastimes as sports. For example, exercise apparatus and driveway basketball hoops are common. Also, such major facilities as home gyms and tennis courts are increasing.

For Further Information

To learn more about managing sports as a leisure services professional, begin with an exploration of the Web site for the National Intramural-Recreational Sports Association (NIRSA, http://www.nirsa.org/). Your exploration here could include the "professional development" and "career services" links. Also, you could visit the Web site for the North American Society for Sport Management (NASSM, http://www.nassm.com/). Then you might check out professional preparation programs in sport management, recreational sport administration, and/or sport marketing in your own university or college catalog.

References

Adams, R. G. (1986). A look at friendship and aging. *Generations, 10,* 40–43.

Barnett, L. A. (1984). Young children's resolution of distress through play. *Journal of Child Psychology and Psychiatry, 25,* 477–483.

Barnett, L. A. (1990). Developmental benefits of play for children. *Journal of Leisure Research, 22,* 138–153.

Bergman, B. (1992). Canada's hot rocks. *Maclean's, 105*(5), 46–48.

Berk, L. E. (2003). *Child development* (6th ed.). Boston: Allyn & Bacon.

Brown, F. (Ed.). (2002). *Playwork: Theory and practice.* Buckingham, United Kingdom: Open University.

Bruya, L. D. (1988). *Play spaces for children: A new beginning.* Reston, VA: American Alliance for Health, Physical Education, Recreation, and Dance.

Canadian Curling Association. (2001). Survey. Retrieved February 5, 2001, from http://www.curling.ca/

Center for Health and Health Care in Schools. (2002). News alerts. Retrieved February 5, 2004, from http://www.healthinschools.org/2002/

Conger, J. J., & Petersen, A. C. (1984). *Adolescence and youth: Psychological development in a changing world.* New York: Harper & Row.

Craig, G. J., & Baucum, D. (2001). *Human development.* Englewood Cliffs, NJ: Prentice-Hall.

Donatelle R. J., & Davis, L. G. (1996). *Access to health* (4th ed.). Boston: Allyn & Bacon.

Durbin, D. L., Darling, N., Steinberg, L., & Brown, B. B. (1993). Parenting style and peer group membership among European-American adolescents. *Journal of Research on Adolescence, 3,* 87–100.

Evans, N. (1993). *Leisure and human development.* Unpublished manuscript, Indiana University, Bloomington.

Freud, S. (1955). Beyond the pleasure principle. In J. Strachey (Ed.), *The standard edition of the complete psychological works of Sigmund Freud* (Vol. 18, pp. 00–00). London: Hogarth.

Freysinger, V. J. (1994). Leisure with children and parental satisfaction: Further evidence of a sex difference in the experience of adult roles and leisure. *Journal of Leisure Research, 26,* 212–226.

Freysinger, V. J. (1999). Life span and life course perspectives on leisure. In E. L. Jackson & T. L. Burton (Eds.), *Leisure studies: Prospects for the twenty-first century* (pp.). State College, PA: Venture.

Fromberg, D. P., & Bergen, D. (Eds.). (1998). *Play from birth to twelve: Contexts, perspectives, and meanings.* New York: Van Nostrand Reinhold.

Goldman, D. (1996). Good news about the aging brain. In *Global aging report: What's happening in aging everywhere* (pp. 8-20). Washington, DC: American Association of Retired Persons.

Graef, R., Csikszentmihalyi, M., & Giannino, S. (1983). Measuring intrinsic motivation in everyday life. *Leisure Studies, 2,* 155–168.

Hendrick, B. N. (1985). The effect of wheelchair tennis participation and mainstreaming upon the perceptions of competence of physically disabled adolescents. *Therapeutic Recreation Journal, 19*(2), 34–46.

Hinden, C. (2000, October 1). Second careers: Four who planned for a retirement of personal fulfillment. *The Washington Post,* pp. H1–H6.

International Council of Shopping Centers, (1996). Retrieved May 14, 2001 from http://www.icsc.org

Iso-Ahola, S. E., Jackson, E., & Dunn, E. (1994). Starting, ceasing, and replacing leisure activities over the life-span. *Journal of Leisure Research, 26,* 227–249.

Jerslid, A. T., & Holmes, F. B. (1935). *Children's fears* (Child Development Monograph No. 20). New York: Teachers College Press.

Kelly, J. R. (1982). *Leisure.* Englewood Cliffs, NJ: Prentice-Hall.

Kelly, J. R. (1999). Leisure and society: A dialectical analysis. In E. L. Jackson, & T. L. Burton (Eds.), *Leisure studies: Prospects for the twenty-first century* (pp.). State College, PA: Venture.

Kowinski, W. S. (1989). Kids in the mall: Growing up controlled. In D. Cavitch (Ed.), *Life studies: A thematic reader* (pp. 192-206). New York: St. Martin's Press.

Lewis, G. J. (1989). Rats and bunnies: Core kids in the American mall. *Adolescence, 24,* 881–889.

Merrell, K. (2003, November). Get smart: Science has found new strategies to help our sharp minds keep their edge. *Real Simple.* 143–147.

National Recreation and Park Association (NRPA). (2003, July). Hearts N' Parks, year 2. *Parks & Recreation,* 46–49.

Piaget, J. (1936). *The origins of intelligence in children.* New York: W. W. Norton.

Ragheb, M. G., & McKinney, J. (1992). *Campus recreation and perceived academic stress.* Paper presented at the Leisure Research Symposium, National Recreation and Park Association, Cincinnati, OH.

Rapoport, R., & Rapoport, R. N. (1975). *Leisure and the family life cycle.* London: Routledge & Kegan Paul.

Research suggests positive attitude could prolong life. (2001, May 8). *The Herald-Times* (Bloomington, IN), p. A5.

Riddick, C. C. (1993). Older women's leisure and the quality of life. In J. R. Kelly (Ed.), *Activity and aging* (pp. 105–119). Thousand Oaks, CA: Sage.

Riddick, C. C., & Daniels, S. (1984). The relative contribution of leisure activities and other factors to the mental health of older women. *Journal of Leisure Research, 16,* 136–148.

Rothschadl, A. M. (1993). *The meaning and nature of creativity in the everyday lives of older women.* Unpublished doctoral dissertation, Indiana University, Bloomington.

Searle, M. S., Mahon, M. J., Iso-Ahola, S. E., Sdrolias, H. A., & vanDyck, J. (1995). Enhancing a sense of independence and psychological well-being among the elderly: A field experiment. *Journal of Leisure Research, 27,* 107–124.

Senior Softball Summit. (2004). Retrieved February 19, 2004, from http://www.softballrating.com/

Special Olympics International. (2004). Retrieved February 10, 2004, from http://www.specialolympics.org

Surgeon General of the United States. (2004). Obesity. Retrieved February 5, 2004, from http://www.surgeongeneral.cov/topics/obesity

Sylva, K., Bruna, J. S., & Genova, P. (1976). The role of play in the problem-solving of children 3–5 years old. In J. S. Bruner, A. Jolly, & K. Sylva (Eds.), *Play: Its role in development and evolution* (pp. 93–105). New York: Basic Books.

Taylor, W. C. (1999). Childhood and adolescent physical activity patterns and adult physical activity. *Medicine and Science in Sports and Exercise, 31,* 118–123.

te Poel Zeijl, E. du Bois-Reymond, Y., Ravesloot, M., & Janita Meulman, J. J. (2000). The role of parents and peers in the leisure activities of young adolescents. *Journal of Leisure Research, 32,* 281–302.

Vandenberg, B. (1980). *Play: A causal agent in problem solving?* Paper presented at the meeting of the American Psychological Association, Montreal, Quebec.

LEISURE AS A CULTURAL MIRROR

SOCIETAL CONTEXT

Leisure is significant to us not only individually, but also collectively. How we express ourselves through our pastimes helps define who we are as a community, as a society, and as a world. Our pastimes are likewise shaped by who we are collectively. It is this cultural interrelationship with leisure that we explore in chapters 5 through 9.

Chapter 5

sets the tone by discussing leisure's uniqueness according to culture and its significance to culture.

Chapter 6

presents the expression of leisure as geographically shaped.

Chapter 7

explores common culture, the most typical pastimes of a majority of people.

Chapter 8

debates the boon and bane of a technological culture and leisure.

Chapter 9

discusses the darker side of the cultural expression of leisure, labeled taboo recreation, because laws, customs, or beliefs make some pastimes forbidden.

Leisure *helps shape who we are as a* **culture**.

Leisure *is both*
a **victim** *and a* **tool**
of moderization.

Leisure *does not always provide for* **people's**
well-being.

CHAPTER FIVE

Leisure's Anthropology

Preview

What is leisure's cultural significance?

Leisure is so much a part of the patterns of life that it can describe how cultures are characterized, change, and are both similar and different.

Did the earliest human cultures have leisure?

Leisure was a part of culture before human civilization developed, even before our ancestors learned to speak.

How is leisure unique in developing cultures?

Leisure can be used as a tool for development. As such, leisure is also typically changed by development.

How does modernity affect a culture's leisure?

Leisure in modern societies is more commercial, diverse, sped up, and technologically oriented. Is it better?

Key Terms

Anthropology	140	Acculturation	152
Holistic	141	Paleolithic era	153
Culture	141	Development	157
Society	141	Gross domestic product	158
Subculture	142	Modernization	161
Enculturation	143	Ethnocentric	161
Cultural change	146	Postmodernism	163
Innovation	146	Cultural pluralism	164
Diffusion	147	Subjective well-being	164
Cultural loss	149		

Before the massive urbanization of black South Africans into white South African areas, which began in the 1930s, few parents of black children had money to buy toys. The result was all sorts of play inventions. For example, the boys, sometimes eagerly assisted by their fathers and elder brothers, made elaborate wire cars, complete with wheels that could turn and a functioning steering system. With urbanization and increased foreign influences, cheap plastic toys became available, which brought an end to this fascinating ingenuity. (Grobler, 1985)

Taoism, one of the three major religions found in China, has served as a primary guiding philosophy in the lives of Chinese people for over 2,500 years. Its influence can be seen in every aspect of Chinese life, including leisure. In fact, Jing Jie is the way leisure is thought of under Taoism—experienced only as a result of making art, admiring nature, and contemplating. (Zhang & Fang, 1998)

As these stories illustrate, in this chapter we consider leisure according to culture. That is, we focus on the anthropology of leisure. **Anthropology** is a discipline that utilizes ideas from the social sciences, the humanities, and the biological sciences. The term itself comes from two Greek words: anthropos, meaning "human beings," and logia, "the study of." Thus, anthropology is the study of human nature, human society, and the human past, so that when we consider leisure as anthropology, we are interested in how leisure both instructs and is instructed by human societies (Fig. 5.1).

> **Anthropology: the study of humanity**

Figure 5.1
A day at the beach on Bali, Indonesia. (© Ruth V. Russell.)

But perhaps more importantly for our interests, anthropology is about a particular perspective as well. Anthropology is holistic, comparative, field based, and evolutionary. Being **holistic** means trying to fit together all that is known about human beings. Thus, when we consider leisure as anthropology, we are interested in a wide range of information (biology, economics, and religion, to name a few examples) about leisure as a cultural phenomenon.

> **Holistic:** all encompassing; a "total picture" of something

In this chapter we explore the anthropology of leisure first in terms of basic concepts about culture. Then we trace the likely role of leisure for humans in the earliest cultures. Finally, we contrast it with the expression of leisure today in relation to cultural developments and modernity.

How Culture Influences Leisure

Culture is the central idea in anthropology. **Culture** is a complex and flexible concept, and there are many definitions for it. Usually culture is used to denote shared values, beliefs, information, and perceptions. Culture also affects people's behavior, including their leisure behavior. This means our leisure behavior fits within what our culture considers appropriate.

> **Culture:** a set of traditions and ideas shared by members of a society

The concept of culture is often confused with the concept of society. Although closely related, anthropologists make a distinction. **Society** refers to a group of people who share a specific locality and who most likely have similar cultural customs and ways of life. Moreover, members of a society are held together by a sense of group identity and group structure.

> **Society:** a group of people who occupy the same locality

Characteristics of Culture

Through the comparative study of many different cultures, anthropologists have arrived at an understanding of the basic characteristics of all cultures (Table 5.1). By understanding these, we can see the importance and function of leisure as a cultural mirror.

The first characteristic is that culture is shared (Haviland, 1990). As its definition suggests, culture is a set of shared ideas and standards of behavior. It is this shared quality that makes the actions of individuals understandable. Because they share a common culture, people can predict how others are most likely to behave in given circumstances. For example, we have expectations for sports participation based on culture. Children in the United States are likely to participate in basketball, whereas children in Chile will consider soccer their most popular sport, and children in Malaysia more likely will grow up learning sepak takraw (Fig. 5.2).

Table 5.1

Characteristics of Culture

Characteristic	Defined	Leisure example	Related concept
Shared	Values and standards of behavior are held in common.	*Sepak takraw* is a favorite sport in Malaysia.	Subcultures based on leisure
Learned	We learn our culture by growing up in it.	The appropriate time to eat is learned from the culture.	Enculturation
Symbols	Cultural "currency" is based on such symbols as language.	Symbols include the visual image in art and the scoring system in basketball.	Whorfian hypothesis
Integrated	All parts of a culture are interrelated.	After communism changes occurred in leisure resources.	Cultural change

Just because culture is shared doesn't mean there are no within-culture differences. That is, it is important to realize that everyone in a culture is not the same. Within American culture, for example, people listen to a wide variety of music, such as country, jazz, classical, rap, or rock. In fact, we can categorize people into subgroups, or **subcultures**, based on their specific musical tastes. Subcultures can be based on demographic factors such as race, ethnicity, geographic region, or social class. They can also be based on leisure interests. For example, leisure-based subcultures exist for playing golf, riding motorcycles, and long-distance running, as well as for the Indianapolis 500 race, gospel singing, and the Monday night poker club.

> **Subculture:** smaller cultures within a dominant culture

A second characteristic of culture is that it is learned (Haviland, 1990). The idea that culture is learned, rather than biologically inherited, prompted anthropologist Ralph Linton (1936) to refer to it as humanity's "social heredity." We learn our culture by growing up with it. The process whereby culture is transmitted from one generation to the next is called **enculturation**. Most animals eat and drink whenever they are hungry or thirsty. Humans, on the other hand, do most of their eating and drinking at certain culturally learned times. Eating times vary from culture to culture, and even from subculture to subculture, and through enculturation we learn what is socially appropriate. This means there is a distinction between the needs themselves, which are not learned, and the learned ways in which they are satisfied.

> **Enculturation:** the process by which culture is transmitted from one generation to the next

Many studies demonstrate this characteristic of culture as applied to the leisure enculturation of immigrants. For example, Tsai (2000), who studied Chinese immigrants in Australia, found that cultural differences initially reduced their opportunities for leisure. Only after the immigrants were sufficiently enculturated into the new culture did their leisure experiences increase.

The third characteristic of culture is that it is based on symbols. The anthropologist Leslie White insisted that all human behavior originates in the use of symbols (1959). For example, art, religion, and money all involve the use of symbols—the visual image in art, the icon in religion, and the coin in money. The most important symbolic aspect of culture is language—the substitution of words for objects (Haviland, 1990).

Figure 5.2
The sepak takraw ball is made of woven rattan. The aim of the game is to keep the ball off the ground using any part of the body except the hands. (© Christopher B. Stage.)

The Study Says

The Leisure-Based College Student Subculture

Box 5.1

In late November, Pete called the second floor meeting of the fall semester on Hasbrouck Fourth, the first one he had scheduled since early September. The floor had to plan its annual Christmas party, he said. Nobody was very interested in the party; the residents were still skeptical about such affairs in the absence of alcohol. Someone suggested that its theme be Dead Rock-and-Roll Stars. Pete, who was fighting a nasty cold, rejected this macabre suggestion out of hand and decided that it would be a toga party. He then indicated he was not pleased with the apathy on Hasbrouck Fourth, and went on to his second piece of business. There was a strict new policy coming out of the dean's office about Secret Santa, he announced.

I had heard rumors about Secret Santa since my first year-long stay in the dorms. It sounded harmless-too innocent, in fact, for the enthusiasm it seemed to generate among the students; they went on talking about Secret Santa for months and even years afterward. By random ballots, the women and men on every coed dorm floor paired off in the last week before exams in early December. I might have a female Secret Santa on Hasbrouck Fourth whose identity I did not know, and be a Secret Santa to a separate female who did not know my identity. Then we all sneak around all week long leaving amusing little presents for each other.

It was Pete who clarified for me the real appeal of Secret Santa. To get each gift, he explained, you had to meet a challenge; you had to perform an embarrassing stunt, sometimes in public outside the dorm, two or three evenings during the Secret Santa week. Pete had made a scrapbook of his own photos of the fun from last year. More than half the photos showed transvestite males, nearly nude females and males, and other outlandish costumes and carryings-on.

The above is an excerpt from the field study of college students at Rutgers University in New Jersey by Michael Moffatt (1989, pp. 103-104). To write this account about college as students really know it, Moffatt did what anthropologists usually do-he lived among the "natives" for a year. His intention was to study college students as a subculture. Among many things, his findings revealed surprising cultural notions about the leisure experience of undergraduates. For example, he specifically studied such college subcultural traditions as drinking, hazing, fraternities and sororities, extracurricular groups, and of course, Secret Santas.

One way of thinking about leisure relative to this characteristic is to consider the word *leisure* itself. According to deGrazia (1962), "leisure cannot exist where people don't know what it is" (p. 3). That is, one must have a symbol (language) for leisure in order to have it. For example, while conducting research with the Sherpa people of the Khumbu region of Nepal, I realized that many people were unable to understand my question, "What do you do for leisure?" because they did not have a translatable word for the English word leisure. This idea has been labeled the Whorfian hypothesis. Named for the anthropologist who first formed a full-fledged theory about it (Benjamin Lee Whorf in 1956), the idea argues that language not only provides a way of communicating among people, but it also becomes the entire definition of the culture itself. The hypothesis states that language provides habitual grooves of expression that dictate people's thinking and behavior (Haviland, 1990).

What do you think? Does the absence of a word such as leisure mean the absence of that concept or experience? The Whorfian hypothesis has received only limited and confusing research support, even though many commonly agree with it (Chick, 1995). Although it may be easier to think about certain things in some languages, concepts do not necessarily need to be governed by the presence or absence of symbols for them (such as words) (Chick, 1995). For example, as I discovered in my own research, the Sherpa people indeed have a life experience characterized by many of the qualities we identify with leisure, even though their word for it does not translate into the English word *leisure*. Thus, we must be very careful in thinking that leisure differs among cultural groups because of language differences.

Finally, culture is integrated. This means that when we examine one aspect of a culture, we invariably find it necessary to examine other parts as well. All aspects of a culture function as an interrelated whole. Like a machine, the parts of a culture must be consistent with one another or it won't run. Conversely, a change in one part of a culture usually will affect other parts, sometimes in rather dramatic ways. Thus, the parts of a culture must be in harmony.

An example of this characteristic as related to leisure is what occurred in Poland with the downfall of communism. Formerly, under the communist system, government-owned companies in Poland were required to generate cultural funds. These funds were used to subsidize holidays and trips for employees; recreational services for employees' children; book purchases for company libraries; and tickets for the theater, cinema, and concerts. When the country shifted away from a communist political system by implementing market-oriented reforms, one essential feature was the privatization of these government funds (Jung, 1992). This meant not only that some establishments formerly used for recreation had shifted to other uses, but also that, with the commercialization of recreation, recreational services were available only to more wealthy consumers. In addition, a new sponsor of recreational services emerged: the Catholic church. The involvement of the church in fine arts, as well as in various forms of youth recreation, has grown tremendously (Jung, 1992). Thus, with one change in the political system, changes were also felt in the economic system, which in turn had an impact on changes in leisure resources and how leisure services were made available in Polish culture. This introduces another related characteristic: cultural change.

Cultural Change

One understanding that emerges from the characteristic that culture is integrated is **cultural change**. All cultures change over a period of time, sometimes gently and gradually, without altering any of the fundamental ways underlying the core of the culture. At other times, however, the pace of change may be dramatically fast, causing radical cultural alteration in a short period of time, sometimes to the disadvantage of the culture. Regardless, certain mechanisms are at work that have implications for leisure. These mechanisms of change are innovation, diffusion, loss, and acculturation (Haviland, 1990).

> **Cultural change:** changes in the lived experience of a culture

One mechanism of cultural change is innovation, meaning any new practice, tool, or principle that gains widespread acceptance within a culture. A significant example of how innovation changes cultural expressions of leisure is the invention of television. In fact, no consideration of leisure prior to television is of anything but historical interest (Kelly & Freysinger, 2000). It has changed everything–and almost everywhere. When television was introduced in 1950, it was in nine percent of U.S. households. It grew quickly, and in just five years TV was in 64.5 percent of households. Today, 99 percent of American households have a television and 74 percent have more than one (Nielsen Media Research, 2003).

> **Innovation:** a chance discovery; something new created out of the deliberate application of a known principle

Yet this innovation has done much more than take up furniture space in our homes. There have been numerous and major changes in culture as a result:

- **People stay at home more.**

- **Household timetables have changed, with "prime time" now devoted to entertainment rather than to family, religion, and education.**

- **There is less socializing in the family, neighborhood, and community and increased social isolation.**

- **Television characters are used as role models.**
  Or "Television characters have become role models"

- **Such forms of leisure as the arts, cooking, travel, and sports have expanded.**

- **New forms of leisure have developed, such as extreme sports.**

Not all leisure innovations cause cultural change. If an innovation is to be accepted, it must be reasonably consistent with a society's needs, values, and goals. People will also reject an innovation from force of habit. For example, a new form of professional football made its debut in American culture a few years ago. It was tagged the "X" league because it used violence to appeal to the entertainment interests of spectators. The XFL lasted only one season because of its inconsistency with society's needs and values.

Diffusion is another mechanism of cultural change. Diffusion is the spread or borrowing of customs or practices from one culture to another. So common is diffusion that anthropologist Linton suggested that borrowing accounts for as much as 90 percent of any culture's content (Haviland, 1990). One major example of cultural change brought about by diffusion is McDonald's restaurants: What began as a single establishment in Des Plaines, Illinois, in 1955 has now expanded to more than 25,000 restaurants worldwide (McDonald's, 2000). Although global in its market, the company also encourages local operators to tailor menu items to local tastes (e.g., the Teriyaki McBurger in Japan and Chile's McPalta, with avocado).

> **Diffusion:** the spread of customs from one culture to another

Figure 5.3

Gridlock of tourist jeeps in Cancun, Mexico. The diffusion of customs from one culture to another is not always compatible. (© Ruth V. Russell.)

This is because people are choosy about their borrowing and pick from multiple possibilities and sources. Usually their selections are limited to those compatible with their existing culture. This includes the diffusion of leisure customs. Why do you suppose Mexican tourism officials borrowed the North American penchant for touring by private automobile (Fig. 5.3)? In addition, particular games, songs, sports, dances, and art forms introduced in one culture spread to others and are often changed in accordance with the dominant values of the receiving culture. For example, Heider (1977) described a game of physical skill that was developed in Java (Indonesia) and later introduced in a highland New Guinea tribe. New Guinean culture valued noncompetitiveness, so when they played the Javanese game, they disregarded scorekeeping and regulations. This was more in keeping with their own cultural values (Chick, 1995).

From Your Own Experience

When Does Cultural Diffusion Become Cultural Invasion?
Box 5.2

So many examples of cultural change mechanisms come from tourism because the movement of millions of people around the world on an annual basis has an extremely significant impact on host cultures. For example, consider the tourist destination of Antarctica. Actually, Antarctica is the least visited continent. Until about 1820, no human had seen it, and it is doubtful whether anyone had landed on it before 1894. Now, each year, approximately 15,000 tourists visit Antarctica, participating in sightseeing, mountain climbing, camping, kayaking, and scuba diving. Is this good or bad? That is, even though the continent is not highly populated (at least not permanently), is the presence of tourism simply the diffusion of cultural change, or would you label it an invasion? Study resources available on the Internet and discuss your resulting opinion with classmates. You might begin with the Web site of the International Association of Antarctica Tour Operators at http://www.iaato.org (International Association of Antarctica Tour Operators, 2004).

Most often we think of cultural change as an accumulation of innovations and borrowings; new things are added to those already there. This is not always the case, however, and frequently the acceptance of an innovation or borrowing leads to the loss of an older one (Haviland, 1990). This is **cultural loss.** When North American and other cultures changed from primarily radio home entertainment to television home entertainment, for example, several pleasurable qualities of leisure were lost. For example, with television we are no longer able to use our imaginations to fill in the "picture" of the action, and the family no longer sits in a circle facing each other while being entertained. With television, someone else's visualization of the action is provided for us, and the family sits in a straight line without eye contact.

> **Cultural loss:** change resulting in the loss of a cultural tradition

In Focus

Torrent of Tourists in the Khumbu
Box 5.3

Nepal packs more geographical diversity into fewer square miles than any other country in the world. The people who inhabit this land mirror this diversity. In Nepal, no majority culture exists–all are minorities. One of the most famous of these cultures is the Sherpa. The Sherpa live in the high valleys in the southern shadow of Mt. Everest in the region known as the Khumbu. They are Buddhists, culturally Tibetan, and a numerically insignificant portion of the population (Fisher, 1990). Their villages, which are situated mostly on rock, ice, and snow at altitudes between 10,000 and 13,000 feet, are connected by narrow mountain footpaths. They have names like Namche Bazaar, Lukla, Tengboche, Thame, and Pheriche.

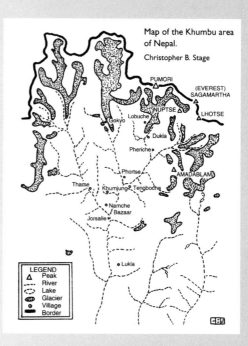

Map of the Khumbu area of Nepal.

Christopher B. Stage

LEGEND
△ Peak
River
Lake
Glacier
● Village
Border

Sherpas have traditionally operated at a very low level of technology, farming potatoes, turnips, and cauliflower, weaving woolen cloth by hand, and repairing rope-soled shoes. They follow their yak herds to higher pastures in the summer and to lower ones in winter. Religious and community celebrations follow a pattern set mostly by the passage of the seasons and often center around local monasteries.

Beginning in 1961, life began to change for the Sherpa of the Khumbu. First, the construction and operation of elementary schools in the villages brought literacy in Nepali and English. The establishment of a hospital in the region also had wide-ranging effects, including the virtual elimination of thyroid deficiency diseases. Clearly, the event inducing the most cultural change for the Sherpas, however, was the construction of an airstrip at Lukla, which shortened the travel time from Kathmandu (the capital) to the Khumbu from 14 days to 40 minutes. This single development has brought more than 18,000 tourists per year to the Khumbu (Fig. 5.4).

Figure 5.4
The airstrip in Lukla brings more than 18,000 tourists a year into Nepal's Khumbu region.
(© Ruth V. Russell.)

What has this torrent of tourists meant for the Sherpa? Those who observe and comment on the impact of tourism generally divide themselves into two camps. One view is that tourism ultimately destroys the cultural integrity of an area. Tourism is considered to place "the whole of the visited culture on sale, distorting its imagery and symbolism, . . . transforming a way of life into an industry" (Smith, 1980, p. 60). As one Khumbu tourist wrote in a visitor's log book, "A hot shower, steaks, and 500-foot viewing tower with central heating would definitely be in order" (Fisher, 1990), which makes the culture-for-sale perspective on the impact of tourism understandable.

The other view is that tourism is good because of the economic benefits it brings to local people. This happens not only by bringing in outside money, but also by increasing employment. Not surprisingly, governments are usually convinced by this second perspective, and for good reason. The government of Nepal's earnings from tourism are substantial.

Which perspective is true for the Khumbu? Let's answer the question both ways.

Residents of the Khumbu now work as guides, cooks, and porters for trekking and mountain-climbing trips. In fact, the word Sherpa has come to describe a particular job: The Sherpa assists the trekking party by setting up tents and managing loads. The village of Namche Bazaar is geographically situated so that all tourists (and all Sherpas, too) who enter the region must travel through it. Namche entrepreneurs have quickly met the challenge by opening roughly 50 shops and hotels. About 85 percent of all households in the village have at least one person working in tourism (Fisher, 1990).

Although most of tourist spending goes to the trekking companies that arrange the trips headquartered outside the Khumbu, Sherpa income has still increased dramatically. From 1964 to 1988, for example, porters' wages increased by 730 percent and those of guides by 369 percent. But inflation has occurred as well: The price of rice in this same period went up by 900 percent (Fisher, 1990).

Partly because of this inflation, partly because the pay is seasonal and unstable, and partly because most Sherpas have little experience in business, they have saved and invested little. Instead, they have spent their earnings on formerly unavailable goods. For example, there is now a wider variety of fruits and vegetables in the region. Jewelry (especially watches) is another popular expense, and there has been a frenzy of activity in repairing and upgrading houses. Some traditional crafts are dying out. With so much ready cash, people now tend to buy manufactured items instead of making them themselves.

Class differences are also emerging as a new "tourist Sherpa" class develops. Formerly, land and yak herds were the sources of wealth and status. Now, an almost nouveau-riche group can be distinguished by their imported hiking boots, down parkas, baseball caps, and American university-labeled sweatshirts. Another result of widespread employment in tourism is that people no longer live the way they used to. For instance, Sherpas who work as trekking guides or porters spend more time, roughly 10 months a year, away from their villages.

Questions to Consider and Discuss

1. *Which perspective do you think best portrays the effects of tourism in the Khumbu? Has it been good or bad? Why do you see it this way? What are the opinions of your classmates?*

2. *If you were managing tourism in the Khumbu, what policies would you establish, and what would you hope these policies would accomplish?*

3. *As a class project, select an undeveloped area near you that has recently promoted itself as a tourist attraction. This could be a small town or a county. Interview local people to find out the impact of tourism on them. Has tourism meant cultural loss or acculturation?*

A final mechanism of cultural change is acculturation. **Acculturation** occurs when groups having different cultures come into intensive firsthand contact, with subsequent massive changes in the original cultural patterns of one or both groups (Haviland, 1990). Acculturation usually involves an element of force, either directly or indirectly. When acculturation occurs, one of several things can happen. Merger or fusion occurs when the two cultures lose their separate identities and form a single culture (the "melting pot" idea), or one of the cultures can lose its autonomy but retain its identity as a subculture (e.g., Native American reservations in the western United States), or one culture can ultimately become extinct.

> **Acculturation:** major cultural changes that occur as a result of prolonged contact between societies

An example of acculturation through leisure may be found in tourism, particularly mass tourism. Mass tourism is what most travelers do most of the time: Large groups of people go to the same destinations. For example, mass tourism means vacationing on one of the cruise ships that go from one seaport to another for shopping, gambling, and to take in sun. It is staying at The Hampton Inn, eating at Cracker Barrel, driving the interstate, and visiting a theme park. Acculturation can occur from mass tourism because of the high-impact developments that are required to support it. When tourism degrades or destroys the host culture with its "gaze" (MacCannell, 1999), the outside influence takes away local autonomy and places the power (economic and social) in the hands of the invading tourists (Fig. 5.5).

Figure 5.5
Tourists often bring customs and demands that are foreign to host cultures. (© Ruth V. Russell.)

Hunches About the Earliest Human Cultures

One of the most illuminating ways to understand present human culture is to view it from its distant origins (Shivers & deLisle, 1997). Leisure was a part of culture before human civilization developed, even before our ancestors learned how to speak. All this makes for a fascinating story.

Humans are classified by biologists as belonging to the primate order, a group that also includes lemurs, tarsiers, monkeys, and apes. Some evidence suggests that humans evolved from the small, apelike ramapithecines, which lived about 15 million years ago. By four million years ago, this apelike creature became fully adapted for moving about on its hind legs, and by 2.5 million years ago, the appearance of the earliest stone tools, along with the gradual enlarging of the brain, set the stage for evolution to the human of the present (Haviland, 1990).

These early tools were choppers, scrapers, gouging tools, and hammerstones for cutting meat, scraping hides, and cracking bones to extract marrow. Their invention marks the beginning of the **Paleolithic era**, or Old Stone Age time, of human existence. Scientists estimate that only a few thousand people lived in all of Africa and that a similar number lived in Asia at this prehistoric time.

> **Paleolithic era:** a period in prehistory characterized by the use of rough stone implements

For more than two million years, people lived by hunting and gathering plants, nuts, and meat left on the carcasses of animals, for it was only about 10,000 years ago that people learned to farm. Instead, Paleolithic people lived in groups and moved from place to place in search of food. A group usually stayed in one place for only a few days. They ate what was available and then moved on. They built shelters only if they found enough food in an area to last a few weeks or months. No one knows when the first clothing was worn—probably not until about 17,000 years ago.

In Profile

Fruh
Box 5.4

He called himself Fruh because of the grunt he emitted when startled. This morning he awoke from his burrow within the tree line bordering on the savannah with that grunt. He had slept fitfully. The night was a fearful time, with prey and predator sharing a common habitat. The first order was to fill his belly. He sniffed the warm air, trying to catch the scent of a carcass that might have some meat left on it. He could always eat grubs, grass, or roots.

When his hunger pangs abated, he trotted to a cliff face, where the brassy sun reflected on some stones. He picked up two. The stones were round and fit easily into his hands. He tossed them into the air, rubbed them together to enjoy the sound, and finally threw them over the cliff with all his might, watching them fall for a long time. Then he sat down under the shade of a tree to take a nap.

About 2.5 million years later, a paleontologist would unearth a fragment of Fruh's skull near Lake Baringo in Kenya and claim it as the earliest corroborated fossil of the human race (based on Shivers & deLisle, 1997, p. 4).

What we know about the leisure expressions of Paleolithic people is, of course, very limited, but we do have surviving cave paintings to offer clues. During the last 50 years, archeologists have discovered thousands of paintings and carvings on the walls of caves and on the surfaces of rocks at sites in Europe, Africa, Australia, and North America. Many discovered as recently as 1996 in southeastern France contain images of animals, birds, fish, and other signs and symbols, all of which reveal a high degree of artistic and technical sophistication (Fiero, 1998).

These artistic artifacts document a great deal about the culture of Paleolithic people. For example, the cave paintings found in France reveal the culture of a hunting people. Realistically depicted bison, horses, reindeer, and other creatures are shown standing, running, and wounded by spears and lances. Because they are located in the most inaccessible regions of the caves, and frequently drawn one over another, it is unlikely that the paintings were intended as decorations or even as records of the hunt. According to the interpretations of some scholars (Fiero, 1998), the cave art reflects a kind of prayer, that is, a means of engaging superhuman forces to advance human needs and efforts. Further, scholars believe that the prayer not only included the drawings, but also was accompanied by song and dance. In other words, perhaps this represents the very earliest use of leisure as ritual.

Beyond these art legacies, we don't know much more about the leisure of the Paleolithic era. There are conjectures, however. For example, the standard anthropological view of this hunting-and-gathering culture is that because they were constantly on the move in search of food for minimal survival, these people must have lacked free time for leisure.

Yet there is an alternative view. Marshall Sahlins, an American anthropologist, has suggested that prehistoric people were the original leisure society (1988, p. 257). Sahlins based this claim on two conjectures. First, Paleolithic people may not have spent as much time hunting and gathering food as formerly assumed. Second, Paleolithic people had comparatively few material goods and thus were free from the effort of protecting and maintaining them. Let's ponder each suggestion in turn.

First, Sahlins cited research about two hunter–gatherer groups living in Australia in the 1960s as examples of what life could have been like for Paleolithic people. The results are surprising. As shown in Figure 5.6, the number of hours per day spent by one of the groups in hunting-and-gathering activities was not great. The most obvious conclusion Sahlins drew from the data was that the people did not have to work hard to survive, particularly by modern standards. The average length of time each person spent per day collecting and preparing food was three to four hours. What might they have done in their spare time? As indicated in Figure 5.7, much of the time freed from the necessities of food-connected tasks could have been spent in rest and sleep. According to Sahlins, other free-time activities may have included chatting, gossiping, and general sociability.

Sahlins' second conjecture about the leisure of Paleolithic cultures has to do with what today we call materialism. In contrast to the many affluent societies of today, with their focus on the acquisition of stuff, early people possessed very little. Most likely their possessions included a few pieces of clothing, portable housing materials, a few ornaments, spare flints, some medicinal quartz, a few tools and weapons, and a skin bag to hold it all. In contrast to the collection of possessions we have today and to the time we spend purchasing, repairing, cleaning, putting away, transporting, sorting, finding, protecting, and storing it all, Sahlins reasoned that Paleolithic people were comparatively free. Although some might consider hunter–gatherers poor because they didn't have anything, another view is to think of them as rich in free time and leisure.

Figure 5.6

The hours per day spent in hunting and gathering activities by one of Sahlins' groups.

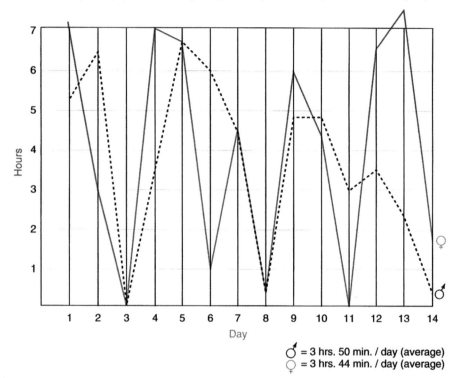

♂ = 3 hrs. 50 min. / day (average)
♀ = 3 hrs. 44 min. / day (average)

Figure 5.7

Amount of daytime devoted to sleep. According to Sahlins' hypothesis, free-time activities could have included rest, sleep, chatting, and general sociability.

Day	♂ Average	♀ Average
1	2'15"	2'45"
2	1'30"	1'0"
3	Most of the day	
4	Intermittent	
5	Intermittent and most of late afternoon	
6	Most of the day	
7	Several hours	
8	2'0"	2'0"
9	50"	50"
10	Afternoon	
11	Afternoon	
12	Intermittent, afternoon	
13	—	—
14	3'15"	3'15"

Leisure and Cultural Development

The story of humankind after these prehistoric times is one of cultural development. **Development** simply means the extent to which the resources of an area or country have been brought into full productivity. In common usage it refers to the amount of economic growth and modernization, and to the production and consumption of goods. Today, countries can be identified according to the extent of their development. For example, Canada, Australia, Great Britain, France, the United States, and Japan are categorized as more developed, whereas India, Paraguay, Nepal, Senegal, and Afghanistan are considered less developed. In this section of the chapter we discuss what cultural development means to the expression of leisure. The conclusion is that with development come both advantages and disadvantages.

> **Development:** the process of improving the material conditions of people through the diffusion of knowledge and technology

"Developing" was the term U.S. President Harry S. Truman introduced in 1949 as a replacement for "backward," the unflattering reference then in use. This new term implies that, sooner or later, all portions of the world will reach a highly industrialized stage. Development is a fluid condition, however, so this may not necessarily be the case. Although the standard of living in most cultures of the world has improved, one serious trend is the widening of the development gap. Rich countries have grown richer, and poor countries have become relatively poorer (Table 5.2). It is more difficult now for a less-developed society to advance to full modernization by its own efforts. Thus, such organizations as the Peace Corps and the World Bank attempt to marshal some of the resources of more-developed areas to help less-developed ones.

Table 5.2

Gross Domestic Product per Capita for Selected Countries, 2001

More than $30,000	Less than $1,000
Iceland	Angola
Ireland	Chad
Luxembourg	Ethiopia
Norway	Liberia
Switzerland	Mali
United States	North Korea

Note. Retrieved February 12, 2004, from http://www.childpolicyintl.org.

A country's level of development can be determined according to three factors: economic, social, and demographic. Accordingly, the Human Development Index (HDI), created by the United Nations, recognizes that a country's level of development is a function of all three of these factors. To create the HDI, the United Nations selected one economic factor, two social factors, and one demographic factor that, in the opinion of their analysts, best reveal a country's level of development. The economic factor used is the **gross domestic product** (GDP) per capita; the social factors are the literacy rate and amount of education; and the demographic factor is life expectancy. These four factors are combined to produce a country's HDI. The highest HDI possible is 1.0, and the country with the highest HDI in the past decade has been Canada, at 0.932. The lowest ranked country most years has been Sierra Leone, with an HDI of 0.254 (Rubenstein, 2003).

> **Gross domestic product:** the value of all goods and services produced domestically

Thus, we see that development is a multifaceted concept with interrelated conditions. This includes such "softer" indicators as social and cultural customs and structures. Although development can enhance an area's HDI, it may be detrimental to other aspects of a culture's uniqueness. The accumulation of wealth, whether on a national or individual level, is not necessarily a recipe for a high quality of life. One way to comprehend this is to notice the impact of development on leisure.

The Study Says

The Material World
Box 5.5

To recognize the United Nations' Year of the Family in 1994, a research team headed by Peter Menzel set out to learn about families of the world. Using country statistics and photographs, Menzel provided a comparative analysis of the material goods of typical families from 30 U.N. member nations.

Data experts at the U.N. and World Bank helped determine what an "average" family was in a country according to location (rural, urban), type of dwelling, family size, annual income, occupation, and religion. To find an actual family that represented what was average, researchers knocked on doors of typical houses looking for cooperative families that fit the statistics. Then each of the 30 families' precious belongings were moved outside to the front of the house for the photographs, to provide a visual means of analyzing the typical material goods.

In studying the photographs, many things can be understood about the material condition of families in various cultures. For example, the researchers noted that the possessions of the family in Uzbekistan overwhelmingly consisted of carpets, and that those of the average Icelandic family were focused on playing music, whereas the photo of the typical family in Kuwait was crowded with four shiny new automobiles, including one Mercedes.

Figure 5.8

The Regzen family outside their ger with all of their possessions, Ulaanbaatar, Mongolia. (From Material World, pp. 40–41 © Peter Menzel/menzelphoto.com. Used with permission.)

Most visible, however, was the common denominator of the television in typical households across the globe. In the photo of the family in Mongolia, the television is located in the front center of the photograph with the family positioned behind it (Fig. 5.8). The South African and Vietnamese families are also pictured with a television nearby, and the Albanian family is seated directly in front of their television in the center of the photograph. The family from Cuba is shown with two televisions, as are the families from the United States, Russia, Italy, and Great Britain. In fact, in all but the very poorest countries (Mali and Haiti), the television is located in the photograph in such a way as to suggest its primacy among the prized possessions of the world's families (Menzel, 1994).

Leisure can be an important consideration in enhancing a country's quality of life. As we've already learned, it can be instrumental in the personal development of each inhabitant and important to social harmony. Leisure can widen every person's relationship to the environment and help build the social identity of a community. As we'll learn in a later chapter, it can even be an important source of economic growth. Yet the ability of leisure to be good for people and societies can be stifled if development is unchecked and unconsidered. Here's how.

Leisure in developing countries such as Costa Rica, Indonesia, Slovakia, and Tunisia is richly laced with the traditions and folkways of the culture. Music, dance, and art forms are woven into the fabric of society in ways uncommon in developed countries such as The Netherlands, Singapore, and the United States. As a country (or any underdeveloped area) seeks to develop, it embraces new income-generating efforts. Sometimes this means the ruin of traditions and folkways. Yet ironically, leisure can also become an important means through which to develop. Traditional arts and crafts are "updated" and exported (Fig. 5.9). Sporting events are held to bring in outside money. Today, perhaps the single largest use of leisure as a development tool is via tourism. In Malaysia, for example, tourism is the third largest foreign exchange earner. It is also the prime motivator for enhancing the country's infrastructure.

Figure 5.9
Art/graffiti on the Berlin Wall before the reunification of East and West Germany. One outcome of the wall was the establishment of ethnocentric views between West and East Germans. (© Beth Elliot.)

Leisure and Modernity

Those cultures considered "developed," are also considered "modern." Our purpose in this section of the chapter is to explore what it means to be modern and then to connect modernity to leisure in two specific ways: through the ideas of postmodernism and well-being.

First, the concept of **modernization** is a cultural process that has several different connotations. To many people, modernization is what happens when undeveloped societies seek to acquire some of the characteristics common to developed societies. Looking at this connotation more closely, we see that "becoming modern" really means "becoming like us." Accordingly, there is a clear implication that not being like us is to be antiquated and obsolete. We realize that this perspective is an **ethnocentric** notion, because it insists that these other societies must be changed to be more like us, irrespective of other considerations, including traditional customs. Ethnocentrism generates emotional reactions to cultural differences and reduces people's willingness to understand different cultures.

> **Modernization:** involving the implementation of recent techniques, methods, or ideas

> **Ethnocentric:** the belief that one's own culture is superior in every way to all others

Although people in every culture, developed and undeveloped, have at least some feelings of ethnocentricity, it seems that Western cultures are particularly good examples. Let's demonstrate this by considering baseball in Japan. Even though the traditional combative sports of judo and sumo continue to be popular, baseball has grown to such an extent that the Japanese are now providing strong competition with major league teams in the United States. An ethnocentric response to this trend would be to assume that the Japanese version of baseball is inferior to the American version. After all, since baseball was invented in the United States, it follows that it is played there the best.

Since this ethnocentric connotation of the concept of modernization is often unfortunate, let us explore a more anthropologically sound one. The process of modernization may be best understood as made up of four subprocesses: technological development, agricultural development, industrialization, and urbanization (Haviland, 1990). These elements are interrelated and occur simultaneously. First, with modernization, traditional knowledge and techniques are replaced by scientific knowledge and techniques. Likewise, the culture shifts from an emphasis on subsistence farming to commercial farming. Industrialization is the third subprocess, in which work is done by machines rather than by humans and animals. Finally, the population becomes urbanized by moving from rural settlements into cities.

From Your Own Experience

Ethnocentricity Scale
Box 5.6

Circle the level of agreement you have with each statement:

	Strongly Agree	Agree	Disagree	Stongly Disagree
1. I am against buying foreign imports.	4	3	2	1
2. I find it frustrating when someone from another country doesn't understand what I'm saying.	4	3	2	1
3. I would have a hard time living in another country.	4	3	2	1
4. I feel uncomfortable when I'm around people from another country.	4	3	2	1
5. I do not care for ethnic food.	4	3	2	1

As you may have already determined, the higher your score, the more ethnocentric you are in your views of other cultures.

As these modernization processes take place, other changes are likely to follow. Some of these changes seem to be for the good; others do not. For example, in the political realm, political parties and some sort of electoral system frequently appear, along with a bureaucracy. In education, there is an expansion of learning opportunities, and literacy increases; typically, there are also major improvements in health care. The environment usually becomes more precious as industrial pollution renders the air and water quality and supplies more fragile. Traditional religion becomes less important as new ideas develop. The mobility of people increases, as does the diversity of roles they assume in the culture. For example, in modern societies, the majority of adult women are in the labor force. As a result of modernization, the status of people shifts from one ascribed by birth to one based on achievements. In fact, in modern cultures, privilege is associated with the good jobs.

People's daily lives usually change as a result of modernization as well. With modernity we become busier as time efficiency becomes more important. In fact, one of the most noticeable signs of modernity is that efficiency becomes the most important cultural value (Godbey, 1997). This modern value shapes much of leisure. In essence, leisure in modern societies is more commercial, diverse, and sped up; it is thus more cherished, as it has to compete with the busyness of work and family lives. Leisure becomes more of a competition to collect fun experiences and recreational equipment. To explore the impact of modernity on leisure more fully, let us finally turn to two specific concerns: postmodernism and well-being.

Postmodernism

Because the impact of modernity is considered to be so extreme and dramatic, a special concept has been adopted by cultural scientists to describe it. This is **postmodernism**. The term is very slippery to define because it can mean different things. For example, in architecture it means a particular style of aesthetic representation. Our use of the concept here comes from anthropology and means a radical break with the past, a new cultural logic for our daily lives.

> **Postmodernism:** a reaction to modernism in various fields (art, film, literature, sociology, anthropology, etc.)

In the last few decades, the nature of Western societies in particular has changed radically. Social theorists have imagined these changes through the development of such labels as a "media society," a "society of spectacle," and a "consumer society." Today, the Western world is dominated by consumption, media, and new technologies. This postmodern "condition," argue scholars, is the result of the benefits of a commitment to modernity, namely, prosperity, equality, and efficiency (Lavenda & Schultz, 2000). From a postmodern perspective, this means that we live in a fragmented way. All the old certainties and standards seem to be breaking down. Old identities and common interests have become fragmented and diffused.

For example, new technologies have made it possible both to make and to lose friends quickly and easily. Societies are more **culturally pluralistic**. That is, they are made up of a multiplicity of heterogeneous subgroups whose

Cultural pluralism: societies in which a diversity of subcultural patterns exists

ways of thinking and living vary. As a result, groups in postmodern cultures are engaged in struggles against each other to create their own identities as separate from those of the others.

Much is being written today about postmodernism, and much of it that applies to leisure carries a negative tone, as though leisure has lost something as a result. For example, in addition to being more commercial, sped up, and technology based, postmodern leisure is also expected to be more concerned with individual self-fulfillment, self-reliance, and a focus on image. For example, modern sports now call attention to differences within a culture. This contributes to the number of perceived gender differences, sexual-orientation differences, ethnic and racial differences, and class differences. A child who plays in a youth basketball program wearing Michael Jordan shoes plays with the style and attitude of a wealthy, black male.

Not everyone agrees that the condition of leisure in modern cultures is as described in the concept of postmodernism. Some continue to argue that leisure is largely unchanged by economic and social progress. For example, Crouch and Tomlinson (1994) suggest that leisure is still lived in communities and social groups, and is not dependent on commodities and forms of electronic media. Similarly, Kelly (1999) contends that most leisure still takes place in and around the home and serves to integrate communities and personal relationships. What do you think?

Well-being

Regardless of your response, a discussion of postmodernism naturally brings forth the question of well-being. Are people in modern societies truly better off? This has been an intriguing question for researchers recently, especially from a cross-cultural perspective (Diener & Suh, 2000). This collection of studies about **subjective well-being** explains some of the ingredients of quality of life in different cultures around the world. Subjective well-being is defined as people's evaluations of their own lives. These evaluations can include positive feelings, judgments about one's life being satisfying, and the view that one's life is fulfilling.

Subjective well-being: people's evaluations of their own lives

Different studies associate different factors with subjective well-being. For example, Ryff and Keyes (1995) found self-acceptance, positive relationships with others, autonomy, mastery of the environment, purpose in life, and personal growth to be associated with well-being. On the other hand, Diener and Diener (1995) showed that high income, individualism, human rights, and social equality were decisive factors in well-being. These factors discovered by researchers are more likely to be compatible with Western cultures. In fact, research has shown that the self-views of East Asians are comparably less positive than those of North Americans.

This is because factors associated with well-being vary from culture to culture, and this is not always according to whether a culture is modern or developing. Indeed, placing a high value on subjective well-being itself varies across cultures. That is, East Asian perspectives on happiness are different from those in the West. For example, to members of East Asian cultures, unhappiness is believed to arrive after happiness, and vice versa (Kovacs, 2003). It is taught in these cultures that happiness should not be embraced with excessive joy; therefore, East Asians do not feel as obligated to be happy and satisfied with their lives. Such cross-cultural comparisons are intriguing.

Yet it remains tempting to ask whether people living in modern cultures feel they are better off. To answer this question, let's look at a study that measured cultural happiness with a "hedonometer." Norman (as cited in Cole, 1988) created the hedonometer to compare Great Britain ($21,200 GDP per capita at the time) with Botswana ($3,300 GDP per capita at the time). However, happiness was measured in terms of psychological satisfaction rather than money. That is, happiness was considered to come from:

- **understanding the environment and how to control it**

- **social support from family and friends**

- **the satisfaction of species drives (such as sex and parenting)**

- **the satisfaction of drives for physical well-being (such as hunger and sleep)**

- **the satisfaction of aesthetic and sensory drives**

- **the satisfaction of exploratory drives (such as creativity and discovery)**

According to these measures, Norman judged the people of Botswana to be higher in all but one factor–physical well-being. Although this is arguably a subjective way of measuring how well off a society is, the point is that determining individual and collective well-being is based on more than economic indicators.

Summary: What We Understand

From the perspective of anthropology, leisure can be understood as a significant cultural phenomenon. That is, leisure helps to shape a culture's characteristics and change, and like a reflection in the mirror, leisure is a result of a culture's characteristics and change. As a result of reading this chapter, you should know that

- As a cultural phenomenon, leisure is characterized as shared, learned, based on symbols, and integrated.

- Leisure contributes to and is affected by the cultural change mechanisms of innovation, diffusion, cultural loss, and acculturation.

- Contrary to the standard view, new data suggest that prehistoric people had abundant free time and spent it relaxing.

- Leisure can contribute to cultural development.

- Leisure in today's cultures is subject to the processes of modernity. The result may be both good and bad.

Applications to Professional Practice

One of the obvious conclusions from this chapter is that leisure is global. Although specific activities may be somewhat unique to societies around the world, people everywhere express themselves through leisure. In addition, through such avenues as tourism, people are crossing borders for leisure more and more often. Godbey (1999) has referred to these people as a "nomad elite" (p. 392) because ties with any particular place are loosening. Television also allows us access to information from all over the world.

One way of learning more about the global nature of leisure is through World Leisure. Founded in 1952, World Leisure is an international, nongovernmental association of individuals and organizations dedicated to fostering conditions that permit leisure to serve as a force for human growth, development, and well-being (World Leisure, 2004). The premise of World Leisure is that access to meaningful leisure experiences is no less a need than the need for shelter, education, employment, and health care.

To accomplish this mission, World Leisure sponsors research and scholarship; disseminates information; and advocates through legislation, infrastructure development, leadership, and programming. These initiatives are carried out in cooperation with other worldwide organizations such as the United Nations.

For Further Information

To learn more about World Leisure, explore the Web site at http://www.worldleisure.org. From the home page, also check out the international jobs link, "World Leisure Jobs," and options for scholarships to world congresses from the "World Leisure Scholarship Program" link.

References

Chick, G. E. (1995). The anthropology of leisure: Past, present, and future research. In L. A. Barnett (Ed.), *Research about leisure: Past, present, and future.* Champaign, IL: Sagamore.

Cole, J. B. (1988). *Anthropology for the nineties.* New York: The Free Press.

Crouch, D., & Tomlinson, A. (1994). Collective self-generated consumption: Leisure, space, and cultural identity in late modernity. In I. Henry (Ed.), *Leisure: Modernity, postmodernity, and lifestyles* (Publication No. 48, pp. 309–321). Brighton, United Kingdom: Leisure Studies Association.

deGrazia, S. (1962). *Of time, work, and leisure.* New York: Twentieth Century Fund.

Diener, E., & Diener, M. (1995). Cross-cultural correlates of life satisfaction and self-esteem. *Journal of Personality and Social Psychology, 68,* 653–663.

Diener, E., & Suh, E. M. (Eds.). (2000). *Culture and subjective well-being.* Cambridge, MA: MIT Press.

Fiero, G. K. (1998). *The humanistic tradition: The first civilizations and the classical legacy.* New York: McGraw-Hill.

Fisher, J. F. (1990). *Sherpas: Reflections on change in Himalayan Nepal.* Berkeley: University of California Press.

Godbey, G. (1997). *Leisure and leisure services in the 21st century.* State College, PA: Venture.

Godbey, G. (1999). *Leisure in your life: An exploration.* State College, PA: Venture.

Grobler, J. E. H. (1985, April). The developing patterns of leisure time activities in South Africa's black cities since ca. 1930. *World Leisure and Recreation Association Magazine,* 35–41.

Haviland, W. A. (1990). *Cultural anthropology.* Orlando, FL: Holt, Rinehart, and Winston.

Heider, K. (1977). From Javanese to Dani: The translation of a game. In P. Stevens (Ed.), *Studies in the anthropology of play.* West Point, NY: Leisure Press.

International Association of Antarctica Tour Operators. (2004). Antarctic tourism overview. Retrieved February 10, 2003, from www.iaato.org

Jung, B. (1992, Winter). Economic, social and political conditions for enjoyment of leisure in Central and Eastern Europe of 1992—The Polish perspective. *World Leisure and Recreation Association Magazine,* 8–12.

Kelly, J. (1999). Leisure and society: A dialectical analysis. In E. L. Jackson, & T. L. Burton (Eds.), *Leisure studies: Prospects for the twenty-first century.* State College, PA: Venture.

Kelly, J. R., & Freysinger, V. J. (2000). *21st century leisure: Current issues.* Boston: Allyn & Bacon.

Kovacs, A. (2003). *Culture and subjective well-being.* Unpublished manuscript.

Lavenda, R. H., & Schultz, E. A. (2000). *Core concepts in cultural anthropology.* Mountain View, CA: Mayfield.

Linton, R. (1936). *The study of man: An introduction.* New York: Appleton.

MacCannell, D. (1999). *The tourist: A new theory of the leisure class.* Berkley: University of California Press.

McDonald's. (2000). Timeline. Retrieved February 11, 2004, from www.media.mcdonalds.com

Menzel, P. (1994). *Material world: A global family portrait.* San Francisco: Sierra Club Books.

Moffatt, M. (1989). *Coming of age in New Jersey: College and American culture.* New Brunswick, NJ: Rutgers University Press.

Nielsen Media Research. (2003). Statistics. Retrieved February 10, 2004, from www.nielsenmedia.com

Rubenstein, J. M. (2003). *The cultural landscape: An introduction to human geography.* Upper Saddle River, NJ: Pearson Education.

Ryff, C. D., & Keyes, C. L. M. (1995). The structure of psychological well-being revisited. *Journal of Personality and Social Psychology, 69,* 719–727.

Sahlins, M. (1988). The original affluent society. In J. B. Cole (Ed.), *Anthropology for the nineties.* New York: The Free Press.

Shivers, J. S., & deLisle, L. J. (1997). *The story of leisure: Context, concepts, and current controversy.* Champaign, IL: Human Kinetics.

Smith, A. (1980). *The geopolitics of information: How Western culture dominates the world.* New York: Oxford University Press.

Tsai, E. H. (2000). The influence of acculturation on perception of leisure constraints of Chinese immigrants. *World Leisure, 3,* 33–41.

White, L. (1959). *The evolution of culture: The development of civilization to the fall of Rome.* New York: McGraw-Hill.

World Leisure. (2004). Home page. Retrieved January 30, 2004, from www.worldleisure.org

Zhang, D. H., & Fang, L. K. (1998). *An introduction to Chinese culture.* Beijing, China: Beijing Normal University Press

Leisure's Geography

Preview

What is the geographical significance of leisure?

Leisure takes place in space and place, the basic concepts of geography.

How is leisure explained as space?

The distribution of leisure according to pattern, density, and concentration explains both where and why people engage in pastimes.

How is leisure explained as place?

People have a strong attachment to specific leisure places.

What does the geographical significance of leisure mean for the future of leisure?

The environmental impact of leisure must be managed; otherwise, many forms of it will be lost.

Key Terms

Geography 172
Climate 173
Density 175
Concentration 175
Pattern 176
Crowding 178
Distance decay 180
Space-time compression . . .181
Smellscape 182
Place attachment 184

Place identity 185
Conservation 188
Preservation 188
Multiple use 190
Single use 190
Dispersed use 190
Carrying capacity 190
Wilderness 190
Sustainable tourism 191

R ecent world events lend a sense of urgency to understanding geography. Does the world face an overpopulation crisis? Will the planet have an adequate energy supply? Why are world refugee flows at unprecedentedly high levels? Why can't people from different world regions get along?

Geography is the scientific study of where things are located on the earth's surface and the reasons for the location (Rubenstein, 2003). Geographers investigate the way people respond to place and how space is shaped by human behavior (Smale, 1999). For example, we know that the home is a more satisfying place of leisure for men than it is for women (Henderson, Bialeschki, Shaw, & Freysinger, 1996). Or we know how differently we feel when we are in a large crowd at a football game versus in a large crowd along a wilderness trail. We also know that some neighborhoods are more compatible for having backyard cookouts with neighbors than other neighborhoods.

> **Geography:** the study of location on the earth

One major geographic factor that helps us understand leisure is climate. Climate determines not only those pastimes we choose for different seasons of the year, but also where we choose to travel for vacations. Climate is determined by location; thus, pastime choices are also location related. For example, the beaches in the northeastern United States are among the finest in the world. However, the area's climate limits their use for sunning and swimming only to the summer months. In contrast, the climate of Hawaii makes it attractive for beach activities throughout the year.

From Your Own Experience

Climate Change and Your Leisure
Box 6.1

Scientists agree that climate changes occurred during the 20th century. The earth's surface temperature rose one degree (Fahrenheit), with most of this warming happening at night. Spring now comes earlier and fall now leaves later. The higher temperature caused the sea levels to rise, mountain glaciers to recede, and permafrost to melt. The warmer air held more moisture, so the amounts of clouds, precipitation totals, and heavy downpours increased.

Scientists also agree that the rate and magnitude of climate change will increase in the current century. In fact, temperatures could rise as much as eight degrees worldwide by 2100. Accordingly, scientists expect plant and animal species to migrate poleward, upslope, and inland. Warm-water fish will replace cold-water species in lakes and streams.

Is it possible that these current and expected climate changes will affect your own pastimes? In the table below, using the information from scientists presented above, prophesize about some climate-related changes possible in your favorite recreational pursuits. Share and discuss these with your classmates.

	Possible positive changes	Possible negative changes
My winter pastimes?		
My summer pastimes?		

What is climate? **Climate** refers to the average conditions of temperature, barometric pressure, and precipitation in an area over a long period of time (Davidoff, Davidoff, & Eyre, 1988). It is different from weather, which refers to the current condition. Climate is primarily determined by latitude. The earth is divided into five basic climatic zones, based on latitudinal position (Fig. 6.1), and expressions of leisure are determined accordingly. For example, for people in the colder climatic zones, the impact of temperature makes a difference in their activities. Cold affects us like a stimulant, inspiring us to get our heat-producing muscles moving. We stamp our feet and rub our arms to warm up at a football game. On the other hand, for people living in warmer climatic zones, heat is a sedative. Since we don't want to warm up, we lounge under shade trees and take naps.

> **Climate:** the average conditions of temperature, barometric pressure, and precipitation in an area over a long period of time

Other climatic variables are involved in determining leisure behavior. These include altitude (mountain skiing has a longer season than valley skiing), prevailing wind patterns (wind surfing is great on Lake Champlain), and water and air currents (the warm winters in Iceland extend the hiking season even though it is on the same latitude as Canada and Greenland).

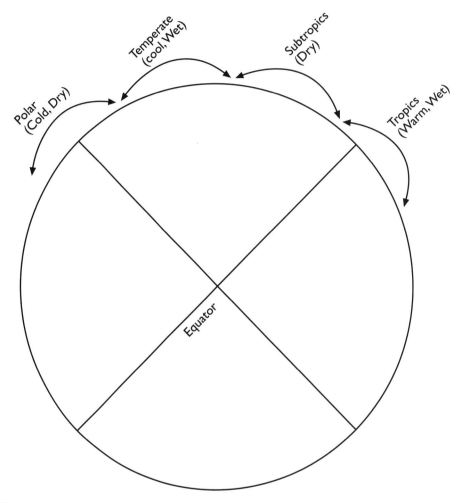

Figure 6.1
The earth's basic climatic zones.

Another geographically determined explanation of leisure is the amount of urbanization. As we considered in Chapter 3, living in urban, suburban, or rural locations determines our leisure interests and choices. As demonstrated in Table 6.1, leisure activities are distributed differently according to geography.

Place and space are central aspects of all human behavior. In this chapter we explore some of the ways we can understand leisure behavior as a geographical concept according to the ideas of space and place. We conclude the chapter by reviewing a particularly relevant geographic leisure concern: environmental impact.

Table 6.1

Distribution of Leisure According to Urban/Rural Differences

Environment	Activities	Facilities
Urban	Shopping, dining, drinking, tourism, plays, concerts, films	Shops, malls, theaters, bars, restaurants, museums, libraries
Suburban	Walking, bicycling, shopping, working out, swimming, youth sports, picnicking	Malls, sports fields, gyms, parks, lineartrails, courts, swimming pools
Rural	Hiking, sightseeing by car, visiting friends and family, boating, snow skiing, horse back riding	Parks, country roads, lakes and reservoirs, mountains, rivers, beaches

Leisure as Space

The famous German philosopher Immanuel Kant (1724–1804) compared the concern of geography for space with the concern of history for time. Historians identify the dates of important events and explain why human activities follow one another across time. Geographers identify the location of important places and explain why human activities are located beside one another in space. Whereas historians ask when and why, geographers ask where and why (Rubenstein, 2003).

To do this, the basic principles of density, concentration, and pattern are of interest. The frequency with which something occurs in space is its **density**. This frequency of something in space could be people, houses, cars, parks, green open spaces, or almost anything. The space could be measured in square kilometers, square miles, hectares, acres, or any other unit used to measure area. **Concentration** is the extent of a feature's spread over space. If the objects in an area are close together, they are clustered, or if they are relatively far apart, they are dispersed.

> **Density:** the frequency with which something occurs in space

> **Concentration:** the extent of a feature's spread over space

Concentration is not the same as density (Rubenstein, 2003). For example, in North America the distribution of major-league baseball teams changed during the second half of the 20th century (Fig. 6.2). On the one hand, the number of major-league teams expanded from 16 to 30 between 1952 and 2000, thus increasing the density. At the same time, six of the 16 original teams moved to other locations. In 1952 every team was clustered in the northeastern United States, but after the teams moved, they were dispersed to the west coast and the Southeast as well. This resulted in a more dispersed concentration of teams.

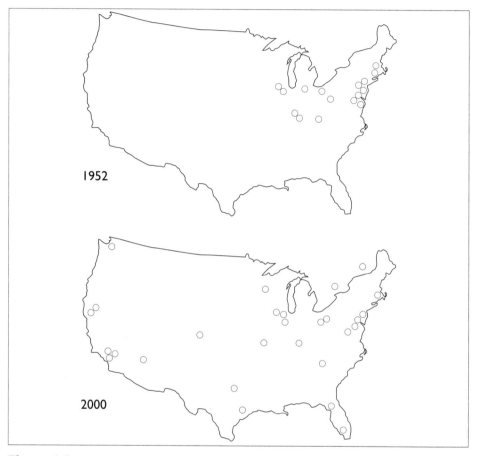

Figure 6.2
Density and concentration of baseball teams in North America from 1952 to 2000. (Adapted from Rubenstein, 2003, p. 6. Used with permission.)

The third property of space is pattern. **Pattern** is the geometric arrangement of objects in space. Objects such as boat slips at a marina and campsites at a campground can be arranged linearly, in squares, in circles, and so on. For example, Figure 6.3 shows the campground map for the Kentucky Horse Park in Lexington. The planners of the campground consider it an efficient use of the available space to arrange campers in two sets of concentric circles. As a camper, what might the camping experience be like with this pattern?

> **Pattern:** the geometric arrangement of objects in space

Let's now consider two specific applications of our understanding of the concepts of density, concentration, and patterns of leisure in space: crowding and distance.

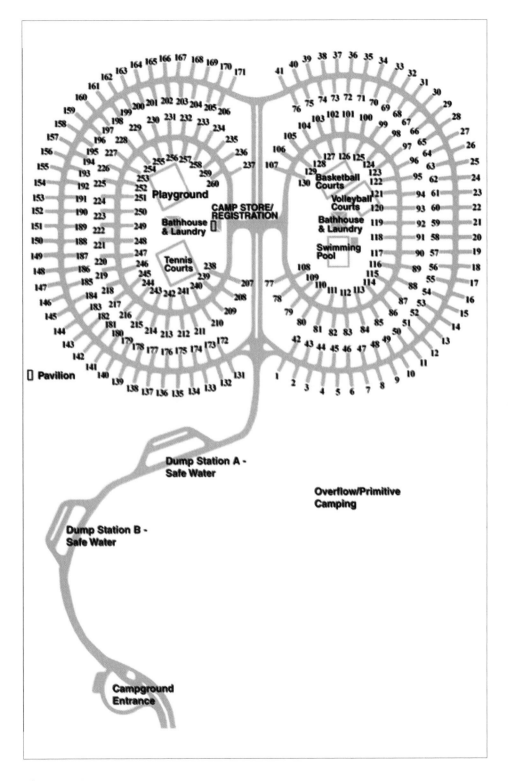

Figure 6.3

Campground map of the Kentucky Horse Park, Lexington, Kentucky,
(http://www.kyhorsepark.com/khp/campground/campmap.asp. Retrieved 2/16/04).

Crowding in Leisure

All of us who visit parks have probably already noticed. Because more of us are visiting parks than ever before, parks are becoming more crowded (Manning, 1999). Unfortunately, this means that not only are more people experiencing this important leisure resource, but they are also experiencing automobile congestion; full parking lots, campgrounds, and lodges; long lines for services; overtaxed rangers and staff; more stringent rules and regulations; higher fees and mandatory use permits; conflicts among visitors; and often degraded parks (Lime, 1996).

At Mount Rainier National Park in Washington, for example, park rangers have become "parking rangers" as they regularly try to cram up to 600 cars into a 250-space parking area for the daily sunrise. At Gettysburg National Military Park in Pennsylvania, monuments are being hit and even knocked down by motorists seeking a parking spot. Such urban-style congestion has spawned urban-style solutions. For instance, at Yosemite National Park in California, a shuttle service has been put into place to transport people from their cars in parking lots outside the park (as many as 7,000 cars daily during peak season) into the park's central valley. At the Grand Canyon National Park in Arizona, lower entrance fees are offered for visitors who use buses to shuttle from viewpoint to viewpoint (Foster, 2001).

Crowding is a value judgment applied to density. That is, the number of visitors to parks (density) may increase to a point where visitors and managers perceive that their use of the park is interfered with. The result is crowding. Whereas density is a neutral concept, crowding is a negative evaluation of density. It's the sort of concept that is difficult to pin down, but we know it when we see it! For example, think of a recent vacation you've taken. If you've returned home realizing you've experienced a different type of trip than expected, or if you've taken steps to avoid encountering other people during the trip, your vacation was crowded.

> **Crowding:** a subjective and negative judgment about the number of people in a given space

Researchers, particularly those in outdoor recreation, have studied how we determine perceptions of crowding. For example, studies have found that perceptions of crowding can result from

- **the personal characteristics of visitors**

- **the characteristics of other visitors encountered**

- **the nature of the outdoor setting**

First, in terms of the personal characteristics of visitors, several studies have demonstrated differences in visitor motivations are the source of differences in perceptions of crowding. A study of visitors to the Buffalo National River found a wide diversity in the perceived crowding among a sample of river floaters. Those visitors who felt crowded reported significantly higher ratings on the motivation "to get away from other people." Other visitors who did not feel crowded while floating down the river rated the motivation "to be part of a group" higher (Ditton, Fedler, & Graefe, 1983). Also, one's experience level has been found to affect perceptions of crowding. For example, in one study (Murray, 1974), more experienced hikers on the Appalachian Trail expressed stronger preferences for low-density hiking.

In terms of the characteristics of other visitors encountered, it seems only reasonable to think that tolerance for meeting lots of other people in a leisure setting would depend to some extent on what these other people were like. For example, studies in the Boundary Waters Canoe Area Wilderness (Manning, 1999) found that paddling canoeists sharply disliked encountering motorboats, were less resentful of encountering motorized canoes, and were relatively tolerant of at least some other paddled canoes. Thus, canoeists tolerated crowding at much lower levels when motorboats were present.

The third characteristic determining perceptions of crowding is situation specific. From my own interests in camping, I know that I have a sliding scale for feeling crowded depending on whether I'm in a highly developed RV campground or an unimproved campground reached by walking (Fig. 6.4). Certain design aspects of a site, such as trees or hedges between sites, can also affect one's sense of crowding. Similarly, research has shown that the level of environmental disturbance is also related to crowding. That is, those trails, campsites, and rivers that are trashed from overuse are perceived as crowded (Vaske, Graefe, & Dempster, 1982).

Figure 6.4

Crowded conditions are often more tolerated at a commercial campground than in government-sponsored campgrounds. (© Ruth V. Russell.)

Leisure and Distance

In addition to crowding, distance is another consideration of geographic space and leisure. Are we likely to work out at the gym every day if it is across the street from our house, across town, or across the region? How fantastic does the gym need to be for us to be willing to travel across our region to use it? Distance is important in influencing our behavior, including our leisure behavior. Notice in Figure 6.5 how distance affects participation rates for different types of recreational sites.

As this figure illustrates, a neighborhood park might attract large numbers of users from nearby, but participation drops off as distance to a shopping center or theme park increases. Participation results from a combination of the distance from the user's residence and the type of recreation facility available. As a site's appeal becomes more specialized, smaller proportions of people are willing to travel farther distances. Geographers call this **distance decay**. Different recreational sites have varying abilities to draw participants to them (Smale, 1999).

> **Distance decay:** increases in distance that bring about decreases in most forms of behavior

But, of course, it is not always so simple. In today's world, more rapid connections among places and regions have reduced the distance between them—

not literally in miles, of course, but in the effort to get there. Geographers call this **space–time compression**. Thanks to technological advances in transportation and communication, distant places seem less remote and more accessible to us. Thus, distances to recreational sites might be perceived in terms of time or cost rather than by miles or kilometers. To demonstrate this for yourself, ask your friends who live in large metropolitan areas how far away something is. Their responses are likely to be in terms of the number of minutes it takes to drive there rather than the mileage.

> **Space–time compression:** the reduction in the time it takes to travel to a distant place as a result of improved communication and transportation systems

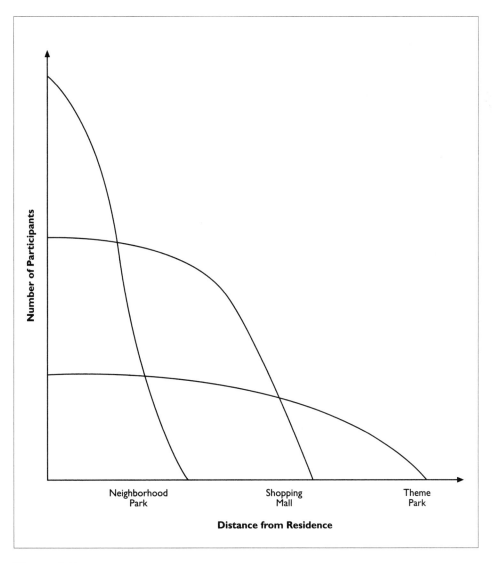

Figure 6.5

Impact of the distance from a residence on the number of participants. (Adapted from Smale, 1999.)

The principle of space–time compression suggests that if the distance to a recreation site is perceived to be less or greater than its actual physical distance, the perception may have more influence on potential participation in the recreational activity than does the actual distance. What this means is that it may not really matter how far away a leisure opportunity is if it is perceived to be attainable. As with crowding in leisure, the perception of distance is what controls leisure behavior.

Leisure as Place

We humans have a strong sense of place. That is, we have feelings for the distinctiveness of particular places. The Golden Gate Bridge in San Francisco, Graceland in Memphis, Yankee Stadium in New York City, Vieux-Quebec in Quebec City, and Horseshoe Falls at Niagara are all particular places to which many people attach strong feelings. What might it be for you? When you think about leisure places that have been meaningful to you, what comes to mind?

> *Imagine red and brown sandstone towers rising out of the desert floor. Imagine the sun setting with black silhouettes of ocotillo cacti vertically slicing the horizon. This describes Juniper Canyon in Texas' Big Bend National Park, which is a special place to me. (Presley, 2003, p. 22)*

And we are not limited only to the visual for our sense of place. The sense of smell is also important. Scholars refer to this as **smellscape**, a concept that suggests that, "like visual impressions, smells may be spatially ordered or place related" (Porteous, 1985, p. 359). Think of the community gym you knew as a youth. Do you associate this fond memory with a smell? There is perhaps no better illustration of this concept than the calculated management of smell at The Magic Kingdom in Disney theme parks. Frontierland smells like leather and gun smoke, and the ride "Pirates of the Caribbean" smells of musty spices.

Smellscape: a concept that suggests that smells are place related

We can perhaps learn most about smellscape from descriptions of travel. For example, in E. M. Forster's novel *A Room With a View*, Miss Lavish proclaims she senses "true Florentine smell" (1928, p. 37), and an advertisement for a suite in Los Angeles' Hotel Bel Air describes "a fire roaring with scented avocado wood, and the French windows can open onto a private herb garden" (Mather, 2001, p.1). Indeed, many travel writers and promoters of tourism fill their accounts with the aromatic framing of places. Even Plato referred to the genuine pleasure of a delightful smell (Tefler, 1996).

This is a difficult area to discuss, because just as beauty is in the eye of the beholder, so too are aromas. Nonetheless, a study by Dann and Jacobsen

(2003) examined the association of smell with tourist sites by studying classical and contemporary travel diaries and essays. In all, they analyzed 65 accounts, 20 that referred to rural settings and 45 that described urban settings. The findings suggested a definite trend toward romantically portraying the countryside as smelling more pleasurable than the city. Thus, the study pointed out that for an urban tourist destination to succeed, it must have the aromatic equivalent of a voyeur—the rich, sensory experience of hot dogs and pizzas on Lexington Avenue in New York, and the spices and flowers of ethnically diverse Kuala Lumpur in Malaysia.

In addition to sight and smell, our emotional attachment to special leisure places is based on a kinesthetic sense. For example, the vast number of mountain resorts scattered over the earth is testimony to the fact that many of us feel emotionally elevated at moderately high altitudes—a kind of mountain high. This is perhaps why we associate certain spiritual practices, such as meditation, with high mountains. As naturalist John Muir observed in 1901, "Thousands of tired, nerve-shaken, over-civilized people [have found] that going to the mountains is going home; that wildness is a necessity" (p. 1).

When you ask people who love mountains to explain what is so special there, the reply is likely to be "just something in the air." So is the connection respiratory? It's less humid in the mountains; there is a better quality of air. But while there are "mountain people," there are definitely also "ocean people," who would describe their favorite places in euphoric terms as well. So perhaps mountain magic and ocean magic are a matter of simple, unexplainable aesthetics.

The Study Says

The Evolution of Our Preferences for Nature

Box 6.2

Some intriguing studies have been reported that explain our preferences in nature according to our evolution as human beings. Findings maintain that Homo sapiens, like other species, are inclined to favor the environment that helped to establish their genetic script. For example, during our long evolution as hunters and gatherers on the East African savannah, we developed a taste for the kind of terrain we as modern humans continue to prefer in paintings, drawings, and photographs. We like natural scenes the best, with a meandering creek and a thundering waterfall. Next comes our preference for open vistas, such as an open meadow punctuated by trees, bushes, and shelter. According to Orians (1986),

In studies of preferences for natural things, the bottom line is that we're attracted to widely spaced trees and smooth ground textures that allow easy locomotion. If a setting is forested, we like open spaces in it, and if it's prairie-like, we like some trees. This preference is consistent across cultures. Around the world people create open parkland and gardens reflecting this same sensibility. (p. 42)

Yet the fact remains that most people do have places that are special to them, and perhaps it is this association with a particular place that is so vital to what leisure means. Researchers have explored the role of places in leisure experiences. Two primary areas of inquiry are centered on the concepts of place attachment and leisure identity through place. Let's explore both of these.

Place Attachment

Researchers have measured the strength of place attachment between recreation participants and settings. **Place attachment** is the label used for the emotional bond between people and particular places. For example, Bricker and Kerstetter (2000) investigated how place attachment varied with levels of specialization among whitewater boaters. They found that more specialized whitewater boaters had stronger place attachments. Why is this so? What is the meaning of a strong place attachment?

> **Place attachment: an emotional bond that develops between a person and a certain place**

To understand this, researchers have also begun to investigate the complex and differing meanings recreation participants attach to places. For example, various studies have suggested that people develop place attachments in leisure for different reasons. According to the research of Bricker and Kerstetter (2002), whitewater river place meanings included repose, peace, beauty, wildness, an appreciation of nature, reverence, and a need to protect the river. And Williams and Patterson (1999) found that the meanings people generally assign to natural places fall into the categories of aesthetic, instrumental goal-directed, cultural symbolic, and individually expressive.

These differences in the meanings of place attachment help to explain why there are conflicts over places. Different people and cultures prioritize place meanings differently. For example, white Americans attach the highest priority to an individually expressive meaning of place, followed by an instrumental goal-directed meaning, and then a cultural symbolic meaning. For many Native Americans, the priority given to the meaning of a place is just the opposite (McAvoy, 2002).

From Your Own Experience
Campus Places
Box 6.3

An easy demonstration of how people attach feelings to places can be made on your own campus. Interview alumni of your college or university and ask them to recall the places on campus that hold special meaning to them. What is the meaning attached to these places? How did these places become meaningful for them? When they return to visit campus, must they visit these places? How do these visits make them feel? After the interviews, think about your own place attachments on campus. What places will you miss, and why?

Thus, places are an important part of the leisure experience. People value their relationships to leisure places just as much as they might value relationships with other people or with specific recreational activities (Presley, 2003). According to Williams (2002), "we choose leisure places not merely because they are useful for leisure, but to convey the very sense of who we are" (p. 353). You might consider such place identity as a specific case of place attachment. Let's explore this idea of identity through leisure places a bit more.

Place Identity

As we have explored in earlier chapters, leisure provides opportunities for people to create and develop personal and group identities. In leisure in particular, place meanings help translate individual values and behaviors. This is the concept of **place identity**. Leisure places have meaning to us because of who they affirm us to be: "I'm a mountain person" or "Only a Winnebago for me."

> **Place identity:** a place as a source of identification and affiliation for a person

Indeed, some scholars (e.g.,Williams, 2002) maintain that because of the process of modernization in society, leisure places are becoming an increasingly important source of identity. As modernity sweeps away tradition, our sense of self is no longer passively awarded to us by our original homes and neighborhoods. We can't go home again! No longer do things stay the same from generation to generation, where hometowns create and anchor our sense of identity. As Godbey (1999) declares, we have become nomads. Yet we still need a sense of self associated with a place. Perhaps leisure places provide for this now. Perhaps this is what the youth are seeking when they hang out at the mall, or what explains the allure of the "leisure world" village for retirees, or why the neighborhood sports bar is "home" for men.

In Profile

The Motor Home
Box 6.4

It is hard to say when the motor home began. In the 1880s a horse-drawn replica Gypsy wagon was a favorite vacation vehicle in England. Americans did not own camping vehicles in large numbers, however, until automobiles were mass-produced in the early 20th century. By 1920 millions of auto campers were sleeping in cars or in tents attached to their cars, and hundreds had purchased trailers with built-in folding tents. Hundreds more built wooden house bodies and placed them on automobile chassis. Called a "housecar," they offered a portable parlor and bedroom, and a picture window on America (Fig. 6.6).

But it wasn't until the 1960s that Americans chose factory-built motor homes over their own inventions. Nationwide sales of housecars began when a small manufacturer of house bodies in Michigan linked up with the Dodge Division of Chrysler Corporation to manufacture

Figure 6.6

Mr. And Mrs. Kinnear with their housecar, Yellowstone National Park, 1925. (Courtesy of Yellowstone National Park, National Park Service Historic Photograph Collection.)

the Frank Motor Home. This wood-and-aluminum motor home sold for about $7,000. Since then, with Winnebago in the lead, between 1961 and 1973 output soared from 200 to 65,300 motor homes per year. In 1992 Winnebago rolled out its 250,000th motor home, and today, with 87 different floor plans (Fig. 6.7), Winnebago has come to symbolize and reaffirm the American identity as both staying home and wandering away (White, 2000).

Figure 6.7
The interior of a Winnebago Adventurer (2004, Model 37B). All the comforts of home.
(© Ruth V. Russell.)

Oldenburg (1989) calls these the "great good places." Accordingly, these great good places are categorized as "third places," a term he uses to describe the many public places that host "regular, voluntary, informal, and happily anticipated gatherings of individuals" (p. 16) beyond the home (the first place) and work and school (the second place). Third places may take many forms, such as cafes, coffee shops, bars, beauty shops, general stores, community centers, and street-corner hangouts. Oldenburg sees them has having virtue in relieving stress and providing identity. They do so, according to him, by providing a home away from home. The third place provides an accessible, socially neutral ground that encourages a playful mood for regulars to engage in their main activity: conversation (Wenner, 1998).

One analogy for understanding the significance of leisure places as identity makers might be religious holy places. As you know, religions elevate particular places to a significant position. This could be Mecca for Muslims, the Ganges River for Hindus, or Bethlehem for Christians. Further, to practice a religion often means making a pilgrimage to these holy places. We can perhaps relate this idea of making a pilgrimage to a holy place with tourism. What does it mean to a tourist's sense of identity to hike in the shadow of the world's tallest mountains in Nepal and Tibet, or to fit one's own foot into the concrete foot indention of John Wayne or Marilyn Monroe at Grauman's Chinese Theatre in Hollywood? Anyone who has ever crawled off a plane after a long flight only to perk up as if by magic at the sight of the Eiffel Tower or Lake Louise knows something about the spiritual power of leisure places.

Environmental Impact

As suggested earlier in this chapter, growth in outdoor recreation and tourism has fueled global concern for a special case of leisure's geography, namely, the pressure on the environment applied by people's expressions of leisure. Considerable debate surrounds the question of the extent and significance to the environment of the impact of leisure, and the appropriateness of policy priorities and management strategies to address these problems (Swinnerton, 1999).

For example, in Canada the impact of human use on the country's most visited national park, Banff, has been the focus of particular attention. Park officials there and elsewhere have called for a "regreening" of national parks–their reinstatement as models of ecological harmony (Sellers, 1997). In many respects, the future of leisure depends on this. With the destruction of soil, water, forest, energy, and animal resources, many forms of recreation would be possible only as indoor, artificial, or simulated experiences.

At the root of the solution are the concepts of conservation and preservation. **Conservation** involves the scientific and rational planning of natural resources for their best use. Conservation also implies the renewal of resources as they become damaged. Conservation is a different concept from preservation. The **preservation** of natural resources means they are protected from human influence. Preservation applies mainly to non-renewable resources, whereas conservation involves primarily renewable resources (Jensen, 1995). Conservation refers to managing deer populations with hunting, whereas preservation is keeping recreationists out of bald eagle habitat.

> **Conservation:** the most efficient use of natural resources over the long term

> **Preservation:** protection of natural resources from human damage

But it wasn't always this way. It wasn't until around the turn of the last century that North American scientists and political leaders became concerned about natural resources. Before then, during the 18th and 19th centuries, North Americans tended to view their natural environment as something to be mastered. This attitude not only encouraged the movement westward and the settlement of nations from ocean to ocean, but it also led to the exploitation of nature. Settlers cut forests, leaving denuded landscapes; farmers grew crops until the soil could no longer nourish them; industrialists used water without much thought for purity. These traditions began to change as the United States and Canada became urbanized. Accordingly, various "movements" emerged with slightly different agendas for what to do about the problems. The conservation movement was different from the preservation movement, and thereafter, both were different from the various environmental movements of today.

The Study Says
Swatting Litter Bugs
Box 6.5

Among various types of visitor impacts to natural resources are those caused by littering, collecting specimen samples, feeding wildlife, not picking up after pets, and other nonconservation behaviors. With increasing participation in outdoor recreation, these problems are likely to intensify. Researchers and managers have implemented numerous direct and indirect actions to encourage conservation, although not always with complete success.

For example, one study evaluated the effectiveness of using fear and morals in written appeals to reduce deer feeding by visitors. Changes in visitor behavior were measured as a result of reading signs placed on picnic tables. The fear appeal (there are risks to people from feeding deer) reduced the feeding of deer by 39 percent, and the moral appeal (feeding deer is not good for the area's ecology) reduced this behavior by only 25 percent (reported in Wirshing, Leung, & Attarian, 2003).

Many management strategies are available to achieve the conservation and preservation of natural resources for leisure. These include multiple use, dispersed use, single use, knowing the carrying capacity, and assigning a wilderness designation (Jensen, 1995). The concept of **multiple use** encourages managers to make resources in a region available for a variety of uses. This is the strategy chosen for some government-owned land. For example, in the United States, the Bureau of Land Management and the Forest Service have a policy of using land and water resources for a variety of purposes including timbering, watershed protection, and outdoor recreation. On the other hand, the concept of **single use** stipulates that some resources have restricted use. Perhaps the most prominent example is the national park system. The historical, archaeological, cultural, and scenic qualities of the parks are managed solely for the benefit and enjoyment of people. The management concept of **dispersed use** encourages spreading use over an entire area, rather than concentrating it in a particular area. For example, a deer herd habitat extends over an entire region; thus, hunting activities are dispersed to a wider range.

> **Multiple use:** within a locale, the use of natural areas in several ways

> **Single use:** the use of natural areas for one major purpose, such as recreation

> **Dispersed use:** making sure that all parts of a natural area are used evenly to avoid damage from overuse of a particular area

Originally used for managing wildlife and range animals, determinations of **carrying capacity** have been a very useful management strategy for outdoor recreation as well. Using this strategy, standards are determined for the "saturation point" of recreational use of a natural resource. Although the main concern is for the biological carrying capacity, such as the impact of people on soil compaction, altered stream flows, and the destruction of vegetation, it also includes the idea of psychological carrying capacity—the impact of people on people. Unfortunately, we are well aware of the social impacts of exceeding the carrying capacity of an area. Not only do these impacts include perceptions of crowding, as discussed earlier in the chapter, but they also may mean increased crime.

> **Carrying capacity:** the number of a species that a habitat can support without permanently damaging it

Finally, conservation and preservation also can be achieved through the establishment of wilderness areas. **Wilderness** areas include desert, forest, water, and coastal resources. The point is that minimal human intervention is allowed in these specified remote and rugged areas. In the United States, with the passing of the 1964 Wilderness Act, areas with this legal designation are protected from all human changes and impact. No motorized equipment can enter wilderness areas, few signs or recreational facilities can be added, and commercial activities are very limited. Because of its many restrictions on use, the wilderness concept is controversial.

> **Wilderness:** nationally designated and protected wild areas where human use is very restricted

In Focus

Trouble in the Woods
Box 6.6

In today's parks, while families camp and boat and enjoy the beauty of nature, park rangers are suiting up in camouflage to fight drug dealers, smugglers, and even, on occasion, terrorists. "We've had rapes, we've had murders in the park," said Dale Antonich, chief ranger at the Lake Mead National Recreation Area, located about an hour outside Las Vegas. Lake Mead is one of America's busiest parks. Each year 36 rangers try to safeguard some eight million visitors, policing more than 1.5 million acres of land and nearly 750 miles of shoreline. Annually, rangers respond to more than 20,000 incidents, ranging from drunken driving, to assault, to suicide. Of these, nearly 1,400 warrant criminal investigation ("Trouble in Paradise," 2003).

Questions to Consider and Discuss

1. *How prevalent are these kinds of problems in the parks where you live? Contact the manager of a city or county park near you. Inquire about the incidence of crimes there and the actions managers are taking to attempt to reduce the impact of these crimes.*

2. *Why do you think these crimes take place in parks? As geographic places, what might be the qualities of parks that provide opportunities for crime?*

3. *How might crimes in parks relate to concepts of the distribution of leisure in space? Are there clues for understanding this from the geographic concepts of density, concentration, or pattern?*

One of the best illustrations of the usefulness of these conservation and preservation measures is the recent concern for sustainable tourism. Because tourism depends almost wholly on the environment, if the environment is degraded, most forms of tourism diminish. Sustainable tourism implies not consuming natural resources at a higher rate than they can be protected or replaced. Mass tourism is usually not sustainable. Sustainable tourism promotes low-impact forms, including small tour groups and low-energy-consuming modes of transportation. Other labels for sustainable tourism might be eco-tourism or green tourism.

> **Sustainable tourism:** controlling visitation to tourist sites, even over economic gain

In Profile

Backroads
Box 6.7

Backroads is an adventure travel company. It offers luxury accommodations, fine dining in five-star restaurants, and tours to some of the world's most unique and beautiful regions. But this is not what makes Backroads special. It is its attention to sustainable tourism. Very small groups of Backroads tourists travel to these hotels and restaurants via their own efforts–walking, biking, and kayaking. They abide by the "leave no trace" philosophy and directly support the wildlife, cultures, and natural resources of the areas visited. Check them out at http://www.backroads.com.

Summary: What We Understand

From the perspective of geography, leisure can be understood as having meaning in space and place. As a result of reading this chapter, you should know that

- The distribution of leisure in space differs according to density, concentration, and pattern.

- Crowding in leisure is a contemporary problem of density.

- Distance affects participation rates for different types of leisure sites.

- Attaching strong sentiment to leisure places comes from our visual, olfactory, and kinesthetic senses.

- Strong leisure place attachments contribute to our self-identity.

- Considerable debate surrounds the question of the extent and significance of the environmental impact of leisure.

Applications to Professional Practice

In this chapter, parks were frequently used to demonstrate geographical concepts. Indeed, parks are a fundamental component of leisure resources. Although essentially all parks can be defined as tracts of land or water that serve the aesthetic and recreational needs of people, they accomplish this goal in different ways. Usually these distinctions are made according to the type of park (Table 6.2).

Table 6.2

Types of Parks

Park type	Definition	Purpose	Example
Minipark	A small park of up to one acre	To be within a 10-minute walk	Park Ridge Mini-Park, Bloomington, Indiana
Neighborhood park	Serves up to 5,000 people in an immediate locale	To serve a single residential area	Huber Village Park, Westerville, Ohio
Community (city) park	Serves an entire town or city	To serve multiple neighborhoods	Balboa Park, San Diego, California
Regional park	Serves users from several communities and rural areas. Often governed by coalitions of city and county governments	To serve users from a wide area	Fort De Soto Island Park, Tampa Bay area, Florida
State/provincial park	Serves an even broader jurisdiction, with historical or natural significance. Governed by state or provincial governments	More remote from population centers	Amherst Shore Provincial Park, Nova Scotia
National park	An area of special scenic, historical, or scientific importance set aside and maintained by a national government	To protect natural resources and provide enjoyment for users	Great Smokey Mountains National Park in Tennessee and North Carolina
Linear park	Area designated for walking, biking, skiing, horseback riding, driving	To provide for travel-related, self-propelled leisure	Cape Cod Rail Trail, Massachusetts

The smallest type of park is the minipark. This is a small area (up to about one acre) that typically provides shade trees and benches for sitting and some children's play equipment. Most miniparks are located in residential areas or downtown business areas, as they are designed to be within a 10-minute walk of users.

Next in size are neighborhood parks. As the label suggests, these parks are intended to serve a particular residential locale. Communities are divided either officially or attitudinally into neighborhoods by such physical or social boundaries as main streets, highways, and ethnic backgrounds. A typical neighborhood has 2,000 to 5,000 people and is up to one mile wide. City planners usually try to locate a neighborhood park (and an elementary school) near the center of each neighborhood. Neighborhood parks range in size from one to 50 acres and provide a wider variety of facilities than miniparks, including swimming pools, sports fields and courts, playgrounds, picnic tables and shelters, and undeveloped natural areas.

Community parks are tracts of land and water that serve several neighborhoods. Some also call these city or district parks. Ideally, each community of 10 to 20 neighborhoods (50,000 to 100,000 people) should have at least one large central park. Community parks range in size from 50 to 300 acres or more. Because they are larger, they are able to provide for larger crowds of users. Facilities often include golf courses, sports fields, picnic areas, playgrounds, swimming pools, bicycling and walking trails, and a special natural feature, such as a lake or stretch of river. Some have beaches, boat rentals, fishing, nature centers, zoos, or gardens.

Major parks, typically located on the outskirts of large cities, are called regional parks. Regional parks are larger (up to about 2,000 acres) and provide a wide range of recreational offerings. They are called regional parks (or metroparks) because they attract users from a wide area and include features not usually found in community parks. These may include ski slopes, marinas, campsites, or nature preserves.

State and provincial parks have an even broader jurisdiction. They differ from community and regional parks in that they usually are more remote from population centers, are of greater historical or natural significance, attract visitors from greater distances, may be larger, and focus more on providing services that relate to the natural environment. State and provincial parks, however, can differ from each other in their purposes. Several state parks in Florida, for example, offer underwater exploration, those in Indiana feature environmental education, and parks specifically for the use of all-terrain vehicles have been created in Delaware. Some parks, such as those in Kentucky and West Virginia, emphasize their appeal as tourist attractions and provide hotel, restaurant, and resort services.

When we think of the "great outdoors," however, many of us immediately picture the Grand Canyon, Old Faithful, or the Banff glaciers. This is because national parks are the finest examples of a nation's heritage. They feature superlative scenery and natural phenomena, and they preserve historic, prehistoric, and scientific areas of great value. A national park is the label reserved for the most superb of natural treasures. National parks have dual roles. They protect the natural resources and provide enjoyment for people who use them.

This means that lodges, restaurants, campgrounds, trail systems, and visitor centers are common services, as are endangered wildlife reintroduction projects, reenactments of historical events, and archeological digs (Fig. 6.8).

Figure 6.8
An example of a national park, the USS Arizona Memorial in Hawaii. Visitors are viewing the sunken ship through observation windows. (© Ruth V. Russell.)

In addition to this park classification, which is primarily organized by size, another park type is becoming more important as a recreation resource. This is the linear park. Linear parks provide leisure experiences for people in the form of travel through them. For example, a lengthy walkway (or promenade) enables people to stroll along a beach, river, or lake shoreline or through a section of a city. The parkway, another form of linear park, is a landscaped road along which people can take slow, relaxing drives. Some parkways are developed as elongated community parks with occasional parking lots, picnic areas, and scenic overlooks. Hiking, bicycling, and horse trails can also be planned as linear parks. These are usually narrow strips of land designated for specific forms of recreational travel and are more frequently built on abandoned railroad beds, on the banks of old canals, along power line right-of-ways, and on easements between private properties. Usually motorized vehicles are not allowed on these trails.

For Further Information

To learn more about parks, explore the park links from the Web sites of towns, cities, counties, states, and provinces near you. Or try these: Alaskan state parks may be found at the state's Department of Natural Resources site at http://www.dnr.state.ak.us/parks/. This site also has a jobs link. The Web site for the National Park Service in the United States is http://www.nps.gov, and for Parks Canada it is http://www.pc.gc.ca. From both of these sites, there are links to more information about employment opportunities.

References

Bricker, K. S., & Kerstetter, D. L. (2000). Level of specialization and place attachment: An exploratory study of whitewater recreationists. *Leisure Sciences, 22,* 233–257.

Bricker, K. S., & Kerstetter, D. L. (2002). An interpretation of special place meanings whitewater recreationists attach to the South Fork of the American River. *Tourism Geographies, 4,* 396–425.

Dann, G. M. S., & Jacobsen, J. K. S. (2003). Tourism smellscapes. *Tourism Geographies, 5,* 3–25.

Davidoff, P. G., Davidoff, D. S., & Eyre, J. D. (1988). *Tourism geography.* Englewood Cliffs, NJ: Prentice Hall.

Ditton, R. B., Fedler, A. J., & Graefe, A. R. (1983). Factors contributing to perceptions of recreational crowding. *Leisure Sciences, 5,* 273–288.

Forster, E. M. (1928). *A room with a view.* London: Edward Arnold.

Foster, G. (2001, May 29). Park ranger now "parking ranger." *Seattle Post-Intelligencer.* Retrieved February 16, 2004, from http://seattlepi.nwsource.com/local/25049_parks29.shtml.

Godbey, G. (1999). *Leisure in your life: An exploration.* State College, PA: Venture.

Henderson, K. A., Bialeschki, M. D., Shaw, S. M., & Freysinger, V. J. (1996). *Both gains and gaps: Feminist perspectives on women's leisure.* State College, PA: Venture.

Jensen, C. R. (1995). *Outdoor recreation in America.* Champaign, IL: Human Kinetics.

Lime, D. W. (Ed.). (1996). *Congestion and crowding in the national park system.* (Minnesota Agricultural Experiment Station Miscellaneous Publication 86-1996). St. Paul: University of Minnesota.

Manning, R. E. (1999). Crowding and carrying capacity in outdoor recreation: From normative standards to standards of quality. In E. L. Jackson, & T. L. Burton (Eds.), *Leisure studies: Prospects for the twenty-first century.* State College, PA: Venture.

Mather, V. (2001, December 9). Heaven on earth. *Sunday Telegraph Travel,* pp. 1–2.

McAvoy, L. (2002). American Indians, place meanings and the old/new West. *Journal of Leisure Research, 34,* 383–396.

Muir, J. (1901). *Our national parks.* Boston: Houghton Mifflin.

Murray, J. B. (1974). *Appalachian Trail users in the Southern national forests: Their characteristics, attitudes, and management preferences* (Research Paper SE-116). Asheville, NC: USDA Forest Service, Southeast Forest Experiment Station.

Oldenburg, R. (1989). *The great good place: Cafes, coffee shops, community centers, beauty parlors, general stores, bars, hangouts, and how they get you through the day.* New York: Paragon House.

Orians, G. H. (1986). An ecological and evolutionary approach to landscape aesthetics. In P. Rousell, & D. Lowenthal (Eds.), *Landscape meanings and values.* London: Allen & Unwin.

Porteous, J. (1985). Smellscape. *Progress in human geography, 9,* 356–378.

Presley, J. (2003, July). In praise of special places. *Parks & Recreation,* 22–29.

Rubenstein, J. M. (2003). *The cultural landscape: An introduction to human geography.* Upper Saddle River, NJ: Pearson Education.

Sellers, R. W. (1997). *Preserving nature in the national parks: A history.* New Haven, CT: Yale University Press.

Smale, B. J. A. (1999). Spatial analysis of leisure and recreation. In E. L. Jackson, & T. L. Burton (Eds.), *Leisure studies: Prospects for the twenty-first century.* State College, PA: Venture.

Swinnerton, G. S. (1999). Recreation and conservation: Issues and prospects. In E. L. Jackson, & T. L. Burton (Eds.), *Leisure studies: Prospects for the twenty-first century.* State College, PA: Venture.

Tefler, E. (1996). *Food for thought: Philosophy and food.* London: Routledge.

Trouble in paradise [television episode]. (2003, July 25). In *20/20.* New York: ABC News. Retrieved February 16, 2004, from http://www.abcnews.go.com/Sections/2020/US/2020_nationalparks030725.html

Vaske, J. J., Graefe, A. R., & Dempster, A. (1982). Social and environmental influences on perceived crowding. In *Proceedings of the Wilderness Psychology Group Conference* (pp. 35–41), Morgantown: West Virginia University.

Wenner, L. A. (1998). In search of the sports bar: Masculinity, alcohol, sports, and the mediation of public space. In G. Rail (Ed.), *Sport and postmodern times* (pp. 210–231). Albany: State University of New York Press.

White, R. (2000). *Home on the road: The motor home in America.* Washington, D.C.: Smithsonian Institution Press.

Williams, D. R. (2002). Leisure identities, globalization, and the politics of place. *Journal of Leisure Research, 34,* 351–367.

Williams, D. R., & Patterson, M. E. (1999). Environmental psychology: Mapping landscape meanings for ecosystem management. In H. K. Cordell, & J. C. Bergstrom (Eds.), *Integrating social sciences with ecosystem management: Human dimensions in assessment, policy, and management.* Champaign, IL: Sagamore.

Wirsching, A., Leung, Y.-F., & Attarian, A. (2003, November). Swatting litter bugs. *Parks & Recreation,* 16–20+.

Common Culture

Preview

What is common culture?

Common culture, or popular culture, refers to the everyday pastimes of the majority of people in a social group. It is the leisure of the masses.

What are examples of common culture?

In Western technologically oriented societies, such as the United States, Canada, and Australia, examples of common culture are typically the media-based forms of entertainment. For example, television, magazines, and films are people's most popular expressions of leisure.

Why is understanding common culture important?

Mediated entertainment as a form of leisure is perhaps the most obvious reflection of who we are as a society.

Key Terms

High culture 202
Folk culture 203
Orienting response 208
Scopophilia 209
Rap 211
Hip-hop 211
Pluralistic 213
Genre 218
Blockbuster 218
Entertainment 227
Mediated entertainment . .227

D o you remember what you did yesterday? Did you listen to music on your portable CD player and headphones? Did you go to a movie, watch television, read a newspaper, read your e-mail, shop at Abercrombie & Fitch, or eat at McDonald's (Fig. 7.1)? You probably did at least one of these activities, perhaps all of them. In fact, you probably do at least one of these activities every day. If so, you are not unusual at all, because these are what most people in modern societies do with most of their free time. These are examples of common culture.

Figure 7.1

Eating at McDonald's is an example of common culture in many societies. This restaurant is located in Beijing, China. (© Ruth V. Russell.)

Characterizing Common Culture

Common culture, or popular culture, encompasses the most immediate and contemporary activities of our lives. Common culture is not so much defined by its content; it could be music, literature, drama, or even sport. Rather, common culture is defined by its typicality. It is labeled "common" because it offers a common ground as the most visible and pervasive level of culture in a society. Other terms for common culture include pop culture, mass culture, or mass leisure.

Why study common culture? What could be the validity of studying MTV or *The National Enquirer*? Because these things serve as a kind of mirror in which we can see ourselves, we can tell who we are, what we are, and why. We see reflected in common culture certain standards and commonly held beliefs about beauty, success, love, or justice. We also see reflected there important social contradictions—the tension between races, genders, generations, and even societies. As Lipsitz (1990) suggests, "perhaps the most important facts about people have always been encoded within the ordinary and the commonplace" (p. 5).

In Profile

Happy Birthday Mickey Mouse!
Box 7.1

Ever since the king of Disney characters arrived on November 18, 1927, as a scrawny but buoyant black-and-white product of the Jazz Age, Mickey Mouse has been popular. To this day, he is still photographed daily alongside thousands of tourists at theme parks in California, Florida, France, and Japan.

Originally, he was a symbol of American optimism and resourcefulness in his screen debut, *Steamboat Willie*. The film shows an irreverent rodent who takes Captain Pete's steamboat on a joyride and woos Minnie Mouse by making music on the bodies of farm animals. The years have dulled Mickey's personality, however—perhaps the result of his becoming the corporate face of a multibillion-dollar entertainment empire.

For Walt Disney, who created the character, Mickey Mouse is "this friendly little guy" (as cited in Schneider, 2003, p. 00. For some scholars of popular culture, however, he represents the vast reach of American cultural power, symbolizing a company that has turned childhood into a function of consumerism by commodifying children's dreams.

You can see it in his face. Soon after Mickey's overnight success in *Steamboat Willie,* he was gradually transformed, both physically and spiritually. His face was rounded out and his eyes went from black ovals to white eyes with pupils. His face became friendlier and less rat-like, reflecting his less edgy, duller, and less subversive personality. Nonetheless, this face has launched a thousand merchandise products: Watches. Pencils. Bedsheets. Alarm clocks. Telephones. He is one of the most merchandised faces ever, amassing about $4.5 billion a year in sales (Schneider, 2003).

Another argument for studying common culture focuses on the important influence it exerts on us (Petracca & Sorapure, 2004). Today, especially in American society, common culture is driven by the media. The media is the primary fund of ideas and images that inform our daily activities, sometimes exerting a more compelling influence than family, friends, school, or work. When we play sports, we mimic the gestures and movements of the professional athletes we see on TV. We learn to dance from the videos on MTV. We learn how to talk from the dialog of movies. Even if we consider common culture as merely low-quality amusement, it delivers important messages that we internalize and later act on. This means we should examine common culture in order to assess, and perhaps also resist, its influences.

How do we know what pastimes to put on the common culture list? Why is The Simpsons on the list and ballet not? In characterizing common culture, we make these distinctions. It is

- **popular**

- **commercial**

- **trendy**

- **specific to age groups**

Let's discuss each of these characteristics of common culture more fully, beginning with its popularity. Common culture refers to those pastimes that we engage in most often. It is the way we use free time that has the most in common with others in our social group. It is popular because it is a fundamental leisure expression of the culture.

This means that common culture can be distinguished from both folk culture and high culture. **High culture** is a label used to distinguish the typical pastimes of the elite. The elite in a society could be intellectuals or the upper socioeconomic classes of people. Examples of high culture might include classical music by composers such as Beethoven, fine art from the impressionist Manet, the plays of Shakespeare, and the literature of Sartre. In some societies, high culture can also be very popular. For example, classical ballet is one of Russia's most popular pastimes.

> **High culture: typical pastimes of the elite**

Folk culture, on the other hand, refers to the more local pastimes that are shared through direct, oral communication by a specific community or ethnic group. Stories, jokes, urban legends, and children's games are common examples of folk culture. Sometimes folk culture can also be considered popular, such as when a particular pursuit becomes so widespread that it crosses subcultural boundaries and becomes commercial.

> **Folk culture:** local pastimes shared through direct, oral communication

Therefore, a second characteristic of common culture is that it is commercial. It is leisure that is marketed and sold as a product. For example, in 1998 The Rolling Stones grossed over $76 million in concert ticket sales alone (BPI Communications, 1998). And in 2000 McDonald's had sales of over $40 billion (www.media.mcdonalds.com. Retrieved 4/9/04), and the all-time top movie success was *Titanic*, which has grossed over $1.8 billion (http://en.wikipedia.org. Retrieved 4/9/04.) Thus, common culture is for sale.

You are probably wondering which ones are this year's top money-making films, popular music groups, and restaurants. This introduces a third characteristic of common culture: It is trendy. Common culture typically does not last long (The Rolling Stones are an exception, of course!). Although television, magazines, and films as categories of common culture are generally enduring, particular programs or titles are not. Someone new will take the place of Beyonce, who took the place of Britney, who took the place of Madonna, who took the place of Gidget. Thus, what is common responds to what is really contemporary in the lives of people. This means that things once popular are inevitably unpopular later.

This also suggests the final characteristic of common culture: It is unique to specific age groups. For example, college students are watching reality TV, middle-aged adults enjoy *Everybody Loves Raymond,* and some elderly people are still faithfully watching *The Lawrence Welk Show.* Further, popular culture that is common among age groups is usually dependent on the tastes of youth. That is, a culture's interest in music, movies, foods, or sports is largely determined by the interests of its young people. Therefore, the vendors of common culture tend to focus on the youth. Nevertheless, the baby boomers, who are now middle-aged adults, also affect common culture. Because of their sheer numbers and higher incomes, their purchasing power also has an impact on mass leisure trends.

This chapter focuses on the most pervasive forms of common culture in industrialized societies. We begin with the most representative of them all: television. Next, we briefly explore popular music, print, film, and theme parks. Finally, we critique the thread that weaves these common cultures together: the role of mediated entertainment.

The Study Says

Generation Y's Interest in Extreme Sports
Box 7.2

The rise in consumer and corporate interest in extreme sports, also known as action sports, has been phenomenal. But is this all hype? What is the actual level and nature of public interest in these sports? The purpose of a study by Bennett, Henson, and Zhang (2003) was to examine Generation Y's interest in media-presented extreme sports. An analysis of questionnaire results from 367 middle school and high school students revealed that this generation indeed prefers watching extreme sports over the traditional sports of basketball and baseball. A strong interest in soccer was also indicated, but the youth would still rather watch the X Games than the World Cup. Male respondents tended to be slightly more familiar with, and supportive of, extreme sports than female respondents.

Television

At the hub of common culture is undoubtedly television. Not only does it hold a central place in our use of free time, but it also has become a primary means of communicating and validating what is popular (Kelly, 1982). Television tells us what music to enjoy, what history to believe, what is funny, what clothing to wear, and what breakfast cereal to eat. Television has the power to bring together the population of a nation and even the world (Kelly & Freysinger, 2000).

Indeed, the amount of time people spend watching television is astonishing (Fig. 7.2). On average, individuals in industrialized societies devote three hours a day to the pursuit—fully half of their leisure time, and more than on any other single activity save work and sleep (Table 7.1). At this rate, someone who lives to age 75 would spend nine full years in front of the tube (Kubey & Csikszentmihalyi, 2004). And data from a U.S. diary study on time conducted by Robinson and Godbey (1997) indicate that TV watching is increasing. In fact, according to their data, almost all of the gain in free time from 1965 to 1985 was given over to television. Although 49 percent of Americans say they watch too much television, 25 percent say they wouldn't give it up even for a million dollars (http://www.soundvision.com. Retrieved 2/24/04.

Figure 7.2
An average child sees 30,000 TV commercials in a year.
(© Ruth V. Russell.)

Who watches television? Almost everyone, of course, but studies (e.g., Kubey & Csikszentmihalyi, 1990) have suggested that not only do women watch more than men, but also that African Americans watch more than other ethnic groups. People who are married and single by choice seem to watch television about the same proportions of time, whereas divorced and widowed people have reported less TV viewing. Meanwhile, viewing for all adults living with children is slightly higher. More educated people tend to watch less television. Finally, most people do not watch television exclusively. Typical accompanying activities are talking, eating meals, getting dressed, doing chores, caring for children, and even studying.

The word television comes from the Greek word tele, meaning "far," and the Latin word videre, meaning "to see." Thus, the original mission of television was to see far. Experiments leading to its invention began in the 1800s,

Table 7.1
Weekly TV Viewing by Age (1998)

Age	Viewing hours
Children (2–5 years)	23
Children (6–11 years)	19
Teens	20
Women (18–24 years)	22
Men (18–24 years)	19
Women (25–54 years)	31
Men (25–54 years)	28
Women (55 years and older)	42
Men (55 years and older)	37

Note. From Nielsen Media Research (1999).

but television as we know it today was not developed until the 1920s, and it had little importance until the late 1940s. During one decade, the 1950s, television became part of everyday life in North America. People became fascinated with having so wide a range of visual events available in their homes. Those who didn't have a set often visited friends who did just to watch television. Many stores placed television sets in windows, and crowds gathered on the sidewalks to watch.

Since this beginning 50 years ago, television's hold on us has been tremendous. This has fascinated scientists, who have been studying the effects of this passion for about as long. Although television can teach and amuse, allow us to reach aesthetic heights, and provide a healing distraction, most of the research literature has focused on its problematic consequences. In fact, some scholars liken television watching to substance addiction. According to Kubey and Csikszentmihalyi (2004), "The difficulty arises when people strongly sense that they ought not watch."

To study people's reactions to TV, researchers have undertaken laboratory experiments in which they have monitored the brain waves (using an electroencephalograph, or EEG), skin resistance, or heart rate of people watching television. As might be expected, these studies show that when viewing TV, there is less mental stimulation. To determine more about how this is experienced, a study by Kubey and Csikszentmihalyi (1990) sampled people's feelings while they were engaged in various activities, including television watching. Foremost, and in agreement with the EEG studies, they found television viewing to be a passive, relaxing, low-concentration activity. Consequently, in contrasting this with other activities (see Table 7.2), television watching was found to be less challenging, less sociable, and less active. In other words, watching TV is easy.

Table 7.2
Rank Ordering (1=strongest to 5 = weakest) of the Experience Qualities for Television Viewing and Other Activities

Experience qualities	TV viewing	Public leisure (parties, sports, dining out, cultural events)	Working outside the home
Concentration	3	2	1
Challenge	5	2	1
Skill	5	2	1
Cheerful	3	1	4
Relaxed	1	2	5
Sociable	4	1	3
Alert	4	1	2
Strong	4	1	2
Active	4	2	1

Note. From Kubey and Csikszentmihalyi (1990)

Further, results from the study by Kubey and Csikszentmihalyi showed that loneliness and negative feelings often drive the motivation to watch TV. Heavy viewers wish to escape something or avoid negative feelings. In addition, television seems to become less rewarding the longer it is viewed. Although it is relaxing, as we increase the amount of time spent watching TV, our satisfaction and enjoyment in the experience tend to drop off. In the study, heavier viewers generally felt worse than light viewers, particularly when alone.

Ironically, this means that even though people often choose to watch TV to escape bad feelings, they often feel worse as a result.

What is it about TV, then, that has such a hold on us? In part, the attraction seems to spring from our biological **orienting response**. First described by Ivan Pavlov in 1927, the orienting response is our instinctive visual or auditory reaction to any sudden or new stimulus (Kubey & Csikszentmihalyi, 2004). It is part of our evolutionary heritage, a built-in sensitivity to movement from potential predatory threats. Typical orienting responses include dilation of the blood vessels to the brain, slowing of the heart, and constriction of blood vessels to major muscle groups. The brain focuses its attention on gathering more information while the rest of the body quiets. This is why it is very difficult not to watch television when it is on. The simple formal features of television, such as cuts, edits, zooms, pans, and sudden noises, activate the orienting response, thereby keeping our attention on the screen.

> **Orienting response:** the instinctive visual or auditory reaction to any novel stimulus

Producers of educational television for children have found that these formal features can help learning by increasing their attention. But increasing the rate of cuts and edits eventually overloads the brain. For example, music videos and commercials that use rapid intercutting of unrelated scenes are designed more to hold our attention than to convey information. The orienting response is overworked. Because viewers are paying full attention, they may remember the name of the product, but they feel tired and worn out afterward (Kubey & Csikszentmihalyi, 2004).

Another answer to how television is able to have such a strong hold on us comes from the leisure quality of pleasure, as discussed in Chapter 2. For example, British cultural studies scientist John Corner (1999) maintains that we watch television because it is pleasurable. Specifically, it provides four types of pleasures:

- *Pleasures of knowledge:* By radically increasing the range of knowledge available publicly (quiz shows; history, science, and nature programs; etc.), television has extended the pleasure of gaining knowledge.

- *Pleasures of comedy:* Television has created a culture of public comedy that developed from comedy programs on the radio and extended into new forms, including the situation comedy. This has guided society in what is to be considered a matter for laughter and what is serious, beyond a joke.

- *Pleasures of fantasy:* Television is widely used as a fantasy device, stimulating viewers by portaying scenarios that are highly improbable for them in real life. The newest example of this is perhaps reality television.

- *Pleasures of distraction, diversion, and routine:* Television is often used as an easily available and familiar relaxant, either after work or between phases of the day. It is a break that is always available. The regularity and repetition of the viewing week are part of a customized pattern in the household.

In other words, Corner (1999) suggests that the value of television is in the extensive range of pleasures provided by the act of viewing itself. This is labeled scopophilia—being the onlooker to unfolding events. The enjoyment of being "tele-present" at a distant event as it happens can be a powerful one (p. 94). Although the idea of scopophilia is applicable to films, photographs, and other visual forms as well, it is a particularly powerful pleasure in television viewing because of its prevalence. As Freud first suggested, what is so pleasurable in viewing, particularly in viewing other people, is the element of surreptitiousness.

> **Scopophilia:** pleasure in viewing, particularly of attractive people

From Your Own Experience

Do You Enjoy Reality Television?
Box 7.3

Do you watch reality television shows? If so, rank order the following reasons for watching reality TV (1 = best reason to 6 = worst reason):

____   Guessing who will win or be eliminated

____   Seeing real people face challenging situations

____   Imagining how I would act in similar situations

____   Fights and/or strategies among contestants

___   **Nothing better to watch**

___   **Attractive contestants and locations**

Do you avoid reality television shows? If so, rank order the following reasons for not watching reality TV (1 = best reason to 6 = worst reason):

___   **Can always find something better to watch**

___   **Too trashy or low class**

___   **Don't like the values or characteristics they present**

___   **I can't identify with the contestants**

___   **They are faked or rigged**

___   **Too voyeuristic/don't like spying on people**

After completing your rankings, if you do not watch reality television, join in a discussion partnership with someone who does, and vice versa. Compare your rankings and discuss reasons for your differences.

Popular Music

Because of its popularity, music has been a tremendously important barometer of the character of a culture throughout history. As we think back over the 20th century, every decade has a melody, a rhythm, a sound track. The years and the sounds blend together.

In the United States, for example, the century starts off blue: Robert Johnson selling his soul to the devil at the crossroads. Then the Jazz Age: Louis Armstrong and Duke Ellington. By mid-century things start to rock: in the beginning, a confused collage of Buddy Holly's hillbilly style, Little Richard's frenzy, and Elvis Presley's blend of country and African American rhythms. Later, the "boy and girl groups," such as The Coasters and The Shirelles, relayed the trials and joys of young love. By the mid-1960s, Bob Dylan and Joan Baez combined folk lyrics with the beat and instrumentation of rock to produce folk, or progressive, music, while Led Zepplin and Frank Zappa pinned their antiestablishment tone to hard rock. Then on to the Beatles, Aretha Franklin, Bob Marley, and Stevie Wonder. (Are you humming along?) Perhaps the memorable sounds of R.E.M., U2, and Prince can drown out the disco sounds of the 80s.

So powerful have been these musical legacies that they can still be heard on the radio today. But how will we remember the end of that century and the beginning of this one? Added to blues, jazz, country, rock, folk, and disco music is **rap**. "Rock is old," says Russell Simmons, head of a hip-hop label that took in nearly $200 million in 1998. "The creative people who are great, who are talking about youth culture in a way that makes sense, happen to be rappers" (as cited in August, Brice, Harrison, Murphy, & Thigpen, 2004, p. 301).

> **Rap:** a form of rhythmic speaking in rhyme

Originally created by and intended for young African American inner-city audiences, rap music has gained more widespread acceptance, to the point that it appears regularly on television and has been adopted by major recording labels. Rap music has spawned an entire **hip-hop** culture of dance movements, clothing, and films. In 2003, 23 million rap CDs were sold, outpacing every other category of music, thus giving previously disenfranchised urban youth a much more pervasive presence in the culture (Petracca & Sorapure, 2004).

> **Hip-hop:** the backing music for rap, which is often composed of a collage of samples from other songs; the culture of rap

Rap music was once called a fad, but it's close to celebrating a 25th anniversary! Although it started as black music, more than 70 percent of hip-hop albums are now purchased by whites. In fact, some feel that rap has been "appropriated" by white audiences. Much as rock did in past eras, rap has compelled young people of all races to search for excitement, artistic fulfillment, and a sense of identity. Further, rap music is the only art form that openly celebrates capitalism.

In Focus

Hip-Hop
Box 7.4

The hip-hop world began in the Bronx in 1971. Cindy Campbell needed a little back-to-school money, so she asked her brother Clive to throw a party. Back in his hometown of Kingston, Jamaica, Clive used to watch dance-hall revelers. He loved the big sound systems the deejays had and the way they'd "toast" people at the party in a singsong voice. When he moved to the United States at age 13, he used to tear the speakers out of abandoned cars and hook them onto a stereo in his room. Needless to say, the after-school party, held in a rec room of a Bronx high-rise, was a success. Clive and Cindy charged 25 cents for girls and 50 cents for boys, and it went until 4 am. Pretty soon Clive was getting requests to do more parties, and in 1973 he gave his first block party. He was Kool Herc now. At 18 he was the first break-beat deejay, reciting rhymes over the instrumental part of the records.

Joseph Saddler loved music too. He thought Kool Herc was a god, but he thought he could do better. Saddler figured most songs had only about 10 seconds that were good, that really got the party going, so he wanted to stretch those 10 seconds out. He invented "scratching"—spinning a record back and forth to create a scratchy sound.

Things then happened fast. In 1979 came "Rapper's Delight," the first rap song most people remember. Then Grandmaster Flash warned, "Don't touch me 'cause I'm close to the edge," and the Beastie Boys hollered, "You gotta fight for your right—to party!" Then gangsta rap, then Mary J. Blige singing hip-hop soul, then Guru mixing rap with bebop.

According to its enthusiasts, the underlying message of early rap was that the violence, sexism, and lustful materialism of some rap songs are deeply American. Yet corporate America's infatuation with rap increased only after its political content withered a bit. And now, claim popular culture experts, rap no longer attacks racism or institutional power. It's just about the problems of the black community— "Just give me a piece of the action" (August, Brice, Harrison, Murphy, & Thigpen, 2004, pp. 305-307).

Questions to Consider and Discuss

1. *Do you listen to (and dance to) hip-hop music? Why do you enjoy it if you do, and why don't you enjoy it if you don't?*

2. *In the text, what might the claim "Hip-hop is perhaps the only art form that celebrates capitalism openly" mean? From your own experience, cite musical examples that support this assertion and/or examples that disprove it.*

3. *What do you think the popularity of hip-hop reflects about youth culture today? Do you like this reflection?*

However, North American popular music is not just of one form. It is at heart **pluralistic**. Although different forms appeal to different social and ethnic groups, foremost it is always an interwoven reflection of the whole culture. Rock, jazz, blues, country, and rap do not remain pure forms as they become popular; they become amalgamations of all ethnic strands and social group values. In directly interpreting the emotional language of a culture, popular music picks up influences as it goes, much like a snowball rolling downhill.

> **Pluralistic:** ethnically, religiously, racially, and socially diverse

American jazz provides an illustration of the pluralistic nature of popular music. In the beginning, jazz was a simple form of folk music developed by nonprofessional musicians. Although several cities make claims, no one really knows exactly where or when jazz was born. Much of the earliest jazz was performed informally at African American funerals in the South. Between 1910 and 1920, it began to spread out of the South to such places as Chicago and New York City. Jazz flourished. Along the way, it picked up the stylistic phrases that reflected the times. For example, at its source jazz is a mixture of rhythms from West Africa, harmony from European classical music, religious music from the gospel traditions of spirituals, and work songs from the days of slavery. As it traveled through time and subcultures, it added the energy of ragtime. Later, the sadness of the blues attached itself to jazz, and by the 1930s, the next step was swing and the big bands. Bop, and later cool jazz, started in the 1940s and 1950s, when jazz began to lose its reputation as low-class music and gained acceptance among intellectuals and college students. In the 1960s jazz was fused with rock. Today, jazz continues its subtle changes as American culture continues to change its dreams. This is the pluralism of popular music.

Popular Print

Reading has been popular since printing was first possible from woodcuts, through the invention of movable type, to today's electronic publishing tools. In the United States and Canada today, more than 200 popular magazines (not counting professional and trade publications) share a total circulation of over 250 million readers. *Modern Maturity, Reader's Digest, TV Guide,* and *National Geographic* are the most popular, with combined circulations of about 67 million (Magazine Audit Bureau of Circulation, 1998.)

In addition, there are hundreds of daily newspapers in the world. The top daily newspaper in the United States is the *Wall Street Journal,* with a circulation of 1.7 million. In the world, the top daily newspaper is *Yomiuri Shimbun* from Japan, with a circulation of over 14.5 million (Editor & Publisher,

1998). Reading books remains popular as well. In fact, according to some surveys, reading is a particularly popular activity among youth. For example, annual sales of books for young readers have more than doubled to $1.4 billion since 1987 (Beck, 1997). Bookstores have become what local libraries used to be.

Although publishing remains a major industry, annually consuming 10 million tons of paper (Kelly & Freysinger, 2000), it is no longer considered a growth industry. Bookstore chains, for example, have driven independent shops out of business, and most cities have gone from two daily newspapers to only a single one. Yet these circumstances may simply reflect change rather than decline. Even though many general-interest magazines have failed, there is a growth market for specialized publications based on specific leisure interests such as gourmet cooking, sports, fitness, biking, camping, and travel. For example, just within the sports category you can subscribe to thousands of titles, ranging from cheerleading to paintball. For surfing alone, 16 different titles are available.

Even though newspaper subscriptions have dropped overall, the number of people who regularly read electronic versions of newspapers from the Internet has increased. Thus, there is still enough power in print media to consider it common culture. How does popular print reflect a society?

Let's begin with newspapers. People read newspapers for a variety of reasons. For some, the morning ritual of coffee and the newspaper is a means of waking up. Other people study newspapers as they would a textbook; some fill idle time with it while waiting in line or during TV commercials. Businesses follow the financial reports. Politicians pay clipping services to monitor the public's moods. Children race with their parents for the Sunday merchandise flyers. Sport fans consider the paper a daily scoreboard. In any case, about 85 percent of adults in the United States read a newspaper to some extent everyday (Mediamark Research, Inc., 1992).

One of the ways to distinguish people by their newspaper-reading behaviors is to compare their educational levels. For example, a study reported by Kando (1980) found that people in the United States who had not completed high school spent more of their reading time on newspapers, whereas college graduates spent more of their reading time on books. College graduates also spent more time reading overall, whereas persons with less education were more likely to replace reading with television watching.

What about reading magazines? The earliest magazines probably developed from newspapers or from the bookseller catalogs that first appeared during the 1600s in France. In industrialized countries, the first large-scale magazine boom occurred in the middle of the 19th century. Over the years, magazines have had varied purposes and contents, but today's magazine is typically a collection of articles or stories, often with illustrations, that provide a wide variety of information and entertainment. They are usually published on a weekly, monthly, or bimonthly basis.

From Your Own Experience

Magazine Ads
Box 7.5

According to some observers, advertising is an important example of common culture. In modern societies, advertising has become such a dominant force that it's not unusual to be exposed to an average of 3,000 ads every day as we watch television, listen to the radio, and read magazines (Pozner, 2004). Even though we usually spend only a few seconds glancing at ads (except during the Super Bowl), they communicate a great deal about a product and your need for it. In addition, ads teach us who the "cool" people are and how to be one. Even the simplest and most seemingly direct ads carry subtly powerful messages about appropriate modes of behavior, standards of beauty and success, gender roles, and a variety of other markers for normalcy and status. Do you agree with this from your own experience?

Try a little investigation yourself. First, select a copy of your favorite magazine. It can be any title that interests you as long as it includes advertising. Study the content and visual images of only the ads in the magazine. Think about what these ads are instructing you to do to be cool or successful. Why do you need the product? How is the product used to market lifestyle, relationships, beauty, or other values? What are the messages? Who are these messages targeted toward? How do these ads make you feel?

With your magazine sample in hand, discuss your findings with classmates. Together, what do you conclude?

Magazine titles are popular with different readers. So strong is this connection that marketing firms can profile people according to their magazine subscriptions. For example, in no other category of common culture are the sexes considered such separate audiences. Age levels, too, represent typical distinctions among magazine readers. For example, such magazines as *Ebony*,

Parents, Weight Watchers Magazine, The New Yorker, Fortune, Southern Living, Cosmo Girl, Car and Driver, and *Real Simple* make very specific claims about the gender, age, race, occupation, residence, education, income, and even weight of their readership.

Films

As with popular print, in the face of television's growing popularity, movies have also experienced declines in theater attendance in many societies since the 1950s. For example, an average of 80 million Americans went to the movies every week in 1946 (Chubb & Chubb, 1981) compared with about 23 million in 1991 (Motion Picture Association of America, Inc., 1991).

Although some predict that movie theaters will practically disappear as technology continues to affect the visual media, this is doubtful because going to the movies means more than seeing the entertainment on the screen. Indeed, just as there are many reasons for going to the movies, so are there many ways of explaining their popularity and their influence within the fabric of contemporary culture.

From a sociological perspective, movies can reflect, define, or even redefine social norms and depict urgent social problems. From a psychological perspective, viewers can identify with the characters and project their own feelings into the action, giving them a deep emotional tension and, ultimately, a release. From a literary perspective, movies can be interpreted in terms of genre—as action, comedy, disaster, crime, documentary, and such—or in terms of plot, characterization, imagery, and symbolism.

In Focus

Slasher Films
Box 7.6

The Texas Chainsaw Massacre is a popular movie. The series of five films, including a remake in 2003, have earned a worldwide gross income of $128 million. The plot of the films is based on a chainsaw-wielding man hacking his victims to death. In the 2003 version, this begins when five young people, driving through the backwoods of Texas, stop to pick up a traumatized hitchhiker. They try to help the girl, but when they knock on the door of a remote homestead, they suddenly find themselves running for their lives from the disfigured cannibal known as Leatherface, who is in hot pursuit with his chainsaw.

In *Friday the Thirteenth*, the plot originates when a New Jersey camp, closed for 20 years after a series of "accidental" deaths, reopens and the horror begins again. Six counselors arrive to get the place ready. Each is progressively murdered—knifed, speared, or axed. The numerous sequels continue the gruesome murders by a maniacal Jason, who rises from the dead to slice up more teenagers at lakeside cottages and halfway houses.

The Texas Chainsaw Massacre and *Friday the Thirteenth* are examples of the "slasher" genre of film. Also labeled "exploitation" films, other examples are *Children of the Corn*, *Terror Train*, *Halloween*, *A Nightmare on Elm Street*, *Prom Night*, and *Bride of Chucky*. During the 1970s and 1980s, this type of film became part of the common culture in North America. What does the popularity of these films tell us about the nature of the culture that loves them? Based on several content analyses of slasher films, we find some clues to the answer.

First, many of these films are engaged in an assault on all that a society is supposed to cherish: youth, home, and school (Modleski, 1986). The individual, the family, and the institution are dismembered in the most literally gruesome ways. A few of the films, such as *The Texas Chainsaw Massacre*, have actually been celebrated for their adversarial relationship to society. The film has been analyzed as a critique of capitalism, since it shows the horror of people quite literally living off other people. It is also described as a critique of the institution of the family, since it implies that the monster is the family (Wood, 1979).

Another reflection of this is how women are considered. In slasher films, an attractive young woman is always threatened by a maniac. In many of the films, "the female is attacked not only because, as has often been claimed, she embodies sexual pleasure, but also because she represents a great many aspects of the specious good" (Modleski, 1986, p. 163).

More horrifying yet, the camera location seems to place the audience in the perspective of the often unseen and nameless presence that annihilates. This is a strategy that delights audiences as they cheer and applaud each outrage from their own vantage point as the slasher. This kind of joyful destructiveness on the part of the audience has been analyzed to mean that the masses are reveling in the demise of the very culture they appear most enthusiastically to support. For example, *Dawn of the Dead*, which is about zombies taking over a shopping center, has become a midnight favorite at shopping malls all over the United States.

Second, the slasher films often delight in fulfilling the audiences' expectations for nonclosure. In *Friday the Thirteenth* the killer rises and kills over and over again, even after presumed dead. Film analysts claim this reflects the impermanent nature of the culture; these films are allowed to dispense with the need for a plot and character development. Because the characters are so dispensable, they are practically interchangeable, since we learn nothing of them as individuals. Likewise, there is virtually no building of a climax in the plot, only variations on the theme of slashing victims.

Questions to Consider and Discuss

1. *Have you seen any slasher films? What was your reaction to them when you saw them? If you haven't seen them, why not? How do your classmates feel about them?*

2. *What do you think these films portray about the culture? Do you agree with the analyses in this case? Why or why not?*

3. *In your opinion, has cinema improved or deteriorated overall in recent years? Why? Discuss the pros and cons of censorship, self-regulation, and governmental intervention in popular cul-*

From an economic perspective, movies may be seen primarily as a consumable product defined by the marketplace. This economic influence might be viewed as negative, reducing a potentially powerful artistic form to the lowest common denominator. The capitalist observer, on the other hand, might see such forces as positive, because they encourage the worldwide spread of a nation's cultural values. Certainly, as markers of common culture, movies are full of interesting reflections to consider.

> **Genre:** a kind or type, usually applied to films, books, or plays

The movie industry itself now uses multiple avenues to gain popularity. In addition to playing in theaters, films are also marketed on videos or DVDs and via television. Thus, changes in the common culture of films cannot be measured singly. For example, until the early 1970s American film companies produced about 200 feature films per year. Now, about half that number is produced. Nonetheless, revenues from films through the 1980s and 1990s exceeded those produced prior to the 1970s. This is attributed to the phenomenon of the **blockbuster** (Fig. 7.3).

> **Blockbuster:** lavishly produced, expecting to have wide popular appeal and financial success

Another change is the location of film production. Prior to the 1970s, the major American film companies were the world's suppliers of movies.

Although the United States continues to be an important market, fewer films are being produced there. Now other countries (such as Japan, France, and Sweden) generate $600 million per year in film rentals compared with $700 million for American and Canadian rentals. Not only is film universally popular, but according to some critics, the film industries in Asia and Europe have produced the majority of socially and artistically worthwhile works.

Figure 7.3
Perhaps surprisingly, the blockbuster film *Titanic* had a positive economic impact on the cruise industry. (© Ruth V. Russell.)

Today's movie audiences are as varied as the films they watch. They are a heterogeneous collection of ethnic, social, and cultural groups. Yet several studies have supported an already well-known fact: Movie audiences are primarily young. Up to 70 percent of movie theater attendance is by those under age 30, and more than half of moviegoers are under 20 (Nye, 1970). In addition, movies, which began as a form of entertainment for less affluent people, have begun to be a common pastime for the more affluent. In fact, some studies report that those from the lowest educational, occupational, and economic levels are now underrepresented among movie audiences. Audiences are also more likely to be living in urban and suburban areas.

Theme Parks

In addition to television, popular music, popular print, and films, expressions of common culture could also include radio (especially considering the emerging popularity of talk radio), comics, and even spectator sports. Before considering the common thread woven through all of these examples, let's briefly consider the last example: theme parks. They provide a fascinating reflection of culture.

The roots of the amusement park go back to the Middle Ages, with the pleasure gardens located on the outskirts of major European cities. These gardens featured live entertainment, fireworks, dancing, games, and even primitive rides. One of these parks, Bakken, north of Copenhagen, Denmark, which opened in 1583, continues to enjoy the status of being the world's oldest operating amusement park (http://www.napha.org/history.html. Retrieved 2/25/04).

History also points to the ice slides in Russia during the 17th century. The structures were built out of lumber with a sheet of ice several inches thick covering the surface. Riders climbed the stairs attached to the back of the slide, sped down the 50-degree drop on a sled, and then swooped up the slide that laid parallel (and opposite) to the first one. It is said that Catherine the Great was a fan of the thrill of the slides and had a few built on her own property.

In Profile

Roller Coasters
Box 7.7

Why do we love roller coasters? We are drawn to them with our hearts racing and our palms sweating as we crave this perversion of the pleasure-pain principle. Beginning in the early 1990s, roller coastering began its second "Golden Age," and the number and variety of roller coasters show no signs of letting up. Therefore, a little basic instruction is required.

Types

All coasters can be subdivided into either steel or wooden tracked. From here, they can contain multiple combinations of these forms:

Steel:	The track is pressurized steel tubing, and the two sets of wheels on the cars surround both sides of the track. This provides a smoother, quieter ride and wilder track patterns due to the added strength.
Wooden:	Although the actual tracks are still steel, the supports are massive gridworks of wood, usually Southern pine. The "Woodies" are preferred by many purists, because the ride is classically rough, bouncy, and rattling.
Dual:	A themed pair of coasters runs on parallel or interweaving tracks, giving them the appearance of racing or colliding with each other.
Standing:	Instead of being seated, riders stand up, usually supported by a bicycle-like seat.
Reverse:	The coaster runs in reverse direction, with riders facing backward.
Inverting:	This type spends some time with the riders upside down.
Vertical:	This coaster drops the riders straight down, usually after shooting them up quickly.
Suspended:	The coaster hangs from the track rather than rolling on it, thus allowing riders' feet to dangle free.
Water-Hazard:	The coaster spends some time traveling over water, plunging toward water, or appearing to plunge into water.
Underground:	This type travels through a tunnel or underground.
Floorless:	This new breed of coaster has a floor that "falls away" after loading, leaving riders' feet dangling, but the coaster is not suspended. The track is still below the rider.
Launched:	Instead of the slow click-clack uphill climb to begin the ride, cars are shot up very fast.

(see http://www.beardfl.com/coasters/. Retrieved 2/26/04

Must Rides (my own favorites)

The Incredible Hulk: This steel coaster is launched, with the thrust of an F-16 (Islands of Adventure, Universal, Orlando, Florida).

Millennium Force: This is a steel coaster with high, long drops at very high speeds and large banks (Cedar Point, Sandusky, Ohio; Fig. 7.5).

Boulder Dash: This wooden coaster is built into the side of a mountain and careens around trees and boulders (Lake Compounce, Bristol, Connecticut).

Apollo's Chariot: This steel coaster travels at 73 mph, with no front or sides to the car (Busch Gardens, Williamsburg, Virginia).

Cyclone: This wooden coaster is not the highest or fastest, but it is certainly the most nostalgic—one of the originals (Astroland, Coney Island, Brooklyn, New York).

Figure 7.4

(Opposite) Visitors enjoying the Ferris wheel at Gorky Park in Moscow, Russia. (© Ruth V. Russell.)

Figure 7.5

(Left) The Millennium Force, Cedar Point, Sandusky, Ohio. (© Cedar Point. Used with permission.)

In the late 1800s the growth of the amusement park industry shifted to the United States. Following the American Civil War, increased urbanization gave rise to electric trolleys. Utility companies charged the trolley companies a flat fee for electricity; thus, the need to stimulate weekend ridership resulted in the first amusement parks in North America.

Amusement parks entered the beginning of their golden era with the 1893 World's Columbian Exposition in Chicago, which introduced the Ferris wheel and the amusement midway to the world. Built by G. W. Gale Ferris, a mechanical engineer from Illinois, this first Ferris wheel was 250 feet in diameter. Each of the 36 cars could hold 60 people, and one revolution took 20 minutes. The Ferris wheel was quickly copied in parks around the world (Fig. 7.4).

In addition, the midway from the 1893 Exposition, with its wide array of rides and concessions, was a huge success and dictated amusement park design for the next 60 years. Under full swing by the 1930s, the center of this growing industry was Coney Island in New York City, which at its peak was home to three elaborate amusement parks along with dozens of smaller attractions. Around the world as well, hundreds of new amusement parks opened. Innovations provided greater and more intense thrills to the growing crowds. By 1919, over 1,500 amusement parks were in operation in the United States, providing a holiday of revelry and extravagance. Unfortunately, the glory did not last (http://www.napha.org/history.html. Retrieved 2/24/04.)

By 1935, following the Great Depression, only 400 amusement parks remained, many struggling to survive. World War II further hurt the industry, but afterward, new prosperity ushered in new parks. For example, a new concept, the Kiddieland, took advantage of the postwar baby boom. With the advent of television in the 1950s, the industry was again in distress as people stayed home for entertainment. What was needed was a new concept.

That new concept was Disneyland. When Disneyland first opened in 1955, many people were skeptical that an amusement park without any of the traditional attractions would succeed. Instead of a midway, Disneyland offered five distinct themed areas, providing "guests" with the fantasy of travel to different lands and times. Disneyland was an immediate success, and as a result, the theme park era was born. Whereas the attraction of earlier amusement parks was that they allowed visitors to break with accustomed social norms and mock the established order, the new theme parks sought to emphasize wholesomeness. Walt Disney envisioned it thus:

> *Disneyland will be based upon and dedicated to the ideals, the dreams and the hard facts that have created America. And it will be uniquely equipped to dramatize these dreams and facts and send them forth as a source of courage and inspiration to all the world. Disneyland will be something of a fair, an exhibition, a playground, a community center, a museum of living facts, and a showplace of beauty and magic. (as quoted in Mosley, 1985, p. 221)*

Today, numerous theme parks provide this form of entertainment. For example, Sesame Place, a children's water park featuring the characters from the television program, and Knott's Berry Farm, which draws on a western theme, are also representative of the coordinated package of attractions around a single theme. Notable as well are Sea World, which uses marine life to educate and entertain, and Universal Studios, a theme park that celebrates another form of common culture: the movies.

But the Disney theme parks remain the industry leaders and standard-bearers. The four parks (Disneyland in California, Magic Kingdom in Florida, Tokyo Disneyland, and Disneyland Resort Paris are organized around themes or "lands." The basic lands are Adventureland (Fig. 7.6), Tomorrowland (Discoveryland), Fantasyland, and Frontierland (Westernland). A fifth land was added in 1993: Mickey's Toontown (or Starland). Depending on which park you visit, the other main areas can include Liberty Square; New Orleans Square; Main Street, USA; Critter Country; and World Bazaar. In each land and area, the theme is carried out through shops, exhibits, rides, and costumed "hosts."

Recently, critiques have emerged about what the Disney theme parks reveal about the culture. Let's briefly discuss these so that you can make up your own mind about this form of common culture.

First, Rojek (1993) has written that Disney theme parks present not just entertainment but a moralistic and idealized version of the "American Way." Here's how he described it. The moral order of the parks is based on a nostalgic picture of American society: the "authentic" American barbershop quartet; the "real" turn-of-the-century streets of small-town America; shiny-faced youth dressed in red, white, and blue playing their hearts out in a brass band; ever-smiling and lively characters from Disney films; and throughout, a narrative of the moral and economic superiority of the American way of life.

Even the layouts of the parks, claims Rojek, suggest an idealized space. Once past the turnstiles, we are in Main Street, USA, where "everything is freshly painted, neat, tidy and clean: a de-racialized, de-politicized space which symbolizes the original purity of the American community" (p. 127). Then in Adventureland, the armchair traveler goes to far-off and mysterious destinations, such as a tropical jungle and the Caribbean. When guests encounter "ferocious" wild animals and "barbaric" pirates, these dangers are always defeated by the "superiority of white, middle-class power" (p. 128). The next stop is Frontierland, which "symbolizes the triumph of white, male culture over nature" (p. 128), and then Tomorrowland, where a "sense of eternal progress" is portrayed (p. 128).

Essentially, Rojek's criticism is that the Disney theme parks overstep their entertainment role. They are underpinned by powerful political and social values; they present white, male-dominated, upper-class culture as perfect; and they distort history, presenting American society as free of conflict.

Another criticism of the Disney parks comes from Bryman (1995). His critique is directed at the nature of control. Control, says Bryman, is in evidence in a variety of ways. It operates at the fairly mundane level of how the visitor is handled while in the parks to the way in which the parks relate to their immediate environment. For example, there is control over the imagination. One way this is done is through selecting out undesirable elements in the stories. Also, there are no playground-type activities in the parks, so children cannot use the park in their own way and at their own pace. Another control is over the nature of the park experience. Bryman cites how the visitors' movements are controlled, both overtly and covertly, by the park's physical layout and by its built-in narratives. For example, the distinction between a ride and its queue has been eroded. There is also control over the behavior of employees. All staff are trained to behave in the Disney way. There are clearly articulated values, a distinctive language (customers are "guests"), and rules about physical appearance.

Figure 7.6

A view of the Magic Kingdom from The Swiss Family Treehouse in Adventureland. (© Ruth V. Russell.)

Role of Entertainment

So what is the reflection of common culture? What do television, popular print, popular music, films, and theme parks suggest is the character of the society that loves them? We have explored many things that common culture reveals about culture, but in industrialized societies perhaps the overarching reflection is that we crave entertainment.

Entertainment comes from a variety of sources, but its goal is to have someone else or something else amuse us. Entertainment is the basis for the common culture of contemporary societies. Further, today's common culture delivers entertainment primarily through the media. Television, film, CDs, and even theme parks are forms of mediated entertainment. In addition, today's common culture is commercial. Has this always been the case?

Although there were the popular attractions of shooting matches and horse races in the late 17th century in the United States, current popular pastimes are traced to the mid-18th century when opportunities for the masses began to increase. Urban living made entertainments for the masses

> **Entertainment:** various ways of amusing people, especially by performing for them

possible in cheap forms. Public baths, coffeehouses, and seaside amusement centers for music and dancing, as well as gaming, bowling, and shopping, occupied much of people's free time. By 1790, there were 14 morning papers in London (Tuberville, 1933). In 18th-century American colonies, commercialized entertainment

> **Mediated entertainment:** entertainment provided via media

spread as well.

Industrialization in the 19th century also produced new forms of popular pastimes. Public amusements then reflected the new variety possible through technology, such as penny theaters with 30-second pantomimed melodramas viewed on kinescopes, and five-cent theaters that projected slides telling popular stories of murder and revenge. Although literacy was not widespread at the time, the demand for accessible pleasure reading was great. Weekly newspapers (later to become magazines), chapbooks (paper-covered booklets), and cheap reprints of classic books were popular.

American nickelodeons (the first was in Pittsburgh in 1905) ushered in the popularity of movie houses. Since early films were silent, short, and cost only five cents, people could enjoy them on their way to or from work. By the 1920s, radio began to reveal a great deal about the times. It was inexpensive and could be enjoyed by everyone. It provided entertainment for the homebound and companionship for the lonely. During the Depression years, radio provided a major form of tension relief. With the collision of advancing technology and the rise of a consumer-based market, the availability of the television in the 1950s sealed the connection between media, commercialism, and popular pastimes.

The Study Says

Commercial Entertainment and Leisure Participation

Box 7.8

Commercial media-based entertainment options have proliferated in leisure. Do they detract from people's participation and active involvement in leisure? Earlier research shows that media use takes about half of people's free time, whereas sports and various active pursuits take about eight percent, our social life takes 18 percent, and walking, resting, and other activities take the rest (Robinson, Andreyenkov, & Patrushev, 1989). More recent studies, on the other hand, show that the level of media use increases the level of leisure activity if the activity is spectator-based. For example, television has a positive impact on going to an art museum, seeing a play at the community playhouse, and attending a pro baseball game (Jeffres, Neuendorf, & Atkin, 2003).

Is mediated and commercialized common culture a good thing? Some, like Neil Postman, say no. In the book *Amusing Ourselves to Death* (1986), Postman argues that our common culture, particularly television, does not merely reflect our culture, but rather has become our culture. Generations reared on mediated entertainment, he asserts, view the world, and ideas, differently. We come to expect life to be presented in small, disconnected, and amusing pieces. As a result, we can no longer think critically or behave rationally. He feels that our ability to live a meaningful life, both individually and communally, is compromised by "the nature of the medium. . . . It must suppress the content of ideas in order to accommodate the requirements of visual interest" (p. 92). The result of such ignorance is a culture addicted to "fluff," in which we are unable to think for ourselves–a "Huxley-like" nightmare come true.

David Bianculli (2000) also wrote about mediated entertainment, especially television. In contrast to Postman's view, Bianculli believes that television serves critically important educational and social functions. He asserts that TV is actually opening the American mind because it provides positive role models, good storytelling, and likable characters. He considers television a misrepresented art form, deserving of respect and reverence. In fact, according to Bianculli, the history of entertainment, from live theater to television itself, can be described as an unhealthy cycle of undue criticism for the new art form and a canonization of the previous one.

What is your position on the "goodness" of contemporary common culture? Probably somewhere in the middle? Perhaps we can aid our consideration of this debate by remembering distinctions in cultural art forms. There is a lot of "trash" in everything. There has always been low and high art, regardless of the medium. We must all learn to discern for ourselves what we will consume and why. Television, movies, popular music, magazines, and theme parks in and of themselves cannot make or break us as a culture. It is up to each of us and each community to decide this for ourselves.

Summary: What We Understand

Common culture, or mass recreation, is an important mirror of society. Because of its popularity, commercialism, trendiness, and youth-dependent characteristics, it is a pervasive expression of the culture itself. From reading this chapter, you should know that

- Television is by far the pastime we participate in most frequently. It is a potent and intimate presence in culture. Yet research suggests that even though television viewing is freely chosen and provides relaxation and escape, it is the least enjoyable and invigorating of all pastimes.

- Such print media as newspapers and magazines, as well as popular music, films, and theme parks are all powerful expressions of common culture in modern society.

- The positive or negative role of mediated entertainment in shaping and reflecting the values of a society is worthy of debate.

Applications to Professional Practice

At the beginning of the chapter, we distinguished among folk culture, high culture, and common culture. We know that folk culture is passed around primarily by word of mouth, and that common culture is distributed via commercialized media. But how do we manage high-culture resources? Although it may seem that only common culture is growing in contemporary societies, expressions of high culture are also increasing.

Summer day-camp programs for children are now just as likely to include art and drama as swimming and games. Members of older adult centers can now sign up to learn to play the oboe or write haiku poetry. Football players take ballet classes, and executives join potter's cooperatives. Teens perform in live community theater, and young children and their parents join bookstore-sponsored book discussions. Youth in a correctional institution are invited to paint murals on blank walls of downtown buildings.

Communities everywhere typically have orchestras, dance companies, theater groups, and art fairs. Private organizations sponsor photography clubs, Shakespeare interest groups, and craft guilds. The university's string quartet performs weekly at noon on the campus lawn, and the Army base provides musical practice rooms. Governments are rapidly establishing community-wide multiple-arts centers, and shopping malls feature art exhibits. In one town, an old riverboat is converted into a theater, and in another a barn becomes an art gallery. In fact, the options for high-culture resources are almost limitless. To focus on this point further, let's especially mention arts councils and multiple-purpose cultural arts centers.

First, in many communities, special-interest organizations in the arts are coordinated or assisted by umbrella agencies that help promote their joint efforts (Kraus, 2001). These umbrella organizations are often labeled community arts councils. For example, The Arts and Humanities Council of Tulsa, Oklahoma, provides arts education in the schools, after-school and summer youth arts programs, art classes for underserved people, and lifelong learning opportunities.

Second, multiple-purpose cultural arts centers represent a special kind of high-culture resource. In many communities, a cultural arts center is usually a cluster of one or more stages, an art gallery, and rehearsal and workshop areas, all under one roof. The idea is to provide a cost-effective resource for expression in all the arts. One of the first multiple-purpose cultural arts centers was New York City's Lincoln Center for the Performing Arts, which opened in 1962. Covering 15 acres, the six buildings and 13 auditoriums support 12 independent companies, including The Metropolitan Opera, The Julliard School of Music, The New York Public Library for the Performing Arts, the New York City Ballet, and the Film Society of Lincoln Center.

For More Information

To read more about the Lincoln Center for the Performing Arts, the Web site is: http://www.lincolncenter.org. Good examples of community arts councils are the Los Angeles County Arts Commission (http://www.lacountyarts.org), the Seattle Arts Council (http://www.cityofseattle.net/arts/), and the Asheville Area Arts Council (http://www.ashevillearts.com). Many of these and other community arts council sites have employment and internship links.

References

August, M., Brice, L. E., Harrison, L., Murphy, T., & Thigpen, D. E. (2004). Hip-hop nation: There's more to rap than just rhythms and rhymes. In M. Petracca, & M. Sorapure (Eds.), *Common culture: Reading and writing about American popular culture* (pp. 311–328). Upper Saddle River, NJ: Prentice Hall.

Beck, M. (1997, February 3). The next big population bulge: Generation Y shows its might. *The Wall Street Journal*, p. C13.

Bennett, G., Henson, R. K., & Zhang, J. (2003). Generation Y's perceptions of the action sports industry segment. *Journal of Sport Management, 17*, 95–115.

Bianculli, D. (2000). *Teleliteracy: Taking television seriously.* Syracuse, NY: Syracuse University Press.

BPI Communications Inc. (1998). Amusement Business.

Bryman, A. (1995). *Disney and his worlds.* London: Routledge.

Chubb, M., & Chubb, H. R. (1981). *One third of our time? An introduction to recreation behavior and resources.* New York: John Wiley & Sons.

Corner, J. (1999). *Critical ideas in television studies.* Oxford: Clarendon.

Jeffres, L. W., Neuendorf, K., & Atkin, D. (2003). Media use and participation as a spectator in public leisure activities: Competition or symbiosis? *Leisure Studies, 22*, 169–184.

Kando, T. M. (1980). *Leisure and popular culture in transition.* St. Louis, MO: Mosby.

Kelly, J. R. (1982). *Leisure.* Englewood Cliffs, NJ: Prentice Hall.

Kelly, J. R., & Freysinger, V. J. (2000). *21st century leisure: Current issues.* Boston: Allyn & Bacon.

Kraus, R. (2001). *Recreation and leisure in modern society.* Boston: Jones and Bartlett.

Kubey, R., & Csikszentmihalyi, M. (1990). *Television and the quality of life: How viewing shapes everyday experience.* Hillsdale, NJ: Lawrence Erlbaum.

Kubey, R., & Csikszentmihalyi, M. (2004). Television addiction is no mere metaphor. In M. Petracca, & M. Sorapure (Eds.), *Common culture: Reading and writing about American popular culture* (pp. 251–272). Upper Saddle River, NJ: Prentice Hall.

Lipsitz, G. (1990). *Time passages: Collective memory and American popular culture.* Minneapolis: University of Minnesota Press.

Magazine Audit Bureau of Circulation. (1998). Retrieved November 30, 2001, from http://abc.org.tw/html/ehome.htm

Mediamark Research, Inc. (1992, Fall). Multimedia audiences. New York: Author.

Modleski, T. (1986). The terror of pleasure: The contemporary horror film and postmodern theory. In T. Modleski (Ed.), *Studies in entertainment: Critical approaches to mass culture* (pp. 76–89). Bloomington: Indiana University Press.

Mosley, L. (1985). *The real Walt Disney.* London: Futura.

Motion Picture Association of America, Inc. (1991). New York: Author.

Nielsen Media Research, (1999). Retrieved November 30, 2001, from http://www.nielsenmedia.com/

Nye, R. (1970). *The unembarrassed muse: The popular arts in America.* New York: The Dial Press.

Petracca, M., & Sorapure, M. (2004). *Common culture: Reading and writing about American popular culture.* Upper Saddle River, NJ: Prentice Hall.

Postman, N. (1986). *Amusing ourselves to death.* New York: Viking.

Pozner, J. L. (2004). You're soaking in it. In M. Petracca, & M. Sorapure (Eds.), *Common culture: Reading and writing about American popular culture* (pp. 319–341). Upper Saddle River, NJ: Prentice Hall.

Robinson, J., Andreyenkov, V., & Patrushev, V. (1989). *The rhythm of everyday life: How Soviet and American citizens use time.* Boulder, CO: Westview Press.

Robinson, J. P., & Godbey, G. (1997). *Time for life: The surprising ways Americans use their time.* University Park: The Pennsylvania State University.

Rojek, C. (1993). Disney culture. *Leisure Studies, 12*, 121–135.

Schneider, M. (2003, November 23). Happy birthday, Mickey Mouse! *Hoosier Times* (Bloomington, IN), pp. E1–E5.

Tuberville, A. S. (1933). *Johnson's England: An account of the life and manners of his age.* London: Oxford.

Wood, R. (1979). *American nightmare: Essays on the horror film.* Toronto: Festival of Festivals.

CHAPTER EIGHT

Leisure and Technology

Preview

Is technology important to leisure?

Absolutely! And its importance is increasing exponentially in industrialized societies.

In what ways has it been important?

Technology has both enhanced traditional pastimes and also invented completely new ones.

Has technology been good for leisure?

As a form of common culture, the role of technology in leisure has received both accolades and criticisms. The answer most likely lies in individual values.

Key Terms

Technology 236
Technological revolution . .236
Cyberculture 238
Fidelity 247
Internet 248
Cyberhood 251
Social capital 253

From the invention of the wheel for toys in ancient cultures to the perfection of robotic techniques for toys today, **technology** has always had an impact on leisure. For example, vulcanization of rubber by Charles Goodyear in the 1830s led to the development of elastic and resilient rubber balls for tennis and golf. The invention of the printing press also invented pleasure reading. Technology helped cause a tripling in the last 25 years in the number of people who sport fish, as the invention of fiberglass rods made it possible for amateurs to match professionals (Hammel & Foster, 1986). Just as the technological development of radios, motion pictures, television, and sound recordings clearly changed people's leisure in the past, technology continues to create entirely new kinds of play possibilities.

> **Technology: the tools, machines, and systems people use to improve their lives**

Thanks to technology, we can now ice skate year-round, our bowling pins are automatically reset and our bowling scores automatically calculated, snow is manufactured and blown onto our ski slopes, and we can see every player's hand in televised poker tournaments. How would mall walkers survive without Walkmans? Clearly, new pursuits have been created by technology, and technology has changed traditional pursuits.

Even though technology has changed our lives for thousands of years, many consider the rapid changes brought about by technology today to signify a **technological revolution**. The prospects for the future of this revolution are even more exciting, as predictions are that the next quarter century will experience the fastest technological change the world has ever known (Forrester, 2004). Although the future is hard to predict, of course, the acceleration of technological development and the expansion of technology into new fields have encouraged futurists to predict some interesting ideas for leisure (Table 8.1). Indeed, some observers consider the leisure fields to be among the first to be affected by technological change.

> **Technological revolution: the "taking over" of all aspects of life by technological Innovation, also referred to as the information revolution**

Whatever happens in the future, it is clear that people love the technological revolution (Fig. 8.1). They are buying computers at a fast pace, hooking up to the Internet from home, and purchasing handheld devices as soon as they are introduced. Enthusiasm for computers and the Internet runs wide and deep, across all regions of North America and much of the world, all races, all political ideologies, and both genders (http://www.npr.org/programs/specials/poll/technology/. Retrieved 3/3/04).

Still, there are people who find themselves on the other side of the "digital divide," especially those with lower incomes, with less education, and who are over the age of 60. For example, according to a recent poll only about half

Table 8.1

A Collection of Future Predictions for Leisure and Technology

Automatic music composition

Toy soldiers with video camera eyes

Theaters allowing Internet attendance

Personalized health monitoring and care

Night glasses extending outdoor recreation participation

Handheld, voice-activated language translators for tourists

Plane zorbing (jumping out of airplanes in inflatables)

Tourists able to virtually experience their destination before the trip

Tactile virtual reality

Orbiting resorts

Instant replay on the video screen at your stadium seat

DNA-matching dating services

Figure 8.1

In these photographs, this person is on vacation. Or is she? Do both scenes qualify as "taking a vacation?" (© Ruth V. Russell.)

of employed Americans under age 60 with incomes less than $30,000 per year use a computer at work, and lower income Americans are less than half as likely as those with higher incomes to have an Internet connection at home. Nevertheless, a surprisingly high proportion of families with low incomes now have computers, and many also have access to the Internet. Only older Americans, as a group, seem out of the loop. And kids are even more positive about computers. In the poll, 85 percent of kids reported they were keeping up when it came to computers, and kids without computers at home were quite concerned that they were missing something (http://www.npr.org/programs/specials/poll/technology/. Retrieved 3/3/04).

Computer culture, or **cyberculture**, is no longer merely an emerging trend. Electronic mail, word processing, games, chat rooms, hypertext, digital multimedia, and on and on have become driving forces in contemporary societies. Indeed, computer-based leisure is perhaps the second most popular pastime, just behind television. Therefore, we continue our consideration of common culture from the last chapter by investigating in this chapter how the computer has already redefined people's ideas and behaviors about leisure.

Cyberculture: the way of life created by heavy use of computers

Technology and Quality of Life

Is cyberculture good for us? Alas, many people have begun to have some doubts about a universal goodness for leisure arising from technology. Although many extol technology's ability to extend leisure options to more people, many also fear its consequences. Goodale and Godbey (1988), for example, argue that a large amount of the leisure afforded us today by technology is trivial at best. Today's societies produce a life that is wasted in a frenetic rush for meaningless pleasure, they claim—a "sordid route to human happiness" (p. 127).

Advances in technology have given people innovative places to play, better equipment to aid their adventures, and new activities to pursue. The efficiency of technology has also been a boon to professionals working in the leisure fields. Many of these positive advances, however, have come with often-overlooked costs. In this section of the chapter, we compare some of the positive and negative outcomes of technology and leisure.

As listed by Henderson and colleagues (2001), the positive influences of technology on our pastimes include access to information about leisure options, the creation of new leisure pursuits, new horizons in leisure for people with disabilities, and tourism as a global focus.

Numerous examples can be found of how technology has helped people access information to extend their leisure options. Not the least, of course, is the use of the Internet. Within seconds, people can get information about new hobbies and places to go for fun, and they can have conversations with other people interested in the same pursuits. People can buy recreational equipment, make trip reservations, and register for use permits faster, easier, and cheaper than ever before.

In addition, technology has led to major changes in the leisure pursuits themselves, and completely new pastimes have resulted. As Henderson and colleagues (2001) have pointed out, we use technology to make our equipment stronger and lighter, our clothing warmer or cooler, and our activities more exciting. We use sonar to locate fish, we bike in our living rooms, and we climb fake rocks. Computers have brought us new forms of music and art. People spend much of their time with such new pursuits as computer games, online chat groups, and just surfing the Net!

The Study Says

Technology Rescues Older Adults
Box 8.1

Even though only about 25 percent of adults over the age of 60 have computers at home and use the Internet, studies have clearly demonstrated their value (Lee, Godbey, & Sawyer, 2003). Chat rooms, online medical and social services information and assistance, and online gaming have been found to be good for older adults. Following are a few of the research highlights:

- It reduces loneliness.

- It expands social support networks.

- It reduces stress.

- It increases feelings of control and empowerment.

- It maintains former leisure expressions.

- It provides leisure companionship.

- It expands leisure interests.

- It helps them keep up with friends and family.

Technology has also opened whole new vistas for people who, because of a physical disability, are not equally enfranchised in leisure. Today, people who use wheelchairs can ski, climb rock faces, garden, and play golf. People with visual limitations can paint, and children with life-threatening illnesses can go to summer camp.

Finally, technology has had a tremendous impact on the way people travel. Thanks to technology, people are now able to visit the penguin colonies of Antarctica, trek in remote areas of Bhutan, and float the Amazon River in more comfort, with more advance preparation, and with more accurate expectations of what they'll see and experience after they arrive. Thanks to Web sites, people unable to leave home can still experience distant lands. Some futurists suggest that the influence of technology on the future of tourism is "barely tapped as entrepreneurs check out the possibility of space travel, orbiting resorts, and moon-based recreational adventures" (Henderson et al, 2001, p. 334).

The Study Says

Vacations Are a Luxury
Box 8.2

According to a study from Oxford Health Plans, vacations are a luxury for many North American professionals. One in six workers in professional occupations chooses to accumulate vacation days instead of using them, and those who do manage to escape the clutches of the office may leave in body, but most remain connected. For example, an amazing 83 percent of U.S. workers who vacationed for seven or more days in the summer of 2000 remained in contact with their offices. Technology was the leash. Sixty-one percent of vacationers brought mobile technology with them to check office e-mail, receive voice messages, give instructions to staff, and communicate with clients daily (Romita, 2001).

On the other hand, technology has been problematic for leisure. Although the consequences to leisure may not seem all that critical, social and environmental scientists, teachers, and other professionals are worried. The issues are complex, and examining them invariably brings forth differences in personal values. Again, from the lists of Henderson and colleagues (2001), the negative consequences of technological advances in leisure include environmental damage, passivity, violence, consumerism, and social isolation.

For example, although many people get tremendous enjoyment from such vehicles as jet skis and snowmobiles, other people see them as incompatible with leisure because of the noise, pollution, resource depletion, and habitat destruction they cause (Henderson et al., 2001). Although technology has allowed the use of conservation measures that can actually improve the quality of our environment (such as polar fleece from recycled plastic), much more needs to be accomplished to keep our pastimes from spoiling the water, land, and air that provide our leisure settings.

When we began to realize the power of technological development, an often-touted claim was that it would save labor. People would be set free from the drudgeries of work and be able to pursue more enjoyable lives. Although some would argue that we are actually working harder, thanks to technology, the technology that has saved labor has also made us less active. Passivity is considered a negative outcome of our enthusiasm for the computer. For example, even though some data suggest that television watching may be declining slightly, the difference is being picked up by an increased use of computer-based entertainment (Kaufman, 2000).

Violence also seems to accompany the use of technology in leisure. Although violence has certainly been a part of leisure for centuries (see chapter 1 on the gladiators in ancient Rome), there is concern today that some technology-based leisure pursuits create too much violence. For example, such new activities as paintball, where camouflaged participants hunt each other down and shoot other players with gel bullets from realistic-looking guns, have raised concern (Henderson et al., 2001). Pornography accessed through the Internet is another example of the perpetuation of violence against women and children. One recent survey discovered that almost one third of kids aged 10 to 17 with computers at home have seen a pornographic Web site, including by accident. The same study also found that many people worry about such potential dangers of the Internet as contact with dangerous strangers and the distribution of dangerous information, such as instructions on how to build a bomb (http://www.npr.org/programs/specials/poll/technology/. Retrieved 3/3/04).

Increased consumerism is also strongly tied to technology. As more activities and equipment are developed at faster rates, the discarding of old activities and equipment and the purchasing of new ones often occurs at breakneck speed. Having the "latest and greatest" in technological advancements symbolizes our expertise, wealth, and status (Henderson et al., 2001). We absolutely must have the most powerful laptop, the largest entertainment center, and the RV with the most extras.

Finally, there is concern for social isolation. Even in specifically social forms of leisure, such as playing games, conversations with friends, and going to parties, technology has made it possible for us not actually to be there. We can e-mail, fax, talk on cell phones, videoconference, and Internet chat without ever leaving our room. In fact, we can lead a pretty "normal" life with only minimal contact with other people, thanks to technology. The result, as some fear, is that we have become more socially isolated.

In the next sections of the chapter, we explore technology and leisure in more depth in terms of computer-assisted leisure and technology as leisure. In these discussions, you can see the positive and negative consequences of technology just discussed.

Computer Assisted Leisure

In this section we consider leisure that has been assisted, improved, or expanded by technology, yet the distinction is often blurry. Although the topics we might include in this category are broad, we focus on games and on simulated sports and outdoor recreation.

Computer games have been part of leisure for over 25 years (Bryce & Rutter, 2003). The black-and-white block graphics of the tennis game Pong first made their way onto people's television sets in the mid-1970s, and since then their popularity has created an industry worth more than $16 billion worldwide (Business Communications Company, 1999). Gaming technologies have evolved from Pong's square ball bouncing between two rectangular bats to realistic images based on the physics of actual human movements. Today computer-based gaming is a very popular form of mass entertainment played on the family television, handheld devices, mobile phones, personal computers, designated "boxes," digital watches, or in game arcades. According to a study by Rideout and others (1999), 50 percent of children aged two to 18 play computer games for more than one hour a day, with 18 percent playing two to three hours daily.

Computer-based games have been the center of controversy almost from the beginning. Although some experts claim the games are useful in developing dexterity and quick thinking, others claim that it would be better for children to develop these abilities through sports. More recently, these games have been criticized for their violent and sexist content. A common game scenario is that of an anonymous character performing an aggressive act against an anonymous enemy. Often a woman is dispensed with in the process. Even the sports games have a certain vitriolic quality.

Even so, computer games continue to be a popular pastime, particularly for children. Interestingly, it seems apparent that these games would never have taken off in such a phenomenal way if they had not been tailor-made for children who had grown up on television. Children gravitate toward video machines if for no other reason than familiarity—they feel comfortable because

In Focus

The Pros and Cons of Video Games
Box 8.3

Eleven-year-old Randy locked his eyes on the target, and with arms straight and steady, raised the gun and fired. His victim screamed and staggered to the ground, but he wasn't dead. The bullet had only grazed his arm. As he was trying to crawl to safety, Randy finished him off with a single bullet to the head. While the victim's body bled and convulsed, Randy had already shifted his attention to a new threat entering through the doorway. Randy has been shooting people for the past two years.

There are arguments on both sides about video and other types of electronic games. What are some of the points of debate?

Pros	Cons
The games are entertaining. At least they're better than staring at the TV.	A lot of things are more entertaining than TV. Since when is TV a good standard?
They're not just passive. They really get kids involved.	Among TV, video games, and school, kids are spending all their time sitting.
They develop good eye–hand coordination. You've got to be fast.	Kids are really expert at pushing a button, but that's because they practice so much.
They can play the games solo; the machine becomes the competition.	Machines are a poor substitute for human beings. Even when they're playing with others, they are not actually playing together.
The games actually help kids develop a greater attention span and train them not to be so easily distracted.	Kids who need flashing lights and beeps to focus on are later going to have problems with a printed page that just sits there.
The games offer an opportunity to learn problem solving.	Problem solving in life is not so simple as triggering a lever.
The games offer a positive release.	The games are aggressive. They focus on violent themes of attack and destroy.
They are a safe form of fantasy.	Kids are pushed into a prefabricated fantasy rather than creating their own.

Questions to Consider and Discuss

1. Which side of the debate do you think wins? What do your class-mates think? Why do you and your classmates support the side you chose?

2. Do some library and Internet investigation to locate research arti-cles on video games. What evidence do these studies offer in sup-port of either the pros or cons of the debate?

3. Take a field trip to your local toy store and/or computer store. As you study the kinds of video games currently available, how would you characterize their play value? Are there games that go beyond blasting and zapping moving targets? Are there games designed to encourage cooperative play? How predominant are they?

they are once again dealing with animated, on-screen images. Yet like televi-sion, computer games are isolating. A visit to any video arcade confirms this. The lights are dim, the kids are serious, and they stand with their backs to one another, hands hammering away in a frenetic motion at knobs and buttons.

In Profile

Manhunt
Box 8.4

The story begins with the staged execution of convicted killer James Earl Cash. He's been strapped to the gurney but unknowingly injected with sedatives instead of lethal drugs. He awakens in the dank confines of the death chamber and discovers he's become the star of a series of snuff films. Cash is ordered around by smarmy Valiant Video Enterprises director Lionel Starkweather. As Cash, you stroll the trash-lined mean streets of Carcer City, a Midwestern Rust Belt town, picking off various thugs and gang members in a variety of bru-tal ways through 20 levels. Delivering the nastiest killings is key—each death is rated on a five-star scale. Lethal weapons include plastic bags for suffocating, glass shards, and metal wire. If you make it to higher levels, you'll obtain sickles, chain saws, and an array of guns. The key to success is stealth: You must lure your victims into shadows where they can't see you, then sneak up from behind for the kill (adapted from Slagle, 2004, p. E5).

Some games present interesting challenges and teach positive values, but the most popular games are those that deal with the martial arts, sports, and fantasy themes. Such games as *Mortal Kombat, Postal, Total Carnage,* and *Street Fighter* have been best-sellers. One game features overdeveloped, tattooed males with shotguns killing similarly ugly characters. The female is dressed in skimpy leather underwear, and she whips the other characters. The winner is the one who kills the most people. Perhaps these are the qualities that kids want because, as one child interviewed put it, "it makes me feel powerful and in control." It's also good business. As one video arcade manager claimed,

> We have boys who come daily in hopes of increasing their score and thereby being able to place their initials on the video screen of the game. Some boys are so committed that they spend upward of twenty dollars a day here. (Russell, 2004)

Although still extremely popular, games played in video arcades have experienced a slight downward trend because of the accessibility of home games (Fig. 8.2). In response, companies are developing virtual reality arcade games as well as bigger, faster, more sophisticated games made with multiple high-speed computers, laser disc players, strobes, large-screen projectors, and booming, discotheque-quality sound.

This brings us to another area of leisure assistance provided by technology: simulated leisure. Leisure activities and settings are being simulated at an unprecedented rate, and some predict that within the next decade, artificial leisure will dominate (Priest & Gass, 2000). There are numerous clues to this: Gaylord Palms Hotel in Orlando, under a biosphere-type dome that simulates Florida's St. Augustine, Key West, and Everglades swamp; the attraction "Mission: Space" at Epcot in Walt Disney World ("as close as you

Figure 8.2
A video arcade in a shopping mall. Games played in public arcades have experienced a slight downward trend because of the accessibility of home games. (© Ruth V. Russell.)

can get to blasting off into space without leaving earth"); and golf simulators at your corner bar. Artificial surfaces have also developed for a wide range of sports: hockey, white-water kayaking, body surfing, rock climbing, and tennis. You can play baseball, swim with dolphins, and hang glide—all virtually. Some leisure scholars envision a day when technology will allow the simulation of any human experience (Forrester, 2004).

Indeed, one of the fastest growing leisure pursuits is indoor rock climbing on artificial walls (Kalaygian, 2002). Since the first one at William G. Long Camp near Seattle, Washington, the sport has now expanded to requiring several regulating bodies. As a result, the Climbing Gym Association currently has members from over 2,000 commercial and public climbing facilities (Attarian, 2000), and numerous regional and international competitions are held.

The Study Says
Simulated Leisure Still Leisure?
Box 8.5

Is simulated leisure still leisure? This was the question for researcher Scott Forrester (2004) in studying the sport of indoor rock climbing. His interviews with climbers at a university-sponsored facility in the United States revealed that the simulated experience of rock climbing can be characterized as:

- **accessible:** More people can learn about and participate in the sport.

- **ecological:** An artificial rock face minimizes environmental disturbances.

- **reduced involvement:** Participants have less personal or emotional investment.

- **reduced mental engagement:** Because the nature of the challenge is predictable, not much thinking is required.

- **reduced sensory:** Because the setting is indoors, absent are the smells, visuals, temperatures, and sounds of the activity.

- passive: It is less physically active.

- social interaction: It provides more of a social setting for many.

So what do you think? Is simulated leisure really leisure?

One of the major questions about simulated leisure is what is called its fidelity. Fidelity is the "realism" of the activity and its environment. How authentic is the simulation compared with the natural or original activity? The **fidelity** of a simulated leisure pursuit is the extent to which it replicates what it is simulating. For example, when playing a game of simulated golf, are your actions, thoughts, and attitudes the same as when you are outside at a real course? In studies investigating this question, virtually all simulated golfers have agreed that the simulator did not reproduce a very realistic experience when compared with outdoor golf (Beggs, 2002; Forrester, 2004). Everything from the teeing and putting surfaces, to the screen images, to the portrayal of shots on the screen, to how people choose to play certain shots, to what they wear and what they do between shots combine to produce a very low-fidelity experience. Other simulated pursuits, such as wave pools and simulated roller-coaster rides, seem to have higher fidelity.

> **Fidelity:** in simulated leisure, refers to the realism of the environment

From Your Own Experience

Let's Ride Some Thrill Rides!
Box 8.6

Go to the Internet and visit sites that have video experiences simulating a leisure pursuit. For example, you could visit Cedar Point Amusement Park in Sandusky, Ohio, by going to http://www.cedar-point.com/. You can "ride" some of the roller coasters, including the new "Top Thrill Dragster." Or, you could go to the site for Walt Disney World (http://disneyworld.com), and from there to Epcot park and experience the new "Mission: Space," which at the time of this writing you could ride with Tiger Woods!

Afterward, reflect on what kind of "fun" you had in these simulated leisure experiences. Share your experiences with classmates and together seek to answer the criticisms about fidelity in simulated leisure.

Of course, as with all matters of technological development, simulated leisure has its critics, and this question of fidelity is at the heart of it. It appears to be a matter of values and preferences. For example, which would you rather see, a robotic crocodile at Disneyland or a real crocodile in the River Gambia? The Disney version rolls its eyes, moves from side to side, and disappears beneath the surface and rises again, just like a real crocodile. But the best part is that it does this all the time, unlike a real crocodile, which actually spends most of its time sleeping. Some of you may prefer the Disney crocodile because it's easier to get to Disneyland than to Africa, but then others of you may prefer the crocodile in the River Gambia, primarily because it is harder to get to (or because they are reputed to have supernatural healing powers).

Another related criticism of simulated leisure is that the fake sometimes seems more compelling than the real. That is, Disney's crocodile might seem more fulfilling because you are able to experience its full range of behaviors. In *The Future Does Not Compute: Warnings from the Internet* (1995), Stephen Talbott quotes educators who say that years of exciting and up-close nature programming on television have compromised wildlife experiences for children. As overheard at the Brooklyn Botanical Gardens, a child asked the attendant to make the flowers open fast—just as she'd seen in the time-lapse photography of Disney films (Turkle, 2004, p. 373).

Perhaps it doesn't come down to a choice between simulated and real leisure pursuits at all. Perhaps we can have both! The important question is more likely, "How can we get the best of both?"

Technology as Leisure

Finally, we consider technology itself as a leisure pursuit. Our topics of discussion might still be computer games and simulated leisure, but our focus here is on technology for its own recreational value. In other words, we go beyond thinking about the computer as an aid to leisure expression and feature it as the goal of leisure expression. An appropriate illustration of this is perhaps the Internet.

It is difficult to exaggerate the importance of the **Internet** in the way people access information, communicate with others, and do business with people in other firms or within their own company. In particular, the World Wide Web, a distributed software facility that organizes the information on the Internet into a network of interrelated electronic documents, has changed the face of communication, information exchange, and commerce (Allen, 1999). It has also become the "superhighway" of leisure: For many it is an entertaining way to spend most of their free time.

> **Internet:** a global network of networks (such as the World Wide Web) on the computer that is a source of communication, information, commerce, and entertainment

In Profile

Geocaching
Box 8.7

Geocaching is an adventure game for global positioning system (GPS) users. A GPS is an electronic device that can determine your approximate location on the planet (within around six to 20 feet). Coordinates are normally given in longitude and latitude. You can use it to navigate from your current location to another location. Broken out, the word *geocaching* is *geo* for *"geography"* and *caching* for "the process of hiding a cache." A cache in computer terms is information usually stored in memory to make it faster to retrieve, but the term is also used in hiking and camping as a hiding place for concealing and preserving provisions. The activity is deceptively easy. The basic idea is to have individuals and organizations set up caches all over the world (currently over 200 countries) and share the locations of these caches on the Internet. GPS users can then use the location coordinates to find the caches. Once found, a cache reward may be of almost anything, such as maps, books, software, CDs, videos, tickets, games, and so on. The rules stipulate that when you take something from a cache, you also leave something for the next person to find (see http://www.geocaching.com).

The Internet is expected to increase in popularity even more. For example, in 1995, approximately 18 million people worldwide were regularly using the Internet. By 1999, just four years later, about 92 million were regular users, and four years after that, 459 million were using the Internet regularly. This is an unprecedented growth rate. The United States and Canada account for about 40% of this usage (CommerceNet/Nielsen Media Research, 2003).

As with anything this powerful, it receives both accolades and criticisms. On the one hand, as one enthusiast commented, the Internet is "by far the greatest and most significant achievement in the history of mankind" (Lohr, 1999, p. C-1). Certainly the use of the computer for fun would be greatly limited without it. Some estimate that people typically use the Internet for pleasure about half of the time. Through the Internet, we can realize savings on travel purchases, make new friends, and gain information that contributes to the overall quality of life. People play games by themselves and with other people in real time through the Internet. But recreational uses of the Internet also include cyberporn and online gambling.

This suggests that the Internet promotes taboo forms of recreation. The criticism is difficult to understand, however, because of the contradictions. For example, let's consider "Net casinos." According to Rolling Good Times Online (http://rgtonline.com/), there are thousands of gambling links, from blackjack to baseball to bingo—all this in spite of the fact that in the United States, several states have outlawed gambling, and current federal law prohibits betting on sports over telephone lines. Yet online gambling can be credited with converting a traditionally solitary pursuit—sitting alone in front of a slot machine at a casino—into a party! Indeed, some gaming sites play host to hundreds and sometimes thousands of players of a single game at a time, match players of comparable skill, and run tournaments—things that bring people together.

Another worry on the minds of some leisure scientists is whether the Internet is replacing other forms of popular culture. Is the use of this technology affecting the use of more traditional media, such as television and newspapers? The significance of the Internet relative to traditional media is its interactivity (Robinson & Godbey, 1997). Rather than being a passive recipient of entertainment, the Internet user is directly involved in a multiway network of communication. For example, people can now discuss their favorite topics with like-minded others through chat rooms or discussion groups. We all know people who spend massive amounts of time in these chat rooms, so it does seem likely they would watch less television or read the newspaper for shorter periods of time.

Figure 8.3
What kind of neighborhood is the cyberhood? (© Ruth V. Russell.)

To submit this hunch to research scrutiny, 3,603 American respondents were surveyed about their use of television, newspapers, magazines, books, radio, movies, and the Internet (Kohut, 1995). In contrast to the expected lower usage of these traditional media by users of the Internet, the results suggested a more reinforcing or supplemental relationship. In general, home Internet users were more likely to use traditional media as well, particularly books. Some media researchers explain this as a pattern of "the more, the more," whereby those already committed become more committed (Robinson, 1968). What was troubling from the survey, however, was that among heavy Internet users, the number of times they called a friend or relative just to talk dropped, even though the number of times they visited with a friend or relative stayed the same.

The umbrella issue in all this is the idea of the cyberhood. **Cyberhoods** are virtual communities formed in chat rooms, through mailing lists, and in discussion groups on the Internet. How closely can they reproduce the qualities of real neighborhoods in terms of human interaction and shared interests, diversity, and meaningfulness? Does it matter if they can't?

> **Cyberhood:** virtual communities formed in chat rooms, on mailing lists, and through discussion groups on the Internet

Barlow (2004) claims that a lot is still missing from the communities of cyberspace (Fig. 8.3). To his thinking, foremost, is *prana. Prana* is the Hindu term for both "breath" and "spirit." Barlow uses the term to mean that even though the cyberhood offers information, it does not offer experience. When we're in a chat room, for example, we cannot really sense the others—their smell, the breeze from their bodies, their tone of voice—the qualities that Barlow claims make an experience. We don't really know if someone is shy or outgoing, because the medium flattens everyone out to rather standard beings.

There is something else missing in the cyberhood, claims Barlow (2004): diversity. At present there are very few older people, poor people, illiterate people, and people from the entire continent of Africa. He writes, "There is not much human diversity in cyberspace, which is populated, as near as I can tell, by white males under 50 with plenty of computer terminal time, great typing skills, high math SATs, strongly held opinions on just about everything, and an excruciating face-to-face shyness, especially with the opposite sex" (p. 364).

From Your Own Experience

Survey of Futures
Box 8.8

Use your individual responses to the following survey as a basis for a group discussion.

Scenario	+ Agreement -
Use of the Internet will continue to increase in importance as a leisure resource.	5 4 3 2 1
Use of the Internet will result in accessing more resources for leisure participation.	5 4 3 2 1
Increasing use of the Internet will mean leisure resources are primarily available only to wealthier and better educated people.	5 4 3 2 1
Tighter regulations against violence and sexism will be applied to video games.	5 4 3 2 1
New uses of technology will be developed that increase social interaction among people.	5 4 3 2 1
Eventually, simulated leisure will become more popular than the original activity it mimics.	5 4 3 2 1
In general, the use of technology as a leisure expression will harm the essential qualities of leisure.	5 4 3 2 1

Summary: What We Understand

Cyberculture is no longer an emerging trend. It is of major importance to everything we know and do, both as individuals and as a society, particularly for leisure. From reading this chapter you should know that

- Advances in technology have given people innovative places to play, better equipment to aid their adventures, and new activities to pursue.

- The positive influences of technology on our pastimes include access to information about leisure options, the creation of new leisure pursuits, new horizons in leisure for people with disabilities, and tourism as a global focus.

- The negative consequences from technological advances in leisure include environmental damage, passivity, violence, consumerism, and social isolation.

- Pastimes have been assisted, improved, or expanded by technology. We focused on games and on simulated sports and outdoor recreation.

- As with all matters of technological development, computer games and simulated leisure have received both accolades and criticisms. Concerns with computer games stem from their impact on children and the question of fidelity, which is at the heart of the concern about simulated leisure. It appears to be a matter of values and preferences.

- Entirely new pastimes have been developed by technology. We focused on the use of the Internet as leisure.

- The Internet has become the "superhighway" of leisure: For many it is an entertaining way to spend most of their free time.

Applications to Professional Practice

As has been made clear throughout this book, leisure resources are needed to enhance the success of societies. As this chapter has pointed out, technologically based leisure resources have become increasingly important. But some worry about the "goodness" of this type of resource for leisure. Primary in the concern is fear of losing what is labeled social capital. **Social capital** refers to the interpersonal networks that make a community cohesive. It is participation in Parent Teacher Associations, the League of Women Voters, and the Canadian Red Cross. It is volunteering in the Boy Scouts and at the hospital. Research by Putnam (1995) documented that there has been a decline in social capital in North American societies. He claims that people are not participating as much as they used to in making their communities good places to live, citing a roughly 25 percent decline in the time spent in informal socializing and visiting since 1965 and a nearly 50 percent decline in memberships in clubs and organizations. Although Putnam's research did not reveal why this may be happening, guesses include a rise in

> **Social capital:** features of community life, such as interpersonal networks, volunteering, and participation in self-governance

the amount of time spent with technological forms of leisure, including video games and the Internet.

Some social critics disagree with Putnam, however. They have argued that Putnam's research has ignored grassroots political groups, religious organizations, and youth sports leagues. For example, Perlstein (1997) claimed that just as many social-good organizations exist but that people in them are more interested in excluding other people. Also, Stengel (1996) proposed that Americans may be redefining the forms and nature of their participation with the community. For example, more of the work of social capital may now be done on home computers and is therefore not as visible.

Regardless, social capital is necessary, and possible declines in it are ominous for our communities. This is because a decline in social capital has numerous negative consequences, including a lack of participation in democratic governance, increased alienation and loneliness, and a decreasing ability to solve problems in groups. It may also mean a decline in a sense of caring about one's neighborhood and community (Godbey, 1997).

Building, or rebuilding, social capital is an important role of leisure, because informal socializing, volunteering to help others, and participating in organizations that work toward a common good are in themselves leisure experiences. In fact, Putnam's (1995) research was published under the title of "Bowling Alone," meaning that people no longer even participate in leisure in groups, such as in bowling leagues. What would a community be like if there were no community-wide festivals and celebrations? What if basketball were no longer played in face-to-face teams or leagues, but only by one player, on one computer, and with a virtual court and opponents? Leisure plays multiple roles that can help restore social capital. Therefore, the professional in leisure services will increasingly need skills in community development, group dynamics, and community organization—as well as access to a computer.

For More Information

Read about Putnam's (2000) book, *Bowling Alone: The Collapse and Revival of American Community* at http://www.bowlingalone.com. From this site you can also listen to a National Public Radio program, read ongoing survey results, and find out how actual communities are increasing their social capital.

References

Allen, J. (1999). *Selected materials for management information systems. S302: Spring 2000, Indiana University*. New York: McGraw-Hill.

Attarian, A. (2000). Artificial climbing environments. In J. C. Miles, & S. Priest (Eds.), *Adventure programming* (pp. 392–415). State College, PA: Venture.

Barlow, J. P. (2004). Cyberhood vs. neighborhood. In M. Petracca, & M. Sorapure (Eds.), *Common culture: Reading and writing about American popular culture* (pp. 211–236). Upper Saddle River, NJ: Prentice Hall.

Beggs, B. (2002). *Activity satisfaction in golf and simulated golf.* Unpublished doctoral dissertation, Indiana University, Bloomington.

Bryce, J., & Rutter, J. (2003). Gender dynamics and the social and spatial organization of computer gaming. *Leisure Studies, 22,* 1–15.

Business Communications Company. (1999). *RG230: The electronic entertainment industry.* Norwalk, CT: Author.

CommerceNet/Nielsen Media Research. (2003). *Demographics of the Internet survey.*

Forrester, S. A. (2004). *The grounded theory of the leisure experience in simulated environments.* Unpublished doctoral dissertation, Indiana University, Bloomington.

Godbey, G. (1997). *Leisure and leisure services in the 21st century.* State College, PA: Venture.

Goodale, T., & Godbey, G. (1988). *The evolution of leisure: Historical and philosophical perspectives.* State College, PA: Venture.

Hammel, R., & Foster, C. (1986). A sporting chance: Relationships between technological change and concept of fair play in fishing. *Journal of Leisure Research, 18,* 40–52.

Henderson, K. A., Bialeschki, M. D., Hemingway, J. L., Hodges, J. S., Kivel, B. D., & Sessoms, H. D. (2001). *Introduction to recreation and leisure services* (8th ed.). State College, PA: Venture.

Kalaygian, M. (2002, January). Advice from the pros: The climbing wall industry sounds off. *Government Recreation and Fitness, 9,* 18–20, 41–42.

Kaufman, W. (2000, June 26). The way we play: The changing face of America [Radio broadcast]. On *National Public Radio Morning Edition.* Retrieved March 3, 2004, from http://www.npr.org/programs/morning

Kohut, A. (1995). *Technology in the American household.* Washington, D.C.: Times-Mirror Center for the People and the Press.

Lee, B., Godbey, G., & Sawyer, S. (2003, October). Senior Net, v. 2.0: Research update. *Parks and Recreation.* 22–29.

Lohr, S. (1999, December 20). The economy transformed, bit by bit. *New York Times,* p. C-1.

Perlstein, R. (1997, January). Blind alley? Field notes. *Lingua Franca,* 12–13.

Priest, S., & Gass, M. (2000). Future trends and issues in adventure programming. In J. C. Miles, & S. Priest (Eds.), *Adventure rogramming* (pp. 416–432). State College, PA: Venture.

Putnam, R. (1995, January). Bowling alone: America's declining social capital. *Journal of Democracy, 6*(1), 65–78.

Putnam, R. (2000). *Bowling alone: The collapse and revival of American community.* New York: Simon & Schuster.

Rideout, V. G., Foehr, U. G., Roberts, D. F., & Brodie, M. (1999). *Kids & media @ the new millennium.* Menlo Park, CA: Kaiser Family Foundation.

Robinson, J. (1968). World affairs information and mass media exposure. *Journalism Quarterly, 44,* 23–30.

Robinson, J. P., & Godbey, G. (1997). *Time for life: The surprising ways Americans use their time.* University Park: The Pennsylvania State University Press.

Romita, T. (2001, May 15). Overworked: Vacations are a luxury for U.S. professionals. *Business2.com.*

Russell, R. V. (2004). Unpublished raw data.

Slagle, M. (2004, February 1). Manhunt redefines video game violence. *Hoosier Times* (Bloomington, IN), p. D2.

Stengel, R. (1996, July 22). Bowling together. *Time,* 35.

Turkle, S. (2004). Virtuality and its discontents. In M. Petracca, & M. Sorapure (Eds.), *Common culture: Reading and writing about American popular culture* (pp. 181–205). Upper Saddle River, NJ: Prentice Hall.

CHAPTER NINE

Taboo Recreation

Preview

Is leisure always wholesome?

No. In spite of leisure's vital importance to the health and well-being of individuals and societies, our pastimes can also produce harmful outcomes.

What is taboo recreation?

Pastimes that are forbidden by law, custom, or belief are taboo. Examples are gambling, substance abuse, vandalism, and harmful sex.

Why does taboo recreation occur?

There are at least three explanations. First, the concept of anomie says that once-viable social norms no longer control people's actions. Second, the concept of differential association claims that deviant behavior is learned through interaction with others. Third, the concept of retreatism explains that taboo recreation is the result of personal expression.

Is taboo recreation leisure?

This question is at the crux of the dilemma. If leisure is a condition of personal attitudes, preferences, and values, labeling leisure as harmful is useless. On the other hand, if leisure is a matter of making moral choices, labeling certain pastimes as unworthy is possible.

Key Terms

Taboo 259
Deviance 260
Anomie 262
Leisure boredom 263
Differential association . . .265
Retreatism 267
Ideational mentality 268
Substance abuse 269
Sensate mentality 274
Wellness 278
Prole leisure 279

L eisure is a major contributor to the well-being of people and their communities. As we've already explored, leisure can help relieve tensions, maintain physical fitness, enhance mental equilibrium, and teach us how to get along with others. It is one of the best methods of health insurance, it builds unified communities, it yields a productive workforce, and it can serve as a catalyst for protecting and rehabilitating the environment. Specially trained professionals working in treatment centers use leisure activities to help ill and injured patients return to the mainstream. Leisure is, in simple fact, one of the most positive and wholesome aspects of contemporary life.

However, leisure also has a negative side. Unpleasant results, as well as pleasant ones, are possible through our pastimes. People can be injured while participating in leisure pursuits. Exhaustion, apprehension, nervousness, disappointment, and frustration can be experienced through participation in outdoor pastimes and sports in particular (Lee, Howard, & Datillo, 1992).

The Study Says
Compulsive Running
Box 9.1

As a leisure activity, drinking alcohol and using mood-altering drugs can become addictive and a problem for users, their family and friends, and society in general. Can this also be true for those leisure activities we typically consider wholesome? What about running, for example? Is it possible that running can become addictive and thus a problem?

Forty males who are regular runners were divided into two groups and studied for six weeks. One group continued their normal running (three times a week for a total of 10 miles). The other group was stopped from running for the middle two weeks of the study. Everyone completed questionnaires at the end of each week.

According to the findings, symptoms of depression were greater for those who stopped running for two weeks. Such complaints as anxiety, insomnia, and feelings of being under strain were also greater after both the first and second weeks of the withdrawal period in the group that stopped running. These complaints disappeared by the last two weeks of the study when both groups were running again.

The researchers concluded that stopping regular physical exercise produces psychological problems and that physical exercise may therefore be considered addictive (Morris, Steinberg, Sykes, & Salmon, 1990).

Beyond this, leisure has an even darker side. Under certain circumstances, individuals engage in pastimes that society considers deviant. In American society, for instance, only certain forms of gambling are legal, and only in certain locations. Buying sexual pleasure is considered a problem in several countries of the world. Vandalism can be fun for the participants, but it costs other individuals and the society billions of dollars each year. Binge drinking is a pastime increasingly practiced by college students. The examples go on. Sometimes these "dark" pastimes are labeled "purple" recreation, implying they are off-color (Curtis, 1988).

Pursuits such as these are considered **taboo** in many societies. The word taboo comes from the Polynesian word *tapu*, which means "something sacred, special, dangerous, or unclean." We use the term here to signify behaviors that are restricted by social custom. All social groups of people have taboos, but the same taboos are not universal. For example, Australian aborigines must not say the name of a dead person aloud, and the left hand is never used for eating in Malaysia.

> **Taboo:** restriction of a behavior based on social tradition

Taboo is a useful descriptor of the pastimes we consider in this chapter because they are typically forbidden by custom or belief, and often by law. That is, a recreational activity wears the label "deviant" because of a subjective value held by society. It is "socially unacceptable." Societies differ in which pastimes are considered taboo. In addition, even within the same society, taboo recreation can be applied differently and change its degree of "wrongness" over time. For example, in colonial America in the 1700s, Puritan taboos were observed. There were laws forbidding card playing, dancing between women and men, and theatrical performances. These laws are no longer enforced in the United States; in fact, governments frequently contribute financial support so that these pursuits might thrive.

The label taboo is appropriate because what is considered deviant also differs according to age groups. For example, one group in particular tends to be associated most with deviant leisure—adolescents (Dormbusch, 1989). In addition to the problems of alienation and changing identities that might inspire more deviant leisure expressions by youth, there is also an age bias in many societies. Indeed, what might be understood as an appropriate activity at an older age (such as sexual activity and alcohol consumption) is often seen as deviant, and perhaps illegal, when carried out by young people (Epstein, 1998).

The purpose of this chapter is to expand our understanding of leisure by considering the relationship between leisure and acts of deviance. We begin by describing a system for classifying taboo recreation and then consider three possible explanations for it. This is followed by examples of taboo recreation that can be injurious to participants and injurious to others.

Leisure and Deviance

What is deviance? Although it may be simple to define **deviance** as any behavior that is different from what is socially accepted, distinguishing when an action is deviant is much more complex and ambiguous. As in all things, there are two sides to the story. Going for a jog may build fitness levels, but so might hooking hubcaps. Joining a Scout troop may provide outlets for socialization and building self-esteem, but so could hanging out with an urban gang.

> **Deviance: behavior that is different from an accepted norm**

In modern industrial societies, everyone is involved at least occasionally in deviant behavior. We have all bent the rules, taken shortcuts, and told white lies. This is because the rules and laws governing social life are inherently ambiguous and therefore open to different interpretations. To some extent, deviance is nothing but the activity that exploits this ambivalence (Rojek, 1999).

Some theorists offer a more precise definition of deviance. For example, Becker (1963) argues that the label of deviance is not a quality of the act itself but a question of the rules and sanctions applied by others. That is, reactions to behavior are value laden and cannot be understood in absolute terms. So instead of being a matter of seeing right and wrong in social acts, deviance is a matter of who or what has the power to shape our judgments about social acts. Later, Foucault (1981) also pinpointed power relations as the crux of deviance. Differences in power mean that if an action is considered wrong or bad by those in power (such as elected officials, religious groups, or those in the majority), then it is labeled deviant.

The occurrence of deviance in leisure is not only documented in police records and social work files but in research as well. For example, in one study (Agnew, 1990), a sample of adolescents indicated the reasons for their participation in 14 types of taboo recreational activities. These reasons included personal pleasure, thrill seeking, social pressure, and boredom—all qualities associated with leisure. Further, Aguilar (1987) provided a rationale for considering delinquent behavior a game:

> In theft or vandalism activities, the object of the game is to complete the task without getting caught. . . . If one youth gets caught, the unwritten rule is never to identify the others. A violation of the rule means exclusion from future delinquent games with friends and peers. (p. 5)

In spite of difficulties in defining deviance precisely, we do have a system that helps us categorize deviant leisure. It is a model developed by J. B. Nash that shows in pyramid form a hierarchy of leisure values (Nash, 1953). As shown in Figure 9.1, creative activity is the highest use of free time. Other positive uses of free time are active participation, emotional participation, and entertainment, although the lower on the hierarchy, the more personally dulling and the more socially mediocre the activity is. Nash designated taboo recreational activity as falling at the lowest two levels of the model, the subzero levels. One level below zero on the model represents pastimes that are unwholesome for the individual participant. At two levels below zero, pastimes that are harmful to others (including society) are represented.

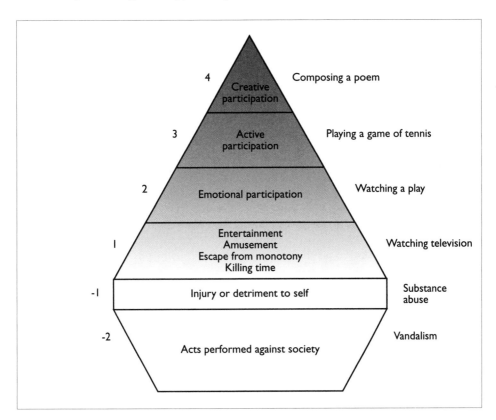

Figure 9.1
An illustration of the Nash pyramid.

Although certainly subject to differences in personal and subcultural values, Nash's pyramid will help us discuss selected taboo recreational pursuits later in the chapter. But before moving on to that, let's try to understand more about why people engage in socially unacceptable pastimes.

Why Taboo Recreation?

Why do people participate in leisure pursuits that are considered harmful, immoral, or wrong? As with most problems in society, explanations for taboo recreation have been sought in attempts to reduce its incidence. Typically, deviant behavior is studied in general, and the findings are then extended to deviant recreational behaviors specifically. As a result, several theoretical explanations are currently available. We'll consider three: anomie, differential association, and retreatism.

The first explanation for taboo recreation is the concept of anomie. **Anomie** occurs when once-viable social norms no longer control people's actions (Merton, 1968). For example, at American River College in Sacramento, California, table games were banned—including chess, checkers, cards, and dominoes. Why? The disruptive behaviors of players in the cafeteria and library required the campus police to restore order because the formerly workable, informal social norms no longer controlled students' behaviors while playing the games. Anomie can be traced to an imbalance between a goal and the means to attain it.

> **Anomie:** a lack of purpose and identity in a person or a society resulting in the demise of formerly useful social norms

Simmel (1971) blames the changes and disruptions of life in modern society in general as creating ripe conditions for the development of anomie. Although it does not cause deviant forms of leisure, perhaps modern stress does provide an environment in which taboo pastime choices are nurtured (Moore, 1982). Boredom may be another environment conducive to the creation of deviant leisure choices. Boredom is a human emotion that occurs when one's life experience is not meaningful enough. As the contemporary philosopher Bertrand Russell (1968) put it, boredom is "essentially a thwarted desire for events, not necessarily pleasant ones, but just occurrences such as will enable the victim of ennui to know one day from another" (p. 36). Although we typically consider leisure as an antidote to boredom, scholars Iso-Ahola and Weisinger (1990) have proposed that boredom can occur in leisure. They called this **leisure boredom**. How would you answer the following questions?

1. For me, leisure time just drags on and on.

2. In my leisure time, I usually don't like what I'm doing, but I don't know what else to do.

3. I waste too much of my leisure time sleeping.

4. Leisure-time activities do not excite me. (p. 10)

These and other questions in a study helped Iso-Ahola and Weisinger discover that boredom can occur during leisure. If you agreed with these questions, your perception is likely to be that leisure can be boring. Leisure boredom results when people feel they cannot escape a meaningless leisure routine.

This often happens because of insufficient leisure skills and an unawareness that leisure can be psychologically rewarding. It seems likely that leisure boredom leads to anomie.

> **Leisure boredom:** results when people feel they cannot escape a meaningless leisure routine

A useful example of anomie as an explanation for taboo recreation is the pastime of sports spectating. Around the world, watching sports competitions is a major pursuit (Fig. 9.2). Television has a constant stream of sports programming 24 hours a day. Universities have multimillion-dollar sports programs with stadiums that seat up to 100,000 spectators. Sporting events are a daily topic of conversation wherever people gather, and attachments to particular teams and athletes seem to provide a kind of social identity for many of us. A wonderful vicarious pleasure results from watching top athletes perform. We see ourselves dancing a pirouette to the top of the hoop for a slam dunk in basketball, or stretching across the court to make an impossible match point in tennis.

Figure 9.2
Thoroughbred horse racing is one of the most popular live spectator sports in the United States, yet it is usually not an example of spectator violence. Why? (© Ruth V. Russell.)

Yet something has gone wrong! With greater frequency, we read about rioting and violence in the crowds at sporting events. Fires have been started in the stands and property destroyed. Fans have crossed barricades to attack and sometimes kill the fans of the other team or an athlete. Referees have been assaulted. It seems the attitude has quickly gone from "It doesn't matter whether you win or lose, but how you play the game" to being "in your face."

Eitzen (1984) examined newspaper accounts of 68 episodes of collective violence among spectators during or after sporting events and concluded that in three quarters of the cases, the precipitating event was violence in the game. Indeed, violence is part of the playing of some sports. American football is a contest of violent collisions; the physical struggle under the basket in basketball has become an essential part of the game. And as the saying goes, "I went to a fight and a hockey game broke out." Stupendous accidents are accentuated in auto racing, and of course, boxing is the practice of beating another person into unconsciousness.

Eitzen's research, then, explains spectating violence as a matter of aggression breeding aggression. When athletes are violent on the field or court, there is a greater likelihood for violence by the fans. Confirming this, a study by Leonard (1988) found a slight tendency for spectators of violent sports to score higher on a hostility scale after an event than spectators of nonviolent events.

From Your Own Experience

Aggressive or Nonagressive?
Box 9.2

Psychologists define aggression as "any form of behavior directed toward the goal of harming or injuring another living being who is motivated to avoid such treatment" (Baron & Richardson, 1994, p. 7). Using this definition as a basis, determine whether you consider the behavior in each of these situations to be aggressive (A) or nonaggressive (N).

A   N   1. A football safety delivers an extremely vicious but legal hit to a wide receiver and later indicates he wanted to punish the receiver and make him think twice about coming across the middle again.

A   N   2. A basketball coach breaks a chair in protesting a disputed call.

A   N   3. Pat, a field hockey midfielder, uses her stick to purposely hit her opponent in the shin in retaliation for her opponent's doing the same thing to her.

A   N   4. Barry knows that Andy is sensitive and self-conscious about his ability to putt under pressure, so he tells Andy that Coach Hall said if he does not putt better he will be replaced in the lineup. Coach Hall never said this.

A   N   5. Terri beans Audrey with a fastball that got away from her.

Answers

1. Aggressive (Although the hit was legal, the intent was to harm.)

2. Nonaggressive (The action was not directed at another human being.)

3. Aggressive (Although the athlete felt she was hit first, her intent was to harm.)

4. Aggressive (Even though no physical harm resulted, the intent was to cause fear or anxiety.)

5. Nonaggressive (Even though harm resulted, there was no intent to harm.)

(adapted from Weinberg & Gould, 1999, p. 477)

How do we explain recent increases in spectator violence? The concept of anomie may provide a useful clue. According to the theory of anomie, society prescribes norms of success for people. For many roles in sports—for example, the athlete, coach, and trainer—this success means winning. However, since virtually all sports contests create both winners and losers, someone is always thwarted in the quest for victory. Ways of coping with losing include conforming and rationalizing, but there are also socially deviant responses, such as cheating. Thus, the social norms that customarily rule sports may no longer have control over the players' (and spectators') behavior, and violence may result.

Other explanations for taboo recreation are plausible. For example, the theory of **differential association** simply claims that delinquent behavior, including taboo recreation, is learned through interaction with others. If a person's social group is delinquent, deviant forms of leisure may be learned. These social groups could include one's family, peers on sports teams, housemates at college, classmates, and friends in the neighborhood or at work. These group behaviors affect young people in particular.

> **Differential association:** delinquent behavior learned from others

Research also supports the differential association explanation of taboo recreation. A study of 3,000 adolescents in Canada (Bippy & Posterski, 1985) found that the majority considered friendships to be more important than family. Agnew (1991) found that the level of attachment and the amount of time spent together conditioned the impact of delinquent peers on delinquency behaviors. When time or attachment was minimal, deviant behavior was less likely to result. These data suggest that to reduce socially unacceptable behavior in leisure, adolescents' emotional closeness with delinquent peers needs to be minimized.

An obvious example of the differential association explanation of taboo recreation is youth gangs. In the United States there are an estimated 28,700 gangs with over 780,000 active members. Gangs are located in urban, suburban, small-town, and rural areas. Their activities include robbery, drug sales, and aggravated assault. Ninety-two percent of gang members are male (Moore & Cook, 1999).

Youth gangs provide an example of the differential association explanation of taboo recreation in that members are attracted to participate because the gangs offer power, recognition, excitement, and independence (Manson, 1990). The gangs create associations that can potentially lead to antisocial actions, depending on the strength of the relationships. A study of gangs in a southern California beach community (Lowney, 1984) reported that gang members felt that although basic needs were fulfilled through their family, the gang provided them with opportunities for the pursuit of pleasure. Further, condemnation by society strengthened the bonds of individuals to the gang, alienating them further from society and limiting their access to socially acceptable forms of leisure (Virgil, 1988).

In Focus

Freaks Talk Back
Box 9.3

Nobody wants to watch anything that's smarmy or tabloid or silly or unseemly—except the audience. (talk show host Sally Jessy Raphael, 1990)

Jerry Springer, Montel Williams, Oprah Winfrey, and others are daytime television talk show hosts. With the shrillness of fingernails on the blackboard, they get show "guests" to reveal nasty personal secrets on national television, rile them up, and then scold them for being so malicious. Cheating spouses, drag queen makeovers,

Christian pornographers, a black man who wants to join the Ku Klux Klan, and all manner of other different lifestyles are paraded before the television audience in a way that makes the fairground freak show seem contemporary.

Talk shows, critics repeat over and over, redefine deviance. The shows blur the lines between what is bizarre and alarming and what is typical and inconsequential. Talk shows boost abnormality by exaggerating its frequency and embellishing its consequences. Talk shows are defining deviancy down.

One person's trash, though, is another person's gold mine. Supporters claim the topics and style of the shows simply mirror society—they operate at the level of real everyday life, where real people are. In addition, the shows could be considered democratic in that they give people whose lifestyles are so heavily tilted toward invisibility and nonconformity 30 minutes of conformity and visibility. Here people can speak in their own voices (based on Gamson, 1998).

Questions to Consider and Discuss

1. *If you can, watch an episode of a daytime talk show, particularly* The Jerry Springer Show. *As you watch, ask yourself what are the appropriate boundaries between public and private, classy and trashy, normal and abnormal, deviant and not deviant.*

2. *These shows have been labeled "paradoxes of visibility." That is, with dramatic fury they democratize through exploitation, tell truth wrapped in a lie, and normalize through a freak show. Do you think this is a correct interpretation? Why or why not?*

3. *How might daytime talk shows be explained through the retreatist theory of deviance? Does anomie or differential association provide a better explanation?*

Finally, a third explanation for taboo recreation may be the idea of retreatism. **Retreatism** is a lifestyle that pulls away from dominant social norms as a matter of personal expression (Rojek, 1999). Dropping out, taking drugs, sexual experimentation, and engaging in other pastimes that are antithetical to the conventional order of life may be considered as an expression of self, in which a lifestyle centered around an alternative personal identity is created. Merton (1968) provided the classic description of retreatism as those who have "relinquished culturally prescribed goals, and

Retreatism: difference from the dominant social norms as a matter of personal expression

their behavior does not accord with institution norms" (p. 207). By this he meant that retreatism is a social problem. More recently, retreatists are considered not so much as having rejected culturally prescribed goals, but as having adopted "alternative" ones that better express how they see themselves.

One of the most interesting studies of a retreatist lifestyle is Willis' (1978) account of motorcycle subcultures. He found that lifestyle disengagement constituted their basis for existence. That is, they violated certain dominant social norms because of their passion for engine technology, not because they rejected dominant society. Simply, the motorcycle culture was felt by its members to be superior, where real life happened for them.

Taboo Recreation That Injures Self

Perhaps you've heard the expression "victimless crime." As described by sociologist Stephen Pfohl (1985), this label applies to a wide range of social exchanges punishable by criminal law, even though there is no specific victim. For example, substance abuse may be considered deviant because society deems it so, although its harm is mainly only to those who participate. Even though it may certainly be argued that substance abuse has the potential to harm others (e.g., drunk driving can kill innocent people), victimless crimes are primarily focused on the participant's pursuit of enjoyment.

A concept that attempts to explain these activities is an **ideational mentality** (Heise, 1988). Laws based on an ideational mentality are primarily morally derived. That is, people have an "idea" that something is bad. Even though they do not wish to participate in it themselves, they feel the need to prohibit others from being involved because they have the idea that such a restriction is for the public good. They have labeled a behavior, such as drug use, as deviant,

Ideational mentality: the belief or idea that something is bad

and they use the powers of law to make the label stick, even though its primary harm may be to the participant only. Let's explore two examples: substance abuse and gambling.

Narcotics are essential in the practice of medicine; they are often effective for the relief of particular diseases and pains. They can literally keep people alive. Alcohol is also useful. In modest amounts it provides a means of relaxation from hectic pressures, providing both physical and psychological benefits. A daily glass of wine or beer is considered by experts on old age to increase longevity. However, when drugs and alcohol are abused (i.e., overused) problems can result.

Substance abuse is perhaps the most prevalent type of taboo recreation. Illegal "experience-enhancing" drugs are everywhere, in every region of the world, and every society has alcoholics. No society is too poor and none too knowledgeable about the costs and consequences (Kelly & Freysinger, 2000).

Nor is the abuse of alcohol and drugs for recreation a new phenomenon. It has existed since ancient times. In fact, the invention of agriculture seems to have been motivated by a need for a constant food supply and the discovery of the use of cultivated grains for beer (Lazare, 1989).

> **Substance abuse:** using drugs, alcohol, and other substances in ways that threaten one's health or impair one's social or economic functioning

Drugs and alcohol can be considered recreational: They provide temporary escapes from everyday life, and they warm up a social group. Interestingly, a euphemism for using drugs is "taking a trip"—meaning to enjoy a change of pace, just as we do when we go on a vacation. Thus, alcohol and drug use often begin in a leisure context (Fig. 9.3). Alcohol and drugs are also combined with other recreational activities because it is believed these substances can enhance the fun. Cocktails are served at parties; beer is sold at baseball games; hallucinogens are popped at a concert. In The Netherlands, marijuana "bars" are common.

Figure 9.3
Substance abuse often begins in a leisure setting. (© Ruth V. Russell.)

In an effort to understand more about the relationship between drinking alcohol and leisure, a researcher interviewed 1,706 Canadians from all 10 provinces. Of the sample, 78 percent drank alcoholic beverages. The first reason given was companionship, followed by entertainment (Cosper, Okraku, & Neuman, 1985). Another study showed that social drinking is second only to television viewing as America's favorite pastime (Gross, 1983).

Unfortunately, alcohol and drugs provide only short trips, and overuse to make the trip longer can lead to insurmountable social and personal problems. Witness the more than two million members of Alcoholics Anonymous, an organization that helps people with alcohol-related problems (Alcoholics Anonymous, 2004). In addition, drug- and alcohol-related problems cost law enforcement agencies billions of dollars in crime management, and they cost employers billions of dollars in lost working time. Families and friends lose loved ones to disease and accidents associated with substance abuse. Indeed, one entire generation of Chinese was essentially wiped out by extensive opium use early in the 20th century (Godbey, 1989).

Good leisure experiences enrich and improve the participant. Although the use of drugs and alcohol may provide momentary sociability and relaxation, their abuse prevents any real leisure benefit from taking place. The more heavily we indulge in alcohol or drugs, the more destructive the effect, including to leisure. Leisure is about joy, freedom, intrinsic rewards, and spirituality, as well as pleasure and risk. Abuse of drugs or alcohol inhibits these qualities. Therefore, the relationship between dysfunctional substance use and dysfunctional use of leisure is a reciprocal one. Although substance use often begins in a leisure setting, as the use of the substance increases, the individual's leisure becomes secondary to the substance.

The Study Says
Recovery from Alcoholism Through Leisure
Box 9.4

A study by Hood (2003) investigated the role of leisure in the recovery from alcoholism among women. Data from an in-depth case study of three women, collected over a six-month period, were examined. The results indicated that these women found leisure involvement to be critical to their moving beyond simply "not drinking" toward true recovery. Specifically, they found that leisure involvement allowed them to learn about themselves. However, they also stated that, for them, learning how to experience leisure without the mediation of alcohol was extremely difficult.

Now we turn our attention to another form of recreation considered taboo because of an ideational mentality: gambling. How can gambling provide many of the qualities of leisure but also be harmful to the participant?

Nevada is the driest state in the United States, with an average annual rainfall of only about seven inches. As a result, much of Nevada is uninhabited, sagebrush-covered desert. In 1931 the state created a new industry: gambling. Today in almost every public place, visitors and residents can enjoy slot machines, and the casinos of Reno, Tahoe, and Las Vegas are legendary (Fig. 9.4). Today, gambling taxes account for about 38 percent of state revenues.

Figure 9.4
Las Vegas gambling. (© Ruth V. Russell.)

Dedicated gamblers in many parts of North America who were once satisfied to visit Las Vegas once or twice a year now scarcely have to leave home to play the slots. In 1971 voters in New Jersey approved legislation allowing legalized casino gambling in Atlantic City. Midwesterners are now revisiting the days of riverboat gambling with casinos on the rivers, and Native Americans managing reservations have realized that by establishing casinos, gambling can solve economic shortfalls without government interference. In fact, gambling, in both its legal and illegal forms, takes place in just about every North American town through dog and horse racetrack betting, poker games, bingo, sport bookmaking, state lotteries, and church raffles. With the advent of Internet-based gambling, wagering has increased, primarily by middle-income people. With an established line of credit, it is possible to wager on a variety of games without leaving home.

The growth of gambling as a favorite pastime has been phenomenal. In 1995, almost 100 million Americans legally wagered $400 billion and lost $39 billion to the house. In 1999 the estimate was up to $600 billion a year for legal gambling. Additionally, the FBI estimates that $80 million is bet illegally each year on the NCAA basketball tournament alone. This means people spend more on legal gambling than on films, books, amusement attractions, and recorded music combined. Prior to 1988 in the United States, gambling was legal in only the two states of Nevada and New Jersey. Now gambling is illegal in only the two states of Hawaii and Utah (http://www.sims.berkeley.edu, Retrieved 3/10/04; Kelly & Freysinger, 2000).

In Profile

Bingo
Box 9.5

Bingo descended from the lotteries first organized by the Italian government in the 1530s. It was an alternative version of the lotteries that existed at the time, with three horizontal rows and nine vertical rows with numbered and blank squares in random arrangements. The columns were broken into sets of 10 numbers, 1-10, 11-20, all the way up to 90 in the last column. The bingo balls were chips in those days, and were pulled out of a sack by the caller. The first player to cover one of the three horizontal rows was declared the winner. Beginning in the 1800s, bingo variations began to be used as teaching devices. Germany, for example, used a version to teach its youth multiplication tables.

Up until this point, though, bingo was not bingo. It was still known as a "lotto" game because of its original designation as a lottery. The coining of the term bingo is most often attributed to a slip of the tongue. As it happened, Edwin S. Lowe was searching for a game to rescue his struggling toy company when he first played "beano" at a traveling carnival. Lowe tells the story of going home and gathering up beans, rubber stamps, and cardboard cards to hold his own beano get-together with friends to test the game's viability. In one of these first games, a friend of Lowe's was fast approaching a winning card, and as the momentum became more and more exciting and tense, he jumped up and tried to stammer out "beano!" but it came out garbled as "bingo!" Lowe recalls knowing right away that he would be marketing the game as bingo (Fig. 9.5).

Figure 9.5
The "picture frame" and "railroad tracks" in bingo. (© Christopher B. Stage.)

Gambling is betting on the outcome of a future event. Although people bet on almost anything with an unpredictable outcome, they bet most often on games of chance and skill. Indeed, the basis of gambling in games is reflected in its other label: gaming. As a pastime, gambling awards the player with the thrill of competition and winning. For most gamblers, it is a form of recreation. Psychologists believe that the real attraction of gambling lies in the thrill of uncertainty, the daring involved in taking chances, and the challenge of testing one's skill. In a study conducted by Smith and Preston (1985), 45 percent said they gamble to relieve boredom and generate excitement.

Unfortunately, some gamble because they also believe it is a quick way to make money without the effort of working. According to one study at Indiana University (School of Public and Environmental Affairs, 1993), state lottery gaming is on the rise, particularly among the poor. The study claimed that lottery players in the lowest income bracket (under $15,000) spent a whopping 8.42 percent of their money on lottery tickets. Another study confirmed that low-income families wagered on average seven percent of their income, whereas those in the middle- and higher-income brackets wagered less than three percent (Abbott & Cramer, 1993).

Government sponsorship of gambling raises a question about the taboo label for this pastime. A contradiction exists when state laws continue to maintain that gambling is immoral and prosecute people for engaging in it (about 20,000 each year) yet increasingly sponsor state lotteries. We might be tempted to conclude that all gambling from which the government doesn't earn money is illegal!

Other forms of recreation that harm participants also demonstrate a taboo contradiction. For example, such pastimes as street racing, although obviously providing thrill and a sense of risk taking, can have deadly outcomes. But so can hang gliding. Do we think of street racing as taboo but hang gliding as not taboo? What is the difference? The likely outcome of death from both activities does not automatically place them in the same category. The concept of ideational mentality does. Although both pursuits are perhaps even equally dangerous, in our societies we believe street racing to be wrong but not hang gliding.

Taboo Recreation That Injures Others

Gambling and substance abuse are taboo activities because of an ideational mentality—people believe they are wrong. Their primary damage is to the participant. Activities that directly result in damage to other people or property are based on another concept, termed **sensate mentality**. This explanation focuses on the more tangible and physical aspects of laws: antisocial acts or crimes with victims (Heise, 1988). These are behaviors

Sensate mentality: a behavior known to be wrong because of our experiences

that our own senses tell us through our own experiences are harmful. Let's explore vandalism and taboo sex as examples.

According to Steve Goodwin, regional manager for the Louisville/Jefferson County Parks Department in Kentucky, an average of 9,765 person-hours per year in his department are devoted to dealing with vandalism. This equates to $103,216 and five full-time employees (Patrick, 2003). Typically occurring in the evening during the summer and fall, vandalism takes many forms: walls covered with graffiti, broken streetlights, stolen signs, doors ripped off hinges, litter, or writing on the pages of library books. According to the National Crime Prevention Council (as cited in Patrick, 2003) vandals tend to be male, ranging in age from grade school to young adults. Whereas vandalism toward facilities (60 percent) is done mainly by children, vandalism toward the environment (30 percent) is done mainly by adults (Patrick, 2003).

There are many forms of vandalism. For example, slovenly vandalism is an expression of bad manners and carelessness, such as littering. Although the least destructive, slovenly vandalism is the most expensive to solve. No-other-way-to-do-it vandalism results from such actions as sitting on a fence because there is no bench, or leaning a bicycle against a tree because there is no bike rack. In addition, conflict vandalism occurs from doing what is most logical and natural, regardless of the intent of a design, such as paths that result from people choosing the most direct route through an area and not using the designated sidewalks. Malicious vandalism usually results from people feeling mistreated and wanting to get back at society or a particular agency, such as by defacing a park sign.

Some people declare that vandalism is a form of recreation for them, and ironically, places of recreation, such as parks, suffer the most. Indeed, the most common forms of vandalism are the ones that can be considered the most recreational. For example, self-expression vandalism, such as graffiti, is usually an attempt to be noticed, and thrill vandalism arises from the goading or daring of friends or from an individual's desire for excitement, such as through damage to private property from swimming in limestone quarries. Ironically, even though a frequent site of and a typical reason for vandalism is linked to leisure, the best solutions for reducing vandalism also have their source in leisure. Among the "best practices" for preventing and stopping vandalism listed by the National Crime Prevention Council (2001) are supporting recreational programs for young people in the community, working with arts councils to paint murals on areas that are vulnerable to graffiti (Figs. 9.6 and 9.7), adopting a park, and planting trees, shrubs, and flowers.

Figure 9.6
Outdoor art—or is it graffiti? (© Ruth V. Russell.)

Figure 9.7
Graffiti—or is it outdoor art? (© Ruth V. Russell.)

In addition to vandalism, some forms of sex can be considered examples of taboo recreation that harms others. If leisure is considered a voluntarily chosen experience that is playful and provides pleasure, then many kinds of sexual activities can be considered leisure. In fact, one of the important uses of sex in contemporary societies is recreational, or physical, play (Comfort, 1973). Satisfying sexual encounters can be a pleasing opportunity to enjoy and communicate with another person. However, particular forms of recreational sex are considered inappropriate, immoral, or illegal by some societies. Among these could be grouped such actions as rape, pandering, and exhibitionism. Here we consider two specific forms of commercialized sex—pornography and prostitution—because they demonstrate the taboo nature of recreational sex. That is, they are pursuits that may provide the benefits of leisure to the participant but that are sometimes forbidden by societies because of the harm possible to inflict on others.

People participate in many forms of pornography today. Sex films, books, and magazines may be purchased legally, and rental of X-rated video and DVD movies for home viewing is widespread. In addition, there is an increase in the amount of pornography on television programs, and "cyberporn" is becoming a very large source of entertainment. By some estimates, in the United States, pornography is a $10 billion annual business, despite innumerable legal battles, zoning restrictions, and community censorship (Cordes & Ibrahim, 2003).

Erotic literature and art are found in most societies, but whether they are considered obscene or lewd varies from society to society and from time to time, according to custom and tradition. For example, today it is hard to imagine that the actor Clark Gable once shocked the nation in the film *Gone with the Wind* when he said the word "damn"! Nonetheless, what is lewd and what is not are frequently and hotly debated. Within North America, for example, the range of opinion concerning what is considered pornography is extremely broad.

Pornography has historically been a product of the male imagination (Godbey, 1999). This dominance by male interests is changing, however, with the availability of more magazines, books, and films that appeal to women's erotic interests. Yet some pornography victimizes women and children by making them the target of degradation or violence. Further, although the relationship between exposure to pornographic material and committing sex crimes is not clearly understood, some rapists have reported they were carrying out fantasies first suggested in a film. Further, even though a few scholars have argued that pornography acts as a useful substitute for antisocial sexual behaviors, others maintain that it increases the incidence of such behaviors. Perhaps the most disturbing research finding about particularly violent pornography is that it tends to desensitize those who view it regularly (Godbey, 1999).

Prostitution, on the other hand, is the business of selling sexual expression. With a long history dating back to ancient cultures, today prostitution is a major tourist attraction. It is a useful example of the taboo quality of leisure because of contrasting views of tolerance. For example, in some Southeast Asian and European countries, and in several counties in the state of Nevada, prostitution is both legal and government controlled. Meanwhile, prostitution has been tolerated only haphazardly elsewhere. Although estimates are difficult, the National Task Force on Prostitution (2001) reports that over one million people in the United States have worked as prostitutes. Further, there are on average 100,000 arrests made for prostitution annually, costing governments an average of $2,000 to manage each arrest. New York City spends more than $23 million each year on prostitution control. The Kinsey Institute also estimates that 70 percent of adult men in the United States have been clients at least once.

What is the harm of prostitution? As long as those who participate in prostitution are consenting adults, why is there such concern? One answer, of course, is in the definition of taboo recreation; prostitution has been considered immoral by many in society as a matter of personal belief and tradition, but there is another more frightening answer as well. When prostitution is not licensed by the government or controlled by legitimate institutions, opportunities for life-threatening diseases are greatly amplified. In fact, AIDS has made many of our sexual practices dangerous, not just prostitution. In addition, prostitution is often linked with serious criminal activity, such as drug trafficking and kidnapping.

The Dilemma of "Goodness"

We close this chapter where we began. There is widespread proof that leisure is good for us. Theoretical, empirical, and anecdotal testimony abounds demonstrating the economic, physiological, environmental, social, and psychological benefits of leisure. But these benefits are not always possible in all situations. Some leisure expressions harm participants as well as other people, including societies as a whole. According to Mannell and Kleiber (1997), for leisure to be of genuine benefit, it must meet the following two criteria:

- **Involvement in a particular pursuit is responsible for a change or the maintenance of a desired condition.**

- **The change or maintenance must be recognized as an improvement over what would have otherwise occurred.**

Based on these criteria, it is clear that some leisure expressions are not beneficial. Indeed, as pointed out by Rojek (1999), "an obvious and indisputable fact about leisure in modern society is that many of the most popular activities are illegal" (p. 82).

Does this mean that leisure is only leisure when it is healthy and moral? This is the "dilemma of goodness." Aristotle wrote in *Politics* that the cultivated ability to use leisure properly is the basis of a person's and a society's entire life. In other words, making good and healthy free-time choices is leisure, not simply doing anything one pleases. To Aristotle, leisure was making the right choices among life's many alternatives and doing them well (Sylvester, 1991). Today, we call this idea of positive life choices **wellness**.

> **Wellness:** making good choices that lead to social, mental, physical, and spiritual health

Indeed, this is the very premise of professionals who work in leisure agencies. Helping people achieve healthy free-time choices is why the YMCA, Girl Scouts, municipal parks and recreation departments, camps, and other organizations and services exist (Fig. 9.8). Professionals in leisure services consider leisure a force of good that allows us the space and time to develop our healthy selves—to be well. This suggests, then, that experiencing a mood uplift from walking through an inspiring natural landscape is leisure, but experiencing a mood uplift induced by a hallucinogenic drug is not. Leisure is a matter of social responsibility.

Contrary to the teachings of Aristotle and the goals of recreation agencies, some contemporary philosophers answer the question differently. This alternative perspective maintains that leisure is derived from personal feelings alone. By this distinction, leisure is in the heart and mind of the individual and has nothing to do with outside factors, such as what other people think. Leisure is considered a private choice based on intrinsically motivated joy and freedom and is not a matter of morality. This suggests, then, that experiencing a mood uplift from walking through an inspiring natural landscape and experiencing a mood uplift induced by a hallucinogenic drug are equally leisure experiences, because leisure is in the mind of the beholder. Leisure is a matter of private feelings and not of social responsibility.

Figure 9.8

Recreation and park agencies provide services in order to contribute to the wellness of people and society. (© Ruth V. Russell.)

What do you think? Of course, this dilemma of goodness is not as simple as it may appear. If leisure is not a matter of private feelings alone—if it can be rated, so to speak, on a goodness scale (such as in the Nash pyramid presented earlier in the chapter)—then some leisure expressions are clearly better than others. Even though it is easy to see a distinction in goodness between child pornography and a family picnic, other comparisons reveal the complexity of the dilemma more sharply. For example, is attending the opera better than attending a rock concert? Is playing golf at the club better than riding a motorcycle through the countryside?

Some would argue that expressions of **prole leisure** such as motorcycling, demolition derbies, rock concerts, and professional wrestling are just as worthy as any others, because leisure is a matter of personal definition. It would be elitist to conclude otherwise. On the other side is the argument that a society in which prole and taboo leisure dominate is mediocre and even debased. As Rojek argues (1999), "one of the most important facts about social life is that it is founded upon obligations to others" (p. 92).

Prole leisure: the recreational activities of the lowest social or economic classes of people

This means that taboo pastimes dehumanize and ultimately demolish "good" culture. But we also know that leisure is at the heart of our obligations to ourselves and others. Thus, leisure is both the problem and the remedy for deviance. Leisure produces socially productive behavior as well as immoral and socially unproductive behavior.

In Focus

Raves
Box 9.6

Raves are all-night dance events held in abandoned warehouses, open fields, airplane hangars, and clubs, where predominantly young adults (teens to mid-20s) dance amid often elaborate lighting and visual displays to the beats of techno, acid house, ambient house, brutal house, progressive house, trance, jungle, and related music (Tomlinson, 1998, p. 195). In addition, there is typically pervasive use of drugs.

Raves are definitely a manifestation of youth culture. Participants are predominantly white, and equally males and females (Glover, 2003). Ravers are typically from middle-class backgrounds, which is perhaps because after paying for clothes, accessories, admission fees, and drugs, raving is an expensive leisure activity. The dress code at raves, for both males and females, is baggy pants, baseball hats, t-shirts emblazoned with cartoon characters, running shoes, and knapsacks—all in very large sizes. Children's and infants' toys (e.g., stuffed animals, lollipops, and pacifiers) are common accessories.

Ecstasy is the drug of choice because attendees believe it enhances the sense of community. Surprisingly, alcohol is often unavailable at raves. Although violence is uncommon at raves, documented deaths associated with overdoses have been reported across North America. For example, in August 2000, CBS News reported that in Florida alone at least 40 deaths between 1997 and 2000 had involved Ecstasy. Deaths associated with Ecstasy also have occurred in other states and in Canada. When a 20-year-old man died after consuming some Ecstasy he had purchased at a rave near Chicago, then-mayor Richard Daley introduced an ordinance that made it a crime for Chicago landlords to rent out facilities for rave parties. Similar actions have been taken by officials in Toronto (Glover, 2003).

What is it about raves that make them fun? According to Thorton (1996), like many subcultural groups, raves are a "taste culture," that is, rave culture is associated with a specific taste in music, a specific style of dress, and people with the same interests. Being at a rave, then, provides a feeling of social harmony. This can be observed in the crowd behavior. Ravers report that they are not afraid of violence or crowd aggressiveness. They also say that social barriers are reduced at raves. There's no "attitude" at events. Participants demonstrate openness to everyone, including traditionally marginalized groups, such as gays and lesbians, ethnic and racial minorities, and women (Glover, 2003).

Questions to Consider and Discuss

1. *Have you attended a rave? Was your experience similar to that described in the case? How? How was it different? Share your experiences with classmates.*

2. *What do you think is the role of the children's accessories for ravers? Ravers are not children, so why might they deliberately use children's culture?*

3. *What are the advantages of raves? What are the disadvantages?*

4. *How might raves serve as an illustration of the "dilemma of good-ness" discussion in the text? Do you think raves are "good" or "bad"? Why?*

Summary: What We Understand

Leisure holds tremendous potential for people's well-being, but at times leisure can have negative outcomes. This occurs when people choose pastimes that society considers taboo. As a result of this chapter you should understand that

- Taboo recreations are those pastimes that are typically forbidden by law, custom, or belief.

- According to Nash's pyramid, taboo pastimes that are primarily injurious to oneself include substance abuse and gambling.

- According to Nash's pyramid, taboo pastimes that are primarily injurious to others and/or society include vandalism and commercial sex.

- As an explanation of taboo recreation, anomie occurs when once-viable social norms no longer control people's actions.

- As another explanation of taboo recreation, differential association is the idea that delinquent behavior is learned through our social groups.

- As a third attempt to explain taboo recreation, retreatism claims that deviance is simply a matter of personal expression.

- Underneath all this is a "dilemma of goodness." If leisure is a matter of personal attitudes and preferences, distinctions of worth for specific pastimes are useless. Or if Aristotle is correct and leisure requires making moral free-time choices, certain pursuits are unworthy.

Applications to Professional Practice

In Buenos Aires, Argentina, burning newspapers thrown from the top of a stadium stairway caused the deaths of 71 persons. In Ankara, Turkey, a shooting battle over the outcome of a soccer match led to the deaths of 42 people. In the United States, Latrell Sprewell, Golden State Warrior NBA star, was fired and suspended from the league for a year after he attacked and threatened to kill his coach. Professional boxer Mike Tyson became frustrated in the ring and responded by biting off part of his opponent's ear. And these are just the well-publicized extreme examples.

Daily, and in our own towns, we see bench-clearing brawls, brushback pitches and retaliatory beanings, and ice hockey fights. There are citywide, or campus-wide, "celebrations" after a championship win that damage property; stalkers prey on star athletes; and fans attack players during a break in the game. Just last evening I watched a Little League coach settle an altercation with his fists after a father complained over his son's lack of playing time.

Unfortunately, leisure service professionals must deal with aggression in sport more and more often. Incidents involving athletes, coaches, officials, and spectators have reached shocking proportions. Yet sport has the potential to be both an instigator of and a solution to the aggression. For example, midnight inner-city basketball leagues have become popular because they help keep gang members off the street. More programs in boxing, wrestling, and football are now provided as socially acceptable channels for aggression. Rules in some sports for young athletes have been adjusted to minimize the emphasis on winning.

Specific strategies to control aggression in sport and physical activity settings are needed to reduce its incidence and teach appropriate behavior (Weinberg & Gould, 1999). It is recommended that sport managers

1. *Understand when aggression is most likely to occur.* Expect certain situations to provoke aggressive behavior. For example, aggression is likely when athletes are frustrated because they are losing, perceive unfair officiating, are embarrassed, are physically in pain, or are playing below their capabilities. An overemphasis on winning is often the root cause. Sport managers should be particularly sensitive to detecting and controlling aggression in these situations by helping players put winning into perspective.

2. *Modify aggressive reactions.* We cannot always control these situations, but we can observe participants more closely and remove them from the situation at the first signs of aggression.

3. *Teach appropriate behavior.* We can also teach athletes skills to control their emotions and their reactions to frustration. We can teach them how to resolve conflicts and disputes in non-violent ways.

4. *Control spectator aggression.* This could include developing strict alcohol consumption policies, penalizing spectators immediately for aggressive acts (such as by kicking them out), hiring officials who won't tolerate aggression, training coaches on fair play and conflict management, and working with the media against glorifying aggressive acts in sports coverage.

For More Information

For more ideas on handling aggression and violence in sport, guidelines are available through The International Society of Sport Psychology. Other sport organizations, such as the National College Athletics Association and the International Ice Hockey Association offer policies as well. A useful site to begin a Web search is www.indiana.edu/~cspc/violence.htm, which also offers other links.

References

Abbott, D. A., & Cramer, S. L. (1993). Gambling attitudes and participation: A Midwestern survey. *Journal of Gambling Studies, 9,* 247–263.

Agnew, R. (1990). The origins of delinquent events: An examination of offender accounts. *Journal of Research in Crime and Delinquency, 27,* 267–294.

Agnew, R. (1991). The interactive effects of peer variables on delinquency. *Criminology, 29*(1), 47–72.

Aguilar, T. E. (1987). *A leisure perspective of delinquent behavior.* Paper presented at the Fifth Canadian Congress on Leisure Research, Halifax, Nova Scotia.

Alcoholics Anonymous, Home page. Retrieved March 10, 2004, from http://www.alcoholics-anonymous.org

Baron, R. A., & Richardson, D. R. (1994). *Human aggression.* New York: Plenum Press.

Becker, H. (1963). *Outsiders.* New York: Free Press.

Bippy, R. W., & Posterski, D. C. (1985). *The emerging generation: An inside look at Canadian teenagers.* Toronto: Irwin.

Comfort, A. (1973, February). Future sexual mores: Sexuality in a zero growth society. *Current, 29*–34.

Cordes, K. A., & Ibrahim, H. M. (2003). *Applications in recreation and leisure for today and the future.* Boston: McGraw-Hill.

Cosper, R., Okraku, I., & Neuman, B. (1985). Public drinking in Canada: A national study of a leisure activity. *Society and Leisure, 8,* 709–715.

Curtis, J. E. (1988). Purple recreation. *SPRE Annual on Education, 3,* 73–77.

Dormbusch, A. (1989). The sociology of adolescence. *Annual Review of Sociology, 15,* 233–259.

Epstein, J. S. (1998). Introduction. Generation X, youth culture, and identity. In E. S. Epstein (Ed.), *Youth culture: Identity in a post-modern world* (pp. 172–191). Malden, MA: Blackwell.

Eitzen, D. S. (1984). *Sport in contemporary society.* New York: St. Martin's Press.

Foucault, M. (1981). *The history of sexuality* (Vol. 1). Harmondsworth, United Kingdom: Penguin.

Gamson, J. (1998). *Freaks talk back: Tabloid talk shows and sexual nonconformity.* Chicago: The University of Chicago Press.

Glover, T. D. (2003). Regulating the rave scene: Exploring the policy alternatives of government. *Leisure Sciences, 25,* 307–325.

Godbey, G. (1989). *The future of leisure services: Thriving on change.* State College, PA: Venture.

Godbey, G. (1999). *Leisure in your life: An exploration.* State College, PA: Venture.

Gross, L. (1983). *How much is too much: The effects of social drinking.* New York: Random House.

Heise, D. R. (1988). Delusions and the construction of reality. *In Delusional beliefs* (pp. 45–69). New York: John Wiley & Sons.

Hood , C. D. (2003). Women in recovery from alcoholism: The place of leisure. *Leisure Sciences, 25,* 51–79.

Iso-Ahola, S. E., & Weisinger, E. (1990). Perceptions of boredom in leisure: Conceptualization, reliability and validity of the leisure boredom scale. *Journal of Leisure Research, 22*(1), 1–17.

Kelly, J. R., & Freysinger, V. J. (2000). *21st century leisure: Current issues.* Boston: Allyn & Bacon.

Lazare, D. (1989). Drugs 'r' us. In *Drugs, society, and behavior 91/92* (pp. 26–39). Guilford, CT: Dushkin.

Lee, Y., Howard, D., & Datillo, J. (1992). *The negative side of leisure experience.* Paper presented at the Leisure Research Symposium, National Recreation and Park Association Congress, Cincinnati, OH.

Leonard, W. M. (1988). *A sociological perspective of sport.* New York: Macmillan.

Lowney, J. (1984). The wall gang: A study of interpersonal process and deviance among twenty-three middle-class youths. *Adolescence, 19,* 527–538.

Mannell, R. C., & Kleiber, D. A. (1997). *A social psychology of leisure.* State College, PA: Venture.

Manson, G. W. (1990). *Why join a gang?* Burnaby, British Columbia: Burnaby Parks and Recreation Department.

Merton, R. K. (1968). *Social theory and social structure.* Glencoe, IL: Free Press.

Moore, J. P., & Cook, I. L. (1999). *Highlights of the 1998 National Youth Gang Survey.* Washington, D.C.: Office of Justice Programs, Office of Juvenile Justice and Delinquency Prevention.

Moore, T. J. (1982). *A study of leisure choices of young offenders and young non-offenders and the impact of social structure and anomie on these choices.* Unpublished master's thesis, Acadia University, Wolfville, Nova Scotia.

Morris, M., Steinberg, H., Sykes, E. A., & Salmon, P. (1990). Effects of temporary withdrawal from regular running. *Journal of Psychosomatic Research, 34,* 493–500.

Nash, J. B. (1953). *Philosophy of recreation and leisure.* Dubuque, IA: Wm. C. Brown.National Crime Prevention Council. (2001). Retrieved June 6, 2001, from http://www.ncpc.org/2vandals.htm

National Task Force on Prostitution. (2001). Prostitution in the United States—The statistsics. Retrieved June 6, 2001, from http://www.bayswan.org/stats.html

Patrick, A. (2003, September). Unwelcome signs. *Parks & Recreation,* 78–81.

Pfohl, S. J. (1985). *Images of deviance and social control: A sociological history.* New York: McGraw-Hill.

Raphael, S. J. (1990). *Sally: Unconventional success.* New York: Morrow.

Rojek, C. (1999). Deviant leisure: The dark side of free-time activity. In E. L. Jackson, & T. L. Burton (Eds.), *Leisure studies: Prospects for the twenty-first century* (pp. 81–96). State College, PA: Venture.

Russell, B. (1968). *The conquest of happiness.* New York: Bantam.

School of Public and Environmental Affairs. (1993). *Lottery sales higher from lower-income groups.* Bloomington: Indiana University.

Simmel, G. (1971). *On individuality and social forms.* Chicago: Chicago University Press.

Smith, R., & Preston, F. (1985). Expressed gambling motives: Accounts in defense of self. In B. Bunter, J. Stanley, & R. St. Clair (Eds.), *Transitions to leisure: Conceptual and human issues* (pp. 100–119). Lanham, MD: University Press of America.

Sylvester, C. (1991). Recovering a good idea for the sake of goodness: An interpretive critique of subjective leisure. In T. L. Goodale, & P. A. Witt (Eds.), *Recreation and leisure: Issues in an era of change* (pp. 83–96). State College, PA: Venture.

Thorton, S. (1996). *Club cultures: Music, media, and subcultural capital.* Hanover, MA: University Press of New England.

Tomlinson, L. (1998). "This ain't no disco" . . . or is it? Youth culture and the rave phenomenon. In E. S. Epstein (Ed.), *Youth culture: Identity in a post-modern world* (pp. 133–148). Malden, MA: Blackwell

Virgil, J. D. (1988). Group processes and street identity: Adolescent Chicano gang members. *Ethos, 16,* 421–445.

Weinberg, R. S., & Gould, D. (1999). *Foundations of sport and exercise psychology.* Champaign, IL: Human Kinetics.

Willis, P. (1978). *Profane culture.* London, United Kingdom: Routledge & Kegan Paul.

LEISURE AS A SOCIAL INSTRUMENT
SYSTEMS CONTEXT

In the book's final section, we turn our attention to the more functional side of leisure: the ability of leisure to be a useful tool.

Chapter 10

explores the use of leisure as an instrument of social good. By tracing the history of leisure in the United States, we are able to see illustrations of leisure being used as a positive and important force in developing community.

Chapter 11

considers how leisure mirrors a nation's level of economic development and drives its economy.

Chapter 12

demonstrates how an instrumental web among leisure, time, and work dictates our lives.

Chapter 13

focuses on leisure as a means for achieving human equity.

Leisure *can be an instrument of social* **good**.

Leisure *both restricts and enables* **equity**.

Leisure *is a* **powerful** *economic force.*

Using Leisure for Social Good

Preview

Can leisure be functional?

Yes. Today leisure is seen as an important force in community well-being.

How does leisure become functional for communities?

As nations become more industrialized, they become more reliant on leisure as a tool for solving problems.

How did this view of leisure as a tool develop?

In the United States, what began simply as a play movement became an entire social movement. Sport, music, dance, and enjoying the outdoors became the means to create better community lives. The movement was so sweeping that it involved cities, states, and the federal government. In addition, people formed organizations, raised funds, and wrote and spoke volumes to teach people how to use their leisure time productively.

Key Terms

Public good	290	Social movement	301
Panacea	290	Settlement house	301
Utilitarian	291	The New Deal	309
Industrial Revolution	297	Urban sprawl	311
Lyceum	299		

As nations of the world have become more industrialized, they have become more reliant on leisure as a tool for social good. Unlike some earlier societies such as the ancient Greeks, for whom leisure was an end in itself, many contemporary societies see a more functional side of leisure. Today leisure is seen as a public good and capable of solving social problems.

> **Public good:** resources that benefit everyone, usually provided by governments

Because leisure plays a key role in civic celebrations, family vitality, counteracting deprivation, and social communication and cooperation, it is useful in creating higher quality lives.

Although leisure is not a **panacea** for social difficulties, it is a major contemporary problem solver. It accomplishes this through the concept of community. Communities take life-sustaining actions, and members of communities work together because they care for each other. It is through community that leisure can accomplish so much (Fig. 10.1).

> **Panacea:** a remedy for all ills

In Canada, for example, the importance of leisure in creating Canadian

culture is considered to be so great that since the 1880s Canadian provinces and cities have played a vigorous role in promoting outdoor recreation, the arts, tourism, and sports. As of the 1980s 64 federal government agencies have been significantly involved in these efforts (Searle & Brayley, 2000). The importance of these services today is emphasized in the development of a national business plan for Canadian parks. The plan outlines fiscal and management strategies for the national park system, marine conservation areas, and historic sites, emphasizing the importance to the public good of these areas (Kraus, 2001).

Figure 10.1

Leisure accomplishes good things by facilitating social communication and cooperation. (© Ruth V. Russell.)

In this chapter, we use the United States to demonstrate the **utilitarian** role of leisure, beginning with the colonial era and continuing on to the present.

> **Utilitarian:** something useful

Colonial America

As late as the 1400s, Native American and Inuit people were the only inhabitants of the western hemisphere, but following Columbus' voyage of 1492, for the next 400 years, large waves of people, mostly from European countries, sailed across the Atlantic Ocean to North and South America. Among them were colonists, chiefly British, who settled along the East Coast of North America between what are now the states of Maine and Georgia. They came because they thought there were opportunities for wealth, power, freedom, and adventure.

However, those who settled in the northern regions of the East Coast did not find great riches; instead, they found rugged wilderness. Yet beyond the legendary hardships they experienced as they established settlements lay a vast and unbelievably rich and varied area—resources of fertile soils, abundant water supplies, and plentiful minerals that would later help the United States become one of the world's most prosperous nations.

In the meantime, the great danger and difficult terrain of the wilderness of the early 1600s meant the earliest colonists suffered from a lack of food and from disease. Little time and energy could be squandered on leisure. Leisure, with its assumed emphasis on things nonproductive, was felt by the colonists not only to be dysfunctional but also to be dangerous. For example, the Virginia Assembly declared in 1619 that any person found idle would be condemned to prison.

Yet it was not just the difficulty of taming a wilderness that sent leisure into the realm of the forbidden; the religious heritage of the new settlers also played a role. Many were motivated to cross the Atlantic because of a belief in a "divine mission," a calling that rebelled against the pleasures of the privileged classes of the English aristocracy. Thus, all amusement, entertainment, and travel were forbidden on Sundays. Merrymaking on religious holidays such as Christmas was also forbidden (Kraus, 2001). In addition, many ordinances banned drama, nonreligious music, card playing, bowling, and shuffleboard. Penalties even existed for wearing decorative clothing.

In spite of religious dictates and the hard work to be done, the early European colonists did have some fun. For example, boys in the town lanes played football. Each town had its own tavern where the British love of games and sports was carried on. They also served as places for dances and cockfights. The wealth of deer, moose, and turkey made hunting more than just a way of getting food. In Boston, for example, close to 1,000 men would gather to attend training days for marksmanship. The wealthy also enjoyed private pastimes, including the oft-banned theatrical amusements. In summer, they attended horse races, and dances and card parties were fashionable. Some of the pastimes of the New England colonists actually had a functional purpose. Celebrations while making a quilt or building a barn, for example, made it possible for many hands to help with the task.

Social activities were favorite pastimes of the settlers in the southern East Coast areas as well, but for different reasons. Unlike their northern counterparts, the lifestyle of the southern colonies more closely resembled that of the British aristocracy—they shared in their tastes for lavish entertainment and hospitality. Weddings and funerals, as well as horse races, cockfights, and bowling matches brought people together for festivities. Dances, parties, barbecues, and little plays were popular forms of home entertainment. Gambling was celebrated with cards, dice, coin tossing, and lotto. A notable southerner, Thomas Jefferson, was an avid reader, writer, and gourmet cook! The nature of leisure in the southern colonies, then, was similar to that of the ancient Greeks. Leisure was more an end in itself rather than a means to another goal.

And like the ancient Greeks, what made all this devotion to pastimes possible for the antebellum South was a system of slavery for black people brought from Africa beginning in the 1600s. By the Civil War, about four million slaves supported a privileged leisure lifestyle for about one fourth of southern white people. Although American folklore portrays cheerful slaves dancing to banjo music, in reality they experienced very little leisure. Those who worked in the fields worked daily from sunrise to sunset. If there was a full moon during the cotton-picking season, the field slaves usually worked until late at night.

It wasn't just the hard work that made leisure for the slaves rare; they also did not have the freedom for leisure. It is symbolic, then, that many of the musical and dance forms that were prevalent in the slave culture featured the theme of freedom, a cornerstone of leisure. There was typically one break in this routine of work, however, and that was the Christmas season. Then owners allowed a few days for feasting, dancing, music, and games.

The Study Says

Nicodemus, Kansas
Box 10.1

During the late 1700s, slavery began to decline. Soon after the end of the Civil War in 1865, slavery was outlawed with the adoption of the Thirteenth Amendment to the Constitution. Many years later, in 1992, the U.S. Congress authorized a feasibility study to determine the eligibility of a site important to the postslavery era to be added to the national park system.

In the 1870s, Nicodemus, located in north-central Kansas, witnessed great movements of African Americans from the horrors of Reconstruction in the South to the Midwest. They were known as "exodusters." Coming to Nicodemus primarily from Kentucky, these former slaves arrived to begin a new life. And by 1881, 35 residential and commercial structures had been erected to form the town.

At first, Nicodemus colonists had to cope with many hardships on the Kansas frontier. Their early shelters were burrows dug in the sides of dirt banks. Wooden structures eventually replaced the burrows, but finding food was a far more difficult problem. Few of the settlers had any money, as most had spent all their funds just to get there. The Nicodemus Town Company was established to secure food from across the state. In 1879 the school district was initiated, with most of the classes being taught in people's homes. By the 1880s, Nicodemus had a baseball team, a literary society, social lodges, and an ice cream parlor. But by 1910 Nicodemus began a gradual decline in population, and with the closing of the post office in 1953, the importance of this Reconstruction-era African American settlement ended.

In conducting the feasibility study on Nicodemus, the National Park Service identified and evaluated regional land uses and trends, analyzed comparative data on the management of similar sites, and inventoried remaining structures. The study team conducted an environmental impact assessment as well as economic and social impact analyses. They formulated alternative management strategies and evaluated their costs. There were frequent interviews with members of the Nicodemus Historical Society.

All this research paid off, because in 1996 Nicodemus was established as a national historic site. Today it stands as symbolic of the pioneer spirit of African Americans who dared leave the only region they had known to seek personal freedom and the opportunity to develop their talents and capabilities (National Park Service, 2002).

Transitions of the 1800s

During the early 1800s, European settlers moved westward by the thousands over the Appalachian Mountains into the new states and territories. As before, these hardy people were searching for a better life, and through hard work and sacrifice, settled the western wilderness as earlier settlers had done in the East. When they arrived, they took over much of the land that native people had occupied for centuries. As these Native Americans were forced from their land, they also endured the hardships of much sickness and death.

Meanwhile, for the European settlers the relationship with the wilderness they were conquering began to shift. It became less and less hostile, and in their collective minds, wilderness began to represent the unique value of their new country. This new reverence for nature was assisted by the artists and writers of the time. For example, the novels of James Fenimore Cooper describe those who lived on the frontier as pure of heart and noble in deed. Such poets as Ralph Waldo Emerson swore undying love to nature, and artists such as Thomas Cole and Thomas Moran made adventuresome forays into the thick woods to paint their majestic beauty.

Such high regard for preserving the American wilderness was challenged, however, by the economic value of expansion into the rich interior of the continent. The westward progress enabled the United States to become a leading agricultural nation. Developments in transportation also contributed to major economic growth as new and improved roads eased the shipping of goods by land. For example, the invention of the steam-powered railroad engine led the way for about 9,000 miles of railroad lines to be laid crisscrossing the country. Accompanying these economic and industrial upheavals were changes in how people lived that eventually meant a more utilitarian role for leisure.

For example, the demand for entertainment became insatiable. City people flocked to plays performed in theaters. Groups of entertainers and magicians toured the country performing for small-town audiences. P. T. Barnum, the most famous showman of the time, fascinated the public with unusual attractions; he often used exaggeration and deception to create interest in his shows. His "museums" included tightrope walkers, pantomimes, tumblers, lectures, and plays. The variety musical show also became popular. By the 1860s, entrepreneurs such as New Yorker Tony Pastor enticed men, women, and children to his "Opera House" on the Bowery for a program of singers, comedians, and animal and acrobatic acts. The traveling circus also became popular, and by about 1879, during the Golden Age of the American circus, more than 10 large circuses toured the country, including the most successful ones of the P. T. Barnum and James A. Bailey partnership, and the five Ringling brothers.

This was also the tourism era of taking a spa treatment at a resort. With roots in ancient Greek and Roman times, and a rich tradition in Western

Europe, American spa development originally focused on the curative powers of spring water. Each year the affluent from the urban North and the southern gentry engaged in a seasonal migration: summer at Newport, winter at Palm Beach, spring and autumn at one of the inland spas such as White Sulphur Springs (Fig. 10.2). These socially exclusive resorts were preeminent until the 1850s, when a wider social base began to be served by such seaside resorts as Atlantic City in New Jersey and Coney Island in New York (Towner, 1996).

Figure 10.2
The Greenbrier Hotel at White Sulphur Springs, West Virginia, continues to be a popular resort today. Still noted for its curative spa, it has also gained distinction in gourmet cuisine and golf. (© Ruth V. Russell.)

Another transition in the pastime patterns of the 1800s was the increasing respectability of sports. Previously associated with gambling, drunkenness, and violence, sports gradually gained legitimacy (Cross, 1990). A new attitude toward the human body helped. It no longer was thought of as merely the source of devilish temptation. Instead, the body became a symbol of physical courage and disciplined will. The change in sports also resulted from the influence of other countries. For example, German immigrants introduced gymnastics when they arrived, and Scottish immigrants imported track-and-field events.

As concern for the nation's health increased, public schools began to embrace the idea of fitness and sports for youth. Although colleges initially offered little leadership in the growth of other sporting activities, they did introduce and promote football. The first intercollegiate game was played between Princeton and Rutgers in 1869, arousing spectator enthusiasm from the start. Private athletic clubs were also founded to provide indoor exercise, primarily for businessmen. The American country club, originating in 1882 near Boston, first provided cricket and tennis and later offered golf to its exclusive membership. By 1891, with the invention of basketball by James Naismith of Springfield, Massachusetts, American sports were based on a kind of gentleman's amateur athleticism. Indeed, because the player in basketball had to throw the ball softly in an arc, the sport was considered more "civilized" (Cross, 1990).

The sports cult of the late 1800s, however, was militantly male, reaffirming the view that the vulnerable female was unsuited for vigorous physical activity. In the 1860s women were allowed to play croquet, and in the 1870s an easy form of lawn tennis was introduced for women. However, so powerful was the lure of sports that women gradually entered into it in spite of social constraints (Fig. 10.3).

Along with the transitions in entertainment, tourism, and sports that evolved during the 19th century, later decades of this period witnessed the beginning of the modern concept of leisure as a tool. As the nation continued to expand in commerce and industry, there were new challenges. Many of these challenges resulted directly from the development of industrialization. Historians refer to this period as the **Industrial Revolution**. Beginning in Great Britain during the 1700s, it spread to other parts of Europe and to North America in the early 1800s. Widespread by midcentury, industrialization created an enormous increase in the production of many kinds of goods because of the introduction of power-driven machinery: the spinning mule replaced the spinning wheel, and the power loom replaced the hand loom. This revolu-

Figure 10.3

Ina Gittings pole vaulting in the late 1800s at the University of Nebraska–Lincoln. A little ahead of her time? (© University of Nebraska-Lincoln Photography.)

tion in industry took work out of the rural home and workshop and into the urban factory. This caused significant changes in people's lives.

Most of those who tended the machines lived and worked under harsh conditions. In the factories, the machines forced workers to work faster and without rest. Jobs became specialized, so the work was monotonous. Factory wages were low. Women and children worked as unskilled laborers and made only a small fraction of men's low wages. Children, many under age 10, worked up to 14 hours a day. Housing in the growing industrial cities of New York, Chicago, and others could not keep up with the migration of workers from rural areas and other countries. Severe overcrowding resulted, and many people lived in filthy conditions that frequently led to outbreaks of disease and death.

> **Industrial Revolution:** a rapid and major change in an economy brought about by the introduction of power-driven machinery

As an obvious consequence, some Americans came to believe that social reforms were needed to correct these "inequalities of condition." Churches and social welfare groups set up charities to aid the poor. Reformers lobbied to reduce the working day of laborers. People such as Dorothea Dix worked to improve the dismal conditions in the nation's prisons and asylums, whereas others such as Horace Mann demanded better schools for all American children.

Most significant, from our perspective, were those reforms that used leisure. Some reformers believed wholesome and enriching leisure experiences would solve the inevitable consequences of the Industrial Revolution. The belief that all Americans had a natural right to a high quality of life was fundamental. We will use as examples the early park developments, the adult education movement, developments in therapeutic recreation, and the birth of voluntary agencies.

In Focus

Tragedy of the Commons
Box 10.2

The city park is a relatively recent phenomenon in the United States, and its beginnings are obscure. Some historians assert that the plaza in St. Augustine, set aside in 1565, should be considered the first city park, whereas others refer to the Boston Common, established in 1634, as the first city park.

The common was originally a British tradition, and the plaza a Spanish one. At first, both were used as a communal pasture. People had unlimited access to this commonly held land for grazing their livestock. As cities grew and open space was lost, the common or plaza became a commonly held recreation resource. In recent years, the consequences of this idea have been destructive. In an essay published in 1968, Garrett Hardin explained this "tragedy of the commons."

Hardin asks us to imagine a pasture, fixed in size, which is accessible to all the livestock owners of a village. Each herdsman, being rational, wants to maximize his use of the pasture by grazing as many cattle as possible. Therefore, he continually expands the size of his herd, recognizing that the benefits from this will be his alone, whereas any costs associated with the increased grazing will be shared among all the village members. What each herdsman fails to recognize, however, is that every other herdsman in the village is following the same logic, and the cumulative effect of their independently rational action destroys the pasture.

Dustin, McAvoy, and Schultz (1982) have extended Hardin's story to city parks and other public recreation places. They ask us to consider an urban resident who wishes to escape the heat, congestion, and noise of the city on a summer weekend. She looks to the mountains or to the beach, lake, or river for a cool and refreshing two-day rest. She gathers the family, packs the car, and heads for one of America's public recreation areas. What this person doesn't take into account is that thousands of other city dwellers are making the same logical decision. Instead of a cool, quiet, and refreshing leisure experience, they are treated to traffic jams, noise, and crime—the very problems they attempted to escape—and to the ultimate destruction of the public recreation site.

Questions to Consider and Discuss

- *What is meant by the tragedy of the commons? Develop a paragraph that explains it in your own words.*

- *Is Hardin's logic applicable to public recreation settings as Dustin et al. suggest? What other examples support an extension of the tragedy of the commons?*

- *Visit a public recreation area in your community. Can you find traces of the tragedy of the commons there? What are these?*

In the face of increasing industrialization, concern for the resulting destruction of natural resources increased. One solution was parks. The need for open spaces for leisure was first felt in the larger cities. Following the example of William Penn, who set aside five undeveloped squares for a park in Philadelphia in 1682, and James Oglethorpe, who designed public gardens and squares in Savannah, Georgia, in 1733, New York City planners provided the grandest example of the park solution at the time: Central Park. Using a design by Frederick Law Olmsted and Calvert Vaux, city planners created the 850-acre park beginning in 1853. Designed to provide relief from the cramped, concrete conditions of the city with the joys of the countryside, this model was followed by other cities. By the turn of the century, over 750 cities had set aside land for public parks.

Concern for the preservation of the natural heritage also began to be answered by the federal government. In 1832 Congress passed legislation authorizing federal control of the Arkansas Hot Springs; the medicinal qualities of its water were reserved for everyone's use. In 1865 Congress set aside Mariposa Big Tree Park for the state of California. The intention was to preserve significant natural resources for the enjoyment of future generations. New York, Michigan, Minnesota, and New Jersey followed this lead and claimed open spaces for the benefit of their citizens as well. Later, the Mariposa Big Tree Park in California became Yosemite National Park. The establishment of Yellowstone National Park in 1872, however, marked the real beginning of the national park movement in the United States.

Considerable civic concern also developed for improving the intellectual capacity of Americans. One solution was universal public education, where there was a growing conviction that leisure, properly used, could contribute to an elevated intellectual character of the people. An example of this was the Lyceum movement. This was a national organization with more than 900 local chapters during its peak. Its program consisted of lectures, readings, and other educational and cultural events. The idea that all citizens should be educated to improve their quality of life was also promoted by the Chautauqua organization, which took lectures and other programs on the road.

> **Lyceum:** originally the name of the ancient Athenian gymnasium and garden where Aristotle taught; also the 19th century American association for popular instruction of adults by lectures and concerts

The prevalence of the humanistic philosophy evident in the 1800s also led to the use of leisure in health care. The utility of chess, gardening, reading, needlecraft, and walking as treatments became most prevalent in the psychiatric hospitals of the time (Carter, vanAndel, & Robb, 1985). Florence Nightingale, the pioneer of modern nursing, recommended in *Notes on Nursing*, published in 1873, the use of music and pets to improve the hospital environment.

Finally, the development of voluntary agencies provided additional leisure tools for the social reforms called for at the time. In 1851, groups of young men copied a British organization and formed the Young Men's Christian Association (YMCA) in Boston and Montreal. At first this organization provided only religious discussion groups for youth and adults. It gradually enlarged its program to include gymnastics, sports, and other recreational activities. By 1860, the first Boys' Club had been established in Hartford, Connecticut, to counteract the ills of city life by providing a play alternative to the streets for young boys. Girls' Clubs, which grew from a concern for disadvantaged girls, weren't established until 1945. By the turn of the century, a few corn-raising clubs for boys and canning clubs for girls began a rural program that led to the founding of 4-H (MacLean, Peterson, & Martin, 1985). Its purpose was to help youth gain life skills and attitudes that would enable them to become productive members of society.

Birth of Organized Leisure Systems

Meanwhile, the industrial boom helped some people amass huge fortunes. For example, in 1900 there were about 3,000 millionaires, compared with only 20 in 1850. American author Mark Twain called this era the Gilded Age, describing the leisure-based culture of the newly rich. Attending operas and horse races, holding balls and parties in large mansions for over 1,000 guests, yachting, relaxing at luxurious resorts, and pursuing other "signs of refinement" created a lavish display of pleasure—the most to date in American history.

Yet for most people, the industrial boom meant that the laborers who toiled in the factories, mills, and mines did not share in its benefits. In spite of social reform efforts, things didn't get much better for most people. Uncontrolled growth of urban areas continued. Workers usually worked at least 60 hours a week for an average of 20 cents an hour. The more than 25 million (mostly European) immigrants who had entered the country by 1916 compounded the problem. They continued to crowd into cheap apartment buildings called tenements. The crowded slum neighborhoods also bred crime, and poor sanitation and inadequate diets continued to make people vulnerable to disease.

However, the strong spirit of reform that swept through the country during the late 1800s persisted into the early 1900s. Now many people were calling for changes in the economic, political, and social systems. Workers' strikes for better wages and shorter work schedules erupted. Even though little progress was made during the 1800s, by 1917 the reformers had many successes, and it was through their work that organized leisure services began. The "leisure solution" was envisioned as a positive alternative to the troubles of the time. In tracing this development, we'll explore two early 20th century **social movements**: settlement houses and playgrounds.

> **Social movement:** a significant change in the social conditions and patterns of behavior in a society

Copying the British model of Toynbee Hall in London, **settlement houses** were established in the United States as an important tool for helping the urban poor and uneducated. Stanton Coit in New York City established the first settlement house in 1886. The movement then spread to Chicago three years later when Jane Addams and Ellen Gates Starr established the settlement house that became famous as the Hull House.

> **Settlement house:** an institution providing various community services

In Profile

Jane Addams and Ellen Starr
Box 10.3

In 1889 Jane Addams and Ellen Starr went to live and work among the poor. They founded the Hull House, one of the earliest settlement houses in the United States. It quickly became a model for efforts nationwide to improve the lives of people coping with urban poverty. What influenced them to leave their safe upper-middle-class existence and venture into the world of urban strife when they had no experience and no guarantees that their efforts would be well received?

Both women were products of their time. The late 19th century in the United States was an era of philanthropy. Both came to this era from gentle Victorian experiences as children and eye-opening travels to Europe as young women. So when the heir of Charles Hull granted Jane and Ellen a rent-free, four-year lease on his large, dilapidated old home that had become surrounded by the sprawling, densely packed, and deteriorating immigrant slums of Chicago's 19th ward, they took it. A few days after Jane's 29th birthday, the two former college roommates moved in. They intended to share with the poor their gifts of culture.

From the beginning, Hull House was the center of social and intellectual activity (McBride, 1989). A day-care center and kindergarten were available in the morning. In the afternoon, classes and clubs for teens were available, and adult education programs were held in the evening. Training was given in cooking, dressmaking, woodworking, photography, printing, and other employment skills. Classes were offered in pottery, rhythm and dance, and chorus. Nearby buildings were acquired and converted into a coffeehouse, gymnasium, and playground. Carefully supervised recreation in these facilities was central to their efforts to help children resist the effects of the city.

Hull House made a special reputation for itself, not so much for its efforts to correct social ills but in the methods used. The Hull House specialty was "the exaltation of art for the benefit of the masses" (Smith, 1890). Concerts, dramatic readings, and lectures were weekly events; the audience was always packed. There were art history classes, literary reading groups, and art exhibits.

The Hull House was not an isolated enterprise in Addams' and Starr's lives. Because of her other well-known activities in organizing labor unions, establishing the women's Peace Party, and leading large antiwar (World War I) demonstrations, Addams was for a time labeled the most dangerous woman in America (Duncan, 1991). Starr, too, reached beyond Hull House to embrace radical politics, including worker strikes—where at one she was arrested. Indeed, Addams and Starr were complex human beings trying to bring better lives to people living in complicated times. Their example set the stage for future generations.

The objective of settlement houses was to improve living conditions in city neighborhoods, particularly for the foreign born. To accomplish this, the houses offered educational classes, nurseries, civil rights and fair employment advocacy, and recreational services. The recreational services—typically play apparatus for young children, sports activities and social clubs for older children, and cultural arts programs for adults—not only provided a more positive balance in their desperate lives but also taught the skills needed to create productive lives.

Meanwhile, the first organized use of play specifically as a tool is traced to Friedrich Froebel, the "father of the kindergarten movement." His kindergarten was founded in Germany in 1837. He believed children should be schooled early in a gentle manner that allowed them to develop freely. Thus, using free play as a tool in child development led the way for another social movement.

Initially, the insight of public-spirited members of the New England Woman's Club led to some children's play areas in Boston, Massachusetts. This led to the establishment of the Boston Sand Garden in 1885, which is considered by many historians to be the first actual playground in the United States. The idea was borrowed from the public parks of Berlin, Germany, where huge piles of sand were given to the city's children for playing. By 1887, when 10 sand play centers were opened, women were employed to supervise the children (Fig. 10.4).

Figure 10.4

A turn-of-the-century Boston playground. (© Joseph Lee Memorial Archives, National Recreation and Park Association.)

Later, additional strides for promoting playgrounds were made by Joseph Lee, who helped create a model playground that included an area for small children, a boys' section, a sports field, and individual sand gardens. In 1889 the Charlesbank Outdoor Gymnasium opened; it provided apparatus for gymnastics, a running track, and space for games for older boys and men. A section for women and girls was added to this playground two years later. By 1899 Boston had 21 playgrounds.

In Profile

Joseph Lee
Box 10.4

Although he received a law degree from Harvard Law School in 1888, Joseph Lee never pursued that career. Instead, he chose a life dedicated to promoting playgrounds.

It began with his participation in a 10-year study of child delinquency in Boston. As a part of the study, he researched play in Boston playgrounds, sand gardens, and streets. He made observations, drew descriptive maps, compiled statistics, and studied the relationships among play, population density, and lawbreaking (Sapora, 1989).

To the confusion of Lee, and in spite of setting aside special places for play, activities in the new Boston play areas did not differ much from those on the streets. Fights frequently broke out, often over card games. Older boys and men monopolized the game areas, and gangs prevented the smaller children from playing. Lee's solution was leadership.

In 1900 he proposed that a model playground be developed. He chose for the experiment the North End playground, a barren two-acre site on the Charles River. Lee supervised the installation of play equipment. He had areas marked off for different age groups, and with his own money, he hired two Harvard students as play leaders, and recruited several more volunteers. Before the playground opened in May, the staff had completely planned the program. All this organization was a new idea at the time, and despite the lack of understanding by the local neighborhood, the program attracted over 300 children per week (Sapora, 1989). Lee had been able to demonstrate the importance of organized and supervised play.

Other playground developments sprang up elsewhere. For example, Jacob Riis, a newspaperman who recognized a great need for play spaces in crowded cities, initiated the movement for publicly sponsored playgrounds in New York City. Chicago established a system of small-park playgrounds. School buildings began to be used as community centers in Pittsburgh, and Philadelphia moved ahead with full playground program services in the summer. Unfortunately, most of these playgrounds were segregated. In general, playgrounds for African American children "were less numerous, smaller, poorer in equipment and less adequately supervised than playgrounds for white children in the same city" (H.J. McGuinn, as cited in Johnson, 1930, p. 91).

In Profile
Janie Porter Barrett
Box 10.5

Janie Porter was born to former slaves in Athens, Georgia, in 1865. She grew up in a white household because her mother was a nurse to the white children. When she reached an age at which it was considered proper for her to leave home, she was enrolled at Hampton Institute in Virginia. Upon graduation, she felt her role as an educated African American was to help all African Americans improve their lives, so she began teaching.

In 1889 Porter married Harris Barrett, also a Hampton graduate, and while raising four children, started a school to teach life skills to other neighborhood children. What began as a sewing class for a few girls in her home on Tuesday afternoons soon became a club. The response to the club was so enthusiastic that two years later it became known as the Locust Street Social Settlement. Like other settlement houses of the time, Locust Street activities included handicrafts, poultry raising, homemaking, gardening, and reading classes. Athletics programs and a playground were also established (Fig. 10.5).

Figure 10.5
Janie Porter Barrett works with a Girls' Club. (Courtesy of Hampton University Archives.)

One of Porter Barrett's most appreciated programs was the summer excursion. Mothers of all ages, without their children, were treated to a day of relaxation and reflection through outings on Chesapeake Bay. During the summer of 1915, 2,200 mothers benefited from these excursions ("Work of Uplift Shown Results," 1912).

These early, scattered efforts of more than 14 cities to provide space, leadership, and facilities for playgrounds finally began to come together when, in 1906, Jane Addams, Joseph Lee, Luther Gulick, Henry Curtis, and others met at the White House. Their goal was to establish some way of connecting their individual efforts (MacLean et al., 1985). They felt a great sense of urgency. Their decision was the establishment of the Playground Association of America. This organization became the Playground and Recreation Association of America in 1911, the National Recreation Association in 1930, and ultimately the National Recreation and Park Association in 1965. It laid the foundation for today's organized use of leisure for social good.

There were other initiatives using leisure as a problem solver at this time as well. By 1910, for example, 336 cities had supervised recreation programs. Schools explored ways of providing recreation programs and facilities, and therapeutic recreation services began to appear in state hospitals. President Theodore Roosevelt encouraged the acquisition of numerous new areas for the national park system, and colleges began offering professional training for recreation leaders. In addition, the organized camping movement began with the first private camp set up to offer a healthy outdoor experience to boys in poor health.

Agencies serving youth also organized to help the cause. Sir Robert Baden-Powell of Great Britain started the Boy Scout movement in 1907 when he organized a camp for 20 boys. Baden-Powell was convinced after his experiences in the Boer War that training in citizenship and outdoor skills was essential for young men. As a result of a British Boy Scout helping him find his way in a thick London fog, William Boyce, an American businessman, brought the idea to the United States in 1909. The movement spread throughout the world, and today approximately 25 million boys, girls, and adult leaders in 154 countries are members (http://www.scouting.org/. Retrieved 3/10/04).

When Baden-Powell began the Boy Scouts in Great Britain, 6,000 girls registered too. As he "could not have girls traipsing about over the country after his Boy Scouts," he got his sister, Agnes Baden-Powell, to help. They formed the Girl Guides program in 1909 (Schultz & Lawrence, 1958). Their first law was that they must not even speak to a Boy Scout if they saw him in uniform.

A few years later, while visiting Britain, Juliette Gordon Low met the Baden-Powells and became fascinated with their organizations. When she returned to her home in Savannah, Georgia, she brought the idea with her. Changing the name to Girl Scouts, Daisy, as her friends knew her, held the first troop meeting in her home on March 12, 1912 (Fig. 10.6). Today, Girl Guides and Girl Scouts involve more than 8.5 million girls and adult leaders in about 144 countries (http://girlscouts.org/. Retrieved 3/10/04).

Figure 10.6
Juliette Gordon Low with Girl Scouts. (Courtesy of Girl Scouts of the USA Archives.)

What have we learned from all the strides made during this turn-of-the-century period? The historian Rainwater (1922) has identified nine transitions that summarize the expanded use of leisure for social good from about 1880 until the end of World War I:

1. Initial limited provisions of activities to young children were expanded to services for all ages.

2. Summer-only programs became yearlong.

3. Indoor activities became just as important as outdoor activities.

4. Services were expanded into rural areas in addition to urban centers.

5. Support shifted from the voluntary efforts of private citizens to government and other community agency support.

6. Play became organized instead of being freely expressed.

7. Projects became more complex and varied.

8. The philosophy shifted to include the provision of programs and leaders and not just the provision of facilities.

9. Community and group activities became more important than individual interests. (p. 192)

What began as a play movement shifted to an entire social movement. Sports, games, music, dance, and enjoying the outdoors became means to create better community lives. The movement was so sweeping that it involved cities, states, and the national government. Hospitals, clinics, social work agencies, and voluntary welfare efforts relied more and more on leisure as a tool. People formed organizations, raised funds, held interminable meetings, wrote volumes of handbooks, and conducted numerous training sessions to discover better ways to teach people how to use their leisure time productively.

From Your Own Experience

Web Explorations
Box 10.6

Explore more about the topics of this chapter on your own. To begin, check out these Web sites:

http://www.fscwv.edu/users/mdobbins1/wvnd.htm, to find examples of actual New Deal projects still of benefit today

http://www.nrpa.org/, for the home page of the National Recreation and Park Association, originally the Playground Association of America

http://www.bsamuseum.org/home.html, to see the official museum of the Boy Scouts of America, including a video overview

http://www.uic.edu/jaddams/hull/hull_house.html, to visit the official museum site for Jane Addams and the Hull House, with a link to the "urban experience of 1889"

http://www.cr.nps.gov/aad/peoples/overview.htm, for an introduction to the national parks associated with African Americans

http://www.ymca.net/about/cont/history.htm, to read some little
known stories about the origins of the YMCA

The Movement's Zenith

The period of time following World War I continued to bring monumental
changes to the people of the United States. Initially, the economy entered a
period of spectacular growth. Spurred on by the good times and a desire to be
"modern," large numbers of Americans adopted new attitudes and lifestyles.
There was greater acceptance of the individual pursuit of pleasure. People young
and old visited supposedly secret nightclubs called speakeasies, where they
danced the Charleston and listened to jazz. Labeled the "Roaring Twenties,"
this fun decade ended with the stock market crash and long economic depression.

The Great Depression of the 1930s in the United States (and in much of
the industrialized world) resulted in mass unemployment that engulfed nearly one third of the labor force in involuntary idleness. In spite of this, the
Depression did provide a benefit for organized leisure services. The federal
government soon instituted a number of emergency work programs—many
related to recreation—to reduce unemployment and stimulate the economy.
President Franklin Roosevelt introduced this as the **New Deal**. Federal workers
hired under New Deal programs built concert halls and community theaters,
developed outdoor recreation areas and camps, and helped establish state park
systems. Such federal work projects built
or improved 12,700 playgrounds, 8,500
gymnasiums, 750 swimming pools, 1,000
ice-skating rinks, and 64 ski jumps
(Knapp, 1973).

> **The New Deal:** the federally sponsored programs to provide jobs and stimulate economic recovery created by President Roosevelt when he took office in 1933

The New Deal relieved some of the hardship of many Americans, but
hard times dragged on until World War II military spending stimulated the
economy out of its depression. The war also brought another emphasis by the
federal government on the utility of leisure. This time it was in war. The goal
was to relieve the tensions, increase morale, and decrease the psychological
impact of being away from home. For example, the approximately 40,000 officers and enlisted men and women of the Special Services Division of the U.S.
Army provided recreation facilities and programs with units based around the
world. About 1,500 officers provided recreation programs for the Navy, and
even the Marine Corps offered expanded programs. Nongovernmental organ-

izations redirected their efforts to the war as well. In 1941, the United Service Organization (USO) was formed to provide recreation services at airports, hospitals, hotels, lounges, and special clubs near combat areas and rest centers.

When World War II ended in 1945, the United States entered the greatest period of economic growth in its history. Because the war had taken place elsewhere, no widespread destruction demanded attention, so postwar prosperity again resulted in a new lifestyle. Vast numbers of Americans moved out of cities to suburbs, where new housing was available. A rise in automobile ownership accompanied suburban growth. By 1960 over three–fourths of all American families owned a car, paving the way for a nationwide network of superhighways. These new roads enabled more people than ever to take vacation trips, and motels and fast-service restaurants sprang up to serve them.

Accordingly, outdoor recreation interests boomed in the 1950s. This boosted the services of such federal agencies as the National Park Service and the U.S. Forest Service. The Land and Water Conservation Fund was created in 1965 to provide federal aid in outdoor recreation development to states and local communities. The 1950s also witnessed new concerns for physical fitness because the effects of television and cars had already made their mark. This led to such organizations as the National Collegiate Athletic Association and the President's Council on Physical Fitness and Sport. This was also a growth period for the performing arts. The 1958 act of Congress that established the National Cultural Center for the Performing Arts (later named the John F. Kennedy Center for the Performing Arts) signaled their importance.

Against the backdrop of the Civil Rights movement, the first crack in the segregation of sports and recreation facilities was at last possible. First, the Brooklyn Dodgers brought Jackie Robinson up from their farm team in 1947. A series of legal test cases were also initiated, including one against the state of Maryland for racial segregation in its state parks. African American citizens of many cities bravely asserted their right to use segregated beaches, swimming pools, and amusement parks. Not until 1964 did the Civil Rights Act outlaw discrimination in public facilities.

Other problems demanded solutions, too. Crime and violence soared after 1960, and the war in Vietnam during the 1960s and 1970s brought civil strife at home. Pollution followed industrialization and population growth. During these years, leisure service organizations grappled with these problems, which also meant tremendous growth for an emerging new profession.

Leisure as a Community-Maker Today

Today, the ability of recreation and park services to create better lives pervades practically all domains of human need—mental and physical health and wellness, family and community relations, maintenance of ethnic identities, formation of social networks and systems of social support, respite from overwork, enhanced environmental stewardship, and assistance to at-risk youth (Driver, 1998). Accordingly, in taking the pulse of today's society, and through reading the crystal ball of the future, we can estimate the important pending social problems that leisure might be useful in helping solve. Those we discuss here are the contemporary problems of urbanization and suburbanization, the environment, changing demographics, juvenile delinquency, and intergroup relations.

First, might organized leisure services be a positive solution to the problems of urbanization and suburbanization? The trends in population location have clearly meant that cities are growing incrementally at the edges to produce the megalopolis and its rings of suburbs (Kelly & Freysinger, 2000). Central cities have remained the centers of culture and finance, but production, retailing, education, and services have gone to the suburbs along with housing. Inner-city areas have deteriorated, as they have been abandoned by almost all economic enterprises. In this process, transportation has become less efficient and more costly, as the private car is required for most everything. What is necessary is an effective reinvestment in the cities. Organized leisure services and initiatives have the potential to help our society realize that it can no longer afford urban slums with all of their social costs, in much the same way this was realized by Jane Addams and others at the turn of the last century.

In addition, as the suburbs expand, **urban sprawl** into wild lands destroys the habitats of wild species, another problem leisure services could help solve. Thus, a second source of problems is the condition of the environment. The degradation of the natural environment that has resulted in the loss of crop and grazing lands, depletion of the world's rain forests, extinction of animal and plant species, shortages of fresh water, air and water pollution, and other problems, provides a tall mandate for organized leisure services. Thus, it is essential to protect and beautify both our rural and urban heritage.

> **Urban sprawl:** when residential and business development outside cities threatens open space

One specific example is the use of once-abandoned waterfronts to create attractive spaces for leisure. In a number of cities, dilapidated freight yards, wharves, waterfront ports, and even junk-filled streams winding through inner-city slums have been dramatically transformed into parklike settings for boating, outdoor theater, shopping, dining, museums, and strolling. For example, in downtown Indianapolis, Indiana, a stretch of the White River, once the site of abandoned factories, was reclaimed as a state park featuring walking and biking pathways, several museums, a zoo, gardens, a baseball park, and an amphitheater.

Third is the challenge of changing demographics. Today leisure services are expected to play a vital role in responding to a rapidly aging population, a more diverse population in terms of ethnicity and lifestyles, the changing roles of women and men, modifications in family structures and functions, issues of crime and safety, and a society with more education. One role for leisure suggested by these changes is in the creation and maintenance of relationships. Today no one family pattern is in the majority; "family" now designates a variety of household compositions. For example, because of higher divorce rates and single-person births and adoptions, most children experience some period of being raised by a single parent. In addition, small families have reduced the child-rearing years; thus, the postparental period before retirement is now the longest period in the family life cycle. More adults are living alone. Committed relationships with and without children are now same sex as well as opposite sex. Leisure may need to become a more important context for building and developing relationships, and for redefining healthy families and communities.

Next, juvenile delinquency remains a social problem appropriate for leisure services. Although it is difficult to prove the specific benefits of organized recreation programs for reducing the problems of youth, a great number of studies have demonstrated positive outcomes (see McKay, 1993). In addition, a number of cities and professional recreation and park societies have recently taken action to offer alternatives to crime for at-risk youth. For example, in such cities as Chicago, Richmond, and Atlanta, highly successful midnight basketball leagues have been initiated that provide older youth exciting league play during the hours of the night when much criminal activity takes place. Additionally, organized leisure service organizations are prepared to offer such problem-solving tools as teen centers, special-interest clubs, employment assistance, cultural enrichment, and other programs as a means of reducing the opportunities for juvenile delinquency.

Finally, cooperation among various ethnic, racial, generational, and special-interest groups could benefit from leisure services. The challenge is for recreation and park organizations to provide opportunities suited to the interests and traditions of these different groups while maintaining a core of shared values and interests. This includes ways of overcoming the hostility and tension that have been building in many communities due to economic competition, negative stereotyping of minority populations, and other social factors that promote bigotry (Kraus, 2001). The arts, in particular, represent a major area of opportunity for sharing cultural traditions and for increasing racial and ethnic pride and tolerance.

Summary: What We Understand

As societies have become more industrialized, they have also become more reliant on leisure as a tool for solving problems. Although leisure is not a panacea for social problems, it is certainly one of the most potent solutions. This chapter traced the development of the utilitarian notion of leisure through its history in the United States. From this chapter you should understand that

- During the colonial period, leisure pursuits were tolerated in relation to the difficulties of survival in a new land.

- The 1800s was a period of transition leading to the "birth" of organized leisure services.

- In the 1900s leisure became part of a social conscience movement striving for humanitarian goals.

- As the use of leisure as a social problem-solving tool grew, services initially available only to young children expanded to include services for all ages, and support shifted from the voluntary efforts of private citizens to governmental and community agency support.

- As a result, leisure is now highly organized, with specific agendas for solving particular social problems.

Applications to Professional Practice

Early in the 20th century, as communities focused on providing organized leisure services, most of the hired leadership came from the fields of education, physical education, and social work. Park personnel were trained in such fields as landscape architecture and forestry. One of the earliest leadership training programs specifically for recreation professionals was a summer-school program conducted in the 1880s by Luther Gulick, then a professor of physical education for the School of Christian Workers (now Springfield College) in Massachusetts (Butler, 1965).

In 1905, Gulick joined the faculty of New York University and offered the first university course on play, called Principles of Physical Education, which included units on sports and games, the theory of toys, and play and the exceptional child (Sessoms, 1993). Later, the awareness of the need for special training for recreation leaders increased, resulting in the start of a one-year graduate curriculum sponsored by the National Recreation Association. Known as the National Recreation School, its founding in 1926 confirmed the desirability of educating recreation professionals. Located in New York City and relying heavily on the faculty of New York University, its curriculum included the construction and planning of play facilities and administering city and county recreation departments. It graduated over 295 students in its nine years of operation.

From this beginning, professional preparation programs in recreation began to appear in the curricula of forestry, education, social work, and physical education at colleges and universities across North America. Among the first academic programs were those at the University of Minnesota (1937) and the University of North Carolina (1939). Soon other colleges and universities that had developed clusters of recreation courses in their physical education curricula began to offer specialized undergraduate degrees in recreation. At the end of World War II in 1945, 37 such degree programs were available, and by the 1960s the number had nearly doubled (Kraus & Bates, 1975). Supporting a burgeoning number of job opportunities, by the end of the 1970s there were approximately 500 academic programs in recreation in the United States and Canada (Kraus, 1993). Although some of these programs were still linked to physical education, many were administered autonomously. They had their own faculty and offered separate courses.

Through the 1980s, professional preparation programs in recreation at colleges and universities were consolidated, and a number of weak and marginal programs were discontinued. Today, professional preparation programs, awarding associate's through doctoral degrees, are provided in more than 600 colleges and universities. The predominant subjects of study include administration and management, programming and leadership, outdoor recreation and resource management, commercial and tourism services, therapeutic recreation, and sports management.

For More Information

The best source of information about recreation and park curricula in North America is the Society of Park and Recreation Educators (SPRE). For example, from their Web site (http://www/nrpa.org) select "branches" and then "SPRE"; one of the items worthy of knowing about is the "Curriculum Catalog." Also, check out the "On-line Course Directory."

References

Butler, G. D. (1965). *Pioneers in public recreation.* Minneapolis, MN: Burgess.

Carter, M. J., vanAndel, G. E., & Robb, G. M. (1985). *Therapeutic recreation: A practical approach.* St. Louis: Times Mirror/Mosby College.

Cross, G. (1990). *A social history of leisure since 1600.* State College, PA: Venture.

Driver, B. (1998, February). The benefits are endless . . . but why? *Parks and Recreation, 26,* 28.

Duncan, M. (1991). Back to our radical roots. In T. L. Goodale & P. A. Witt (Eds.), *Recreation and leisure: Issues in an era of change* (210–229). State College, PA: Venture.

Dustin, D. L., McAvoy, L. H., & Schultz, J. H. (1982). *Stewards of access, custodians of choice: A philosophical foundation for the park and recreation profession.* Minneapolis, MN: Burgess.

Hardin, G. (1968, December 13). The tragedy of the commons. *Science.* 1243–1248.

Johnson, C. S. (1930). *The Negro in American civilization.* New York: Henry Holt.

Kelly, J. R., & Freysinger, V. J. (2000). *21st century leisure: Current issues.* Boston: Allyn & Bacon.

Knapp, R. F. (1973, July). Play for America: The New Deal and the NRA. *Parks and Recreation, 23,* 00.

Kraus, R. (1993). *Leisure in a changing America: Multicultural perspectives.* New York: Macmillan College.

Kraus, R. (2001). *Recreation and leisure in modern society.* Boston: Jones and Bartlett.

Kraus, R., & Bates, B. (1975). *Recreation leadership and supervision: Guidelines for professional development.* Philadelphia: W. B. Saunders.

MacLean, J. R., Peterson, J. A., & Martin, W. D. (1985). *Recreation and leisure: The changing scene.* New York: John Wiley & Sons.

McBride, P. (1989). Jane Addams. In H. Ibrahim (Ed.), *Pioneers in leisure and recreation* (pp. 35–37). Reston, VA: American Alliance for Health, Physical Education, Recreation, and Dance.

McKay, S. (1993). Research findings related to the potential of recreation in delinquency prevention. *Trends, 30*(3), 27.

National Park Service. (2002). Nicodemus. Retrieved June 6, 2002, from http://www.nps.gov/nico/

Rainwater, C. E. (1922). *The play movement in the United States.* Chicago: University of Chicago Press.

Sapora, A. (1989). Joseph Lee. In H. Ibrahim (Ed.), *Pioneers in leisure and recreation* (pp. 38–39). Reston, VA: American Alliance for Health, Physical Education, Recreation and Dance.

Searle, M., & Brayley, R. (2000). *Leisure services in Canada: An introduction.* State College, PA: Venture.

Sessoms, H. D. (1993, October). Quo vadis physical education and recreation. Paper presented at the Leisure Research Symposium, National Recreation and Park Association, San Jose, CA.

Schultz, G. D., & Lawrence, D. G. (1958). *Lady of Savannah: The life of Juliette Low.* Philadelphia: J. B. Lippincott.

Smith, S. (1890, August 7). Sophia Smith collection (SSC), Starr Family Papers, box 1, folder 3 [Newspaper clipping].

Towner, J. (1996). *An historical geography of recreation and tourism in the Western world, 1540–1940.* New York: John Wiley & Sons.

Work of uplift shown results. (1912, August 31). *Afro-American Ledger,* p. 2.

CHAPTER ELEVEN

Paying for It All

Preview

Is leisure of economic value?

Leisure is an economic balancing tool. For example, leisure mirrors a nation's level of economic development and its economic system. Leisure also drives an economy by fostering consumerism.

What is the positive economic impact of leisure?

Leisure makes good economic sense. It benefits investments, employment, taxes, and property values.

What is the negative economic impact of leisure?

Sometimes leisure results in undesirable costs. Examples are the negative economic impacts of leisure accidents and a nation's unfavorable balance of payments.

Key Terms

Economics 318
Standard of living 319
Gross domestic product (GDP) . . .319
Purchasing power parities (PPPs) 319
Human development index (HDI) .319
Capitalism 324
Consumption 326
Harried leisure class 329
Balance of payments 339
Foreign exchange leakage 339

Every society has a system for organizing the production and distribution of goods needed by its citizens. This organizational system is called the economic system, and it differs from society to society. Individuals also have a system for organizing the acquisition of the goods and services they need or want. This, too, requires an economic system. For both the society and the individual, the resources used to produce and acquire the goods and services are usually scarce. For example, a teen may have to chose between seeing a movie or buying a video game, and a nation may have to choose between weapons for defense and a good educational system. Few persons or societies are prosperous enough to buy everything they want when they want it. Thus, economic systems are based on economizing—using resources wisely to produce the things wanted the most. This is the most essential task of **economics**.

Leisure is at the heart of economics. Opportunities for leisure depend on how much money people have to spend, how much time away from the production of goods and services they have, and what leisure goods and services are available for purchase. The desire and ability to purchase leisure goods and services are expanding in contemporary societies. Despite the ups and downs of the economies in many of the wealthiest nations, personal income is rising over the long run, making more discretionary resources available to spend on pastimes. Such expenditures make the leisure industry among the fastest-growing segment of an economy. Leisure is, therefore, an economic tool.

> **Economics:** how people use their scarce resources to satisfy unlimited wants

Leisure operates as an intricate and fragile economic balancing tool. Changes in the economy create shifts in leisure, and shifts in leisure have an impact on the economy. A healthy economy depends on the relative stability of leisure. For example, if we reduce the amount of leisure time (perhaps if people worked longer hours) there would be less time to use the extra money earned. People would buy fewer boats, take fewer vacations, and attend fewer sporting events. These industries would, in turn, earn fewer profits, and their employees would be without work. Taxes generated from these industries would be reduced and thus harm the government's economy, and so on. The balance would be out of kilter.

In this chapter we begin with the intricacies of the balance between leisure and economics. Specifically, we consider the relationships between leisure and economic development, capitalism, and consumerism. Then we contrast the positive and negative effects of leisure economics. The power of leisure to affect economic health positively through expenditures and investment, employment, taxes, and property values is compared with leisure's negative impact from the cost of accidents and a negative balance of payments.

The Web of Leisure and Economics

Again, the point is that leisure is an economic balancing tool; it both helps shape an economy and is affected by changes in the economy. An examination of economic development, capitalism, and consumerism illustrates this function of leisure.

Economic Development

An economy must grow if its people want a higher standard of living. As an economy grows, it satisfies more and more of its people's needs and wants. Economists measure an economy's rate of growth by studying its gross domestic product (GDP). For example, the GDP of the United States recently increased by 4.1 percent (Bureau of Economic Analysis, 2003). Although widely used to measure economic growth for individual countries, the GDP is problematic for comparing countries. Hence, there are two additional ways of measuring economic well-being: purchasing power parities and the human development index.

> **Standard of living:** the economic, physical, social, and psychological level at which an individual, family, or nation lives

Purchasing power parities (PPPs) are the ratios in the prices of the same good or service in the national currencies of different countries. A well-known example is *The Economist's* "BigMac Currency Index," whereby the BigMac PPP is the conversion rate that would mean hamburgers cost the same in America as abroad (Schreyer & Koechlin, 2002). When nations are compared according to their PPP, the comparison ratio is set to 1.0 for the United States and then the purchasing power of citizens of other countries is compared to this. For example, Americans have a purchasing power of 1.0, whereas Koreans have a purchasing power of 733.0 (Organisation for Economic Co-operation and Development, 2003).

> **Gross domestic product (GDP):** the value of all goods and services produced

> **Purchasing power parities (PPPs):** the ratio of the prices in national currencies of the same good or service in different countries

In addition, a comparison of countries can be accomplished through a measure labeled the human development index (HDI). The HDI, published annually by the United Nations, ranks nations according to their citizens' overall quality of life rather than strictly by traditional economic figures. The criteria for calculating rankings are the combination of life expectancy, adult literacy, school enrollment, and per capita GDP. In other words, the HDI indicates "livability." For example, in 2000 Norway had the highest HDI in the world (.942) (see Fig. 11.1), whereas such developing economies as Sierra Leone (.275) and Niger (.277) had the lowest.

> **Human development index (HDI):** ranks nations according to citizens' overall quality of life rather than strictly by economic figures

Figure 11.1
Oslo, Norway, has Old World charm with a highly developed economy. (© Ruth V. Russell.)

Table 11.1 compares the ranking of the top 10 nations according to the PPP and HDI. The point is that even though citizens of a particular economy may be able to buy more, living there might not always make them feel well-off. For example, although the PPP for Koreans is the strongest in the world, their HDI ranks the country 27th.

Table 11.1

Comparison of Countries According to the PPP and the HDI

The wealthiest countries the PPP (2003)	The most livable countries according to the HDI (2000)
Korea (733)	1. Norway (.942)
Japan (140)	2. Sweden (.941)
Hungary (124)	3. Canada (.940)
Iceland (95.5)	4. Belgium (.939)
Slovak Republic (17.2)	5. Australia (.939)
Czech Republic (14.9)	6. United States (.939)
Sweden (9.69)	7. Iceland (.936)
Norway (9.48)	8. The Netherlands (.935)

Denmark (8.67)   9. Japan (.933)

Mexico (6.88)   10. Finland (.930)

Note. PPP = purchasing power parity; HDI = human development index. PPP statistics are from the Organisation for Economic Co-operation and Development (http://www.oecd.org/statisticsdata. Retrieved 3/23/04), and HDI statistics are from GeoHive.com (http://www.geohive.com/global/linkg.php. Retrieved 3/23/04).

How is economic development related to leisure? The relationship web differs considerably according to the level of economic development. For example, in developing economies, such as Sierra Leone and Niger, leisure is possible only for those who, because of their status, do not need to be directly involved in producing food or shelter. Often such a "leisure class" is supported by a working-class system.

Thorstein Veblen's (1899) classic ideas correspond here. Veblen was a late-19th-century scholar who concluded that, as a nonproductive consumption of time, leisure is an aristocratic possession. He claimed that throughout history, leisure was available only to the rich and powerful social classes. Their pastimes demonstrated their superior status; they were the leisure class. To Veblen, leisure was a decadent economic exploitation because it was characterized by idleness and conspicuous consumption. Only the wealthy could have leisure; only the wealthy could afford to have nothing to do with work. Veblen's writing reflected a satire of his own time, for in the late 19th century, the pastimes of the wealthy few in Europe and North America contrasted starkly with the poverty of the masses. Today, do television shows that expose the lifestyles of the "rich and famous" continue to mirror Veblen's critique?

In Focus

Are Veblen's Ideas Still Contemporary?

Box 11.1

Today we consider leisure to be an important life force for everyone. One hundred years ago, however, economist Thorstein Veblen (1899) argued that leisure had become the main way in which the affluent demonstrated their status. Is his claim still pertinent today? Does leisure still designate wealth and affluence? Based on a debate published elsewhere (Kelly & Freysinger, 2000), which case are you prepared to make?

Yes, Leisure Remains a Status Symbol

- Leisure is our social ID. With our "toys" we make a clear statement about our place in society. More expensive leisure goods designate a higher social status. This is particularly noticeable for children, who are well aware of their status among their peers when wearing $150 sport shoes.

- The leisure activities we choose clearly designate status. The poor do not engage in golf or snow skiing. Softball and bowling are considered to be working-class activities. Symphony concerts carry a higher status than square dances.

- Our playmates also appoint status. Kids wear clothing that identifies their social group. Adults join the "right" clubs. Even churches are clearly divided according to social status.

- Tourism is also a symbol of wealth. For Americans, a trip to Europe carries a higher status than a trip to Walt Disney World; a condo in Aspen is a far cry from visiting relatives in Indiana.

No, Leisure Is No Longer a Status Symbol

- Veblen's (1899) argument applied only to the "leisure class" who wanted to demonstrate that they did not have to work. They could live a life of leisure. Most people now have to work and even want to work.

- Expressions of leisure are quite diverse. We do many things for many different reasons. Leisure is now more personal and reflects our own unique histories.

- Expressions of leisure are also now more likely to be based on satisfaction. We stay involved in particular activities because they relax or excite us.

- Most of our leisure is private and not on display. For example, we read, watch television, and garden. We do things that don't attract attention or impress anyone.

Questions to Consider and Discuss

1. *Which side of the debate rings true from your experience? Why? Which side of the debate matches the perspectives of classmates? Why?*

2. *Can you name any leisure goods you've purchased lately or experiences you've had that may, at least in part, carry a high status for you? How did you feel right after purchasing them or having that experience? How do you feel about these purchases or experiences now?*

3. *If the "yes" side of the debate wins, what implication does this have for the quality of leisure itself? Or, if the "no" side of the debate wins, what implication does this have for the quality of leisure itself?*

Meanwhile, when industrialization reaches a successful level of output such that many people have command over consumption, a modern economic system is achieved, as is the case in Norway. People's basic needs for food, shelter, and clothing are satisfied, and they can focus on services. High amounts of discretionary income and time abound. In mature economic systems, leisure itself is an industry. Tourism is an excellent example of this. Tourism is an aggregate of many different businesses: Tourist attractions, transportation systems, lodging, restaurants, entertainment, and advertising focus on generating a profit from people's desires to travel for pleasure. In Greece, for example, a majority of those working in the service sector of the economy work in tourist industries (Fig. 11.2).

Figure 11.2
Fifty-two percent of those in the labor force in modern-day Greece work in the service sector of the economy, with tourism as its primary service industry. (© Ruth V. Russell.)

In addition, in the United States, tourism is one of the top three sources of income for 46 of the 50 states. States such as Hawaii, where tourists outnumber residents six to one, are almost pure tourist economies. Hawaii's annual 6.4 million visitors directly account for about one third of all jobs in the state, 28 percent of the state's GDP, 64 percent of its exports, and 27 percent of total taxes (Hawaii Department of Business, Economic Development, and Tourism, 2004).

Capitalism

The relationship between leisure and a mature, developed economic system is not always so positive. From some viewpoints, economic systems can be harmful to leisure. We'll use capitalism to illustrate this point. **Capitalism** is an economic system in which individuals or private business enterprises develop, own, and control much of the capital and means of production. Also labeled the free-enterprise system, the central ideas of capitalism date back to as early as 1656 when the philosopher Lee suggested that "the advancement of private persons will be the advantage of the public" (Goodale & Godbey, 1988, p. 74). Adam Smith later expanded on this idea in his book *An Inquiry into the Nature and Causes of the Wealth of Nations* (1937, originally published in 1776), in

> **Capitalism: an economic system characterized by private ownership of goods and resources**

which he promoted the view that an individual's work automatically contributes to the welfare of others.

According to Smith (1937), the basic premises of economic order were that (a) self-interest is the prime motivation, (b) individual striving will lead to a common good, and (c) no regulation of the economy is best (1937). Smith's argument—that individualism will lead to economic progress—served as the basis for today's capitalist economic system. How does leisure fare under capitalism?

"In capitalist society . . . leisure time for a privileged class is produced by converting the whole lifetime of the masses into labor time" (as cited in Cunningham, 1980, p. 515). This statement, made in the 1800s by Karl Marx, the father of communism, criticized the suppression of leisure under capitalism. Because Smith's ideas of free enterprise were based on human progress possible only by the labor of individuals, leisure was considered an obstruction, even by Smith himself: the more leisure, the less progress; the more progress, the less leisure (Smith, 1937).

In contrast, since Smith's time, many people have come to believe that capitalism has created more leisure time for people. For example, in the 1960s economic progress through capitalism was projected to yield steady reductions in working time. Because of this economic system, people in the United States, for example, now have a 40-hour workweek, two weeks a year for a paid vacation, and extended years of schooling and retirement.

Yet some commentators consider this not to be the progress expected. Economist Juliette Schor (1992) and others argue that capitalism tends to expand work to the detriment of leisure. Indeed, almost all other nations have an average of twice the paid vacation days as Americans! Schor maintains that this is because capitalist economies contain biases toward long working hours. As a result of these "long hour jobs," capitalism has created a crisis of leisure time (p. 7).

Other economic systems have also had roller-coaster relationships with leisure. For example, those associated with communism have been successful in creating free time for people but unsuccessful in producing the goods and services people want for leisure. People in these economies have not been able to "buy leisure" because the products are simply not available on the retail market. A few years ago, under the communist system in what was then the Soviet Union, the consumption of "luxuries" was discouraged. At the time, a 21-inch color television typically cost more than $1,000, and a VCR was more than $2,500. Even more problematic was that there were only a few videotape rental stores with very few titles. In spite of all this, there was a 10-year waiting list to purchase a VCR.

This might all mean that when leisure is defined as buying experiences, a communist-based economic system is prohibitive, whereas if leisure is defined as free time, a capitalist system may be disadvantageous.

In Profile

Veblen, Smith, Marx, and Schor
Box 11.2

Do Thorstein Veblen, Adam Smith, Karl Marx, and Juliette Schor consider the relationship between leisure and economics in a similar way? Separated by many years, is there still a common thread in the ideas of these economists? Briefly, let's compare them. What is your conclusion?

Time Period	Smith Late 1700s	Marx Mid-1800s	Veblen Late 1800s	Schor Late 1990s
Biography	Born in Scotland in 1723. Professor of moral philosophy at the University of Glasgow. Generally considered the founder of the free-enterprise economic system (capitalism).	Born in Prussia (now Germany) in 1818. Working with colleague Friedrich Engels, is known as communism's most zealous intellectual advocate. Spent much of his life exiled for radicalism.	Born in Wisconsin in 1857. Professor at the University of Chicago. Coined the expression "conspicuous consumption."	Contemporary economist; professor at Harvard University.
Economic premise	Individual self-interest with no regulation provides for a common good.	Exchanges of equal value for equal value, where value is determined simply by the amount of work put into whatever is being produced.	Life in modern industrial society is a conflict between making money and making goods; the market mechanism of capitalism interferes with production.	Economies based on a consumerist mentality (spending for social meaning) harm people and communities.
Consequence for leisure	Leisure is an obstruction to progress.	Leisure is harmed when not equally available. To gain more leisure, the lower classes must overthrow the upper classes.	Leisure belongs only to the upper classes. To gain more leisure, the lower classes must climb up to the level of the upper classes.	Keeping up with the Joneses requires working more, which means less leisure time and energy.

Consumerism

Let's look at the idea of "buying" leisure a bit more. A fundamental part of any economic system is the function of **consumption**. In most economies, it is the largest spending category. Along with services, it includes purchases of non-durable goods, such as soap and steak, and durable goods, such as stereos and suitcases. You can usually tell a lot about an individual's or family's economic status by observing their consumption patterns. Do they drive a new Hummer or an old VW bus? What do they eat? What do they wear? Although you sometimes come across people who live well below or above their means, consumption and income tend to be closely related. This is demonstrated in Table 11.2.

> **Consumption:** all household purchases of goods and services

The higher the incomes of people, the more they are likely to spend. Consumption, then, is an expected characteristic of mature economies.

Table 11.2

Per Capita Income and Personal Consumption Expenditures in the United States (in current dollars)

Year	Personal income	Personal consumption
1950	$1,516	$1,270
1960	$2,283	$1,838
1970	$4,101	$3,164
1980	$10,205	$7,741
1990	$19,614	$15,327
2000	$30,205	$24,429

Note. From U.S. Department of Commerce, Bureau of Economic Analysis (2001).

From Your Own Experience

Buy Nothing Day
Box 11.3

Can you go for one day without spending any money? Try it. The day before, load up your refrigerator with the food you'll need for the next day, buy the gasoline for your car that you'll need to get you to school or work, and acquire whatever other absolute necessities (such as medicine) you'll need for the day.

Now, for 24 hours, live without consumption. Spend absolutely nothing. Keep a personal journal about your experience and feelings during this experiment. Afterward ask yourself, "How hard was it?" Even though you had life's necessities, did you miss spending money? What was it like not to go to a movie, have a beer with friends, or shop at the mall?

So that you don't feel so unusual, link onto the numerous "spend nothing" campaigns available on the Internet. Just type in "spend nothing day" in your search.

Spending money for leisure is a common focus of consumption. Indeed, expenditures for leisure are at the center of some economies. People buy tennis rackets, basketballs, fishing licenses, amusement park admissions, gasoline for power boats, golf clubs, pets, DVDs, flower seeds, jogging shoes, health club memberships, violins, and magazine subscriptions. Buying these goods is good for the economy, but the web entangling leisure and consumption is more dynamic than this. In some societies, consumption is actually a form of leisure (Fig. 11.3). Let's consider shopping as an illustration.

Figure 11.3
Shopping for leisure goods or shopping as leisure? (© Ruth V. Russell.)

Although we have no clear estimates of how many of us spend time wandering around the stores, a number of research studies have pointed to the prevalence of shopping as a favorite pastime for North Americans. Visiting shopping malls is for many a preferred form of evening or weekend recreation. In fact, when people are given more free time, participation in shopping often increases. In one study of the effects of converting to a four-day workweek and thus a 3-day weekend, one third of the workers surveyed filled the extra time by spending more money on shopping (Maklan, 1977).

In Profile

Mall of America
Box 11.4

When the Metropolitan Stadium in Bloomington, Minnesota, closed, the city was left with what amounted to a huge white elephant. What could be done with 78 acres of land near the Minneapolis-St. Paul airport?

At 10:00 am on August 11, 1992, the most discussed retail project in the United States opened and answered the question. Everything about it is big. Mall of America is 4.2 million square feet of "buying leisure" under one roof. It includes 2.5 million square feet of retail, a seven-acre Camp Snoopy theme park; Underwater Adventures, featuring 3,000 living sea creatures; a LEGO Imagination Center; a bowling center; and an entertainment complex of four night clubs, 14 theater screens, and 17 restaurants plus a food court (see http://www.mallofamerica.com). There are also 400 trees, nearly 13,000 parking spaces, 109 surveillance cameras, and 700 tons of monthly garbage (Guterson, 1993).

Promoted as "one of the nation's most popular vacation destinations," this mall was always envisioned as an event. No clocks or windows remind people of realities like the time and the weather outside. It is divided into four themed "streets." North Garden features a heavily landscaped summer décor. East Broadway is a contemporary, chrome-filled street; South Avenue features a 1920s grand hotel look, and West Market resembles a European train station. At night, the outside is lit in the manner of a Las Vegas casino.

"I believe we can make Mall of America stand for all America," asserted the mall's general manager in a promotional video accompanying its opening. The idea was to position Mall of America as a giant pleasure dome (Guterson, 1993). And it has worked. Faced with threats of catalogue purchasing, large discount stores, cable television's shopping networks, and Web-based shopping, Mall of America prospers. It understands that shopping and fun go hand-in-hand.

Yet is this really leisure? As one philosopher observed, what we want are things, but things cost money, and money costs time (deGrazia, 1962). This leads us to the concept of the **harried leisure class**, which is also the title of Staffan Linder's (1970) book. The theme of this classic is that consumption greatly limits leisure; in fact, Linder considers it the antithesis of leisure. The increased work required for the money to buy things, the increased time needed for upkeep and maintenance on the things we buy, and of course, the time devoted to the process of buying it all result in a hectic, never-satisfied, materialistic frenzy. Is it leisure? Linder says no.

> **Harried leisure class:** when spending money for leisure spoils leisure by making us feel frantic

We already know that if we own more and more material possessions and work longer hours so we can purchase them, we will not necessarily find happiness. In fact, some studies indicate no relationship between money spent and the personal satisfaction obtained from the purchases. For example, going diving in top-of-the-line scuba gear sounded like fun from the advertisements, but one time out was enough! The ocean was cold and you felt woozy the whole time. Now the gear is somewhere in the back of the closet. You feel guilty. In one study of lottery winners, even though the winners were much happier immediately after winning the lottery, one year later their average happiness had increased on a nine-point scale from 6.5 to only 6.8 as a result of winning (Sobel & Ornstein, 1987).

As an economist might say, the marginal utility on more wealth, experience, or success declines dramatically after a minimum acceptable level has been reached. One reason for this is that expectations are easily inflated (Godbey, 1997). When we owned a black-and-white television (some of you may not remember this), we were pleased with it, but now that we own a large flat-screen color TV, our expectations have increased to assuming this is normal. Our expenditure for the television also increased.

In Profile

Affluenza
Box 11.5

Introduced in a Public Broadcasting Service documentary that first aired in 1997, and using the analogy of a disease, "affluenza" is defined as "a painful, contagious, socially transmitted condition of overload, debt, anxiety, and waste resulting from the dogged pursuit of more" (deGraaf, Wann, & Naylor, 2001, p. 2). Amid the prosperity of a healthy economy, this powerful "virus" is threatening our friendships, our families, our communities, and our environment. Untreated, the disease can cause permanent discontent. To treat it, we must stop pursuing more stuff, and reconnect to other values. We must cure our shopping fever, swollen expectations, the stress of excess, and our ache for meaning.

Do you have affluenza? Do you get bored unless you have something to consume (goods, media, food)? Do you try to impress your friends with what you own, or where you vacation? Do you ever use shopping as "therapy"? Do you think about things more than you think about people? Are any of your credit cards "maxed out"? Do your conversations often gravitate toward things you want to buy?

Here are some of the symptoms of affluenza at the societal level:

- In the past several years, more Americans declared personal bankruptcy than the number who graduated from college.

- In America the annual production of solid waste would fill a convoy of garbage trucks stretching halfway to the moon.

- There are twice as many shopping centers as high schools.

- Americans now work more hours each year than do the citizens of any other industrial country, including Japan.

- Although comprising only 4.7 percent of the earth's people, Americans account for 25 percent of its global warming greenhouse gas emissions.

- Ninety-five percent of workers say they wish they could spend more time with their families.

- Since 1950, Americans have used up more resources than everyone who ever lived on earth before then.

Godbey (1989) criticizes consumerism for more than its damage to happiness and the spirit of leisure. He claims that North Americans have developed a style of life and an attitude toward the consumption of material goods that "rapes the world's resources and does untold environmental harm" (p. 17). Many others also decry the problems of too much consumerism, but they throw up their hands in hopelessness because they consider leisure to be impossible in contemporary societies without consumption.

What if we were more conserving in our leisure patterns. Could we still have fun? What would happen if we didn't want faster jet skis, easy travel to unusual places, and hundreds of CDs? What would life be like if we engaged in only those activities that made a minimal demand on material goods, such as walking, yoga, organic gardening, reading, singing, and dancing? How would our health be affected if we chose cross-country skiing over downhill skiing, hiking over all-terrain motorbikes, or playing basketball rather than watching it on TV? How would our environment be affected if we recycled the medals won in sports competitions, repaired and passed on to others toys our children have outgrown, and took our own cup to the refreshment stand at the ball game (Fig. 11.4)? Conserving on our leisure is converting "having" into "being" and "doing." Would we still have a good time?

Figure 11.4
Recycling children's toys and sports equipment would be a good place to begin practicing conserver leisure. (© Ruth V. Russell.)

How Leisure Benefits an Economy

There is no doubt about it, however: leisure has economic value. The presence of leisure facilities and programs attracts businesses and industries to particular locales. Cultural and sporting events have public relations value for the corporations that support them by enhancing the company's image and ultimately increasing profits. Well-planned leisure services can help reduce the costs of vandalism and crime, particularly in urban areas. Although the list could go on and on, the specific positive economic benefits from leisure reviewed here are direct expenditures and investments, employment, taxes, and property values.

The Study Says

How to Spend $30,000
Box 11.6

It costs approximately $30,000 to incarcerate a convicted youth offender for one year. According to research reported by the National Recreation and Park Association (2000), if that money were available to the community recreation and parks department, the same youth offender could instead be taught good behavior through

- swimming twice a week for 24 weeks
- four tours of the zoo plus lunch
- enrollment in 50 community center programs
- visiting a nature center twice
- playing league softball for a season
- touring the public gardens twice
- two weeks of tennis lessons
- two weeks of day camp
- three rounds of golf
- acting in a play
- participating in one fishing clinic
- taking a four-week pottery class
- playing basketball eight hours a week for 40 weeks
- and still have $29,125 left over to spend on someone else. Do you think we'd have a much happier kid spending taxpayer money this way?

Expenditures and Investments

In industrialized societies it is common for people to spend more money on leisure than on any other single category, including housing, food, clothing, health care, or education (Chubb & Chubb, 1981). Every indication is that leisure has become the primary economic base for many cities, states, and provinces. The competition for conventions, tourism, shopping, spectator sports events, entertainment, festivals, and fine arts has become a major tool for urban renewal projects. The promotion of leisure expenditures and investments makes good economic sense.

For example, in the United States, total annual expenditures for pastimes are estimated to be higher than $500 billion per year. This includes video, audio, and computer products ($89.7 billion); toys and sporting supplies ($45.4 billion); and commercial amusements ($46.2 billion) (U.S. Department of Commerce, 1999). It does not include travel, which is estimated to carry an annual price tag of another $500 billion (Cordes & Ibrahim, 2003). According to many researchers, however, these estimates are conservative, because they do not take into account money spent on restaurants, all shopping, and the operational expenses of thousands of public and private leisure service organizations. In fact, some authorities have estimated that annual leisure expenditures in the United States alone are now over two trillion dollars.

Further, economists report that expenditures for leisure goods and services in the United States have been increasing at a faster rate than other merchandise. That is, in the late 1800s, less than two percent of household expenditures were devoted to recreation, but by 1985, the recreational portion of the budget had increased to 6.6 percent, and by 1996 to 8.3 percent (U.S. Department of Commerce, 1999). This means that leisure is a growth industry.

Economic data in the United Kingdom give a similar story. For example, a study of the economic importance of sports alone demonstrates that it has grown substantially. Sports-related consumer expenditures accounted for 2.33 percent of the total in 1995, representing 1.61 percent of the GDP (Gratton & Taylor, 2000). The value of private investing in new leisure projects in the United Kingdom has also shown a significant growth pattern (Tribe, 1999).

In Focus

The Credit Card Crisis
Box 11.7

More than one-third of kids acquire their first credit card in high school. By college, they carry an average of three cards, with balances totaling around $2,500. Like 48 percent of adults, they pay only their minimum charge each month. Kids are quickly learning to use high-interest plastic to live well beyond their means.

Questions to Consider and Discuss

1. *Do you have more than one credit card? Do you pay off your balance every month, or do you make only the minimum payment? If you make only the minimum payments, have you calculated how*

long it will take you to pay off your balance even if you charge nothing more? Surprised?

2. *About what proportion of your monthly charging on these cards is for things or experiences you'd label as recreational? For these, would you say you are borrowing off of future employment earnings to live the good life now?*

3. *Do you think there is a credit card crisis in our society? If so, to what extent do you think the pursuit of leisure is responsible?*

Employment

It is also difficult to estimate the number of people whose income is leisure-related, yet available statistics suggest that many occupations have something to do with leisure. Those in the entertainment fields, supervisors in city recreation agencies, managers in parks and forests, employees of health and fitness facilities, workers in factories manufacturing recreational goods, employees of restaurants and hotels, managers of bowling centers, travel agents, recreation therapists in hospitals, and many more types of leisure-related employment provide benefits to an economy.

For example, the U.S. state park systems employ over 45,000 people (Association of State Park Directors, 2001). More than 12,000 permanent and 6,000 seasonal employees are hired to operate the recreational facilities and programs of federal agencies. In addition, it is estimated that American hotels employ about 1.5 million people, the motion picture industry about 404,000, amusement services about 1.1 million, and social services (museums, zoos, and private organizations) about 1.9 million (U.S. Department of Commerce, 1995). This represents billions of dollars in income, which is fed back into the economy. Many other occupations, such as transportation system workers and child-care specialists, are indirectly or partially related to leisure and provide economic benefits as well.

There is another way to view the positive impact leisure has on employment. Substantial research data indicate that participation in some leisure activities leads workers to become more productive. Since labor is a factor in production, when that factor becomes more productive, the costs of production decrease. This results in financial gain to employers. Activities that are strenuous and that increase participants' strength and endurance, for example, allow them to be more productive at jobs that require both physical and mental labor. It reduces health-care costs, lowers absenteeism, reduces on-the-job accidents, and provides other benefits that mean better profits for employers

(Ellis & Richardson, 1991). Otherwise, according to the Centers for Disease Control and Prevention (2001, see http://www.cdc.gov/), about $5.7 billion is spent in the United States each year on medical bills and lost productivity of people who could have fought off at least heart disease with even a little physical exercise.

Taxes

Generating local, state or provincial, and federal revenues through the taxes typically paid in connection with leisure also contributes to the economic health of a society (Fig. 11.5). These include sales taxes from the purchase of leisure goods and services, income taxes on wages earned in leisure-related jobs, property taxes from private and commercial properties that are partly or totally leisure oriented, gasoline taxes, and taxes on entertainment, restaurant meals, and hotel accommodations.

Figure 11.5
Mayesville, Ohio, town scene, in duplicate! Leisure is good business for communities. (Wall mural painted by Robert Dafford. © Ruth V. Russell.)

The fees for hunting, trapping, and fishing licenses, and the taxes on hunting and fishing equipment usually benefit the upkeep of fish and game habitats. Excise taxes are levied on certain imported leisure goods. Liquor taxes in some areas are quite high, and the taxes garnered from legal gambling, such as lotteries and pari-mutuel betting, have been very useful to local and state governments. In many cases, these tax revenues are used to enhance the leisure services available to people. For example, the National Endowment for the Arts allocates millions of dollars in federal tax money to be used as matching funds by local arts organizations.

Property Values

The value of land is often affected by the presence of leisure-related development. For example, large and well-maintained parks usually increase the value of adjacent property, such as the land near Central Park in New York City and Golden Gate Park in San Francisco. In some situations, the highest priced residential property adjoins golf courses, developed lakes and reservoirs, resorts, wildlife refuges, and other leisure sites.

Perhaps the most visible examples of the positive impact of leisure on property values are found in such places as Palm Springs, California. Once barren desert land, today Palm Springs has a population of approximately 40,000 residents. Why? Sometimes the best economic use of an area is for leisure. Palm Springs has made itself into a playground. The Palm Springs industries are tennis, golf, cultural events, bicycling, lounging by the pool, pleasure walking, and eating fine foods. These industries bring in not only permanent residents but also conventioneers and tourists. Two million visitors a year flock to this land of 350 days of sunshine. It is estimated that in this area there are some 109 golf courses, 600 tennis courts, and 8,000 swimming pools. Based on an almost purely leisure-focused industry where there was once nothing, Palm Springs now has one of the highest median family incomes, city revenues per capita, and average single-family home values in the United States (Information Publications, 1993).

How Leisure Harms an Economy

Hawaiian studies professor Haunani-Kay Trask pleads, "Please stay home." Why? Trask believes that Hawaii doesn't need any more tourists: "My advice is, if you're thinking about Hawaii, don't come. Stay right where you are. If you do come, remember that you're contributing to the oppression of a native people in their home country" (as cited in Olson, 2001, p. 78). Although businesses in Hawaii benefit from tourism, not all its residents do. Today, Hawaii's 6.4 million tourists a year not only contribute positively to the state and local economies, but they also drive up inflation, and thus the cost of living for residents. As a result, according to Trask, the native people are finding it harder and harder to remain on their homeland because they can't afford it. About half of the native Hawaiian population now lives stateside, and nearly one fifth of Hawaii's entire resident population is classified as near-homeless. Beach shanties have sprung up throughout the islands, but this image is, of course, bad for tourism.

As this situation in Hawaii illustrates, sometimes leisure results in costs rather than benefits to an individual's finances and a community's economy. There are many more examples, such as the decreased productivity of workers that often happens at holiday times. The opening of baseball and hunting seasons, and the two-week holiday period around Christmas and the New Year typically experience the highest rates of absenteeism, inattentiveness, and lethargy. In addition, leisure businesses are among the most susceptible to the whims of public taste. Fads come and go, and expensive leisure industries come and go with them. What happened to trampoline parks? Financial headaches can also be caused by the seasonal nature of some forms of leisure. Ski resorts are a good illustration.

Frequently, members of a society must pay high costs to solve some of the problems that result from leisure. These problems include public money spent on pet-related problems. For example, about 53 million dogs are kept as pets in the United States (American Veterinary Medical Association, 1997), and the cost to taxpayers for managing the dogs, such as dealing with strays and removing fecal waste from public places, is about $500 million per year. Another example is the $1 billion spent annually by the U.S. Coast Guard to rescue small pleasure boats, and it is estimated that dealing with the problems of pleasure drinking, such as sick pay, accidents, and lost production, costs about $15 billion a year.

To understand in more depth how leisure harms an economy, let's consider accidents and the negative balance of payments.

Accidents

Every day, on average, 24,384 Americans suffer disabling injuries. These accidents cost the U.S. economy about $323,287,671 per day in lost wages, indirect work loss, medical expenses, insurance payments, rescue and emergency care, and lawsuits (Heymann, 1989). What proportion of these accidents and costs is leisure related? Perhaps you can conduct your own survey to investigate the role of leisure in accidents. Every time someone you know is injured, ask him or her whether the injury was the result of something he or she was doing for fun. You will probably find that a large proportion of the injuries have some connection to leisure. To emphasize the point, lawsuits for injuries sustained while pursuing recreational activities have become economically significant. About half of all sports-related lawsuits, for example, result in financial recovery for the injured; frequently, the amount awarded is over $1 million.

Heymann (1989) estimates that every day in the United States, 222 people are injured using skateboards, 1,546 are injured using bicycles (Fig. 11.6), and 523 children are treated at hospitals for playground injuries. In fact, injuries due to falls from playground equipment result in a higher proportion of severe injuries than either bicycle or motor vehicle crashes, according to a study conducted by the Children's Hospital Medical Center of Cincinnati (http://www.eurekalert.org/pub_releases/2001-07/chmc-pim071801.php. Retrieved 4/25/04).

How do accidents in leisure occur? There are multiple ways. Lack of sufficient or appropriate information can give people a false sense of security when they engage in pastimes. For example, diving into murky water of an unknown depth is an uninformed action that creates an unnecessary risk to safety. Limited performance skills can also lead to accidents. Sometimes people participate in activities before they have mastered the needed skills. For example, drowning victims are likely to be poor swimmers, and novice skiers are more likely to be injured than experts. One hospital's estimate is that most of the more than 10 million sports injuries per year can be prevented with proper conditioning and training (http://www2.jeffersonhospital.org. Retrieved 3/29/04).

Figure 11.6
Risks to bicyclists have increased. © Ruth V. Russell

Another category of leisure-related accidents is caused by a lack of proper management by sponsors of recreational services. Poor maintenance of facilities can lead to accidents, such as when someone is cut falling on broken glass on a ball field. Also, if recreational facilities and programs provided by organizations are not adequately supervised, such as lifeguards failing to control rowdy behavior at the pool, accidents are more likely to occur.

Accidents can also be attributed to careless behaviors. Bouncing on a trampoline without spotters present, not using protective eyewear in racquetball, starting down a water slide before the one in front is off, running on a wet pool deck, using alcohol while playing volleyball, and not wearing a helmet when bicycling are likely to lead to injuries. Such careless behavior is different from dangerous behavior. Careless behaviors produce at least 90 percent of all accidents that occur at places of recreation (Bucher, Shivers, & Bucher, 1984). This means that participation in high-risk activities, such as scuba diving, hang gliding, caving, rock climbing, and extreme skiing are not more likely to produce injuries when pursued cautiously and wisely.

Balance of Payments

A nation's balance of payments is the comparison of its imports against its exports. Although exchange rates are an important part of the picture, so are the differences between economies in the transactions of buying and selling merchandise. In recent years such countries as the United States, Canada, and the United Kingdom have experienced a deficit in this trade balance. That is, their imports exceed the value of their exports. In 1998, for the United States, this deficit amounted to $231 billion (Foreign Trade Division, 1999). This means that during most of the 1980s and all of the 1990s, Americans were consuming more than they were producing.

> **Balance of payments:** a statement of all goods and services, as well as investments, that flow in and out of a country

How does this relate to leisure? Inventory your own leisure-related equipment and clothing. Do you own athletic shoes, golf clubs, snow skis, a bicycle, a television set, a CD player, a DVD player, or a musical instrument? What proportion of your leisure possessions were made in your own country? If more of them were made outside your country, you have just demonstrated a negative balance of payments related to leisure. According to the Foreign Trade Division (1999) leisure-related commodities significantly contribute to a negative balance of payments.

Tourism provides a ready illustration. During the past decade in the United Kingdom, more British tourists vacationed outside the country than the number of international tourists who arrived in the country. This created a negative balance of payments for the U.K. tourist industry (Tribe, 1999). On the other hand, during this same time period, there were more international tourist arrivals in Australia than resident departures out of Australia. This created a positive balance of payments.

In tourism, one of the factors complicating the balance of payments ledger is the extent to which tourist attractions are foreign owned. Disneyland Resort Paris is a good example. Although the location of this theme park attracts many more tourists from other European countries into France, a large portion of the income generated there goes back out of France to owners in the United States. This occurrence is called **foreign exchange leakage** and is a strong determinant of whether tourism really provides an economic advantage for the locale hosting the attraction. In particular, for developing countries using tourism as an economic development tool, foreign

> **Foreign exchange leakage:** money generated in a country that is removed out of that country because of foreign ownership of the goods and services sold there

exchange leakage caused by foreign ownership of the airlines, hotels, resorts, souvenirs, alcohol, and other tourist goods and services can be significant.

Summary: What We Understand

Leisure is a powerful economic balancing tool. In this chapter we explored the relationship between leisure and economics. You should now understand that

- Leisure is a mirror of a nation's level of economic development and its economic system.

- In economically mature countries (especially under capitalism), leisure drives the economy by fostering consumerism. Sometimes consumption itself is viewed as a leisure experience.

- Leisure has both positive and negative economic impacts.

- On the one hand, leisure makes good economic sense; it benefits expenditures and investments, employment, taxes, and property values.

- On the other hand, leisure has monetary costs. Two examples are the costs of leisure-related injuries and a negative balance of payments.

Applications to Professional Practice

The commercial recreation sector is a collection of industries that capitalizes on the economic power of leisure by providing a wide range of recreation, entertainment, and amusement services in order to make a profit. These businesses range in size from a family-run commercial campground to a professional sports franchise. Indeed, the range of leisure services provided commercially is quite wide. Included are amusement and theme parks, show businesses, retail outlets, restaurants, tour buses, circuses, bowling centers, campgrounds, marinas, ski resorts, malls, and all manner of other facilities and programs. Every form of leisure can be sold commercially.

In the United States and Canada, the market for such services is one of the fastest growing elements of the economy. Further, in comparison with services offered to the public by governments, and services offered to members by private organizations, some consider commercial recreation enterprises to have significant advantages. For instance, they are often better able to develop new projects that require large capital investments and expose owners to financial risks. Commercial recreation also is usually the first provider to try new things, often capitalizing quickly on trends and fads and expanding into new markets for pastimes (Fig. 11.7).

Figure 11.7
Commercial leisure enterprises are often trendsetters in delivery of services to people.
© Ruth V. Russell

On the other hand, since the motivation of commercial recreation industries is to make money, they have less responsibility to serve underrepresented or disadvantaged members of a community. In addition, many commercial recreation operators consider themselves less obligated to educate and inform customers than to "give them exactly what they want" (Henderson et al., 2001, p. 265). This sometimes means that they regard as acceptable some activities such as drinking or pornography that are considered inappropriate for government or private agencies to provide. Retailers of jet skis, snowmobiles, and all-terrain vehicles, for example, have very different views on the value of their products than do professionals in other leisure service organizations who are charged with preserving natural resources.

For More Information

Many jobs are available in commercial recreation. The sector is growing rapidly, and knowledgeable and socially responsible professionals are needed there. To learn more about your options, check the Web site for the Resort and Commercial Recreation Association at http://www.r-c-r-a.org/.

References

American Veterinary Medical Association. (1997). *U.S. pet ownership and demographics sourcebook*. Schaumburg, IL: Author.

Association of State Park Directors. (2001). Home page. Retrieved July 21, 2001, from http://naspd.indstate.edu/index.html

Bucher, C. A., Shivers, J. S., & Bucher, R. D. (1984). *Recreation for today's society*. Englewood Cliffs, NJ: Prentice Hall.

Bureau of Economic Analysis. (2003). News release: Gross domestic product. Retrieved March 23, 2004, from http://www.bea.doc.gov/bea/newsrel/gdp-newsrelease.htm

Chubb, M., & Chubb, H. R. (1981). *One–third of our time? An introduction to recreation behavior and resources*. New York: John Wiley & Sons.

Cordes, K. A., & Ibrahim, H. M. (2003). *Applications in recreation and leisure for today and the future*. Boston: McGraw-Hill.

Cunningham, H. (1980). *Leisure in the Industrial Revolution*. London: Croom Helm.

deGraaf, J., Wann, D., & Naylor, T. H. (2001). *Affluenza: The all-consuming epidemic*. San Francisco: Berrett-Koehler.

deGrazia, S. (1962). *Of time, work and leisure*. New York: The Twentieth Century Fund.

Ellis, T., & Richardson, G. (1991). Organizational wellness. In B. L. Driver, P. J. Brown & G. L. Peterson (Eds.), *Benefits of leisure* (pp. 314–329). State College, PA: Venture.

Foreign Trade Division. (1999). U.S. Bureau of the Census. Washington, DC: Government Printing Office.

Godbey, G. (1989). *The future of leisure services: Thriving on change*. State College, PA: Venture.

Godbey, G. (1997). *Leisure and leisure services in the 21st century*. State College, PA: Venture.

Goodale, T. L., & Godbey, G. (1988). *The evolution of leisure: Historical and philosophical perspectives*. State College, PA: Venture.

Gratton, C., & Taylor, P. (2000). *Economics of sport and recreation*. London: Spon.

Guterson, D. (1993). Enclosed. Encyclopedic. Endured: One week at the Mall of America. *Harper's Magazine, 281*(17–19), 49–56.

Hawaii Department of Business, Economic Development, and Tourism. (2004). Tourism web guide. Retrieved April 23, 2004, from http://www.hawaii.gov/dbedt/guides/tour-wg.html

Henderson, K. A., Bialeschki, M. D., Hemingway, J. L., Hodges, J. S., Kivel, B. D., & Sessoms, H. D. (2001). *Introduction to recreation and leisure services*. State College, PA: Venture.

Heymann, T. (1989). *On an average day*. New York: Fawcett.

Information Publications. (1993). Palo Alto, CA: Author.

Kelly, J. R., & Freysinger, V. J. (2000). *21st century leisure: Current issues*. Boston: Allyn & Bacon.

Linder, S. (1970). *The harried leisure class*. New York: Columbia University Press.

Maklan, M. (1977). How blue-collar workers on a four-day workweek use their time. *Monthly Labor Review, 100*(8), 26.

National Recreation and Park Association. (2000). *Discover the benefits of parks and recreation* [Brochure]. Ashburn, VA: Author.

Olson, K. (2001, July–August). Please stay home. *UTNE Reader, 106*, 78.

Organisation for Economic Co-operation and Development. (2003). Purchasing power parities. Retrieved March 23, 2004, from http://www.oecd.org/statisticsdata

Schor, J. B. (1992). *The overworked American: The unexpected decline of leisure*. New York: Basic Books.

Schreyer, P., & Koechlin, F. (2002, March). Purchasing power parities—Measurement and uses. *Statistics Brief: Organisation for Economic Co-operation and Development 3*, 1–8.

Smith, A. (1937). *An inquiry into the nature and causes of the wealth of nations*. New York: The Modern Library. (Original work published 1776.)

Sobel, J., & Ornstein, R. (1987). *Healthy pleasures*. Reading, MA: Addison-Wesley.

Tribe, J. (1999). *The economics of leisure and tourism*. Oxford: Butterworth Heinemann.

U.S. Department of Commerce. (1995). *Statistical abstract of the United States*. Washington, D.C.: Government Printing Office.

U.S. Department of Commerce. (1999). *Statistical abstract of the United States*. Washington, D.C.: Government Printing Office.

U.S. Department of Commerce, Bureau of Economic Analysis. (2001, July). Retrieved March 23, 2004, from http://www.infoplease.com/ipa/A0104550.html

Veblen, T. (1899). *The theory of the leisure class*. New York: Macmillan.

Of Time and W   P

Preview

How do we know what time it is?

How people view time differs according to their history, biology, and culture.

How does leisure depend on time?

Leisure is shaped by many factors, including personal perceptions of time, the amount of time, the time needs of activities, and a culture's time sufficiency.

Is time ever a problem for leisure?

Free time for leisure can be problematic because of such time tyrannies as time urgency and time deepening.

Why do we work?

Work (like time) is a modern phenomenon that is the result of the influences of early Christianity and the industrialization of society. It is necessary for human survival, yet it may or may not allow us to live well.

What is leisure's relationship to work?

There are conflicting answers to this question. Some argue that work is less desirable and leisure is needed to overcome it. Others claim that work and leisure are both satisfying. There are also those who claim that work and leisure are separate but equal spheres of life.

Key Terms

Cyclical time	.347	Time famine	.359
Mechanical time	.348	Temporal displacement	.359
Nanosecond	.349	Time sufficiency	.359
Biological time	.349	Homo faber	.361
Endogenous	.349	Homo ludens	.361
Circadian	.350	Work ethic	.362
Cultural time	.350	Workaholic	.367
Time urgency	.351	Play-aversionist	.367
Time deepening	.354	Central life interest	.370

hey lost a weekend. The nearly 3,000 American military and civilian workers living on the remote Pacific atoll of Kwajalein, Marshall Islands, didn't remember Saturday, August 21, 1993. And for good reason. For them, the day didn't happen. Residents went to bed Friday night and woke up Sunday morning. That was because at midnight Friday, Kwajalein switched its system of time from one side of the international dateline to the other.

Kwajalein is west of the line, but for the past 40 years had synchronized its time with the United States mainland to the east in order to match the workday there. They did this by pretending they were located east of the dateline. In 1993, however, The Republic of the Marshall Islands requested the change so that all its islets would be on the same side of the dateline, and on the same time. The residents of Kwajalein still wanted to match the U.S. work schedule, so their workweek shifted to Tuesday through Saturday, which matches Monday through Friday in the United States. Much ado about nothing? Indeed not!

People of many societies take these notions of time and work very seriously. In part, this seriousness is what distinguishes technological cultures and "modern" human beings from others. Also, the concepts of time and work relate like a giant spider's web to leisure. Leisure is frequently restricted to a specific timetable in homage to work, and leisure is often used as a reward for work. Although in this chapter we explore how these assumptions are incorrect and stifling, they represent a typical understanding.

In Focus

Remember Fun?
Box 12.1

Is anyone having fun anymore? Fun does seem in jeopardy as our lives revolve more around work schedules these days. Well, at least kids are still having fun.

Or are they? Protective parents, school officials, and lawmakers are gradually building a safety net that threatens to trap children too in a tangle of scheduled worklike activity. From tampered-with recess in schools, to increased enrollments in structured recreation programs, to the rise of commercial playgrounds, kids are finding fewer opportunities for spontaneous fun (Harris, 2001).

For example, more than 40 percent of school districts across the United States have dropped or are considering dropping recess (Harris, 2001). For those that still have recess, highly structured activities have been established for the kids. The purpose of recess is now to boost academic achievement.

Or take the state park lake beaches in Indiana. Children are not allowed to use inflatable toys, mattresses, snorkels, or fins, or even throw a beach ball around. But an hour's drive down the road, kids can play with an inflatable raft and other toys at a commercial water park— for $30 admission. And in the summer, kids are shuttled off to day-care programs, often held in schools.

Having fun no longer seems to be a spontaneous everyday and everywhere thing for children. It has become a commodity that is formalized, structured, and purchased.

Questions to Consider and Discuss

1.   *Do you think the claim in this case is accurate? Are we all losing out on fun?*

2.   *How much "real" free time do children have these days? According to a University of Michigan study (O'Sullivan, 2000) among children ages 12 and under, unstructured time declined from 40 percent of a child's day in 1981 to 25% in 1997. Do some independent investigation with children and their parents you know to see if you can confirm or contradict this.*

3.   *What are the implications of your findings for your own life?*

Nonetheless, this means we might think of this web between work, time, and leisure as a kind of "symbiotic instrumentalism." Each is used as a tool for the others.

As suggested in the situation for the people of Kwajalein, time, work, and leisure are intertwined in contemporary society.

Time

Time is the most equally distributed of all our culture's resources—we all get exactly the same amount. We each have 24 hours a day for days and weeks and months and years to do with as we choose. Yet time is also considered the scarcest and most fragile of our culture's resources. None of us feel that we have control over our time or that we even have enough time. What is the source of this paradox?

In this section we explore how determinants of history, biology, and culture influence our perceived abundance or lack of abundance of time for leisure.

Types of Time

Time has become one of the most complex phenomena in contemporary life. Indeed, it was Aristotle, in the book *Physics*, who first asked the question, "In what sense, if any, can time be said to exist?" (as cited in Barnes, 1984, p. 369). Scholars still do not dare declare that time is well understood.

Understanding time has nonetheless become important in life because time is the framework on which all our behavior rests, including leisure. Our understanding of time is personal; we continually adhere to the structure of time, often in very emotional ways. Perhaps no other noun in the English language (interestingly, the word is also a verb, adverb, and adjective) is applied to so many different actions. For example, we save time, spend time, hoard time, make up time, speed up time, make good time, kill time, mark time, while away time, and of course, time flies!

We are very time conscious—even in our pastimes. For example, we have the 35-second shot rule in college basketball. The game period in football is four 15-minute quarters, and how much playing time within this scant hour individual players receive is critically important to their success (Fig. 12.1). If we don't get our pizza delivered in an hour, the restaurant pays for it. Having a day off has become increasingly difficult because the beeper, cell phone, and Palm Pilot we carry with us tether us to work.

Today time is measured as seconds, minutes, hours, days, weeks, months, years, decades, and centuries. Has it always been this way? Although time can be measured in a wide variety of ways (for example, there's universal time, international atomic time, and terrestrial time), we focus here on cyclical, mechanical, biological, and cultural time.

One type of time that helps us understand our time legacy is **cyclical time**. To the Navajos of North America, time is the here and now. Similarly, the Balinese in Indonesia

Figure 12.1
Many pastimes are very time conscious.
(© Ruth V. Russell.)

know time only as the present and not as a progression to an end. Such notions of time are assumed to be the original human experience. Early humans are said to have thought of time as part of the regular patterns of nature: the rising and setting of the sun, the tide coming in and going out, the passage of the seasons, the location of the moon in the sky (Green, 1968). Even with the invention of devices to measure time, such as the sundial and the water clock, the human experience of time was like that of nature. It recurred regularly.

> **Cyclical time:** time perceived as constant and returning

This type of time is perceived as circular, that is, constant and returning. Time thought of in this way means that time is never lost or wasted, because, just like the cycles of life, time repeats itself. Scholars guess that people experiencing cyclical time had no concept of getting control over time, since most measures of time came from nature; thus, they felt no responsibility for it.

As best we know, about 5,000 to 6,000 years ago the great civilizations in the Middle East and North Africa began to perceive time differently. They invented clocks. With their emerging bureaucracies, formal religions, and other growing societal activities, these cultures apparently found a need to organize their time more efficiently (http://physics.nist.gov/GenInt/Time/early.html. Retrieved 2/27/04).

For example, the Egyptians were probably the first to formally divide their day into parts something like our hours. Obelisks (slender, tapering, four-sided monuments) were built as early as 3500 BC. Their moving shadows formed a kind of sundial, helping people partition the day into morning and afternoon. Later, in about 1500 BC, the Egyptian sundial became possibly the first portable timepiece. This device divided a sunlit day into 10 parts plus two "twilight hours" in the morning and evening. A few hundred years later, the Egyptians are credited with the invention of the water clock. These were stone vessels with sloping sides that allowed water to drip out a small hole near the bottom. Called *clepsydras* ("water thieves"), these clocks could be used to determine hours at night.

From then, it wasn't until the 14th century that mechanical clocks were developed (Priestly, 1968). All of these early clocks were difficult to regulate accurately, a problem that wasn't solved until 1656 when Christiaan Huygens, a Dutch scientist, made the first pendulum clock, which used the principle of oscillation. A few years later, Huygens developed the balance wheel and spring assembly still found in some watches today. This improvement allowed portable 17th century watches to keep accurate time to within 10 minutes a day.

This was helpful because keeping accurate time was becoming more important. For example, the earlier activities of the monks in medieval monasteries were regulated by dividing the day up into times for prayer, meditation, and work. Later, clock time became a tool for industrialists to regulate the flow of production.

With the invention of the clock, people's experience of time changed. Now set to the rhythm of a machine, it became linear. This meant that a period of time could pass, and when it passed, it could not be recovered. Now time could no longer be accumulated; it could only be spent and wasted. The perception of **mechanical time**, which demands precision, punctuality, regularity, and reliability, was vital to furthering a work-focused civilization. Timekeeping became an economic weapon to eliminate the gaps in the traditional day of work and to ensure a uniformity and continuity of output (Cross, 1990).

The focus of time was now one of using time wisely. As the American statesman Benjamin Franklin recognized, "Do not squander time, for that's the stuff of life" (*Poor Richard's Almanac*, 1733 to 1757). To this day, technology and the belief in the regularity of mechanical time have continued to sever our ties with nature. Lights, and heating and cooling systems that turn on and off automatically, have eliminated the need for any alertness to natural daily and seasonal cycles. Digital alarm clocks wake us up in the morning, even if the sunrise is still hours away. Wristwatches beep out the time it takes us to jog around the block. The post office announces the deadline for sending holiday cards. Today we live by completely artificial distinctions of time.

> **Mechanical time:** time paced by machine, enabling the precise division of the day into equal parts; a linear perception of time

In Profile

Benjamin Franklin
Box 12.2

Benjamin Franklin (1706-1790) believed that one must live an ordered daily life. This idea certainly seemed to pay off for him. Franklin's accomplishments as a printer, publisher, civic leader, statesman, and scientist seem astounding, even by today's inflated standards. How did he get it all done? Perhaps Franklin's greatest legacy was his system for how to organize the day. For example, here's how he did it.

The Morning	5	Rise, wash, contrive the day's
Question: What good shall	6	business, and breakfast.
I do this day?	7	
	8	
	9	Work.
	10	
	11	
Noon	12	Read, or overlook my accounts, and dine.
	2	
	3	Work.
	4	
	5	

Evening	6	Put things in their places, supper,
Question: What good have	7	music or diversion, or conversation.
I done this day?	8	
	9	Examination of the day.
	10	
	11	
	12	Sleep.
Night	1	
	2	
	3	
	4	

Note. From Franklin (1932, p. 93).

This shift to a mechanical notion of time is perhaps the most important change in human life so far. Time has become standardized, and as a result, it rules our lives. Although we still use the word "pastimes," for many of us it is almost impossible to think of simply letting time pass. Perhaps the first to call our attention to this was Sebastian deGrazia in a classic study titled *Of Time, Work, and Leisure* (1962). "Clock time cannot be free," claimed deGrazia (p. 310), and he went on to posit that because of our mechanical notion of time, and because of the alliance of mechanical time with work, few of us will ever experience the sublime state of leisure.

Some predict that our sense of time is switching to the rhythm of another machine—the computer. A computer-driven concept of time speeds us up. After all, waiting a full minute for a program to load on our computer is an eternity! Welcome to the nanosecond! The computer works in a time frame in which the **nanosecond** is the basic time unit. At a billionth of a second, it is the common measurement of read or write access time to random access memory (RAM). A computer-driven time experience is also simultaneous. For example, the circle represented time for ancient peoples, and the straight line suggests society's experience since then, whereas the double helix is considered the time-shape of the future (Rifkin, 1987). This spiral, with its feedback loops, could take us even farther from our rhythms in nature (Fig. 12.2).

> **Nanosecond:** one billionth of a second

But we also experience other types of time. For example, we live according to **biological time**. Biological time is time controlled by a living organism. That is, plants and animals have biologically based ways of knowing what time it is. One source, photoperiodism, is a plant's response to light. The second, celestial orientation, is observed in birds and insects. The third, endogenous rhythms, is common to many plants and animals, including humans. These endogenous rhythms are cyclical physiological functions. For example, the heart beats about 60 to 80 times per minute. For women there is a 28-day menstrual cycle. Hunger occurs on about a 90-minute cycle.

> **Biological time:** time that is controlled by a living organism

> **Endogenous:** caused by factors inside the organism

Figure 12.2
A spiral with feedback loops and simultaneous shapings may be the concept of time in the future. (From Epcot at Walt Disney World in Florida. © Ruth V. Russell.)

Unlike mechanical time, endogenous rhythms are not regulated by a precise 60-minute hour or 24-hour day. Nonetheless, our biological time is precise. Because we have become so dependent on external factors of timekeeping, such as the clock, computer, and even television, we are not always able to experience time according to our own biological sense. Mechanical time and biological time are frequently in conflict.

For example, one endogenous rhythm that has been most problematic in contemporary life is the daily rhythm of activity and rest. This is called the **circadian** rhythm. A single activity-and-rest cycle ranges between 20 and 28 hours. As an illustration, without clocks or light cues, people in experiments who have been free to live according to their circadian rhythms go to bed progressively later each day (Wever, 1985). When we can live according to our circadian rhythms, we feel better.

Circadian: daily rhythm of activity and rest

One reason is that rhythmic flow is experienced as comfort, even pleasure. This is why we particularly appreciate rhythmic experiences such as light, color, music, and poetry. In addition, paying attention to our internal clock means we're at our best. For example, elite athletes have used circadian rhythm charting to help predict peaks in performance. In one study, circadian rhythms and teams' performance in a 24-hour relay race were considered (Krombholz, 1990). The performance of one of the teams was found to be lowest during the night and to increase during the morning hours.

We also live with another type of time: **cultural time**. Whether the cultures we are a part of are schools, homes, shops, hospitals, or even the nation, they also tell us what time it is. For example, in some families, 6:00 pm is always dinnertime. On college campuses, most students attend classes between 10:00 am and 2:00 pm. On the job, most employees are at their desks from 9:00 am to 5:00 pm.

Cultural time: socially established perceptions of time

In each society certain time periods are established as the norm for various life events. It is the cultural context that dictates the appropriate timing of things. People get so used to these time expectations that they become alarmed at deviations. This means that we believe events occur too soon, too late, too far apart, or too close together. For example, in the United States, if a professor is more than 10 minutes late for class, students begin to debate how long they should wait. In Brazil, on the other hand, university students define lateness as slightly over 30 minutes after the scheduled start of a class (Levine & Wolff, 1985).

One explanation for such cultural distinctions is the degree to which a mechanical notion of time is followed. Basically, the greater the reliance on mechanical notions of time, the greater an urgency to live by them. To demonstrate this, let's compare cultures according to waiting in line. Americans spend at least 37 billion hours a year waiting (Denny, 1993), and they do it by forming lines according to the order of arrival. But this is not universal. In southern Europe, it's part of the culture to jockey for position in lines, and Brazilians are notoriously nonqueuing. Meanwhile in Israel, even though people wait for buses by stubbornly resisting forming lines, when the bus comes, they board according to the first-come, first-served principle as if they had been in line all along. Indeed, the fact that forming waiting lines is unknown in some cultures was a fact missed by the Disney Corporation when it opened Disneyland Resort Paris in France and expected attraction riders to line up in an orderly fashion.

Time Tyrannies

Adherence to mechanical time has disadvantages. Recently, one poll found that 62 percent of respondents said they were stressed because they didn't have enough time to get everything done (Barnette, 2004). This is because of time tyrannies, such as time urgency and time deepening.

A truly contemporary condition, **time urgency** refers to a quickened pace of life, that is, feeling rushed. It is to approach the day with speed and impetuosity. Although not everyone or not every culture experiences time urgency, according to the time diary studies of Robinson and Godbey (1997), the "always feel rushed" response on questionnaires has shown a gradual increase since 1965. In 1975, 28 percent of adults reported always being rushed; in 1985 it was 35 percent; and in 1992 this response had risen to 38 percent. Further, those who reported such time urgency tended to be profiled as women, the middle aged, whites, the college educated, the employed, married, and parents. As Rifkin worried in the book *Time Wars* (1987),

> **Time urgency: feeling rushed**

*We have quickened the pace of life only to become less
patient. We have become more organized but less spontaneous, less joy-*

ful. We are better prepared to act on the future but less able to enjoy the present and reflect on the past. (pp. 11-12)

From Your Own Experience

Time Urgency Survey
Box 12.3

Instructions: Circle either True or False for each statement according to how well they reflect you.

1.	Other people consider me a rushed person.	True	False
2.	I feel anxious whenever I am idle.	True	False
3.	I become irritated when I must wait for something.	True	False
4.	I enjoy working against deadlines.	True	False
5.	I often race against time even when there is no reason to.	True	False
6.	Sometimes my schedule seems overwhelming.	True	False
7.	I don't feel like I have time to take a weekend off.	True	False
8.	I perform my best when I have a lot to do.	True	False
9.	I often interrupt people when they are talking.	True	False
10.	I usually move about my day in a hurry.	True	False

Scoring: Give yourself one point for every True response. Add these points up.

0-2	No time urgency
3-6	Moderate time urgency
7-10	Extreme time urgency

The consequence of time urgency for leisure can include participating hurriedly in an activity or choosing particular activities because they take less time. This is a malady for leisure. How much real pleasure and satisfaction can be derived from learning to play the guitar in "three easy lessons," eating dinner in less than 10 minutes, or traveling through Europe in a week? Time urgency might mean condensing a birthday party into a meal at a restaurant where the waitstaff sing a quick chorus of "Happy Birthday," or spending only a few seconds in front of a painting in a museum. Leisure requires tranquility, letting go, not being in a hurry.

Contemporary leisure is often lived as a restless energy that preys on us with speed records and shortcuts—the quick fix. Even in leisure we're on the fast track. Isn't this all rather ironic? The modern world of fast transportation, instantaneous communication, and time-saving technologies was supposed to free us from the tyranny of time. Instead, we rarely have a moment to spare, especially for our favorite pastimes. And there are no signs of this changing.

For example, sports courts are reserved for play with great time precision, and it is considered bad form to fail to give up your racquetball court even a minute past your reserved time. Perhaps the effect on leisure of speed in our contemporary lives is best exemplified by computer games. They are relentless in their demand for our attention. Unlike pinball games or Scrabble, in which the player can dominate time, the players of computer games must totally surrender to the machine's tempo. You have to play with the heartbeat of the computer if you are to win (Turkle, 1984).

So where's the tyranny in time urgency? Beyond losing the ability to enjoy savoring the day, being in a hurry can kill you. It is referred to as type A behavior. The malady was first formulated almost 40 years ago when two cardiologists noted that the majority of their heart attack patients seem to have the same behavioral traits: impatience, talking and eating rapidly, frequent fidgeting, tapping the feet or playing with a pencil in a rhythmic fashion, interrupting or finishing the sentences of others, and other signs of a competitive attitude (Friedman & Rosenman, 1983). It was discovered that these patients had increased amounts of the stress-related hormones known to damage heart muscle. Still supported by today's research, type A behavior has been demonstrated to be as significant a predictor of heart attacks as other risk factors such as high cholesterol, hypertension, and smoking.

In Focus

The Slow Movements
Box 12.4

Japan has a "slow life" movement. Italy has a "slow cities" movement. Spain has a network of siesta salons. Originating in Austria is the Society for the Deceleration of Time, which sets speed traps for pedestrians. People the world over are resurrecting the art of doing things more slowly.

For example, catching on around the world is a "slow food" movement. Slow Food is a fast-growing international organization with 65,000 members in 50 countries, 5,000 of which are scattered among 62 chapters in the United States, where membership has grown 20 times in the last three years alone (http://www.organic-consumers.org/Organic/slowfood.cfm. Retrieved 3/1/04). Chapters declare themselves to be dedicated to supporting and celebrating the food traditions of their locale, including taking the time to prepare and eat foods slowly. Honored are heirloom varieties of fruit and vegetables, handcrafted wine and beer, hand-parched wild rice, and farm-house cheese. Slow Food USA believes that many of these foods are at a growing risk of succumbing to the effects of the fast life.

Slow Food started years ago as a response to the arrival of the first McDonald's on the Spanish Steps in Rome. From here, the growth of Slow Food represents a cry against the indignities of moderniza-tion–the homogenizaton and standardization of food and the aban-donment of the dinner table.

Questions to Consider and Discuss

1. Are the "slow" movements around the world small actions by only a few people? For example, will Slow Food remain a move-ment or develop into a full-fledged force to be reckoned with?

2. Published in 2004 is a new book entitled In Praise of Slowness: How a Worldwide Movement is Challenging the Cult of Speed, by Carl Honore. Read the book and determine your agreement or dis-agreement with its premise. Share the results with your class-mates.

3. If you wanted to slow your own life down, how would you do it?

Another contemporary time tyranny that affects our leisure is time deep-ening (Godbey, 1999). **Time deepening** (Fig. 12.3) means that several activi-ties are done at the same time. Some call this tyranny "multitasking." For example, as you drive to work or school in the morning, are you also drinking a cup of coffee and eating a donut, glancing at your appointment calendar, lis-tening to news on the radio, and brushing your teeth? The goal of time deep-ening is to pile multiple activities into the same time frame. It is a higher rate of "doing" (Robinson & Godbey, 1997).

This means we can, of course, do more in our leisure time—have more leisure experiences. A good example is listening to the radio. Before television, people sat by the radio and listened, doing nothing else. Today, radio is almost exclusively a secondary activity, some-thing we listen to while doing something else, and television is beginning to go the same route. According to the time

> **Time deepening:** doing several activities at the same time

diary studies of Robinson and Godbey (1997), at least one–quarter of television viewing is combined with other activities.

Although time deepening may have some advantages in getting more done, it has some significant disadvantages, particularly for leisure. Time deepening can make us feel rushed, anxious, and unfulfilled. Our leisure becomes packed with activities, but it does not provide pleasure or relaxation. People who suffer from time deepening never experience anything fully. Leisure activities that require a long time to learn are avoided. Do you really have the patience these days to learn bonsai gardening? Perhaps it makes sense to say we have become "unleisurely" in our leisure (Godbey, 1999).

Figure 12.3
Time deepening makes us feel anxious and unfulfilled.
(© Christopher B. Stage.)

Time for Leisure

Up to now, we've mentioned the instrumentality between time and leisure to illustrate basic concepts of time. Now let's discuss this connection more directly. Leisure takes place in time. Although estimates vary, for the majority of adults in industrialized societies, about 40 hours each week are not committed to work or responsibilities. Considered another way, without taking into account evening hours, a conservative schedule of weekends, holidays, and vacations gives us over four months a year of free time (Fig. 12.4).

Figure 12.4
Participating in a model railroad club. How do you choose to use your free time? (© Ruth V. Russell.)

How do we experience all this free time? Time used for leisure is essentially shaped by four factors:

1. personal perceptions of free time

2. personal amounts of free time

3. the time needs of leisure activities

4. a culture's time sufficiency

First, people's perceptions of free time influence how they use it for leisure. If free time is regarded as a privilege, it is likely that it will be used wisely in pursuits that are perceived as personally beneficial and socially constructive. Others may view free time mainly as a chance for temporary escape from the physical and mental environment of work and daily routines. They regard it as an opportunity rather than a privilege; thus, the goal is "getting away from it all." Others see free time as neither a privilege nor an opportunity but as an empty space that, if left unfilled, becomes frightening. These are people who work so hard at leisure that it almost becomes another job. They feel compelled to be busy. Finally, similar behaviors may arise from a perception of free time as a precious commodity. Every spare moment must be crammed with activity to be sure it is not wasted.

From Your Own Experience

Perceptions of Free Time
Box 12.5

From the following set of statements, check the one that best expresses your own view of free time:

___ I like to use my free time wisely on things that are personally and socially beneficial.

___ Free time is my chance to get away from work and daily routines.

___ I am frequently afraid I'll have nothing to do in my free time.

___ I don't like to waste my free time.

> Compare your perception about free time with the description in the text. What are your conclusions about the role of leisure in your life?

Quite related to perceptions of free time, leisure as experienced in time is also based on the amount of free time individuals actually possess. Just how much free time do people have? This has been hotly debated recently because research findings on the question have been conflicting (see Box 12.6). Some findings suggest free time is increasing in contemporary societies, whereas other findings maintain that free time is decreasing. Even without study findings, however, it is clear to us all that some people have more free time than others. As we've already discussed, time tyrannies such as time urgency and time deepening can reduce the time allotted for and the experience of leisure. In addition, notorious deficits in free time are typically ascribed to specific sectors of the population, such as married women who have young children and are employed outside the home. The expression **time famine** has been coined to describe this condition of not having enough free time.

The Study Says

Is Free Time Increasing or Decreasing?
Box 12.6

In the mid-1990s a debate raged about exactly how much free time contemporary Americans have. At the core of the debate were two research studies. Here we compare them and ask that you be the judge.

Study One: Schor

I advocate mandatory increases in free time. (Schor, 1992, p. 150)

Juliet Schor, an economist, published a study in 1993 entitled *The Overworked American: The Unexpected Decline of Leisure.* Her argument was that Americans are working longer; she claimed the average employed person worked an additional 163 hours a year in 1987 compared with 1969 (p. 29). This amounts to a loss of nearly one month of free time per year. The reasons for such changes, Schor suggested, are related to the endless work-and-spend cycle produced by capitalism. To be more specific, people are working longer hours, taking less time for vacation, and feeling the time squeeze at home because we are a consumer culture. Her findings claim we are spending our way through life. This requires us to work harder to be able to have the money to buy more. Schor's findings support people's growing perception that work hours and time pressures have increased substantially in American society.

Study Two: Robinson and Godbey

We argue that free time is likely to increase even more in the future. (Robinson & Godbey, 1997, p. 5)

Leisure scholars John Robinson and Geoffrey Godbey published a study in 1997, and again in 1999, that directly refuted Schor's claims, arguing that Americans actually have almost 265 hours more free time per year today than they did in the 1960s—that's five more hours per week. They claimed that we feel a sense of time famine that doesn't actually exist. Their explanation of this discrepancy is that we feel more rushed and stressed because we try to do many things all at once, having free time in only small segments rather than in a larger time period—such as having full weekends—and investing time in activities that bring us minimal enjoyment and fulfillment—such as watching television. Thus, from Robinson and Godbey's findings we can conclude that the problem is not actually the amount of free time, but people's use of it.

Explaining the Contradiction

How might we explain the difference in findings? Which study is true? One way to approach this dilemma is to compare the ways of collecting information used. Schor's findings are based on estimates of time use from various government reports, such as Bureau of Economic Analysis data. These documents track the market hours of full-time and part-time employees for all industries. Robinson and Godbey's findings are based on individual time diaries. Every 10 years the project asks thousands of Americans to report their daily activities on an hour-by-hour basis. These differences in data collection methods could render differences in findings, suggesting that they aren't really comparable.

To help you make up your own mind, see Schor's "rebuttal" to the debate at http://www.swt.org/putok.htm.

Leisure as experienced in time is also based on the amount of time an activity requires. I often choose to jog three miles because it takes less time than walking the same distance. Some people hold off playing golf until they retire because it takes most of a day to play. One sadness of contemporary society is that activities requiring more extensive time are being displaced in popularity by others with a shorter time frame. For example, the trend in vacations is multiple three-day excursions spread throughout the year rather than the traditional two-week trip in the summer.

> **Time famine:** having insufficient free time

There is another way we demonstrate our sensitivity to the time leisure takes up. This is the concept of temporal, or time, displacement. **Temporal displacement** begins with a conflict in using a leisure resource, so people choose to continue their involvement by shifting the timing of the activity. For example, suppose campers who have frequented a campground in the past become dissatisfied with some type of change at the site. This might be rowdy, noisy neighboring campers on holiday weekends. When guided by temporal displacement, the campers respond to this undesirable condition by altering their timing for camping. For instance, they might switch from weekends to weekdays and never camp on holidays. Spatial displacement is another response to an unsatisfying situation. This involves changing the location of the activity, such as switching allegiance to a different campground. Research has demonstrated, however, that temporal displacement is the most common way to avoid recreational conflicts (Hall & Shelby, 2000).

> **Temporal displacement:** altering the timing of visits as a reaction to adverse changes at a recreation resource

Finally, the expression of leisure in time is a function of how much time a culture has. Referred to as a culture's **time sufficiency**, and contrary to what might be expected, this refers to the observation that as the general welfare of people increases, life becomes more hectic and time more scarce. First noted by Linder (1970), cultures can be categorized according to the amount of time they have. Cultures have either a time surplus or a time scarcity (Table 12.1).

> **Time sufficiency:** the amount of time a culture has, determined by the general welfare of the society

For example, a time surplus is descriptive of the least developed and poorest countries. Production and income are so low that large portions of time remain unused. The mechanical perception of time is not really necessary, because there is no need to pace activities. In fact, in time-surplus cultures, rushing is a sign of rudeness and poverty of spirit (Robinson & Godbey, 1997). What happens to leisure in this situation? It tends to be more spontaneous, lengthy, relaxed, and frequent. Time-surplus cultures also tend to designate a larger number of days as holidays (or holy days). Yet on "the road to riches, a country gradually eliminates more and more holidays," reducing the amount of free time (Linder, 1970, p. 18).

Table 12.1
Cultural Time Sufficiency and Leisure

Distinction	Time surplus	Time scarcity
Time	Time rich; much free or idle time	Time poor; no or little free time
Wealth	Poor	Rich
Production	Low	High
Work	Not dependent on mechanical time; no time-related work stress	Highly dependent on mechanical time; time stress causes illness
Leisure	Numerous holidays Popular recreation activities occupy large time blocks Much spontaneity Little consumption of special equipment	Few holidays Popular recreation activities occupy small time blocks Less spontaneity Much consumption of special equipment

Thus, for wealthier cultures, the pace of life is more rapid and more dependent on mechanical time. As a result, there is a time famine. When the drive for time efficiency is dominant, free time is transferred to active use and becomes scarce. In rich countries, all "waste" in the use of time has been eliminated, efficiency becomes an important value, punctuality becomes a virtue, and rushing is a sign of intelligence and importance. For countries with time scarcity, pastimes are less spontaneous and convenience becomes the rationale for choosing activities. Leisure becomes just another thing that must be worked into the schedule.

Work

In many societies, there is an emphasis on work. Most of us understand from a very early age that work is a constant in life. We also know that work can be a curse and a burden, a benefit and release, fun and fulfilling, boring and miserable. What is work? Why do people work? Why do some people work harder than is required? Is there a work "problem" in society? Today there is a tremendous debate about the worth of work—a debate that affects the worth of leisure. In this section we continue our theme of instrumental connections for work and leisure.

The Intention of Work

Work, most simply, can be defined as the expenditure of effort. Work is the use of energy—human, animal, mechanical, electrical, or solar—to produce something. The answers to questions about why people work are more complex than this, however. For example, some of the answers may be based on the idea that we are all, at least in part, **homo faber** (ancient Greek for "man the toolmaker or worker"). That is, work is more than a necessity; it is part of being human. It is in the fabric of our moral and biological character. As such, work has meaning in and of itself. Work is not just making necessities, but also making ideas and possibilities—something that did not exist before. Of course, there is also the idea of **homo ludens**, which is ancient Greek for "man the player," connoting that play pervades all of life. Leisure too is in the fabric of our moral and biological character. So what's the distinction?

Indeed, the emergence of work as a distinct concept is a relatively modern phenomenon. As you recall from chapter 1, the ancient Greeks had their own unique ideas about work. In fact, the early Greek distinction was really between work and labor. Roughly, labor meant providing for the necessities of life and described the activity performed by a class of laborers,

> **Homo faber:** ancient Greek meaning "human as worker"

> **Homo ludens:** ancient Greek meaning "human as player"

or slaves. Early Greek poets and philosophers found no inherent value in labor, calling it ponos, or "sorrow." Work, on the other hand, was a meaningful way of life in the voluntary pursuit of intellectual and creative ideas—what today we might refer to as leisure.

The ancient Romans began to change this distinction as they faced the practical problem of overseeing a large empire. There were wars, taxes, and barbarians to manage, along with millions of citizens. Such an enormous enterprise began to take precedence over individual freedoms and pursuits. This led into the medieval period in Europe, which brought a more revered notion of work. The powerful influence of early Christianity elevated work to godliness. Monks in the early monasteries practiced self-denial as a way of purification. Work was not for the accumulation of worldly goods but for serving God. Many hours were spent tending the crops in the field, performing charitable work for others, praying, and on religious study. Monks were never to be idle.

Over 1,000 years later, the protests led by Martin Luther and John Calvin against the Roman Catholic Church resulted in a modified interpretation of the way to salvation. The outcome was Protestantism, which also influenced work. Luther's writings were the first to suggest the idea of vocation, performing dutifully that work God wishes you to do. With Protestantism there was a shift from the work of the heavenly world to the work of the earthly world (Kelly

& Freysinger, 2000). Protestantism spread in central and southern Europe, and out of this movement, a group of dissidents emerged. Called Puritans, their political and religious struggles resulted in a wave of migration to North America. They brought with them a **work ethic**. Indeed, without their opposition to idleness and wasting time, the Puritans may not have survived the first several winters. There was no margin of abundance; work was an absolute necessity.

Across several more centuries, industrialization and urbanization brought about more promotion of a work ethic. The transition from a preindustrial to an industrial society during the Industrial Revolution of the late 1800s and early

> **Work ethic:** the idea that work is the center of life

1900s resulted in an even greater regard for work and an increasing separation of work and leisure in everyday life. Work, necessary to feed the voracious machines in common use at the end of the 19th century, now came to be associated with the values of speed and efficiency (Robinson & Godbey, 1997). And leisure was now relegated to that time that was left over. Industrialism also made it possible to produce more goods that could be purchased by everyone. Thus, the acquisition, use, protection, and upkeep of larger amounts of goods made work a human priority, and leisure became associated with consumption.

Indeed, today one of the stereotypical distinctions between work and leisure is that work is economic and leisure is not (although we certainly dis-

In Profile

The Shakers
Box 12. 7

The Shakers were an evangelistic religious group that came to the American colonies in 1774 to establish a utopian society. Separating the men and women in communal housing, they set up settlements, first near Albany, New York, and later in Kentucky and Ohio. Their cleanliness, honesty, and frugality received the highest praise, and their communal approach and belief in hard work provided economic success. The common theme was, "Put your hands to work, and your heart to God" (see Fig. 12.5).

Shakers are known to this day for an exquisitely simple and functional style of furniture. A Shaker chair would take weeks to make because only one craftsman made it and put a great deal of effort into making sure every joint, corner, and leg were correctly in place. They also made leather, applesauce, linen, and knitted underwear, all of which were highly acclaimed for their quality. These industries became both the sustaining income for the Shakers and a form of recruiting. By the mid-1800s, however, as they reached their peak membership, their communities became a sort of tourist attraction that outsiders could observe on Saturday evenings.

Figure 12.5
In addition to a high regard for their work, Shakers are still known today for their music and dances. In just a short time they authored thousands of religious songs. Here tourists observe an interpretation of Shaker singing at Shakertown, Kentucky.
(© Ruth V. Russell.)

covered otherwise in chapter 11!). People must work to have the money to buy things—an important "modern" standard for living.

Worker Rewards and Dissatisfactions

Whether people work today because they have to or because they want to, work provides certain rewards. For example, in a research study reported by Brook (1993), work activities were more likely than nonwork activities to be creative, challenging, require mental activity, offer self-development, and involve others. Nonwork activities, on the other hand, were more likely to be enjoyable, involve emotions, provide a sense of control, be done for others, and include freedom of choice.

What other rewards might work offer? There is the obvious reward of money to buy things. Workers exchange their time, energy, and talent for money. The exact financial value of their work differs according to the nature of the work, the education and training required, and even the culture where it is performed.

Yet anyone who has ever worked, even for the necessity of earning money, knows that work provides other rewards as well. For example, work is often the central identity for adults. When we meet someone new, we typically introduce ourselves by what we do for work. We wear our worker label up front: "I am a lawyer," or "I am a teacher." Even the retired often claim their identity through their former work. No society is without its status symbols or ways of manifesting publicly an individual's worth, and in many contemporary societies, this status is provided by work.

Another reward of work is often human interaction. In many occupations there is ample opportunity to enjoy companionability. Someone who cares for patients in a hospital or works with children in the classroom gains a sense of interrelatedness. Conversations and sharing information satisfy a basic human need for affiliation with other people.

Work can also provide a sense of contributing. Through work we have opportunities to make something, do something, and improve something. Work can provide a sense of accomplishment, creating something good that didn't exist before. The hospital worker rejoices when patients get well, and the teacher celebrates student learning. Work, even such monotonous chores as taking tickets, handing out towels, or digging a ditch, can produce the satisfaction of a job well done.

So work offers the rewards of money, status and identity, social interaction, and a sense of making a difference. Does all work provide these rewards, and is work satisfying to all workers?

"The number-one risk factor of heart attack in people under the age of 50 is job dissatisfaction," says motivational speaker Anthony Robbins (http://charlotte.bcentral.com/charlotte/stories/1998/09/14smallb5.html. Retrieved 6/14/01). It seems that a startling number of people are unfulfilled and unhappy in their jobs. The tangible symptoms show up as tardiness, apathy, and complaining. The intangible symptoms are worse. According to a study of office workers employed by a public service organization (Occupational Safety and Health, 1995), worker dissatisfaction was characterized as boredom, tension, anxiety, depression, anger, fatigue, daily life stress, and ill health.

What is it about work that might create such dissatisfaction? The primary factors are high job demands, lack of supervisor support, and uninteresting job content. For example, some research suggests situations that make the content of work uninteresting include doing a repetitive job, making only a small part of something, and doing tasks that seem useless. Further, in an analysis of the quality of work for those in an urban recreation department (Russell, 1993), employees perceived that having inadequate control over their work, unclear ways of increasing their position in the department, and the lack of meaningful and consistent rewards for good performance instigated their dissatisfaction with work.

Another strain on contemporary workers is that in spite of projections for increases in the number of jobs, many of these new options will be temporary, low-paying, high-turnover, minimally skilled positions. The traditional connection between hard work and a secure position with a career of advancement has been lost in many societies. In the volatile employment market that accompanied the economic restructuring that began in the 1990s, layoffs and downsizing now occur with regularity for workers at all levels.

Leisure and Work

Quite often leisure and work are compared. For example, leisure is typically considered a "solution" to the dissatisfactions of work, other workers love their jobs so much it seems like play to them, and some people feel they don't deserve leisure if they don't have a job. Beyond these common perspectives, there are also complicated views of the relationship between leisure and work in the scientific literature.

For example, in a study of workers in Ontario, Canada, Reid (1995) compared the satisfactions found in work and in leisure. Workers were asked to rank eight possible personal satisfactions in order of importance for both their work and leisure (see Table 12.2). Notice that for some satisfactions, there is a similarity between work and leisure. For example, for the satisfactions of "feeling powerful," "keeping busy," "being competent," and "maintaining fitness," the rankings are closer together. On the other hand, for such satisfactions as "escaping stress," "service to others," and "socializing," the rankings are farther apart, suggesting a minimal comparison between work and leisure.

Table 12.2
Comparison of Work and Leisure Satisfactions

Satisfactions	Rank for work	Rank for leisure
Keeping busy	1	3
Socializing	2	6
Being competent	3	5
Service to others	4	7
Developing friendships	5	2
Maintaining fitness	6	4
Feeling powerful	7	8
Escaping stress	8	1

Note. Adapted from Reid (1995, p. 67).

Let's explore the work and leisure comparisons found in the scientific literature a bit more. There are basically three ways of comparing the relationship between leisure and work. One view is rather pessimistic; it maintains that work is a less desirable human condition and that leisure is needed to control or even overcome its problematic effects. Another, and opposite, view is more optimistic. It suggests that all is well with both work and leisure, and healthy people need the rewards and satisfactions from both. Life is only meaningful when both are in harmony. Finally, perhaps neither an optimistic nor pessimistic understanding of work and leisure is needed. Perhaps work and leisure are simply two separate domains in life and not necessarily related to one another at all. The relationship is neutral.

According to the pessimistic view, leisure is needed to overcome work's inhuman consequences. For example, according to Kelly (1982), the critical difference between work and leisure is that work contributes to the survival and well-being of society, whereas the benefits of leisure are primarily personal and experiential. A specific consequence of this view is the **workaholic**. Workaholism is an addiction to work, and it is the only addiction that wins the admiration of others. It is working long hours in order to gain approval and success. Workaholism is more than being unable to relax when not doing something considered productive; it is the pursuit of the "work persona," an image workaholics wish others to have of them.

This condition is very unhealthy. It can be a major source of marital discord and family breakup, it can create job stress, and it can even bring on poor health and illness. The prescription for workaholism, of course, is leisure; to return to health, work must be in proper balance with leisure. Yet what is particularly interesting is that the compulsive nature of workaholism can be applied to leisure as well. That is, we can engage in pastimes in a worklike way. Some people today overcommit themselves to recreational activities to the point where it becomes work. They find that their weekends are booked full with shopping, social obligations, gardening, youth sports schedules, and planned outings. No free time is left for spontaneity. Workaholism applied to leisure is called play-aversion (Dickens, 1991). A **play-aversionist** is a workaholic in disguise, a person who works hard at playing. Symptoms include placing a high value on always being busy, playing hard, overscheduling activities, and feeling anxious when nothing is scheduled.

> **Workaholic:** a person who is addicted to the control and power of work in order to gain approval and success

On the other hand, according to the optimistic view, work and leisure are not at battle with each other—both are desirable for their respective benefits. For example, according to Murphy (1981), meaning and satisfaction exist in both work and leisure, and both are required for realizing life to its fullest. How can this balance be achieved? People have implemented numerous ways to achieve a more leisurely work schedule. See Table 12.3 for some ideas.

> **Play-aversionist:** a person who applies the behaviors and standards of work to leisure

The need for more freedom to choose when and how much to work is potentially more appropriate for people in today's society. For example, findings in one study indicated that workers who switched to flextime were more satisfied because they had 25 percent more time with their families (Nollen, 1982). These alternatives for work time to achieve balance are based on adjustments made to the hours of the day or days of the week. What about freeing time for leisure that is an adjustment to the lifetime schedule? Most people live on a life plan that follows a straight line. That is, life begins with play, is followed by a period of education, then a long term at work, and finally returns to a life of play again through retirement (Fig. 12.6). Such a traditional approach organizes life by strictly adhering to a single direction as preordained by society. Is there another way to live?

As also shown in Figure 12.6, an alternating life plan would redistribute some years of schooling from the childhood and youth periods and some free time from the retirement phase into the middle years of life. Work wouldn't need to be the dominant theme in middle age, nor leisure in old age. Advantages of

Table 12.3

Better Ways to Schedule Work into Life

Job sharing	Usually involves two persons filling a single job, both dealing with the same workload.
Flextime	A person may choose the time to start and finish the work day.
Compressed workweeks or work-months	Giving employees the right to take time off on one day or week if they make up the time by working longer hours the other days of the week or month.
Four-day workweek	Employees work four days a week with, in some cases, 10-hour-per-day schedules.
Reduced work time	Reduced hours of work in order to create new jobs or to avoid layoffs.
Limiting overtime	Maximum standards set on the amount of over time work allowed.
Early retirement	Employees are given financial incentives to retire from work at an earlier age.
Phased-in retirement	Workers are allowed to retire gradually, cutting back by days, weeks, or months.

Note. Adapted from Godbey (1997).

In Focus

Ninety Percent Unemployment
Box 12.8

Eve Smith heard herself say, "Why not? Let's give it a try." The man from the Department of Creative Technology (DOCT) had left, leaving Eve in a somewhat skeptical frame of mind. Then again, it did sound reasonable.

Eve owns a shoe factory. One thousand workers are directly involved in the production of shoes at an average pay of $20,000 per year or a yearly payroll of $20 million. She produces one million pairs of shoes per year, which she sells for $60 million. The difference between total sales and payroll ($40 million) takes care of other expenses and profits.

The man from DOCT suggested that she install a computer-controlled robotic system that would enable Eve to lay off 90 percent of her workforce, that is, 900 workers. Output of shoes would remain the same: one million pairs per year. Eve would turn over the salary previously paid to the 900 workers (that is, $18 million) to the DOCT. It, in turn, would keep 10 percent ($1.8 million) of that amount to pay for the development of the robotic system and put 90 percent ($16.2 million) into a Guaranteed Income Fund (GIF).

The 900 laid off workers would be paid 90 percent of their previous salary from the GIF, either indefinitely or until they chose to seek other employment. In Eve's profit picture, nothing would change. She would have as many shoes to sell as before and, if anything, would have fewer labor and production problems.

Nine hundred workers, human beings, would be freed from the necessity of wasting their time making a living. They would be able to develop their capabilities, skills, and talents or, if they desired, work for the betterment of society.

Just then, Eve heard a faint ringing, as of a far away bell. Then it became more insistent. She opened her eyes, realizing that she had dozed off. Had it all been a dream?

(Based on Neulinger, 1989, pp. 21–24; used with permission from the American Alliance for Health, Physical Education, Recreation and Dance.)

Questions to Consider and Discuss

- *Is this truly a dream or can you see some real possibility in it? Why? Why not? What might be done to turn the dream into reality?*

- *If you were given the opportunity to receive 90 percent of your salary and not work at a job, would you take it? Why? What about 75 percent of your salary or 50 percent of your salary? By the way, according to one survey (Hymowitz, 1991) almost 50 percent of the respondents said they would give up a day's pay each week for a day of free time.*

- *Is leisure the ultimate good in life, or is work? Read J. B. Nash's classic book Spectatoritis (1932) to form your own opinion.*

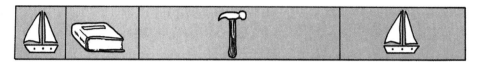

Traditional life plan

Alternating life plan

Figure 12.6
An alternating life plan redistributes schooling, work, and leisure throughout life.
(© Christopher B. Stage.)

an alternating plan are a more even distribution of income over the life cycle and more people having the opportunity to realize personal goals, such as a college degree and child rearing.

Finally, the third view of the relationship between leisure and work is neutral. Unlike the pessimistic view, in which leisure cures us from work, and the optimistic view, in which we need both work and leisure in balance, this last view claims there is no relationship at all between work and leisure. For example, Huizinga (1955) envisioned leisure as outside ordinary life, something special. More important, leisure must remain separate from the rest of life. To integrate leisure with work would destroy it. This is because leisure is spontaneous, a celebration, and even mysterious.

One relevant illustration of this is the concept of **central life interest**. A concept originally identified in 1956, sociologists have explored people's central interests in life, often using work and leisure as the two options. A central life interest refers to the major role in life, and overall, work seems to be losing out. Dubin (1992) writes,

> *A committed gardener, stamp collector, opera buff, jet setter, cook, housewife, mountain climber, bird watcher, computer "hacker," novel reader, fisherman, or gambler (and you can add many more to the list from your own experiences) are usually devoted to their activity as a central life interest [CLI]. Give such individuals a chance to talk freely about themselves and they will quickly reveal their CLI through fixation on the subject and obvious emotional fervor with which they talk about it. (pp. 41-42)*

> **Central life interest: the main or primary focus of one's life**

Enjoying ample and meaningful leisure, and having a stable and thriving family and community are goals that are replacing the centrality of work for some people. For example, in one survey 53 percent of respondents declared that having ample time for leisure is very important, as compared with 44 percent who said having a job that pays above average is very important (Roper Organization, 1987).

Summary: What We Understand

Time, work, and leisure are instrumentally related. That is, each has an impact on the others. For example, although leisure is typically prescribed as a cure for the problems of time and work, it has also adopted many of the characteristics of time and work that make it problematic. As a result of reading this chapter, you should understand that

- Cyclical time is that pace set by the rhythms of nature. In industrialized societies it has been replaced by the concept of mechanical time, of life paced to the machine. In the future, the computer may set an even faster and more artificial pace for life.

- Biological time refers to endogenous rhythms of rest and activity, and cultural time tells us how to pace our lives according to where we live.

- The expression of leisure in time is a function of personal perceptions of free time, personal amounts of free time, the time requirements of particular pastimes, the amount of free time available in a society, and the unique tyrannies to leisure from time itself.

- Although work offers the rewards of money, self-esteem, personal interactions, and the sense of making a contribution to society, some people are dissatisfied with work.

- Will leisure take the place of work? There are three answers to this question: (a) the pessimistic view, which holds that work is a less desirable human condition and that leisure is needed to overcome its negative by-products; (b) the optimistic view, which holds that work can be made more fulfilling by incorporating leisure into the work schedule; and (c) the neutral view, which maintains that leisure and work are not related but rather two separate domains of life.

Applications to Professional Practice

Often in this chapter we saw leisure, time, and work as being entangled in controversy. For example, conditions such as workaholism snub the worth of leisure, and time tyrannies such as time urgency and time deepening steal joy from a leisure experience. Two areas of professional practice take aim at such maladies of time, work, and leisure. These are leisure education and leisure counseling.

The idea of leisure education carries diverse connotations, even among those working in the leisure services fields. The most common image of leisure education is that of teaching what is a worthy and wise use of free time. According to Navar and Tschumper (1999), leisure education seeks to help people

- discover new interests

- explore community resources

- achieve the benefits of leisure

- expand their leisure choices

- learn how to establish and maintain friendships

- overcome barriers to enjoyment

Leisure education is learning to value and prioritize leisure. In contemporary societies, such education is a necessity. Perhaps surprisingly, people need to learn how to live a meaningful existence.

Leisure education has primarily been a technique used by therapeutic recreation specialists. Expanding leisure education opportunities beyond clinical settings is needed, however. Leisure education can be provided in special school, club, and organizational programs. Preretirement planning seminars should be made available by employers. Colleges and universities should require coursework to educate people on the important role of leisure in adult life. Community cable channels on television can help deliver leisure education messages.

Leisure counseling has also been viewed in a number of different ways. Quite similar to other forms of personal assistance services, the object of leisure counseling is to determine an individual's leisure interests and needs, and then to assist him or her in locating activities and options to meet these needs (McLellan & Pellet, 1975). Again, often found in a therapeutic recreation setting, the leisure counselor helps patients examine the feasibility of their

activity choices in terms of cost, accessibility, and personal skills and ca
ties. Often leisure counseling is delivered through individual or group s̲~
sions, uses assessment instruments, and provides referral services. In leisure
counseling, leisure is considered a therapeutic tool that can be directly applied
to improving a person's situation and happiness.

For More Information

To find out more about leisure education and leisure counseling as possible
career roles, contact the National Therapeutic Recreation Society
(http://www.nrpa.org), the American Therapeutic Recreation Association
(http://www.atra-tr.org), and the Canadian Therapeutic Recreation Association
(http://www.canadian-tr.org). An excellent example of leisure education
applied in a therapeutic recreation setting is LEEP (Leisure Education for
Exceptional People) in Mankato, Minnesota (http://mankatoleep.org).

References

Barnes, J. (1984). *The complete works of Aristotle.* Princeton, NJ: Princeton University Press.

Barnette, M. (2004, March). The stressed-out American family. *Ladies' Home Journal*, 134–143.

Brook, J. A. (1993). Leisure meanings and comparisons with work. *Leisure Studies, 12,* 149–162.

Cross, G. (1990). *A social history of leisure since 1600.* State College, PA: Venture.

deGrazia, S. (1962). *Of time, work and leisure.* New York: The Twentieth Century Fund.

Denny, D. (1993, November 2). Waiting on down the line. *The Bloomington Herald-Times* (Bloomington, IN), p. E1.

Dickens, P. (1991, March/April). Playing hard or hardly playing? *Executive Female,* 46.

Dubin, R. (1992). *Central life interests: Creative individualism in a complex world.* New Brunswick, NJ: Transaction.

Franklin, B. (1932). *The autobiography and selections from his other writing.* New York: The Modern Library.

Friedman, M., & Rosenman, M. (1983). *Type A behavior and your heart.* New York: Fawcett.

Godbey, G. (1997). *Leisure and leisure services in the 21st century.* State College, PA: Venture.

Godbey, G. (1999). *Leisure in your life: An exploration.* State College, PA: Venture.

Green, T. F. (1968). *Work, leisure, and the American schools.* New York: Random House.

Hall, T., & Shelby, B. (2000). Temporal and spatial displacement: Evidence from a high-use reservoir and alternate sites. *Journal of Leisure Research, 32,* 435–456.

Harris, M. (2001, March–April). The game of life: As work pressures mount and free time dwindles, it's more important than ever to recapture the joy of play. *UTNE Reader, 104,* 61–62.

Honore, C. (2004). *In praise of slowness: How a worldwide movement is challenging the cult of speed.* San Francisco: Harper.

Huizinga, J. (1955) *Homo ludens.* London: Paladin Books.

Hymowitz, C. (1991, August 5). Trading fat pay checks for free time. *Wall Street Journal,* p. C10.

Kelly, J. R. (1982). *Leisure.* Englewood Cliffs, NJ: Prentice Hall.

Kelly, J. R., & Freysinger, V. J. (2000). *21st centu-ry leisure: Current issues.* Boston: Allyn & Bacon.

Krombholz, H. (1990). Circadian rhythm and performance during a 24-hour relay race. *Perceptual and Motor Skills, 70,* 603–607.

Levine, R., & Wolff, E. (1985). Social time: The heartbeat of culture. *Psychology Today, 19,* 28–30.

Linder, S. (1970). *The harried leisure class.* New York: Columbia University Press.

McLellan, R., & Pellet, L. (1975). Leisure counseling: The first step. *Therapeutic Recreation Journal, 9*(4), 161–166.

Murphy, J. F. (1981). *Concepts of leisure.* Englewood Cliffs, NJ: Prentice Hall.

Nash, J. B. (1932). *Spectatoritis.* New York: Barnes.

Navar, N., & Tschumper, R. (1999, January). *Leisure Lifestyle Center: A combination of teaching, scholarship and service.* Paper presented at the Society of Park and Recreation Educators' Teaching Institute, Myrtle Beach, SC.

Neulinger, J. (1989). *A leisure society: Idle dream or viable alternative, encroaching menace or golden opportunity* [J. B. Nash Scholar Lecture]. Boston: American Association for Leisure and Recreation.

Nollen, S. D. (1982). *New work schedules in practice: Managing time in a changing society.* New York: Van Nostrand-Reinhold.

Occupational Safety and Health. (1995). Examining the relationship between job design and worker strain over time in a sample of office workers. *Ergonomics, 38,* 1199–1211.

O'Sullivan, E. (2000, October). Play . . . for life. *Parks & Recreation, 35*(10), 98–107.

Priestly, J. B. (1968). *Man and time.* New York: Dell.

Reid, D. (1995). *Work and leisure in the 21st century: From production to citizenship.* Toronto, OH: Wall and Emerson.

Rifkin, J. (1987). *Time wars: The primary conflict in human history.* New York: Henry Holt and Company.

Robinson, J. P., & Godbey, G. (1997). *Time for life: The surprising ways Americans use their time.* University Park: Pennsylvania State University.

Robinson, J. P., & Godbey, G. (1999). *Time for life: The surprising ways Americans use their time* (2nd ed.). University Park: Pennsylvania State University.

Roper Organization. (1987, February). The American Dream survey. *Wall Street Journal*, p. C8,11.

Russell, R. V. (1993). *Employee attitudes toward the quality of work and organizational barriers. Indianapolis Department of Parks and Recreation.* Bloomington, IN: The Leisure Research Institute.

Schor, J. B. (1993). *The overworked American: The unexpected decline of leisure.* New York: Basic Books.

Turkle, S. (1984). *The second self: Computers and the human spirit.* New York: Simon & Schuster.

Wever, R. A. (1985). Man in temporal isolation: Basic principles of the circadian system. In S. Folkard & T. J. Monk (Eds.), *Hours of work: Temporal factors in work scheduling.* New York: John Wiley & Sons.

CHAPTER THIRTEEN

Leisure and Equity

Preview

Is there equity in leisure?

No. Barriers exist in society to equal opportunities for leisure. This can be demonstrated by considering the discrimination in leisure against women, persons with disabilities, gays and lesbians, ethnic and racial minorities, immigrants, and at-risk youth.

Does leisure have the potential to enable equity in society?

Yes. Leisure is an important context for creating equal opportunities for a high quality of life for everyone.

Key Terms

Equity	379	Pluralism	392
Constraints	380	Culture shock	395
Inclusion	381	At-risk youth	399
Diversity	381	Disabling condition	400
Feminism	383	Self-determination	403
Ethnicity	391	Self-advocacy	403
Race	391	Normalization	403
Assimilation	392	Integration	403

s leisure a right or a privilege? This is a simple question to ask but much tougher to answer. Leisure has been viewed by some as a privilege—something to be earned after a hard day's or life's work. When leisure is defined as free time, it is often viewed as a reward for work and thus a privilege for those who work. On the other hand, leisure has also been viewed as a right—something that is as essentially human and necessary as eating and sleeping. Much of what you have read in this book supports both perspectives. So what do you think? Is leisure a right or a privilege (Fig. 13.1)?

Figure 13.1

Is it a right or a privilege for these young adults to participate in this drum and bugle corps? (© Ruth V. Russell.)

As a privilege, of course, leisure is something that is distributed unequally. That is the whole point of it. As a privilege, leisure is a reward available only to qualifying people. Sometimes the qualifier is having enough money to pay for certain forms of leisure. Other times, it is the guilt-free sensation that, by the time the weekend is here, you have worked hard enough to qualify for taking some hard-won time off. Or it could also be the gift of a lucky birth into privileged circumstances.

As a right, leisure is supposed to be distributed equally. Many cultures have a belief in natural or inalienable rights—rights that are impossible to surrender. These are often described as life, liberty, and the pursuit of happiness. With these rights comes the belief in equality—that everyone has a right to the good life. Thus, leisure is felt to be the right of everyone.

In many societies, including Canada and the United States, notions of inalienable rights and equality form the basis of political philosophies and governmental policies. In fact, these governments sponsor services considered vital to a happy life, including fire, police, and sanitation services. These services also include provisions for leisure expression. This is because of the belief that leisure can be a way of achieving **equity** in the pursuit of happiness. In fact, the very premise of recreation services provided by local, state or provincial, and federal governments is equity. This is based on the commitment that a full range of opportunities is good for all, regardless of gender, age, income, race, and other distinctions.

Equity: freedom from bias or favoritism

Yet women's roles and responsibilities often constrain them from full participation in leisure, people with disabilities must continually overcome architectural barriers for total access to leisure facilities, racial minorities are sometimes discriminated against in certain leisure settings, and new immigrants to a country may find opportunities for leisure in their own traditions to be nonexistent.

How Leisure Both Restricts and Enables Equity

Two major points can be made about leisure and equity. First, there is not yet equity in leisure. Second, leisure has the potential of being a great equalizer. Our pastimes have been both a hurdle to equity and an enabler of equity in modern societies.

First, let's consider how leisure restricts equity. You are already well aware that, in general, certain pastimes are more likely to be pursued by people in certain ethnic, racial, age, gender, and other social groups. For example, women are more likely to participate in aerobics classes, whereas men are much less likely to do so. Some men feel this leisure option is not available to them because of the stigma of it being a "women's thing." On the other hand, women don't always feel comfortable in a sports bar because the patrons' behaviors, the physical layout, and the décor suggest it is a place for "drinking with the boys" (Wenner, 1998, p. 304).

Another, and more serious, way of viewing inequity in leisure is to cite the numerous incidences of prohibitions against certain leisure expressions for certain groups. For example, gays and lesbians are not permitted equal participation in the programs and services of certain religious denominations, including the Presbyterian Church, the Southern Baptist Convention, and the Catholic Church. Goodale (2004) refers to this as "leisure apartheid," citing studies of recreation and park areas operated by federal agencies where 94 percent of the users are white and only two percent are Latino, even though Latinos are now the largest minority group in the United States (Armas, 2004).

One way of studying leisure as restricting equity in society is through the concept of **constraints**. In fact, investigation of leisure constraints has become a major theme in leisure research over the past two decades. Essentially, the numerous studies in this area have started with the question, "Why do some people not participate in leisure in general or in particular activities for which they might have the desire?"

> **Constraint:** something that inhibits leisure once a preference or desire for it has been formed

A model has been developed to explain the concept of leisure constraints (Crawford & Godbey, 1987; Crawford, Jackson, & Godbey, 1991). This model suggests that leisure participation is dependent on negotiating through a hierarchy of structural, intrapersonal, and interpersonal constraints. Structural constraints are those factors that intervene between a leisure preference and participation. Structural constraints are usually architectural barriers, such as a recreation center that is inaccessible to a person using a wheelchair because of stairs at all entrances, or economic barriers, such as high fees charged for youth sports programs that prohibit economically disadvantaged children from participating.

Intrapersonal constraints are defined as "individual psychological states and attributes which interact with leisure preferences" (Crawford & Godbey, 1987, p. 322). Intrapersonal constraints exist when, as a result of abilities, personality needs, prior socialization, and perceived reference group attitudes, individuals fail to develop certain leisure interests. This last factor might explain why men are constrained in developing an interest in aerobics classes: their reference group of other men perceives this leisure pursuit as unacceptable for men. Intrapersonal constraints restrict leisure according to appropriate or inappropriate, interesting or uninteresting, and available or unavailable.

Finally, interpersonal constraints are those barriers that arise out of social interaction with friends, family, and others. In a family, for example, interpersonal constraints may occur when spouses or partners differ in terms of their leisure preferences (Jackson & Scott, 1999).

In addition to considering constraints as focused on participation versus nonparticipation, another aspect of constraints has to do with inhibitions of the frequency or intensity of involvement in pastimes. For example, a study by Nadirova and Jackson (2000) found that the single most constrained leisure situation was the inability to participate as often as one would like.

Now we turn to how leisure enables equity. In fact, leisure can be one of the most powerful forces for equity. Leisure can be a means by which people who are homeless, unemployed, or migrant are incorporated into mainstream society. And as demonstrated by the Olympic Games, leisure can at least call a temporary halt to international disagreements. In addition, community festivals are able to unify a widely diverse population through a common spirit of cooperation. We will discuss two leisure concepts that have the ability to enhance equity: inclusion and diversity.

In the late 1990s, professionals in leisure services began to focus on the concept of inclusion. **Inclusion** suggests that leisure service organizations should provide mechanisms for individuals who have special life conditions, such as a physical disability, to participate according to typical circumstances and to help them become as independent as possible by joining the mainstream of society. In fact, one of the very principles of equity calls for programs and services that maximize inclusion. On the one hand, this might mean a community supports additional leisure resources for low-income neighborhoods, or, on the other hand, inclusion might mean holding an ice cream social to bring church members and nearby college students together.

> **Inclusion:** the involvement and full acceptance of persons with special needs into a wide range of community settings

This suggests that inclusion means more than access to a wide range of leisure opportunities. It also means that some adaptation may be necessary for those who do not otherwise "fit" into the main interests and behaviors of the others. For example, participation in basketball by players who use wheelchairs could mean modifying the rules. However, such modifications should not go too far when the interest is in inclusion—adaptation of the activity should be as minimal as possible.

Ironically, the second leisure concept that speaks to the ability to create equity—diversity—seems the antithesis of inclusion. A major conclusion from the most recent census of the population of the United States is that **diversity** has increased. Americans are more different from one another than ever before in terms of race, ethnicity, family type, household income, lifestyle, political beliefs, and other factors. As former President Jimmy Carter (1976) once observed: "We become not a melting pot but a beautiful mosaic. Different people, different beliefs, different yearnings, different hopes, different dreams" (p. 00).

> **Diversity:** recognition and celebration of differences within a unifying sense of togetherness

From Your Own Experience

Your Attitudes Toward Diversity
Box 13.1

You might identify your own attitudes toward diversity by remembering certain pivotal moments in your life. Ask yourself these questions:

Recall the incident in which you first became aware of people who were different from you. What was your reaction? Were you the focus of attention or were others?

What are the "messages" that you learned about various "minorities" or "majorities" when you were a child? At home? In school? Have your views changed since then? Why or why not?

Recall an experience in which your own difference put you in an uncomfortable position with the people directly around you. What was that difference? How did it affect you?

Today it is considered very important to support and protect diversity, because by valuing the differences in individuals and groups, and by fostering a climate where not only equity but also mutual respect is intrinsic, a better society is created. Here is an illustration. In July 1996, the deciding game of the U.S. Cup soccer tournament was played in the Rose Bowl stadium in Pasadena, California. The contest matched the U.S. and Mexican national teams and featured important stars from both countries (Gramann & Allison, 1999). More than 98,000 spectators packed the stadium to watch the match. There was great excitement. In fact, the demand for tickets was so great that seats that had been held back because they offered poor viewing of the field were released and sold to fans waiting in lines outside the stadium even after the game began.

Was this situation a testimony to the rising popularity of soccer in a traditionally non-soccer-playing country? Probably yes, in part, but that is not all of the explanation, because most of the fans were cheering for Mexico. Mexican flags and other banners of green, red, and white overwhelmed the red, white, and blue in the stands (Gramann & Allison, 1999). Because of a large Mexican American population living in southern California, it was a home game for Mexico. This shows the potential of leisure to maintain and even strengthen group identity within a diverse society. Latino cultural traditions and pride were celebrated that day.

Examples

There are many more examples of how leisure both constrains and enables equity. To further illustrate the concepts of constraints, inclusion, and diversity, we focus now on leisure and women, gays and lesbians, at-risk youth, racial and ethnic minorities, immigrants, and persons with disabilities.

Women

The woman has played many roles throughout history. She has been a mother, daughter, lover, and mate. She has also been a prime minister, farmer, political activist, CEO, and scientist. Today women combine many of these roles, yet through the centuries, almost every society has developed definite ideas about what activities and behaviors are appropriate for women. Some of these ideas have disappeared or changed greatly over time, but others have changed little or not at all.

What have been the implications for leisure of these changes in women's roles? What is the meaning of leisure for women? Is equitable leisure available to women? Our exploration into these questions considers two themes: feminist theory applied to women's leisure, and research conclusions about the nature of women's leisure.

Although there are many perspectives about **feminism**, it has come to be known as the belief that women should have economic, political, and social equality with men. Even though feminist beliefs have existed in various cultures throughout all of history, it wasn't until the early 1800s that a struggle to have women's equity taken seriously began in the countries of North America and Europe. Early efforts focused mostly on achieving political equality, including the right to vote. This was won in most countries by the early 1900s. After this, efforts for equity nearly disappeared until the mid-1900s, when increasing numbers of women entered the labor force and found many higher paying jobs closed to them. This time the focus was on achieving equity through economics. Through the efforts of such reform organizations as the National Organization for Women (NOW), by the end of the last century, more women were entering law, medicine, and other traditionally male fields, yet full economic equality still has not been achieved. Today in the United States, for example, women earn about 73 cents for every dollar men earn in comparable employment (General Accounting Office, 2004).

> **Feminism:** the theory of political, economic, and social equality of the sexes

Feminism, however, is more than the efforts to achieve political and economic equality. It has a broader philosophical framework that includes ideas of empowerment and social change. For example, liberal feminism, as one of the oldest forms of feminist thought, focuses on gender justice by working to address social and legal constraints to equal opportunity for both women and men (Henderson & Bialeschki, 1999). Particularly relevant for our attention to leisure is ecofeminism. This perspective considers the dominance of men over women and Man over nature to be parallel (Henderson & Bialeschki, 1999).

But the link between feminism and leisure is even more direct than this. In the first place, both are based on the qualities of choice and freedom (Henderson, Bialeschki, Shaw, & Freysinger, 1989). In fact, encouraging freedom of choice is the essence of both feminism and leisure. Women have not had the same freedom to choose leisure as men. Yet through leisure, women have the opportunity to achieve this freedom. This is a unique relationship: Leisure provides women an avenue for achieving equity, empowerment, and social action, and for women, leisure has itself been constrained because of a lack of equity, empowerment, and social action. We can demonstrate this from research.

Through an analysis of professional recreation literature, Henderson (1993) revealed that between 1907 and 1916, girls and women were "discovered" to need recreation, too. Some writers of the time thought that the playground movement in the United States had focused only on boys. Through their writing, they sought to include girls as well. Henderson's analysis also revealed that this early professional literature debated whether girls' sporting activities should be more like boys' or the other way around. This was particularly debatable because of the "corruption" in boys' activities (McKinstry, 1909, p. 11) and because it was believed that boys would be better off if they adopted some of the "gentler and more conventional amusements" of girls (Weller, 1913, p. 209). Today, of course, increasing numbers of girls and women are involved and very successful in all sorts of leisure pursuits. In fact, girls' and women's involvement in sports and physical activity is one factor helping to change stereotypes of what it means to be female (Fig. 13.2).

Other studies demonstrate leisure as an enabler of equity. For example, Kleiber and Kane (1984) found that girls who exhibited playful, exuberant, self-expressive behavior in leisure were able to move beyond societal prescribed roles for women. That is, leisure can help girls to develop their full potential. Leisure has also been studied as a tool of resistance for women. For example, the work of Freysinger and Flannery (1992) and Shaw (1994) demonstrated that through leisure pursuits, women were able to resist oppression by achieving greater autonomy and respect.

Figure 13.2
A women's bicycle racing team at Indiana University's "Little 500." (© Ruth V. Russell.)

Yet significant inequities for women still exist in leisure. Today's research on women reveals the persistence of the theme of constraint. In reviewing the research on women's leisure from the past 20 years (Henderson, 1990; Henderson, Hodges, & Kivel, 2002; Shaw, 1999; Wearing, 1998), we can draw five broad conclusions about women's leisure:

1. ***Women experience inequity in leisure when compared with men.*** Regardless of social class, age, income, race, or educational level, the leisure of men and women varies considerably. Many women have less time for leisure and less of a priority for leisure. Women also tend to have narrower options for choosing particular leisure activities. For example, women have fewer opportunities to play football, soccer, and baseball.

2. ***Combining role obligations with leisure is a common focus for many women.*** Many women perceive themselves as their roles (mother, wife) first and individuals second; thus, they perceive expressions of leisure according to their roles. For example, when a woman marries, her social life often becomes linked with that of her husband. When she has children, her life is further sublimated to the interests and needs of the family. Some studies claim that an important reason many women participate in organized sports is for the chance to socialize outside their dominant roles.

3. ***Women's leisure is more likely to occur in the home and be unstruc-tured.*** This is because pastimes can easily be infused with household chores, and women are socialized

to value home-based activities, such as gardening, reading, and cooking. Fewer leisure opportunities are available to women outside the home because assistance with child care is often not available. Unfortunately, the home does not always provide an opportunity for a change of pace; it is frequently not refreshing. For many women, the home is considered a site with more responsibility rather than one of freedom.

4. *Much of women's leisure is fragmented.* Women seldom find large blocks of time for leisure in their lives. Instead, they have to "steal" free time, such as a spare minute or two in between loads of laundry. They take shorter vacations and have interrupted weekends. Women are also more likely to combine leisure activities with other obligations, such as watching television while folding laundry.

5. *Many women do not feel entitled to leisure.* Many women believe they do not deserve leisure. If leisure is viewed as a reward earned from work, some women who are homemakers may never feel they earned the reward. Even for women who work outside the home, studies have found they too often feel they have no right to take time off.

To conclude, although leisure is an important aspect in the quality of life for people, women are unable to take full advantage of the potential for leisure in their lives. This must be corrected, because leisure experiences provide the opportunity for maintaining personal autonomy, self-definition, and choice often absent from other aspects of their lives.

In Profile

Behind the Veil
Box 13.2

For a significant number of the world's population, Islam is more than just a religion—it is an entire way of life (Taylor & Toohey, 2001/2002). The majority of Muslims live in Middle Eastern and South Asian countries. However, the number of Muslims in countries outside this region, such as in the United States, Canada, and Australia, is rapidly increasing. More Muslims are living in non-Muslim countries than ever before. The United States, for example, has approximately 3 million immigrant Muslims.

What is life like for Muslim women living in a non-Muslim country? Are there systemic constraints in sports and recreational participation due to the requirements of their religious and cultural practices?

Islam requires physical exercise, and activities that are particularly recommended in the Koran include horseback riding, swimming, archery, running, and mountaineering (Zaman, 1997). Do Muslim women in non-Muslim countries have access to these sports? From interviews conducted in Australia by Taylor and Toohey (2001/2002), we can catch a glimpse of the problem.

As Modi, an Iranian Muslim woman living in Australia, pointed out "the recreational side is very important and a vital part of our healthy life. When I was a girl, I loved P.E., but it all changed when we moved here" (p. 100). Natalie said, "part and parcel of our religious requirements is to learn swimming and safety, but you'll find that none of our women here have any idea of water safety" (p. 100).

In response, one of the swimming pool operators indicated that he was sensitive to the requirements of Muslim women, but explained that due to financial constraints, "we can't afford to close the pool to all males when just a handful of women want to go swimming." Another recreation facility manager, explaining why he could not meet all the requirements made by a team of female Muslim basketball players, said, "They didn't want men around when they played but the other teams wanted their boyfriends to come and some had male coaches; it was a tough one." Unfortunately, the Muslim women's team withdrew from the competition when males were allowed access.

Gays and Lesbians

There may well be more openly gay men and women in North America now than in any other region of the world at any other time in history. In fact, in many corners of society, gay and lesbian people are no longer thought of as a counterculture. According to a Time/CNN Poll (Yankelovich Partners, Inc., 1998), whereas 41 percent of respondents felt homosexual relationships were acceptable in 1978, the attitude had shifted to 64 percent by 1998.

In the past, throughout much of the world, religious and governmental authorities have condemned homosexuality. Until more recently it was categorized as a form of mental illness by the psychiatric profession and as a crime by law enforcement agencies. Thus, most gay and lesbian people hid their sexual orientation "in the closet." Change began in the United States in June 1969 when crowds demonstrated following a police raid on the Stonewall Inn, a popular gay bar in Greenwich Village, New York City. The riots were considered a call to arms for the birth of a gay rights movement (Pela, 1994).

The Gay Liberation Front was formed, and it and other groups throughout the country began lobbying for pro-gay political candidates and legislation. In 1961 Illinois became the first state to abolish its laws against people who were homosexuals. Since the 1970s, although still contentious, many U.S. cities and states have passed laws banning discrimination against gays and lesbians in employment, housing, and other areas. Vermont has legalized civil unions for gay couples, and Massachusetts offers marriage to same-sex couples. In all of Canada, human rights legislation prohibits any form of antigay discrimination, and same-sex marriages are legal. Similar attitudes of acceptance exist in some European countries as well. Meanwhile in the United States, some cities have repealed their antidiscrimination policies. Thus, the struggle for equality continues.

Nonetheless, the Civil Rights movement initiated in the 1960s and 1970s, as well as new research evidence suggesting that homosexuality has a genetic basis, have given gays and lesbians greater public acceptance. Numerous universities openly employ gay and lesbian faculty members, have instituted courses and curricula in gay studies, and sponsor student organizations that are gay oriented. Gay and lesbian people are depicted regularly in books, theater, film, and art.

What are the implications of these trends for leisure? Most public and nonprofit leisure service organizations do not deal at all with the issue, or they simply accept gay or lesbian participants as part of their total membership without recognizing their sexual orientation. In some cases, however, leisure service organizations have explicitly sought membership and participation by gay and lesbian individuals.

For example, marketing to gays and lesbians for resorts and other leisure attractions has become quite lucrative for the tourist industry. To illustrate, although not "officially" sponsoring it, Gay Days at Walt Disney World in Orlando, Florida, annually draws some 135,000 visitors. This is because Walt Disney World's official policy is to not discriminate against anyone's right to visit the parks, and over the years it has become more involved in planning and working with the event coordinators.

Another example is the Lavender Youth Recreation and Information Center (LYRIC) in San Francisco, California, a program that promotes comprehensive recreation and social activities for gay, lesbian, transgender, and bisexual youth in a safe and positive social environment.

Some leisure service organizations, on the other hand, have explicitly refused membership to and participation by gay and lesbian individuals. These include recreation and social clubs sponsored by some religious denominations, fraternities and sororities, youth-serving organizations, and schools. Further, in a survey conducted by Parents and Families of Lesbians and Gays (2001), 50 percent of all gay and lesbian youth reported that their parents had rejected them because of their sexual orientation.

Scouting for All
Box 13.3

The following is excerpted from an editorial prepared by David Cole for CNN Interactive:

Few entities are more sacred in mainstream America than the Boy Scouts. With more than five million youth and adult members, the Scouts are an integral part of American childhood. By their own terms, the Scouts are "open to all boys." Yet the Boy Scouts have also gone on record claiming that gays should be excluded from membership because their creed holds that homosexuality is immoral.

A centerpiece for the issue is James Dale, an exemplary Boy Scout for 12 years before he was expelled in 1990 at the age of 19. The Boy Scouts knew of Dale's record and demonstrated commitment to Scouting values and principles. But when they learned that Dale was gay, the Scouts expelled him.

But Dale lives in New Jersey and New Jersey law forbids "public accommodations" from discriminating on the basis of sexual orientation, arguing that the Scouts are a "public accommodation" because they receive governmental support and because they are open to the public.

Both the New Jersey and the Supreme Courts have handled Dale's case. In the courts the Scouts assert that compelling them to accept gay "leaders" violates their rights of speech and association. They argue that they speak through their leaders, and therefore, state control of their leaders is the same as state control of their speech. The Scouts asked: How can we effectively express our message that homosexuality is immoral if we are legally required to tolerate leaders and members who by their very lifestyle contradict that message? If freedom of association means anything, they maintained, it must protect a private organization's right to limit its leaders and members to those who reflect its values and beliefs.

(http://www.cnn.com/2000/LAW/04/20/boy.scout/index.html. Retrieved 7/11/01)

Figure 13.3

The Boy Scouts represent a private organization that provides leisure services to its members on a discriminatory basis. (© Ruth V. Russell.)

Questions to Consider and Discuss

1. How did the New Jersey and U.S. Supreme Courts decide this case? Do some independent research and find out the conclusions to the court deliberations. Do you agree or disagree with them? Why? Why not?

2. How have the local Boy Scout Councils in your own area responded to these court decisions? Do some independent research to find this out. What has been the community's response to the council? Do you agree or disagree? Why or why not?

3. Is this case about discrimination? Should leisure service organizations such as the Boy Scouts be considered truly private organizations with full authority and autonomy over their membership? Or should such organizations be recognized for their public nature as well? Do public organizations have the right to discriminate in membership? Should scouting be open to all?

To conclude, although leisure is an important aspect of the quality of life for people, people who are gay or lesbian are unable to take full advantage of the potential for leisure in their lives. This must be corrected, because leisure experiences provide the opportunity for maintaining personal autonomy, self-definition, and choice often absent from other aspects of their lives.

Racial and Ethnic Minorities

The increase in ethnic diversity in North America is one of the most powerful forces shaping these societies today. As the proportion of the population that demographers classify as white declines in the 21st century, diversity in **ethnicity** and **race** and the societal consequences of this diversity will become even more visible. For example, of the 70 million people projected to be added to the U.S. population between 1980 and 2025, 78 percent will come from increases in its minority populations (Murdock, Backman, Colberg, Hogue, & Harmon, 1990). In turn, much of this will be accounted for by a dramatic growth in Latino American populations, which, for example, increased by 4.7 percent between April 2000 and July 2001 (Armas, 2004). Canada is similarly affected. There, 23 percent of the total population report French as their first language (Statistics Canada, 2004).

> **Ethnicity:** having a unique cultural heritage that is passed on from one generation to another, often identified by patterns of language, family life, religion, and recreational customs

> **Race:** a set of common physical traits, such as skin pigmentation, head form, facial features, stature, and the color and texture of body hair

Often ethnic and racial groups in the United States and Canada are concentrated geographically. For example, the majority of French Canadians live in the province of Quebec. In the U.S. states that border Mexico, Latinos (mostly Mexican Americans) substantially surpass other ethnic groups. Cuban Americans constitute an important population in south Florida, and Asian Americans are concentrated mostly in Hawaii and California.

The increasing ethnic and racial diversity of North America presents increasing challenges and opportunities in virtually every sphere of social life, including leisure needs and provisions. One thing that history has taught us, however, is that ethnic and racial divisions are among the most persistent. Let's demonstrate this by considering the concepts of assimilation and pluralism.

Many "modernization" theories of the 19th and early 20th centuries predicted the disappearance of ethnic differences in industrialized nations (Evans & Stephens, 1988). We were expected to merge into a culturally homogeneous whole. Informally, the idea was called the "melting pot." The basis of this prediction was the judgment that ethnically distinct immigrant groups would assimilate into their host cultures. In fact, the **assimilation** was expected to be rather specific—that is, the various ethnic groups were expected to assimilate into the white mainstream. At least it was felt that such cultural characteristics as speech patterns and clothing styles would become a new homogeneous culture that was a combination of ethnic and racial groups.

> **Assimilation: absorption into the system**

Some of this has happened—rap music is popular with both black and white youth. But by and large, assimilation has not happened. In fact, many members of particular ethnic and racial groups (Native Americans, French Canadians, African Americans) appear to be doing the opposite by emphasizing their ethnic and racial distinctiveness.

Rather, cultural pluralism seems to be happening. Similar to the idea of diversity discussed earlier in the chapter, **pluralism** encourages distinctiveness according to ethnic or racial heritage. According to some sociologists, people from ethnic or racial groups select certain things about the mainstream to adopt because of the economic benefit, but they retain other traditional cultural values from their own group.

> **Pluralism: when members of diverse ethnic and racial groups maintain separate participation in their traditional cultures**

What has been the impact of pluralism on leisure? Have leisure values and behaviors helped or hindered the drive to acceptance of ethnic and racial diversity?

One way to answer these questions is to consider leisure as a tool for distinguishing ethnic groups. In fact, over the years most of the leisure research on race and ethnicity has focused on differences in recreational participation. For example, early research found great differences between whites and blacks in their interests and motivations for outdoor recreation. Later, research focused on the outdoor recreational behavior of Mexican Americans. In general, members of ethnic minority groups tend to participate less frequently than whites in a wide range of outdoor pursuits (Gramann & Allison, 1999). Further, in terms of sports, African American youth show a stronger preference for basketball, whereas white youth are more likely to be found participating in baseball and soccer (Ogden & Hilt, 2003).

Two contrasting explanations have been proposed for such differences in recreational participation patterns among ethnic groups. The first explanation is termed the marginality thesis. This suggests that ethnic and racial differences are due to a group's marginal position in society. For example, socioeconomic status or residence locale may be more associated with particular ethnic or racial groups, and thus constrain their opportunities for specific recreation activities. In addition, a pattern of inequitable treatment may limit opportunities. Children who live in the suburbs are more likely to be of higher socioeconomic status and have more opportunities to join soccer and baseball programs, whereas children who live in the inner city are more likely to have

The Study Says

African Americans Lost to Baseball
Box 13.4

A growing body of research evidence shows a widening gulf between baseball and African Americans. African Americans comprise less that three percent of the players at the highest competitive levels of youth baseball and three percent of NCAA Division I baseball players. African Americans also constitute less than five percent of spectators at some Major League parks, and the percentage of African American players in the Major Leagues has reached a 30-year low.

Why? According to studies, basketball has become the preeminent sport in African American culture. Unlike the bulk of the 20th century, there has been a cultural shift for African American children and youth of both genders away from baseball to basketball. Studies contend this has been brought about by four factors: encouragement by authority figures to pursue basketball, the portrayal of basketball in the media as a form of empowerment, the abundance of black role models in basketball, and the perception of high and fast social mobility in basketball (Ogden & Hilt, 2003).

a lower socioeconomic status and have more opportunities to join basketball programs.

The second explanation for differences in participation is termed the ethnicity thesis (Washburne, 1978). According to this view, ethnic and racial differences in recreational participation are explained by culturally based value systems, norms, and socialization patterns. It assumes that ethnic groups preserve distinct cultural identities that are carried forth into their leisure interests and behaviors. For example, one study (Dragon, 1986) found distinct cultural differences between Native Americans and white Americans in the meanings each attached to the use of national parks.

Another way to consider the impact of pluralism on leisure is to identify leisure as a tool for empowering people in their ethnic differences. Several decades ago it was believed that leisure did just the opposite. For example, writers such as Meyer and Brightbill (1964) claimed that leisure had value in helping assimilate people of different backgrounds—a kind of blending into the American lifestyle could be achieved by playing baseball, for example. In contrast, we now believe that the leisure interests and behaviors of particular racial or ethnic groups helps to explain them. Leisure provides the means for expression of ethnic individuality and identity. For example, Navajo youth often convert an informal game of basketball into a less competitive and more collective game (Allison, 1982).

To conclude, although leisure is an important aspect of the quality of life for people, ethnic and racial minorities are unable to take full advantage of the potential for leisure in their lives. This must be corrected, because leisure experiences provide the opportunity for maintaining personal autonomy, self-definition, and choice often absent from other aspects of their lives.

Immigrants

Part of North America's increasing population diversity can be attributed to immigration. In fact, throughout history, immigration has been an important event that has characterized most nations around the globe, and today the volume of international migration appears to be growing. For example, the number of immigrants who live in the United States has tripled during the last 20 years and is now approaching 10 percent of the population (U.S. Census Bureau, 2000).

Equity for immigrants has always been an issue. For example, when Irish immigrants migrated to the United States in 1841 because of the Great Irish Potato Famine, they were not tolerated for their Catholic faith. Later, when Chinese laborers first came to the United States in 1848 to work the Gold Rush in California, their culture was perceived as strange and evil. Since these early immigrations, the stories of persecution of immigrants from Africa, Europe, and Asia can be added. Today, although their lives are still not free of discrimination, immigrants to North America have come closer to winning full economic, social, and political equity.

One way to understand immigrants and leisure is to consider a typology that describes their experience with discrimination (Ogbu, 1998). This classification includes people who are autonomous, voluntary, and involuntary. Autonomous minorities consist of small groups who differ from the dominant group in ethnicity, religion, and language and who suffer some discrimination. Autonomous minorities are typically not immigrants, including such white minorities as the Amish, Jews, and Mormons (Salazar, 2001).

The involuntary minorities are also not immigrants. They include people who were conquered (Native Americans, Native Alaskans, and Native Hawaiians) or enslaved (African Americans). They may differ in race, language, religion, and ethnicity, but the characteristic they share in common is that, in contrast to immigrants, they do not have a home country against which to compare their present situation. Instead, they compare their status with that of the dominant group and usually conclude that they are worse off (Ogbu, 1991). In addition, involuntary minorities do not see their situation as temporary. Instead, they see discriminating conditions as institutionalized and permanent.

Finally, the voluntary minorities, or what Obgu (1998) officially refers to as immigrants, include people who moved to another country more or less willingly with the expectation of better job opportunities or for political and religious freedoms. Examples of voluntary minorities might include Cubans, Haitians, and Mexicans. Usually voluntary minorities, or immigrants, have a positive attitude toward the host country, especially during the first generation. This is often because they compare their new host country with the situations they left in their home countries. This enables them to assume that the discrimination they suffer in the host country is temporary and due to their lack of education or fluency in the language. They believe that hard work, more education, and the passage of time will make their futures better (Salazar, 2001).

From this typology let's focus just on immigrants, the voluntary minorities. For immigrants, culture shock is usually an important reality. The process of **culture shock** is a multifaceted experience, a product of many stressors activated by contact with a different culture (Winkelman, 1994). Of course, immigrants aren't the only group to experience culture shock. Business people working in other countries and extended-stay tourists also can experience culture shock.

> **Culture shock:** a sense of confusion and uncertainty, and perhaps anxiety, affecting people exposed to a foreign culture without preparation

Winkelman (1994) proposed four stages of culture shock. The first is the "honeymoon or tourist" phase, in which excitement, interest, and positive expectations about the new culture are experienced. Stage two is "crisis." Things start to go wrong, minor issues become major problems, and the cultural differences become irritating. This stage often leads to feelings of helplessness and confusion. The third stage is the "adjustment and reorientation" phase, in which the immigrant begins to learn how to live effectively in the new country. When immigrants begin to understand the host country's culture, they have more fun and experience fewer negative reactions (Salazar, 2001). Thus, the fourth stage is one of "adaptation and resolution." At this point, a bicultural identity can be developed as new cultural aspects are integrated into the previous home-country identity, and stable adaptations to problems are achieved.

How does culture shock influence the leisure behaviors of immigrants? The answer varies, of course, depending on the immigrants' original cultural orientation, their personal traits, and their experiences in the host country. In general, however, all immigrants bring with them "baggage" of their culture, which includes distinct leisure participation patterns (Stodolska, 2000). One view of this comes from the role of family in the lives of immigrants. Family networks often help immigrants when they arrive in the host country (Foner, 1997). For many immigrants, family leisure in particular can reduce the stresses causing culture shock. The extended family is often a prime source of recreational involvement and is often isolated from the rest of the culture in the host country. Research has indicated generally that the less assimilated the immigrant, the lower the involvement in host-culture leisure pursuits. For example, one study found that those Chinese immigrant youth with lower self-esteem were more likely to engage in recreation with Chinese friends and their families (Yu & Berryman, 1996).

Another view of leisure and immigrants is that leisure can be an aid to reducing the effects of culture shock (Fig. 13.4). The studies of Polish immigrants to Canada demonstrate this. In one study, Stodolska (1998) found that the leisure of immigrants was most severely constrained immediately after their arrival. Many of the Polish immigrants in the study even ceased doing the recreational activities that were a part of their regular life in Poland. Reasons for this included language differences, the need to work hard and save money, and unawareness of leisure resources.

Figure 13.4
For young immigrants, the role of leisure is likely to be particularly critical during the initial period in the new country. (© Ruth V. Russell.)

Yet Stodolska (2000) also discovered that leisure can help with this adaptation. Those Poles who continued the various activities they started in their home countries found psychological comfort, stability, and familiarity. Stodolska described these immigrants as consciously using leisure as a tool for retaining their cultural identity. In addition, leisure can be a way to meet and share with other people and learn about the culture of the host country (Stodolska & Yi, 2003). Both preserving part of one's cultural heritage and making adjustments to a new cultural presence are responses to culture shock for which leisure can be helpful.

To conclude, although leisure is an important aspect in the quality of life for people, immigrants are unable to take full advantage of the potential for leisure. This must be corrected, because leisure experiences provide the opportunity for maintaining the personal autonomy, self-definition, and choice often absent from other aspects of their lives.

At-Risk Youth

As a society, we have been loath to recognize the chronic problems that plague the North American household. We prefer to romanticize the family; we want to see rosy-cheeked children coming home after school to a steaming bowl of Campbell's chicken noodle soup, and mothers and fathers tumbling joyously with their kids in a backyard game of touch football. Yet these are fantasies for the great majority of households (Table 13.1).

Table 13.1
The American Family, by the Numbers

	1950 (%)	1998 (%)
Married-couple households	78.2	52.9
Never-married adults	20.0	28.0
Children living with both parents	92.6	68.0
Married couples in the labor force	32.0	68.0
Children reared by a grandparent	3.2	5.5

(From: U.S. Socitety and Values, "The American Family," Department of State, International Information. http://usinfo.state.gov/journals/itsv/0101/ijse/numbers.htm. Retrieved 4/14/04)

Today the typical household is just as likely to be smaller and headed by overworked single parents. In addition, nonmarried adults and people living alone make up an increasing proportion of households, and adoption and surrogacy are more common options for parenting. More children are being raised by a grandparent, and in all households, all adults are more likely to be working outside the home. Horribly, the fastest growing segment of the homeless population is families with children.

One obvious outcome of statistics such as these is the growing concern for children who are regularly without adult supervision. Yet this is not necessarily a new phenomenon. Before the 16th century in England and other parts of Europe, children were not cared for by their parents. The rich had little to do with their children until they were grown. Infants were given to wet nurses, and older children were sent off to boarding school. Children in poorer families fared similarly. They became servants or apprentices at early ages. Time for extended mothering was an unaffordable luxury, and children were routinely left unattended for long periods of time. To make them less of a nuisance, babies were wrapped in swaddling clothes, their limbs completely immobilized. Toddlers were given opium to keep them in a stupor until parents returned home (Razzell & Wainwright, 1973).

Eventually, these child-rearing practices faded away. In fact, more caring attitudes began to emerge in the 18th century in both Europe and North America, when parental affection became more common. However, the biggest changes came in the 19th century when, spurred on by religious reformers, the idealization of mother love, with vigilant attention to the needs of children, came to dominate. By the end of the 19th century, a bona fide "mothers' movement" emerged. When the "century of the child" opened, mothers and fathers in the 20th century were providing their children all manner of new services (Schor, 1992). In fact, the legacy of child neglect gave way to the most intensive parenting process in human history. Today we teach children to read and count before they go to school. We convert whole rooms in the house to playrooms. We give them daily baths, chauffeur them to school and activities, and take them to psychiatrists.

Because current economic conditions require all adults in the household to work, and because single adults increasingly head the typical family, no wonder we feel great concern about the slipping standards of child care. Thanks to the glorification of parenting, and higher standards of parenting, we blame poor parenting for many problems today, ranging from poor academic performance to rudeness, from delinquency to obesity, from bullying to boredom. As parents become busier, television has assumed a major role in rearing children. In addition, social institutions such as schools and recreation programs are expected to make up the slack.

Beginning about 20 years ago, the call came forth that youth in North America were in trouble. For example, Caldwell (1983) summarized a national study of more than 46,000 sixth through 12th graders in the United States that pointed to 26 at-risk indicators, including frequent binge drinking, tobacco use, illegal drug use, sexual involvement, depression, and suicide. The students cited such specific causes as "being alone at home, hedonistic values, television overexposure, and social isolation" (p. 19). Later, in 1992 the U.S. Surgeon

General emphasized the link between youthful drinking and teen suicides, drowning, vehicle deaths, and committing serious crimes, including rape. Also in 1992, a study concluded that teen gambling had grown steadily (Belluck, 1992).

By the early years of the 21st century, the statistics seem to have improved a bit, with teen pregnancy rates declining by about 30 percent, cigarette use reduced by about nine percent, and alcohol consumption down by about 4 percent (Centers for Disease Control and Prevention, 2002). In addition, other studies point to many positive youth trends. For example, a nationwide poll reported that

> *. . . in some ways they are as wholesome and devoid of cynicism as the generation that wore saddle shoes. They trust their government, admire their parents, . . . Ninety-four percent say they believe in God. And, strong majorities say they never drink alcohol and never smoke cigarettes or marijuana. (Goodstein & Connelly, 1998)*

Nonetheless, today's adults still worry about today's youth. In fact, a special term has been coined to designate this concern: **at-risk youth**. At-risk youth research and solution initiatives have focused on those children who have at least two hours of unobligated time every day, most typically after school on weekdays. Although the impact of this on kids' school performance, safety, stability, social adjustment, and other qualities is not well understood, the perception exists that this time should be filled in a meaningful way (Fig. 13.5).

> **At-risk youth:** adolescents who are in trouble at home or school, and who may have been brought into the juvenile justice system

Figure 13.5
Children need healthy and supervised options for play, especially after school when many parents are still at work. This play "wave" is in Halifax, Nova Scotia. (© Ruth V. Russell.)

The most frequent solution has been after-school recreation programs. School systems, city recreation and park departments, churches, voluntary youth agencies, commercial day-care agencies, and others offer a wide array of programs that include sports, crafts, hobbies, cultural arts, adventure activities, and homework tutoring. Frequently, late bus service is also provided. Other solutions tried in some areas are telephone check-in services, where an adult calls the child at home every day after school, and flexible work hours for parents so they can be at home when the children return. In one city, a community program called "police partners" turned children into extra eyes and ears for the police.

Of particular concern is the way free time is spent by adolescents. Too old for traditional playgrounds, yet too young to drive, many youth between 10 and 15 years of age spend their free time not doing much of anything. According to a study by Cordes and Ibrahim (2003), the number-one activity in terms of participation rates for this age group was "hanging out." Sometimes this included watching television, listening to music, and conversation.

Identical to the goal of professional recreation providers over 100 years ago, using leisure services to achieve youth development goals remains central. Although leisure is an important aspect in the quality of life for people, at-risk youth are often unable to take full advantage of the potential for leisure in their lives. This must be corrected, because leisure experiences provide the opportunity for maintaining personal autonomy, self-definition, and choice often absent from other aspects of their lives.

Persons with Disabilities

The U.S. Bureau of the Census has placed the number of Americans with disabilities at close to 49 million. This is slightly more than 19 percent of the total U.S. population (Smith, Austin, & Kennedy, 2001). Approximately one half are considered to have disabilities that are severe (Worsnop, 1997), yet only about 10% are institutionalized (Leitner & Leitner, 2004).

A variety of **disabling conditions** are included, such as visual and hearing impairments, mental retardation and other learning difficulties, motor impairments, psychological and behavior disorders, brain injury, acquired immunodeficiency syndrome (AIDS), and problems normally associated with advanced age. Disabilities cut across age, race, social class, gender, and educational backgrounds, but people with particularly severe disabilities find it more difficult to attend school, pursue a career, live independently, and enjoy leisure.

Disabling condition: a physical or mental impairment that limits one or more of an individual's life activities

During the 1960s in the United States, a movement developed that emphasized the rights of people with disabilities. Philosophically originating in efforts at the turn of the 20th century to overcome the human consequences of industrialization, the crux of the movement was simple advocacy (Kennedy, Smith, & Austin, 1991). A significant turning point for people with disabilities in Canada was the amendment of the Human Rights Act in 1974, which prohibits discrimination against persons for a position of employment for reasons of physical or mental disability (Searle & Brayley, 2000). Such official notice of the rights of persons with disabilities did not occur in the United States until 1990, with the passage of the Americans with Disabilities Act (ADA), which required public institutions to provide fuller and more equitable opportunities for accessibility to buildings, programs, jobs, and other areas.

For equity in leisure, advocacy originally took the form of "separate but equal." Recreation programs in communities were instrumental in addressing the needs of persons with disabilities by establishing segregated programs (Bedini, 1990). These included residential and community services separate from those available to people without disabilities. In fact, these were often labeled as programs for "special populations" (Fig. 13.6).

Figure 13.6
Wheelchair basketball–an example of "separate but equal." (© Ruth V. Russell.)

Later it was realized that segregation encouraged dependence by those with disabilities and invited the community's condescension and pity (Bedini, 1990). Now the focus is not simply on providing access to community facilities or leisure resources through segregated and "special" programs, but on enabling persons with disabilities to become full participants in community life. As an inclusive philosophy, the goal is to create environments that are option rich, responsive, and informative so that people with disabilities can take control of their own leisure expressions. This has been labeled "inclusive recreation."

Yet according to research and personal testimony, people with disabilities report that negative attitudes continue to represent the most devastating barrier they experience (Dattilo & Williams, 1999). Indeed, the notion that individuals who are disabled can participate fully in their communities still meets with controversy and avoidance. This is fueled by intolerance and the devaluation of people who are considered different, and this establishes barriers that are difficult to overcome.

In Profile
Casey Martin
Box 13.5

In February 1998, Casey Martin, a 25-year-old golfer and Stanford classmate of Tiger Woods, sued the Nike Tour for the right to use a golf cart. Martin has Klippel-Trenaunay-Webber Syndrome, a circulatory condition that limits his ability to walk. If he puts too much pressure on his legs, it could necessitate amputation.

His suit used the Americans with Disabilities Act (ADA) to defend three counts: discrimination in public accommodation, inhibition of professional advancement, and employment discrimination. Martin alleged that the Tour was denying him the right to play, and as an employer of sorts, the right to work, based on his disability.

The Tour countered that the ADA didn't apply to professional-level sports and that walking is an essential part of the game. The Tour felt that if Martin could ride in a cart, he would have an unfair advantage over the other players who would tire from walking around the course. Some golfers were on Martin's side; others were not. Arnold Palmer and Jack Nicklaus both stressed how important walking was to golfing, implying that if Martin couldn't play on his own two feet, he shouldn't.

The court ruled in Martin's favor, and even though the Tour quickly appealed, Martin was able to use a cart until his appeal was approved in 2000. This long, high-profile case gave the general public its first taste of the power of the ADA (Shklyanoy, 2000).

This brings to light several important equity issues about leisure and persons with disabilities, namely, self-determination, self-advocacy, normalization, and integration (Searle & Brayley, 2000).

First, one of the most significant ways people with disabilities can be empowered in leisure is through allowing them to make decisions for themselves (Mahon & Bullock, 1992). Such **self-determination** involves acting as the primary causal agent in one's life and making choices and decisions regarding one's life free from influence or interference. Indeed, the role of self-determination is critical to the very essence of leisure itself. For persons with disabilities, it is especially important to have the ability to choose leisure. To do otherwise is in violation of a basic right.

> **Self-determination:** defining goals for oneself and taking the initiative to achieve them

Similarly, **self-advocacy** means that, individually or as a group, persons with disabilities speak for and on behalf of themselves. In many ways, the evolution of the idea of self-advocacy represents true progress in the revolution of rights for persons with disabilities (Searle & Brayley, 2000). In the past 30 years, a great deal has been written and accomplished to facilitate equal rights for individuals with special needs, yet until very recently, much of what was proposed was by nondisabled people. Self-advocacy gives persons with disabilities their own voice in leisure.

> **Self-advocacy:** speaking on behalf of oneself

Next is the principle of normalization. **Normalization** has become an internationally influential idea that has served as the cornerstone of recreation services for persons with disabilities. Normalization does not mean making persons with disabilities like "normal" people. Instead, it refers to the provision of typical experiences so that persons with disabilities can maintain or develop characteristics and behaviors that are as normal to their own culture as possible (Wolfensberger, 1972). People with disabilities should have access to canoeing, pottery, and basketball programs that are typical for those without disabilities. This implies that even if persons with disabilities cannot directly participate in the same leisure opportunities as the nondisabled, their opportunities should be equal and similar.

> **Normalization:** conditions that are as culturally normal as possible, providing typical leisure opportunities

One of the outcomes of normalization is integration. **Integration** requires both social interaction and social acceptance (Bullock & Howe, 1991) because it is based on the idea of integrity, meaning "to be yourself among others" (Fullwood, 1990, p. 3). There are many other ideas that are similar to integration. For example, mainstreaming is an older term meaning that persons with disabilities are included in settings that traditionally serve the general public. The term "inclusive recreation" is a more contemporary expression suggesting that people with disabilities are entitled to the same respect and attention as others receiving recreation services in the community. Regardless of the in-vogue terminology, the principle of integration is opposite the practice of segregation.

> **Integration:** enabling persons with and without disabilities to participate together

All four principles—self-determination, self-advocacy, normalization, and integration—are not mutually exclusive. For equity in leisure, they are all strongly related and all necessary. To conclude, although leisure is an important aspect of the quality of life for people, those with disabilities are often unable to take full advantage of the potential for leisure in their lives. Thus must be corrected, because leisure experiences provide the opportunity for maintaining personal autonomy, self-definition, and freedom often absent from other aspects of their lives.

Summary: What We Understand

Our pastimes are a tool for equity. In this chapter, leisure is presented as both part of the problem and part of the solution. For such groups as women, gays and lesbians, ethnic and racial minorities, immigrants, youth at risk, and persons with disabilities, two major points can be made about leisure and equity:

- **Leisure is not yet equitable; constraints to participation exist.**

- **Leisure has the potential of being a great equalizer; through leisure equality of opportunity can be achieved.**

Application to Professional Practice

The professional specialty of therapeutic recreation has grappled with the principle of integration of persons with disabilities for many years. In delivering leisure services, specialists essentially operate in both segregated and integrated ways. That is, therapeutic recreation models are essentially either community based or clinically based.

By far the majority of leisure services provided to persons with disabilities in the United States and Canada exist within the community. City recreation departments, YMCAs, Boys & Girls Clubs, and many other agencies provide such services either through specially adapted programs or via services that exist for all citizens and members. Thus, within community-based service delivery are examples of both segregation and integration. To facilitate more integration, the Parks and Recreation Department in the city of Dartmouth (Nova Scotia) employs a "recreation integrator" whose job it is to facilitate an individualized integration process (Searle & Brayley, 2000).

On the other hand, an example of completely segregated service delivery is that which takes place in clinical or institutional settings. Here therapeutic recreation specialists use leisure expressions as part of the treatment of patients and residents of hospitals, rehabilitation centers, convalescent facilities, special camps, and other agencies that are aligned with the medical perspective of helping people achieve optimal health. That is, specialists in the clinical setting use purposeful recreation interventions.

For Further Information

Information is available through a large list of government, private, and professional associations. For example, the National Therapeutic Recreation Society (www.nrpa.org) and the American Therapeutic Recreation Association (www.atra-tr.org) can be contacted for information about their current therapeutic recreation service delivery philosophies, upcoming conferences, and careers. The National Council for Therapeutic Recreation Certification (www.nctrc.org), as a professional credentialing group, has a newsletter for certified members, as well as candidate bulletins for those interested in taking the national exam and becoming certified. In addition, the Canadian Federation of Sport Organisations for the Disabled and the Canadian Parks and Recreation Association provide both advocacy and national coordination of programs and services.

References

Allison, M. T. (1982). Sport, culture, and socialization. *International Review for the Sociology of Sport, 17,* 11–37.

Armas, G. C. (2004, January 2). Hispanics now outnumber blacks in U.S. *Herald-Times* (Bloomington, IN), pp. A1, A9.

Bedini, L. (1990, October). Separate but equal? Segregated programming for people with disabilities. *Journal of Physical Education, Recreation and Dance, 40,* 40–44.

Belluck, P. (1992, August 16,). Starting too young, getting in too deep. *Philadelphia Inquirer,* p. A-1.

Bullock, C. C., & Howe, C. Z. (1991). A model therapeutic recreation program for the reintegration of persons with disabilities into the community. *Therapeutic Recreation Journal, 25*(1), 7–17.

Caldwell, L. (1983, March). Research update: On adolescents and leisure activities. *Parks and Recreation,* 19.

Carter, J. (1976). Speech, Pittsburgh, Pennsylvania.

Centers for Disease Control and Prevention. (2002). Home page. Retrieved April 19, 2004, from http://www.cdc.gov/

Cordes, K. A., & Ibrahim, H. M. (2003). *Applications in recreation and leisure for today and the future.* Boston: McGraw-Hill.

Crawford, D. W., & Godbey, G. (1987). Reconceptualizing barriers to family leisure. *Leisure Sciences, 9,* 119–127.

Crawford, D. W., Jackson, E. L., & Godbey, G. (1991). A hierarchical model of leisure constraints. *Leisure Sciences, 13,* 309–320.

Dattilo, J., & Williams, R. (1999). Inclusion and leisure service delivery. In E. L. Jackson, & T. L. Burton (Eds.), *Leisure studies: Prospects for the twenty-first century* (pp. 451–466). State College, PA: Venture.

Dragon, C. (1986). *Native American under-representation in national parks: Tests of marginality and ethnicity hypotheses.* Unpublished master's thesis, University of Idaho, Moscow

Evans, P. B., & Stephens, J. D. (1988). Development and the world economy. In N. J. Smelser (Ed.), *Handbook of sociology* (pp. 192–204). Thousand Oaks, CA: Sage.

Foner, N. (1997). The immigrant family: Cultural legacies and cultural changes. *International Migration Review, 3,* 961–974.

Freysinger, V. J., & Flannery, D. (1992). Women's leisure: Affiliation, self-determination, empowerment and resistance? *Society and Leisure, 15,* 303–322.

Fullwood, D. (1990). *Chances and choices: Making integration work.* Baltimore: Brookes.

General Accounting Office. (2004). Home page. Retrieved April 15, 2004, from http://www.gao.gov

Goodale, T. L. (2004). White paper #2: Leisure apartheid. Retrieved March 3, 2004, from The Academy of Leisure Sciences at http://www.academyofleisuresciences.org/alswp2.html

Goodstein, L., & Connelly, M. (1998, April 30). Teenage poll finds a turn to the traditional. *New York Times,* p. A-20.

Gramann, J. H., & Allison, M. T. (1999). Ethnicity, race, and leisure. In E. L. Jackson, & T. L. Burton (Eds.), *Leisure studies: Prospects for the twenty-first century* (pp. 283–298). State College, PA: Venture.

Henderson, K. A. (1990). The meaning of leisure for women: An integrative review of the research. *Journal of Leisure Research, 22*(3), 228–243.

Henderson, K. A. (1993). A feminist analysis of selected professional recreation literature about girls/women from 1907–1990. *Journal of Leisure Research, 25*(2), 165–181.

Henderson, K. A., & Bialeschki, M. D. (1999). Makers of meanings: Feminist perspectives on leisure research. In E. L. Jackson, & T. L. Burton (Eds.), *Leisure studies: Prospects for the twenty-first century* (pp. 167–176). State College, PA: Venture.

Henderson, K. A., Bialeschki, M. D., Shaw, S. M., & Freysinger, V. J. (1989). *A leisure of one's own: A feminist perspective on women's leisure.* State College, PA: Venture.

Henderson, K. A., Hodges, S., & Kivel, B. D. (2002). Context and dialogue in research on women and leisure. *Journal of Leisure Research, 34*(3), 253–271.

Jackson, E. L., & Scott, D. (1999). Constraints to leisure. In E. L. Jackson, & T. L. Burton (Eds.), *Leisure studies: Prospects for the twenty-first century* (pp. 299–322). State College, PA: Venture.

Kennedy, D. W., Smith, R. W. & Austin, D. R. (1991). *Special recreation: Opportunities for persons with disabilities.* Dubuque, IA: Wm. C. Brown.

Kleiber, D. A., & Kane, M. J. (1984). Sex differences and the use of leisure as adaptive potentiation. *Society and Leisure, 7,* 165–173.

Leitner, M. J., & Leitner, S. F. (2004). *Leisure enhancement.* New York: The Haworth Press.

Mahon, M. J., & Bullock, C. C. (1992). Teaching adolescents with mild mental retardation to make decisions in leisure through the use of self-control techniques. *Therapeutic Recreation Journal, 26,* 9–26.

McKinstry, H. M. (1909). Athletics for girls. *The Playground, 3*(3), 3–7.

Meyer, H. D., & Brightbill, C. K. (1964). *Community recreation: A guide to its organization.* New York: Prentice-Hall.

Murdock, S. H., Backman, K., Colberg, E., Hogue, M. R., & Harmon, R. R. (1990). Modeling demographic change and characteristics in the analysis of future demand for leisure services. *Leisure Sciences, 12,* 79–102.

Nadirova, A., & Jackson, E. L. (2000). Alternative criterion variables against which to assess the impacts of constraints to leisure. *Journal of Leisure Research, 32*(4), 396–405.

Ogbu, J. U. (1991). Immigrants and involuntary minorities in perspective. In M. A. Gibson, & J. U. Ogbu (Eds.), *Minority status and schooling: A comparative study of immigrants and involuntary minorities* (pp. 72–96). New York: Garland.

Ogbu, J. U. (1998). Differences in cultural fram of reference. *International Journal of Behavioral Development, 16,* 483–506.

Ogden, D. C., & Hilt, M. L. (2003). Collective identity and basketball: An explanation for the decreasing number of African-Americans on America's baseball diamonds. *Journal of Leisure Research, 35*(2), 213–227.

Parents and Families of Lesbians and Gays. (2001). Today's gay youth: The ugly, frightening statistics. Retrieved September 1, 2001, from http://www.pflag-phoenix.org/youthstats.html

Pela, R. L. (1994). Stonewall's eyewitnesses. *The Advocate, 654,* 50–55.

Razzell, P. E., & Wainwright, R. W. (1973). *The Victorian working class: Selections from letters to the Morning Chronicle.* London: Frank Cass.

Salazar, C. G. (2001). *Immigrants and recreation in the United States and Canada.* Unpublished manuscript, Indiana University, Bloomington.

Schor, J. B. (1992). *The overworked American: The unexpected decline of leisure.* New York: Basic Books.

Searle, M. S., & Brayley, R. E. (2000). *Leisure services in Canada: An introduction.* State College, PA: Venture.

Shaw, S. M. (1994). Gender, leisure, and constraint: Towards a framework for the analysis of women's leisure. *Parks and Recreation, 26*(1), 8–22.

Shaw, S. M. (1999). Gender and leisure. In E. L. Jackson, & T. L. Burton (Eds.), *Leisure studies: Prospects for the twenty-first century* (pp. 271–282). State College, PA: Venture.

Shklyanoy, P. (2000, September/October). Just how compliant are you? *Recreation Management.* 12–18.

Smith, R. W., Austin, D. R., & Kennedy, D. W. (2001). *Inclusive and special recreation: Opportunities for persons with disabilities.* Boston: McGraw-Hill.

Statistics Canada. (2004). Home page. Retrieved April 19, 2004, from http://www.statcan.ca/

Stodolska, M. (1998). Assimilation and leisure constraints: Dynamics of constraints on leisure in immigrant populations. *Journal of Leisure Research, 30*(4), 521–551.

Stodolska, M. (2000). Changes in leisure participation patterns after immigration. *Leisure Sciences, 22*(1), 39–63.

Stodolska, M., & Yi, J. (2003). Impacts of immigration on ethnic identity and leisure behavior of adolescent immigrants from Korea, Mexico and Poland. *Journal of Leisure Research, 35*(1), 49–79.

Taylor, T., & Toohey, K. (2001/2002). Behind the veil: Exploring the recreation needs of Muslim women. *Leisure/Loisir, 26*(1–2), 85–105.

U.S. Census Bureau, (2000). Population estimates program. Retrieved January 2, 2003, from http://www.census.gov/population/documentation/twps0045/tab09.txt

Washburn, R. F. (1978). Black underparticipation in wildland recreation: Alternative explanations. *Leisure Sciences, 1,* 175–189.

Wearing, B. (1998). *Leisure and feminist theory.* London: Sage.

Weller, C. F. (1913). Life for girls. *The Playground, 7*(5), 199–207.

Wenner, L. A. (1998). In search of the sports bar: Masculinity, alcohol, sports, and the mediation of public space. In G. Rail (Ed.), *Sport and postmodern times* (pp. 213–231). Albany: State University of New York Press.

Winkelman, M. (1994). Cultural shock and adaptation. *Journal of Counseling and Development, 73*(2), 121–126.

Wolfensberger, W. (1972). *Normalization.* Toronto: National Institute on Mental Retardation.

Worsnop, R. L. (1997, January 19). Despite business grumbling, disabilities act here to stay. *Sunday Herald-Times* (Bloomington, IN), p. D1.

Yankelovich Partners, Inc. (1998, October 14–15). Time/CNN Poll.

Yu, P., & Berryman, D.L. (1996). The relation ship among self-esteem, acculturation, and recreation participation of recently arrived Chinese immigrant adolescents. *Journal of Leisure Research, 28*(4), 251–273.

Zaman, H. (1997). Islam, well-being and physical activity: Perceptions of Muslim young women. In G. Clarke, & B. Humberstone (Eds.), *Researching women in sport* (pp. 111–121). Hampshire, United Kingdom: Macmillan.

A

accidents related to leisure, 337–338

Addams, Jane, 301, 306

addictions, 258, 268–270

adolescence

    See also teenagers

    leisure during, 111

    play, importance of during, 114–115

    social development, 127

adventure experience paradigm (AEP), 93–95

African Americans

    See also ethnicity, race

    and baseball, 393

age

    meaning of, 106–109

    and predictors of leisure experience, 73

    television viewing by (table), 205

aggression at sporting events, 263–265, 283

alcohol use, 258, 268–270

amusement parks, 220–226

ancient leisure

    China, 23–25

    Greece, 9, 17–21

    Muhammad's early empire, 25

    Rome, 21–23

    societies in the Americas, 26–28

animal play, 53

anthropology of leisure, 140–141

anti-structure theory of leisure, 96–98

applications to professional practice. *See* professional
    practice applications

Aristotle, 17–19, 44, 278

art

    graffiti and outdoor art, 275–276

    leisure and, 9–13

at-risk youth, 397–400

Aztecs, 26–27

B

Backroads (adventure travel company), 192

Baden-Powell, Sir Robert, 306

balance of payments, and leisure, 339

Barrett, Janie Porter, 304

baseball teams, geographic distribution of, 175–176

Beach Boys, the, 14–15

Bianculli, David, 228

bingo, 272–273

boredom and leisure, 262

Bourdieu, Pierre, 68

Bowling Alone (Putnam), 254

Boy Scouts, 306, 389–390

Boyce, William, 306

C

camping, 178–180

Canadian Tourism Human Resource Council, 101

capitalism, 323–325

Carter, President Jimmy, 381

casinos, 271–274

central life interest (CLI), 370

chapter summaries

    anthropology of leisure, 166

    common culture, 229

    economics of leisure, 340

    explanations of leisure, 98–99

    having fun, 66

    leisure and equity, 404

    leisure for social good, 313

    leisure's geography, 192

    leisure and technology, 252–253

    life span and leisure, 131–132

    meanings of leisure, 34

    taboo leisure, 281–282

    work and leisure, 371

children

    See also adolescence, teenagers

    importance of play to, 114–115

China, leisure in ancient, 23–25

cinema. *See* film

climate's influence on leisure, 172–175

Colonial America, leisure in, 291–292

commercialism

    and fun, 345

    jobs in commercial recreation, 341

    media-based entertainment options, 228

    of modern Olympics, 20

commitment and leisure, 61–62

common culture

    characterizing, 200–204

    film, 216–219

    popular music, 210–213

    popular print media, 213–216

    role of entertainment, 227–229

    television viewing, 203–210

    theme parks, 220–226

commons, decline of the, 297–298

community

    art and cultural centers, 229–230

    leisure as creator of, 310–312

    loss of social capital in, 253–254

computer-assisted leisure, 242–248, 253

conservation, preservation, 187–191

consumerism

    and economics, 326–331

    and leisure, 323

    and technology, 241

contests and games, 53

'core plus balance' concept, 108–109

counseling, leisure, 372–373

countries, international analysis of wealthiest and
    most livable (table), 320–321

credit card crisis, 333–334

crimes

    delinquency. *See* delinquent behavior

    victimless, 268–274

crowding in leisure, 178–180
Csikszentmihalyi, Mihaly, 89–90, 93
cultural
        capital, 67–68, 229–230
        development and leisure, 157–160
        time sufficiency and leisure (table), 360
culture
        characteristics of (table), 142
        common. *See* common culture
        earliest human, 153–156
        influence on leisure, 141–145
        Internet and, 250
culture hearths, 16
culture shock, 395–396
cyberculture, 238, 251–252
cynicism, 47

D

Dale, James, 389
delinquent behavior
        and differential association, 265–266
        and leisure services, 312
        youth-at-risk, 397–400
demographics
        American family, child raising (table), 397
        challenges to leisure services, 312
        of leisure behavior, 72–77
        of movie-watchers, 219
        of vacation goers, 239
deviance, and leisure, 260–261
differential association explanation of taboo recreation, 265–266
diffusion in culture, 147–149
disabled people, and leisure, 400–404
discretionary time. *See* free time
Disney, Walt, 201, 224
Disneyland, 224–226, 248, 388
diversity, 382
drinking games, 7–8
drugs and alcohol, 268–270

E

economics
        benefits of leisure, 331–336
        harmful effects of leisure, 336–340
        and leisure, 318–331
        work and leisure, 362
ecstasy (drug), 280
education
        leisure, Web sites for, 373
        recess, trends in, 344–345
        sports and fitness in, 295–296
educational television, 208
elderly
        See also age
        technology and, 239
emotional development and life span, 114–120
employment in leisure-related sector, 334–335

enculturation, 142–143
endurance contests, 27–28
entertainment
        role in common culture, 227–229
        self-as-entertainment theory, 95–96
environmental impact of outdoor recreation, 187–191
Epicurus, epicureanism, 47–48
equity, how leisure restricts and enables, 379–382
ethnicity
        and 'average' families around the world, 158–160
        ethnic diversity and leisure, 391–394
        and predictors of leisure experience, 73
        and well-being, 164–165
ethnocentric, 161–162
Evolution of Leisure, The (Goodale and Godbey), 47
exercises
        See also self-tests
        ethnocentricity scale, 162
        health and heart, 113
        leisure and nonleisure states of mind, 87–88
        smartening-up strategies, 124
        test your spiritual health, 63
        your leisure preferences, 66
expenditures in leisure, 332–334
extrinsic rewards of leisure, 43–44

F

fairy tales, characteristics of, 7–8
families
        American, child raising demographics (table), 397
        international analysis of, 158–160
fantasy play, 116, 209
feelings. *See* emotional development
feminism and leisure, 383–386
film and common culture, 216–219
flow concept (Csikszentmihalyi), 89–94
free time
        leisure as, 31–32
        leisure as freedom, 40
        perceptions of, 355–360
freedom, leisure and, 40–41, 84
Freud, Sigmund, 52
Froebel, Friedrich, 302
fun, 39–66, 344–345
future predictions for leisure and technology (table), 237

G

gambling
        on the Internet, 250
        taboo recreation, 271–274
games
        computer, 242–246
        geocaching adventure, 249
        leisure and, 54–56
        public, in ancient Rome, 21–23
gangs, youth, 266

gays, lesbians, 380, 387–391
gender
    identity, 125
    and predictors of leisure experience, 73
Generation Y, characteristics of, 107
geography
    geocaching adventure games, 249
    and leisure, 171–192
Godbey, Geoffrey, 358
Goodwin, Steve, 274
Greece, 9, 17–21
Gulick, Luther, 313

H

handicapped people and leisure, 400–404
happiness
    measures of, 165
    qualities of, 44–46
Hardin, Garrett, 298
Hawaii, 336–337
HDI (Human Development Index), 158, 319–321
health
    alcoholism, 270–271
    and physical development, 112–113
    spiritual, 63–64
Heart N' Parks initiative, 113
hedonism, 48
high culture, 202
hip-hop culture, 211–212
history
    of leisure for social good, 307–309
    meanings of leisure throughout, 16–30, 291–300
    of organized leisure systems, 300–310
hobbies, 83, 124
horse racing, 263
Huizinga, Johan, 49–50
Hull House, 301–302
Human Development Index (HDI), 158, 319–321
Human Rights Act of 1974, 401
humor, leisure and, 56–57

I

identity
    during college years, 117
    in children's play, 116
immigrants, 394–397
Impressionism, 9–13
income
    and computer ownership, 237–238
    gross domestic product per capita, selected countries (table), 157
    and predictors of leisure experience, 74
    and well-being, 164
Industrial Revolution, 296–297
injuries related to leisure, 337–339
innovation, and cultural change, 146–147
intellectual development and life span, 120–124
international analysis of wealthiest and most livable countries (table), 320–321

Internet
    cyberporn, 276–277
    video simulation experiences, 247–253
intrinsic reward, 42–44, 84
Inuit's ancient endurance contests, 27–28
investments in leisure, 332–334

J

jazz music, 213
jokes, 56–57

K

Kant, Immanuel, 175
Kelly, John, 82
Kleiber, Doug, 57–58
Knowles, John, 7
Kush, kingdom of, 17

L

language and behavior, Whorfian hypothesis, 144–145
Lee, Joseph, 303–304, 324
leisure
    anthropology of, 140–165
    classical and historical meanings of, 16–30
    community-making aspects of, 310–312
    constraints, opportunities, 380–382
    and consumption, 326–331
    economics of, 317–340
    and equity, 378–404
    explanations of, 71–98
    fun, qualities of, 39–66
    geography and, 171–192
    humanities of, 4–16
    and life span, 105–131
    meanings of, contemporary, 30–34
    and modernity, 161–165
    organized systems, birth of, 300–310
    services sponsor types (table), 35
    taboo. See taboo leisure
    and technology, 235–252
    theory of. See theories explaining leisure behavior
    time and, 344–371
    urban/rural differences (table), 175
    using for social good, 289–313
    values hierarchy (fig.), 260
lesbians, gays, 380, 387–391
life expectancy calendar, 110
life span
    emotional development, 114–120
    intellectual development, 120–124
    meaning of age, 106–109
    physical development, 109–114
    social development, 125–131
lifestyle
    changes, and freedom, 41–42
    described, types of, 75, 77–78
    retreatism, 267–268
Linder, Steffan, 58
Linton, Ralph, 142

literature and leisure, 4–8
Low, Juliette Gordon, 306–307

M

Mall of America, 328
malls, shopping, 117, 328
Martin, Casey, 402
Marx, Karl, 324, 325
Maya Indians, 26–27
McDonald's restaurants, 200
meanings of leisure
    classical and historical meanings of, 16–30
    contemporary, 30–34
    humanities of, 4–16
Menzel, Peter, 158
Mexico, ancient Mayas and Aztecs, 26–27
Mickey Mouse, 201
Middle Ages, leisure during, 28–29
modernity, leisure and, 161–165
Monopoly (Parker Bros.), 55
mood, effects of humor on, 56
motor homes, 186–187
movies. *See* film
Muhammad's early empire, 25
music
    leisure and, 13–16
    popular, and common culture, 210–213
Muslim women, 386–387

N

Nash's leisure/value hierarchy, 260–261
National Intramural-Recreational Sports Association, 133
National Park Service, 196
National Recreation and Park Association, 36, 306
nature, evolution of our preferences for, 183–184
Neulinger, John, 84
Nicodemus, Kansas, 293
North American Society for Sport Management, 133

O

Olmstead, Frederick, 299
Olympic Games, 19–20
optimal experience and 'flow,' 89–90, 94

P

Paleolithic culture, 153–156
Parker Brothers' *Monopoly*, 55
parks
    and employment, 334–335
    origins in America of, 299, 302–303
    theme, 220–226
    types of, 192–196
Pavlov, Ivan, 208
peers
    influence, and social class, 128
    and levels of play (table), 126
personality types and tourist destinations (fig.), 100

Pfohl, Stephen, 268
physical
    development and life span, 109–114
    exercise and addiction, 258
Piaget, Jean, 122–123
Pieper, Josef, 57
place, leisure as, 182–188
play
    comparison of theories (table), 51
    current activity level, 110
    leisure and, 49–54
    level, according to peer interactions (table), 126
    playgrounds, origins of, 302–304
pleasure, leisure and, 46–49
popular print media, 213–216
pornography, 276–277
positive emotions and longevity, 120
Postman, Neil, 228
postmodernism, 163–164
privilege, leisure considered as a, 378–379
professional practice applications
    anthropology of leisure, 166–167
    common culture, 229–230
    economics of leisure, 340–341
    increasing cultural capital, 67–68
    leisure and equity, 404–405
    leisure and technology, 253–254
    leisure for social good, 313–314
    leisure's geography, 192–193
    leisure's meaning, and, 34–36
    sports resources, 132–133
    taboo leisure, 282–283
    theories explaining leisure behavior, 99–100
    work and leisure, 372
property values and leisure-related development 336
prostitution, 277–278
Protestantism, and attitude toward leisure, 361–362
purchasing power parities (PPPs), 319–321

Q

quality of life
    leisure and, 160
    technology and, 238–242
questionnaires. *See* exercises, self-tests

R

race
    ethnic diversity and leisure, 391–394
    and predictors of leisure experience, 73
raves, 280–281
reading
    common culture, 213–216
    in solitude, and leisure, 60–61
reality television, 209–210
recess, trends in, 344–345
recreation, taboo, 261–268
recreational
    activities, leisure as, 32–33
    sport administration, 133

relaxation, 25, 57–58
religion
        and intention of work, 361–364
        and predictors of leisure experience, 74–75
Renaissance, humanities of leisure, 30
resources and further information
        anthropology of leisure, 168
        community art councils, 231
        leisure service agency careers, 36
        park links, 196
        sports management, 133
        taboo leisure, 283
        therapeutic recreation, 405
retirement, 108–109, 119
retreatism lifestyle, 267–268
rewards, intrinsic and extrinsic, 42–44
right, leisure considered as a, 378–379
Riis, Jacob, 304
risk, leisure and, 65–66
ritual
        leisure and, 59–60
        role in children's social development, 125
Robinson, John, 358
roller coasters, 220–223
Rome, leisure in ancient, 21–23
running, compulsive, 258
Russell, Bertrand, 45

S

Sahlins, Marshall, 155
Sarton, May, 61
Schor, Juliette, 324, 325, 357
self-tests
        See also exercises
        ethnocentricity scale, 162
        future use of technology for leisure, 252
        health and heart, 113
        leisure and nonleisure states of mind, 87–88
        test your spiritual health, 63
        your leisure preferences, 66
serious leisure, 62
settlement houses, 301–302
sex and teenagers, 128–129
Shakers, the, 362–363
Sherpa people of the Khumbu, 144–145, 149–152
shopping centers
        and American youth, 117
        Mall of America, 328
simulated leisure, 246–247
situational factors explaining leisure behavior, 72–77
slasher films, 216–218
smell, and attachment to leisure places, 182–183
Smith, Adam, 324, 325
social
        capital, 253–254
        class and peer influence, 128
        development, 124, 125–131
        good, leisure as instrument for, 289–313

solitude
        leisure and, 60–61
        social isolation and technology, 241–242
spectacle, and leisure in ancient Rome, 21–23
spectator sports and violence, 263–265
spirituality, leisure and, 63–65
sponsors of leisure services, types of (table), 35
sports
        in the 1800s, 295
        during adolescence, 111
        aggression at sporting events, 263–265
        in ancient Greece, 19–21
        betting on, 272–273
        extreme, 204
        guidelines on handling aggression in, 283
        resources for participation and spectating,
                132–133
Starr, Ellen, 301
state of mind
        'flow,' 89–90
        leisure as, 33–34
        and Neulinger's paradigm, 84–88
stoicism, 47
subcultures, 142–144
substance abuse, 258, 268–270, 274
surplus energy theory of play, 50

T

taboo leisure
        described, 258–260
        deviance and leisure, 260–261
        dilemma of 'goodness,' 278–281
        reasons for taboo recreations, 261–268
        recreation that injures others, 274–278
        self-injuring recreation, 268–274
Talbott, Stephen, 248
talk shows, 266–267
Taoism, 140
taxes generated by leisure, 335–336
technology
        computer-assisted leisure, 242–248
        and leisure, 235–238
        as leisure, 248–251
        and quality of life, 238–242
teenagers
        See also adolescence
        delinquent behavior. *See* delinquent behavior
        sex and, 128–129
        and shopping malls, 117
        youth-at-risk, 397–400
        youth gangs, 266
television viewing
        and common culture, 203–210, 229
        internationally, 159
        teenagers and, 111
        time spent, 345–345
        talk shows, 266–267
theme parks, 220–226

theories explaining leisure behavior
    anti-structure theory, 96–98
    compensation, spillover effect, 79, 81
    Kelly's types of leisure, 82–84
    Neulinger's paradigm, 84–88
    self-as-entertainment, 95–96
thinking, and intellectual development, 120–121
time
    allocation and leisure, 345
    types of, 346–351
    urgency, tyranny, 351–355
tourism, 59, 99–101, 148–152, 323, 339
Trask, Haunani-Kay, 336
Turner, Victor, 96

U

unemployment, 368–369
Updike, John, 5

V

vacations, demographics of, 239
VALS (Values and Lifestyles) Survey, 77
values, leisure hierarchy (fig.), 260
vandalism, 274–275
Vaux, Calvert, 299
Veblen, Thorstein, 321–322, 325
victimless crimes, 268–274
video games, 242–246
violence
    in computer games, 242–246
    delinquent behavior, 265–266, 312, 397–400
    part of leisure and technology, 241, 253
    recreation that injures others, 274–278
    recreation that injures self, 268–274
    and spectator sports, 263–264
    in sport, guidelines on handling, 283
    slasher films, 216–218

W

weather's influence on leisure, 172–175
Web sites
    See also Internet
    about cultural capital, 68
    about sports management, 133
    Backroads (adventure travel company), 192
    Canadian Tourism Human Resource Council,
        101
    community art councils, 231
    jobs in commercial recreation, 341
    leisure education and counseling, 372
    leisure for social good, 308–310
    life expectancy calendar, 110
    National Park Service, Park Canada, 196
    National Recreation and Park Association, 36
    recreation and parks, 314
    therapeutic recreation, 405
    World Leisure organization, 167
White, Leslie, 143
Whorf, Benjamin Lee, 144–145
Winnebago motor homes, 187
women
    in ancient Greece, 20
    leisure opportunities and constraints, 383–386
word play, 121–120, 124
work
    better ways of scheduling into life (table), 368
    ethic, 28–29, 362
    and leisure, 82–83, 86, 360–371
    unemployment, 368–369
World Leisure organization, 166–167

Y

yo-yos, 52
youth-at-risk, 397–400
youth gangs, 266